THE NEW SCIENCE OF GIAMBATTISTA VICO

THE NEW SCIENCE OF

GIAMBATTISTA VICO

Translated from the third edition (1744) by

THOMAS GODDARD BERGIN

AND MAX HAROLD FISCH

Cornell University Press

ITHACA, NEW YORK, 1948

To ROBERT MORRIS OGDEN

AND GEORGE HOLLAND SABINE

PREFACE

THE FOLLOWING translation of Vico's *Scienza nuova,* begun in 1939 at Naples and on Capri but interrupted by the war, is based on the text edited by Fausto Nicolini which forms volume 112 and the first 166 pages of volume 113 in the *Scrittori d'Italia* (Bari, Laterza, 1928).

That text was based on a word-for-word collation of Nicolini's earlier edition of 1911–16 with the edition of 1744 and with the manuscript in Vico's hand from which the latter was printed. Vico's intolerably long paragraphs and sentences were broken up and the punctuation was otherwise modernized. His countless parenthetical phrases and clauses were enclosed in curved lines to clarify the syntax. The paragraphs were numbered, and the index references were to paragraphs rather than pages.

We have retained Nicolini's paragraphing, and our index, like his, refers to the paragraphs by number; but we have carried the breaking up of sentences much further. With occasional exceptions, we have followed Nicolini's use of parenthesis marks, but the reader should perhaps be warned that they are no part of Vico's own punctuation.

Our thanks are due to William Cherubini for placing at our disposal his translation of paragraphs 365–445, to James Hutton for his careful and helpful scrutiny of our entire translation in the typescript, to Ruth B. Fisch for preparing the index, and to the University of Chicago Library for supplying a photograph of the plate facing page 3 from its copy of the edition of 1744.

For a discussion of the development of the New Science, of its background in European thought, and of its subsequent influence, we may refer the reader to the introduction to our translation of Vico's *Autobiography* (Cornell University Press, Ithaca, 1944). It was our intention, as we stated in the preface to that volume, that that somewhat lengthy introduction should serve for our translation of the *New Science* as well.[1]

Two indispensable aids to the scholarly study of Vico have appeared or been announced since the present translation was completed. Croce's *Bibliografia vichiana* has been enlarged and rewritten by Nicolini (Naples, Ricciardi, 2

---

[1] The essay promised in note 147 of our translation of the *Autobiography* is appearing under the title "The Academy of the Investigators" in a volume of essays in honor of the English historian of science, Charles Singer.

vols., 1947–48), and Nicolini has in press a definitive commentary on the *Scienza nuova* (Bari, Laterza, 2 vols., 1948).

Vico's argument touches so many fields which have been assiduously cultivated since his day (the Homeric question and the general field of folklore for examples) that it is difficult to resist the temptation to annotate the *New Science* in the light of subsequent investigations. But Nicolini's commentary will take care of the needs of scholars in this and other respects, and a commentary would be only a distraction to most of the readers we hope our translation will have. We have therefore chosen to publish it without notes.

A general caveat, however, should perhaps be entered here. The *New Science* abounds in confusions, misquotations and misinterpretations of Vico's sources, arising in part from taking them at second hand, in larger part from unconscious reading of his own views into them, and in still larger part from simply misremembering them. A few of the resulting errors have been indicated in the index and by bracketed insertions in the text. For examples, Vico remembers Arion as Amphion, makes a proper noun out of an adjective in Homer (see index s.v. Eureia), adds Pacca to the name of the troubadour poet Arnaut Daniel, confuses Kronos and *chronos,* attributes to Thucydides what was said by Isocrates, and alters beyond recognition the meaning of a passage in Seneca (at the end of paragraph 1096). A complete exposure of Vico's errors in this kind would require the elaborate commentary which we have foregone, and yet would not touch the heart of his argument.[2] Our general caveat seems therefore sufficient.

Readers new to Vico may find it advantageous on their first reading of the *New Science* to pass over the "Idea of the Work" and the "Notes on the Chronological Table" and begin with the "Elements" (Book I, Section II).

To smooth the way of readers with little Latin and less Greek, we have transliterated the Greek words and phrases in Vico's text, and have usually inserted translations of these and of his Latin words, phrases and quotations. For the literary works he cites, we have often used familiar English titles in the case of Greek and Latin classics; but in the case of modern works we have usually given the title in the language of original publication (Latin for the most part), even when Vico gives an Italian translation or paraphrase. Minor errors in the citations have been silently corrected.

At the expense of occasional awkwardness, we have tried to respect Vico's technical terms. *Certo* and its cognates, for example, are with rare exceptions translated "certain" etc., even when it is not clear that Vico is using them in the technical sense explained in paragraph 321. *Umano* and its cognates, which we were often tempted to render "humane" or "civilized," are usually allowed to stand as "human" etc., in order to preserve a possible reference either (a) to the

---

[2] In addition to Nicolini's forthcoming commentary, the curious reader may consult his *Fonti e riferimenti storici della seconda Scienza Nuova* (Bari, Laterza, 1931), and the notes to his 1911–16 edition.

age of men as distinguished from the age of gods and the age of heroes, or (b) to the ages of heroes and men together as distinguished from the age of gods, as in paragraph 629. An *eterna propietá* remains an "eternal property" even when we are tempted to employ the more secular language of uniformities and correlations. *Principio* we have sometimes rendered "principle," sometimes "beginning." As a technical term with Vico, it means both in one, and it may fairly be said that the ambivalence of this term is one of the keys to Vico's thought. The term *principe,* "prince," has the same ambivalence, and so does *natura,* "nature" or "birth." *Dominio* (Latin *dominium*) we have usually translated "ownership," but sometimes "dominion" or (in the phrase *dominio eminente*) "domain." *Repubblica* is uniformly rendered "commonwealth" to avoid the misleading associations of "republic" in English. A few terms for which there are no exact English equivalents are represented by the corresponding Latin terms, as likely to be less unfamiliar: *connubio* by *connubium, famoli* by *famuli, suitá* by *sui heredes* etc. *Diritto naturale delle genti* we have usually rendered "the natural law of nations" since "law of nations" is the common English equivalent for *ius gentium.*[3]

In general, apart from the breaking up of sentences and an occasional lapse from Italian superlatives into English positives, or from literal translation into paraphrase for clarity's sake, we have aimed at as close an approximation to Vico's style as English will permit. A recent critic [4] has argued that Vico is more poet than philosopher, and that his style is essential to the full communication of his meaning. Perhaps it would not overstrain the point to say that he is even more prophet than poet, and that his language, with all its obscurity, incoherence and magnificence, is the language of one who beholds a vision. Indeed the frequent "as we have already seen" and "as we shall soon see" betray the essential characteristic of the seer. The vision is forever with him in all its dazzling totality; it is a scintillant whole though with many facets, and Vico even while enraptured by one aspect of his revelation is never unaware of the others. His references forwards and backwards connect primarily the parts of the vision, and only secondarily and imperfectly the parts of the book.[5] Not to attempt to convey something of this divine or at least heroic intoxication would be to fail to translate Vico in any real sense of the word.

T. G. B.
M. H. F.

Ithaca and Urbana, April 1948

---

[3] For the meaning of this portmanteau phrase see paragraph 998 below and page 48 of the introduction to our translation of Vico's *Autobiography.*

[4] Mario Fubini, *Stile e umanità di Giambattista Vico,* Bari, Laterza, 1946.

[5] We have inserted paragraph numbers in brackets for all backward references to the Axioms, and for a very few other backward and forward references.

CONTENTS

IDEA OF THE WORK

BOOK FOUR: THE COURSE OF NATIONS

BOOK FIVE: THE RECURRENCE OF HUMAN THINGS IN THE RESURGENCE OF THE NATIONS

CONCLUSION OF THE WORK

THE NEW SCIENCE OF GIAMBATTISTA VICO

IDEA OF THE WORK

EXPLANATION OF THE PICTURE

PLACED AS FRONTISPIECE

TO SERVE AS INTRODUCTION TO THE WORK

1   AS CEBES the Theban made a table of things moral, we here offer one of things civil. We hope it may serve to give the reader some conception of this work before he reads it, and, with such aid as imagination may afford, to call it back to mind after he has read it.

2   The lady with the winged temples who surmounts the celestial globe or world of nature is metaphysic, for the name means as much. The luminous triangle with the seeing eye is God with the aspect of His providence. Through this aspect metaphysic in the attitude of ecstasy contemplates Him above the order of natural things through which hitherto the philosophers have contemplated Him. For in the present work, ascending higher, she contemplates in God the world of human minds, which is the metaphysical world, in order to show His providence in the world of human spirits, which is the civil world or world of nations. The latter has as the elements of which it is formed all the things represented by the hieroglyphs displayed in the lower half of the picture. The globe, or the physical, natural world, is supported by the altar in one part only, for, until now, the philosophers, contemplating divine providence only through the natural order, have shown only a part of it. Accordingly men offer worship, sacrifices and other divine honors to God as to the Mind which is the free and absolute sovereign of nature, because by His eternal counsel He has given us existence through nature, and through nature preserves it to us. But the philosophers have not yet contemplated His providence in respect of that part of it which is most proper to men, whose nature has this principal property: that of being social. In providing for this property God has so ordained and disposed human affairs that men, having fallen from complete justice by original sin, and while intending almost always to do something quite different and often quite the contrary—so that for private utility they would live alone like wild beasts—have been led by this same utility and along the aforesaid different and contrary paths to live like men in justice and to keep themselves in society and thus to observe their social nature. It will be shown in the

present work that this is the true civil nature of man, and thus that law exists in nature. The conduct of divine providence in this matter is one of the things whose rationale is a chief business of our Science, which becomes in this respect a rational civil theology of divine providence.

3   In the belt of the zodiac which girds the celestial globe the two signs of Leo and Virgo, more than the others, appear in majesty, or, as is said, in perspective. The former signifies that our Science in its beginnings contemplates first the Hercules that every ancient gentile nation boasts as its founder, and that it contemplates him in his greatest labor. This was the slaying of the lion which, vomiting flame, set fire to the Nemean forest, and adorned with whose skin Hercules was raised to the stars. The lion is here found to have been the great ancient forest of the earth, burned down and brought under cultivation by Hercules, whom we find to have been the type of the political heroes who had to precede the military heroes. This sign also represents the beginning of time[-reckoning]s, which among the Greeks (to whom we owe all our knowledge of gentile antiquity) began with the Olympiads, based on the games of which we are told that Hercules was the founder. They must have begun among the Nemeans to celebrate his victory over the lion he slew. Thus the time[-reckoning]s of the Greeks began when cultivation of the fields began among them. The second sign, that of the Virgin, whom the astronomers found described by the poets as crowned with ears of grain, signifies that Greek history began with the golden age. The poets expressly relate that this was the first age of their world, when through the long course of centuries the years were counted by the grain harvests, which we find to have been the first gold of the world. This golden age of the Greeks has its Latin counterpart in the age of Saturn, who gets his name from *sati,* "sown" [fields]. In this age of gold, the poets assure us faithfully, the gods consorted on earth with the heroes. For we shall show later that the first men among the gentiles, simple and crude, and under the powerful spell of most vigorous imaginations encumbered with frightful superstitions, actually believed that they saw the gods on earth. We shall see further that by uniformity of ideas the orientals, Egyptians, Greeks and Latins, each in ignorance of the others, afterwards raised the gods to the planets and the heroes to the fixed stars. Thus from Saturn (whose Greek name Chronos means "time") new principles are derived for chronology or the theory of time.

4   You must not think it improper that the altar is under and supports the globe. For it will be found that the world's first altars were raised by the gentiles in the first heaven of the poets, who in their fables faithfully passed on to us the story that Heaven had reigned on earth over men and had left great blessings to mankind. These first men, children as it were of the growing human race, believed that the sky was no higher than the summits of the mountains, as even now children believe it to be little higher than the roofs of their houses. Then as the Greek intelligence developed heaven was raised to the summits of the highest mountains, such as Olympus, where Homer relates that

the gods of his day had their dwelling. Finally it was raised above the spheres, as we are now taught by astronomy, and Olympus was raised above the heaven of the fixed stars. Thither likewise was transported the altar, which is now a celestial sign, and the fire upon it passed into the neighboring house (as you see here) of the Lion. (This, as we have just observed, was the Nemean forest, to which Hercules set fire to bring it under cultivation.) For the lion's skin was raised to the stars in token of the triumph of Hercules.

5 The ray of the divine providence illuminating a convex jewel which adorns the breast of metaphysic denotes the clean and pure heart which metaphysic must have, not dirty or befouled with pride of spirit or vileness of bodily pleasures, by the first of which Zeno was led to put fate, and by the second Epicurus to put chance, in the place of divine providence. Furthermore it indicates that the knowledge of God does not have its end in metaphysic taking private illumination from intellectual things and thence regulating merely her own moral conduct, as hitherto the philosophers have done. For this would have been signified by a flat jewel, whereas the jewel is convex, thus reflecting and scattering the ray abroad, to show that metaphysic should know God's providence in public morals or civil customs, by which the nations have come into being and maintain themselves in the world.

6 The same ray is reflected from the breast of metaphysic onto the statue of Homer, the first gentile author who has come down to us. For metaphysic, directing a history of human ideas from the beginnings of truly human thinking among the gentiles, has enabled us finally to descend into the crude minds of the first founders of the gentile nations, all robust sense and vast imagination. They had only the bare potentiality, and that torpid and stupid, of using the human mind and reason. For that very reason the beginnings of poetry, not only different from but contrary to those which have been hitherto imagined, are found to lie in the beginnings of poetic wisdom, which have for that same reason been hitherto hidden from us. This poetic wisdom, the knowledge of the theological poets, was unquestionably the first wisdom of the world for the gentiles. The statue of Homer on a cracked base signifies the discovery of the true Homer. (In the first edition of the *New Science* we sensed it but did not understand it. In the present edition it is fully set forth after due consideration.) Unknown until now, he has held hidden from us the true facts of the fabulous period among the nations, and much more so those of the obscure period which all had despaired of knowing, and consequently the first true origins of the things of the historic period. These are the three periods of the world which Marcus Terentius Varro, the most learned writer on Roman antiquities, recorded for us in his great work entitled [*Antiquitates*] *rerum divinarum et humanarum,* which has been lost.

7 Moreover, it may here be pointed out that in the present work, with a new critical art that has hitherto been lacking, entering on the research of the truth concerning the authors of these same [gentile] nations (among which

more than a thousand years had to pass in order to bring forth the writers with whom criticism has hitherto been concerned), philosophy undertakes to examine philology (that is, the doctrine of everything that depends on the human will; for example, all histories of the languages, customs and deeds of peoples in war and peace), of which, because of the deplorable obscurity of causes and almost infinite variety of effects, philosophy has had almost a horror of treating; and reduces it to the form of a science by discovering in it the design of an ideal eternal history traversed in time by the histories of all nations; so that, on account of this its second principal aspect, our Science may be considered a philosophy of authority. For by virtue of new principles of mythology herein disclosed as consequences of the new principles of poetry found herein, it is shown that the fables were true and trustworthy histories of the customs of the most ancient peoples of Greece. In the first place, the fables of the gods were stories of the times in which men of the crudest gentile humanity thought that all things necessary or useful to the human race were deities. The authors of this poetry were the first peoples, whom we find to have been all theological poets, who without doubt, as we are told, founded the gentile nations with fables of the gods. And here, by the principles of this new critical art, we consider at what determinate times and on what particular occasions of human necessity or utility felt by the first men of the gentile world, they, with frightful religions which they themselves feigned and believed in, imagined first such and such gods and then such and such others. The natural theogony or generation of the gods, formed naturally in the minds of these first men, may give us a rational chronology of the poetic history of the gods. [In the second place,] the heroic fables were true stories of the heroes and their heroic customs, which are found to have flourished in the barbarous period of all nations; so that the two poems of Homer are found to be two great treasure houses of discoveries of the natural law of nations among the still barbarous Greeks. In the present work this period of barbarism is determined to have lasted among the Greeks until the time of Herodotus, called the father of Greek history, whose books are for the most part full of fables and whose style retains very much of the Homeric. This is a characteristic retained by all the historians who came after him, as they used a phraseology half way between the poetic and the vulgar. But Thucydides, the first scrupulous and serious historian of Greece, at the beginning of his account, declares that down to his father's time (and thus to that of Herodotus, who was an old man when Thucydides was a child) the Greeks were quite ignorant of their own antiquities, to say nothing of those of other peoples (which, apart from the Roman, have all come down to us through the Greeks). These antiquities are the deep shadows which the picture shows in the background, against which there stand forth, in the light of the ray of divine providence reflected by metaphysic upon Homer, all the hieroglyphs which represent the principles, known until now only by the effects, of this world of nations.

8   Among these [hieroglyphs] the most prominent is an altar, because

among all peoples the civil world began with religion, as we have briefly noted a while back and as we shall shortly observe more fully.

9 Upon the altar, at the left, the first object we see is a lituus, the staff with which the augurs took auguries and observed the auspices. This signifies divination, from which, among the gentiles, the first divine things took their origin. The Hebrews thought God to be an infinite Mind beholding all times in one point of eternity, whence God, either Himself or through the angels that are minds or through the prophets to whose minds God spoke, gave notice of what was in store for His people. The gentiles fancied bodies to be gods, that by sensible signs they might give notice of what was in store for the peoples. On account of the attribute of His providence, as true among the Hebrews as it was imagined among the gentiles, all humankind gave to the nature of God the name "divinity" by one common idea, which the Latins expressed in *divinari,* "to foretell the future"; but with the aforesaid fundamental difference from which derive all the other essential differences shown by our Science between the natural law of the Hebrews and the natural law of nations. The Roman jurisconsults defined the latter as having been ordained by divine providence along with human customs themselves. Thus the aforesaid lituus represents also the beginning of gentile universal history, which is shown by physical and philological evidence to have begun with the universal flood. After an interval of two centuries (as fabulous history relates), Heaven reigned on earth and bestowed many and great blessings on mankind, and, by uniformity of ideas among orientals, Egyptians, Greeks, Latins and other gentile nations, there arose equally the religions of as many Joves. For at the end of this period of time after the flood, heaven must have thundered and lightened, and from the thunder and lightning of its Jove each nation began to take auspices. This multiplicity of Joves, which led the Egyptians to call their Jove Ammon the oldest of them all, has hitherto been a marvel to the philologians. The same twofold evidence proves the religion of the Hebrews more ancient than those by which the nations were founded, and hence the truth of the Christian religion.

10 On the altar near the lituus may be seen the water and fire, the former contained in a jar. For with a view to divination sacrifices arose among the gentiles from that common custom of theirs which the Latins called *procurare auspicia,* i.e. to sacrifice in order to understand the auguries well so that the divine warnings or commands of Jove might be properly carried out. These are the divine things among the gentiles, from which came later all their human things.

11 The first of these [human things] was marriage, symbolized by the torch lit from the fire on the altar and leaning against the jar. For marriage, as all statesmen agree, is the seed-plot of the family, as the family is the seed-plot of the commonwealth. To denote this, the torch, although it is the hieroglyph of a human thing, is placed on the altar along with the water and the fire, which are hieroglyphs of divine ceremonies; just as the ancient Romans celebrated

nuptials *aqua et igni,* because it was understood that by divine counsel these
two common things (and, before fire even, perennial water as a thing more
necessary to life) had led men to live in society.

12   The second of human things is burial. (Indeed *humanitas* in Latin
comes first and properly from *humando,* "burying.") This institution is symbolized by a cinerary urn, placed to one side within the forest, indicating that
burial goes back to a time when men ate fruit in summer and acorns in winter.
The urn is inscribed *D. M.,* which means "to the good souls of the dead." This
motto represents the common consent of all mankind in the opinion later proved
true by Plato, that human souls do not die with their bodies but that they are
immortal.

13   The urn indicates also the origin among the gentiles of the division
of the fields, to which is to be traced the distinction of cities and peoples and
finally of nations. For it will be found that the races, first of Ham, then of
Japheth and finally of Shem, without the religion of their father Noah, which
they had repudiated (and which alone, in what was then the state of nature,
could have held them by marriages in a society of families), were lost from one
another by roving wild in the great forest of the earth, pursuing shy and indocile women, and fleeing from the wild animals with which the great ancient
forest must have abounded. They were scattered further in search of pasture
and water, and as the result of it all were reduced, at the end of a long period,
to the condition of beasts. Then, on certain occasions ordained by divine providence (occasions which our Science studies and discovers), shaken and aroused
by a terrible fear, each of the particular Uranus and Jove he had feigned and
believed in, some of them finally left off wandering and went into hiding in
definite places. There, settled with particular women, through fear of the apprehended divinity, in religious and chaste carnal unions they solemnized marriages under cover and begat acknowledged children and so founded families.
By long residence and burial of their dead they came to found and divide the
first dominions of the earth, whose lords were called giants, a Greek word meaning "children of the earth," i.e. descendants of those who have been buried.
Hence they considered themselves noble, justly ascribing their nobility in that
first state of human things to their having been humanly engendered in the
fear of the divinity. From this manner of human engendering and not from
anything else, what is called human generation took its name. The houses which
had branched out into several families thus formed were called the first nations
[*gentes*] because of such generation. As the subject matter of the natural law of
nations begins at so early a time, so in this work the doctrine begins there too.
This is a third principal aspect under which our Science should be viewed. Now
there are both physical and moral reasons, apart from the authority of history,
to show that the giants must have been of disproportionate strength and stature.
Since these reasons did not obtain in the case of believers in the true God, creator
of the world and of Adam the prince of all humankind, the Hebrews from the

very beginning of the world were of proper stature. So, after the first principle of divine providence and the second of solemn matrimony, the universal belief in the immortality of the soul, which had its beginnings in the institution of burial, is the third of the three principles on which this Science bases its discussions of the origins of all the innumerable various and diverse things of which it treats.

14 From the forests where the urn is placed a plough stands forth, signifying that the fathers of the first peoples were the first strong men of history. Hence the founders of the first gentile nations above mentioned were the Herculeses (of whom Varro counted a good forty and the Egyptians claimed theirs to be the most ancient), for these Herculeses subdued the first lands of the world and brought them under cultivation. Thus the first fathers of the gentile nations—who were [1] just in virtue of the supposed piety of observing the auspices which they believed divine commands of Jove (from whose Latin name *Ious* came the old word *ious* for "law," later contracted to *ius;* so that justice among all peoples is naturally taught along with piety); [2] prudent in sacrificing to obtain or clearly to understand the auspices, and thus to take good counsel of what, by the commands of Jove, they should undertake in life; and [3] temperate in the institution of matrimony—were also, as is here indicated, [4] strong men. Hence new principles are given to moral philosophy, in order that the esoteric wisdom of the philosophers may conspire with the vulgar wisdom of lawmakers. By these principles all the virtues have their roots in piety and religion, by which alone the virtues are made effective in action, and by reason of which men propose to themselves as good whatever God wills. New principles are given also to economic doctrine, by which sons, so long as they are in the power of their fathers, must be considered to be in the family state, and consequently are in no other way to be formed and confirmed in all their studies than in piety and religion. Since they are not yet capable of understanding commonwealth and laws, they are to reverence and fear their fathers as living images of God, so as to be naturally disposed to follow the religion of their fathers and to defend their fatherland, which preserves their families for them, and so to obey the laws ordained for the preservation of their religion and fatherland. (For divine providence ordained human things with this eternal counsel: that families should first be founded by means of religions, and that upon the families commonwealths should then arise by means of laws.)

15 The plough rests its handle against the altar with a certain majesty, to give us to understand that ploughed lands were the first altars of the gentiles, and to denote also the natural superiority which the heroes believed they had over their *socii.* (The latter, as we shall see shortly, are symbolized by the rudder which is seen bowing near the base of the altar.) On this superiority of nature, it will be shown, the heroes grounded the law, the science and hence the administration of divine things (i.e. the auspices), which were in their keeping.

16 The plough shows only the point of the share and hides the mold-

board. Before the use of iron was known, the share had to be made of a curved piece of very hard wood, capable of breaking and turning the earth. The Latins called the moldboard *urbs,* whence the ancient *urbum,* "curved." The moldboard is hidden to signify that the first cities, which were all founded on cultivated fields, arose as a result of families being for a long time quite withdrawn and hidden among the sacred terrors of the religious forests. These [cultivated fields] are found among all the ancient gentile nations and, by an idea common to all, were called by the Latin peoples *luci,* meaning "burnt lands within the enclosure of the woods." The woods themselves were condemned by Moses to be burned wherever the people of God extended their conquests. This was by counsel of divine providence to the end that those who had already reached the stage of humanity should not again become confounded with the wanderers who still nefariously held property and women in common.

17   There may be seen at the left side of the altar a rudder, symbolizing the origin of the migration of peoples by means of navigation. And by its seeming to bow at the foot of the altar, it symbolizes the ancestors of those who later were the authors of these migrations. These [ancestors] were at first impious men, who recognized no divinity; they were nefarious, since relations among them were not distinguished by marriages, and sons often lay with mothers and fathers with daughters; and finally, because like wild beasts they had no mind for society in the midst of this infamous communism of possessions, they were all alone and hence weak and finally miserable and unhappy, because lacking all the goods which are necessary for preservation and security of life. Fleeing the several ills they suffered in the dissensions which this savage communism [of possessions] produced, and seeking escape and safety, they betook themselves to the cultivated lands of the pious, chaste, strong and even powerful, that is, of those who were already united in family society. From these lands, it will be found, cities were called *arae,* "altars," throughout the ancient world of the gentiles. For they must have been the first altars of the gentile nations, and the first fire lighted on them was that which served to clear the forests of trees and bring them under cultivation, and the first water was that of the perennial springs, which were necessary in order that those destined to found humanity should no longer wander in bestial vagrancy in search of water, but settle for a long time in one place and give up vagabondage. And since these altars were evidently the first asylums of the world (which Livy defines generally as *vetus urbes condentium consilium,* "an old counsel of founders of cities," as we are told that within the asylum opened in the grove Romulus founded Rome), hence the first cities were almost all called altars. To this minor discovery let us add a major one: that among the Greeks (from whom, as was said above, we have learned all that we know of gentile antiquity) the first Thrace or Scythia (i.e. the first North), the first Asia and the first India (i.e. the first East), the first Mauretania or Libya (i.e. the first South) and the first Europe or first Hesperia (i.e. the first West), and along with all these the first

Ocean, were born within Greece itself; and then the Greeks, going abroad in
the world, extended these names by analogy to its four parts and to the ocean
that surrounds it. These discoveries, we assert, give new principles to geography,
which, like the new principles already promised for chronology, are necessary
if we are to read the ideal eternal history above mentioned. For chronology
and geography are the two eyes of history.

18   To these altars then, the impious-nomadic-weak, fleeing for their lives
from the stronger, came seeking refuge, and the pious-strong killed the violent
among them and took the weak under their protection. Since the latter brought
with them nothing but their lives, they were accepted as *famuli* and given the
means of sustaining life. The family took its name principally from these
famuli, whose status roughly approximated that of the slaves who came later
with the taking of prisoners in war. Hence like several branches from one trunk
spring the origins (1) of the asylums, as we have seen; (2) of families, from
which cities later arose, as we shall explain below; (3) of the founding of cities,
that men might live secure from the unjust and the violent; (4) of jurisdictions
to be exercised within prescribed territories; (5) of the extension of empires,
which comes by the practice of justice, strength and magnanimity, which are
the most luminous virtues of princes and states; (6) of family coats-of-arms,
whose first fields-of-arms are found to have stood for the first seed-fields; (7) of
fame, from which the *famuli* derived their name, and of glory, which is eternally
inherent in serving the human race; (8) of true nobility, which arises naturally
from the practice of the moral virtues; (9) of true heroism, which is to put
down the proud and give aid to those in danger (in which heroism the Roman
people surpassed all other peoples of the earth and so became master of the
world); and lastly, (10) of war and peace, the former taking its start in the
world from self-defense, in which the true virtue of strength consists. In all these
origins one can trace the eternal plan of commonwealths, on which states,
though acquired by violence and fraud, must take their stand in order to survive, as on the other hand those acquired by way of these virtuous origins
afterwards fall to ruin through fraud and violence. This plan of commonwealths
is founded on the two eternal principles of this world of nations, namely the
mind and the body of the men who compose it. For men consist of these two
parts, one of which is noble and should therefore command, and the other of
which is base and should serve. But because of the corruption of human nature,
the generic character of men cannot without the help of philosophy (which can
aid but few) bring it about that every individual's mind should command and
not serve his body. Therefore divine providence ordained human things with
this eternal order: that, in commonwealths, those who use their minds should
command and those who use their bodies should obey.

19   The rudder bows at the foot of the altar because these *famuli*, as men
without gods, had no share in divine things and consequently no community
even of human things with the nobles. Above all, they lacked the right to cele-

brate solemn nuptials, which the Latins called *connubium*. The most solemn
part of the ceremony was the taking of the auspices, by reason of which the
nobles thought themselves to be of divine origin and held the *famuli* to be of
bestial origin, as generated by nefarious couplings. Bound up with this distinction of a nobler nature we find, equally among the Egyptians, Greeks and
Latins, a presumed natural heroism, as is more than sufficiently made plain to
us in ancient Roman history.

20   Finally the rudder is at some distance from the plough, which is in
front of the altar and displays to the rudder a hostile aspect, menacing it with
its point. For the *famuli,* having no share, as we have seen, in the ownership
of lands, which were all in the hands of the nobles, grew weary of being obliged
always to serve their lords. At last, after a long period, they laid claim to the
lands and rose in mutiny to enforce the claim, and revolted against the heroes in
agrarian contests which, we shall learn, were much more ancient than and very
different from those that we read of in later Roman history. Many leaders of
bands of *famuli* which had rebelled and been conquered by the heroes (as the
serfs of Egypt often were by their priests, according to the observation of Peter
van der Kuhn, *De republica hebraeorum*), in order to avoid oppression and to
find escape and safety along with the members of their factions, committed
themselves to the hazards of the sea and went in search of unoccupied lands
along the shores of the Mediterranean, toward the West where the coasts were
not then inhabited. This is the origin of the transmigration of peoples already
humanized by religion, starting from the East (Phoenicia above all) and from
Egypt, as happened later, for the same reasons, in the case of the Greeks. In
such wise not inundations of peoples, which cannot take place by sea; nor the
jealous desire of keeping remote acquisitions by means of recognized colonies,
since we do not read of any empire of the East or of Egypt or Greece being extended into the West; nor reasons of trade, for the western coasts were not yet
inhabited; but rather heroic law made it necessary for such bands of men in
these nations to abandon their own lands, a thing which naturally happens only
under some extreme necessity. By means of such colonies, which will accordingly be called "heroic overseas colonies," the human race was spread abroad in
the rest of our world by sea, just as by means of the savage wanderings a long
time before it had been spread abroad by land.

21   Standing a little further out, in front of the plough, there is a tablet
inscribed with an ancient Latin alphabet (which, as Tacitus relates, was similar
to the ancient Greek) and, underneath, the latest alphabet that has come down
to us. This tablet symbolizes the origin of the languages and letters that are
called vulgar. These are found to have come into being a long time after the
founding of the nations, and letters much later than languages. To signify this,
the tablet rests on a fragment of a column of the Corinthian order, which
came quite late among the architectural orders.

22   The tablet lies near the plough and far from the rudder, to signify the

origin of native languages, which were first formed each in its own land, where the founders of the nations, scattered and dispersed through the great forest of the earth as we have said above, finally came together by chance and ceased their bestial wandering. With these native languages the Eastern or Egyptian or Greek tongues long afterwards mingled, on the occasion of the above-mentioned transmigration of peoples to the shores of the Mediterranean and the Ocean. Here we get new principles of etymology, abundantly illustrated throughout this work, by which the origins of native words may be distinguished from those that are unquestionably of foreign origin. The important difference is that native etymologies are histories of things signified by the words in the natural order of ideas. First the woods, then cultivated fields and huts, next little houses and villages, thence cities, finally academies and philosophers: this is the order of all progress from the first origins. Foreign etymologies, on the other hand, are mere stories of words taken by one language from another.

23 The tablet shows only the first letters of the alphabets and lies facing the statue of Homer. For the letters, as Greek tradition tells us of Greek letters, were not all invented at one time; at least they cannot all have been invented by Homer's time, for we know that he left none of his poems in writing. But of the origin of native languages more particular information will be given further on.

24 Lastly, in the plane most illuminated of all, because the hieroglyphs there displayed represent the most familiar human things, the ingenious artist exhibits in capricious arrangement the Roman fasces, a sword and a purse leaning against the fasces, a balance and the caduceus of Mercury.

25 The first of these symbols is the fasces because the first civil empires arose on the union of the paternal powers of the fathers. Among the gentiles these fathers were sages in auspicial divinity, priests who sacrificed to take the auspices or make sure of their meaning, and certainly monarchs who commanded what they believed to be the will of the gods as shown in the auspices, and consequently were subject to no one but God. So the fasces are a bundle of *litui* or rods of divination, which we find to be the first scepters of the world. These fathers, in the agrarian disturbances we have mentioned above, in order to resist the bands of *famuli* aroused against them, were naturally led to unite and enclose themselves in the first orders of reigning senates (or senates made up of so many kings of families) under certain heads-of-orders. These are found to have been the first kings of the heroic cities. Ancient history tells us, though too obscurely, that in the first world of the peoples kings were created by nature; our studies discover the manner. Now these reigning senates, to content the revolting bands of *famuli* and reduce them to obedience, granted them an agrarian law, which is found to have been the first civil law born in the world; and naturally the first plebs of the cities were composed of these *famuli*, subdued by this law. What the nobles granted the plebeians was natural domain of the fields, civil domain remaining with the nobles, who were the only citizens

of the heroic cities. Thence arose the eminent domain of the orders which were
the first civil or sovereign powers of the peoples. All three kinds of domain were
formed and distinguished one from another at the birth of the commonwealths,
which among all the nations, by one idea variously expressed, are found to have
been called "Herculean commonwealths" or commonwealths of Curetes, armed
men in public assembly. This clears up the origins of the famous *ius Quiritium,*
which the interpreters of Roman law have thought to be peculiar to the citizens
of Rome, as in later times it was; but in the ancient Roman times it was evidently a natural law of all the heroic peoples. And thence, as various streams
from a common source, numerous origins spring forth. (1) The origin of cities,
which arose from the families not of sons only but of *famuli* also. Thus they
will be seen to be founded by nature on two communities, one of the nobles,
to command, the other of the plebs, to obey. Of these two parts is composed the
entire polity or law of civil governments. For it is shown that the first cities, of
this or indeed any other kind, could not arise from families of sons only. (2) The
origins of public empires, which were born from the union of private father-
sovereign empires in the family state. (3) The origins of war and peace, whereby
all commonwealths were brought into being by force of arms and then composed by laws. From the nature of these [two] human things derives their
eternal property: that wars are waged so that peoples may live secure
in peace. (4) The origin of fiefs, for by one sort of rustic fiefs the plebeians
became subject to the nobles, and by another sort of noble or military
fiefs the nobles, who were sovereign in their own families, became subject
to the greater sovereignty of their heroic orders. We find that the kingdoms
of barbarian times have always had a feudal basis. This sheds light on the history
of the modern kingdoms of Europe, which arose in those latest barbarian times
that are more obscure to us than the first barbarian times of which Varro wrote.
For these first fields were given by the nobles to the plebs under burden of a
payment [variously] called tithe of Hercules (among the Greeks) or census
(which we find to be what Servius Tullius ordained for the Romans) or tribute.
The plebs were further obliged to serve the nobles in war at their own expense,
as is plain to be seen in ancient Roman history. Here appears (5) the origin of
the census which remained the basis of the popular commonwealths. Of all
our researches into things Roman, the most difficult has been that of tracing the
process by which this [popular census] developed from that of Servius Tullius,
which will be found to have been the basis of the ancient aristocratic commonwealths. The relation between the two has made everyone fall into the error of
assuming that Servius Tullius ordered the census as a basis for popular liberty.

26   From the same beginning come also: (6) The origin of commerce,
which, in the form we have indicated, began in real estate with the beginnings
of the cities themselves. The term "commerce" is derived from that first *merces*
or payment in the world, the fields which the heroes gave the *famuli* under the

aforesaid law obliging the latter to serve them. (7) The origin of public treasuries, the rudiments of which were there from the birth of the commonwealths
but which assumed the recognizable form properly called *aeraria* (from *aes
aeris* in the sense of "money") when the public had to supply money to the
plebs in war time. (8) The origin of colonies, which are found to have been
bands first of peasants who served the heroes for the sustenance of their lives,
then of vassals who cultivated the fields for themselves under the aforesaid real
and personal obligations. These we shall call heroic inland colonies to differentiate them from the overseas colonies mentioned above. And finally (9) the
origins of the commonwealths, which had at their birth a most severe aristocratic
form, in which the plebeians had no share in the civil law. In this connection
the Roman commonwealth is found to have been an aristocratic kingdom which
fell under the tyranny of Tarquinius Superbus, who sadly misgoverned the
nobles and almost destroyed the senate. When Lucretia stabbed herself, Junius
Brutus seized the occasion to arouse the plebs against the Tarquins, and, having
freed Rome from their tyranny, reëstablished the senate and reorganized the
commonwealth on its first principles. For by substituting two annual consuls
for one king for life, he did not introduce popular liberty but rather reaffirmed
the liberty of the nobles. This is found to have lasted till the Publilian Law,
which won for the dictator Publilius Philo the epithet "popular" by declaring
that the Roman commonwealth had become popular in its form of government.
Indeed it expired only with the Petelian Law, which completely freed the people from the feudal rustic right of private imprisonment which the nobles had
over their plebeian debtors. These two laws, which contain the two major points
in Roman history, have been pondered neither by statesmen nor by jurists nor
by the learned interpreters of Roman law. For they have been misled by the
fable that the Law of the Twelve Tables came from free Athens to set up popular liberty in Rome, whereas these two laws declare it to have been set up at home
by the natural customs of the Romans themselves. (This fable was exposed in
the *Principles of Universal Law,* printed many years ago.) Therefore, since
the laws of a commonwealth must be interpreted according to its form of government, these principles of Roman government involve new principles for
Roman jurisprudence.

27   The sword leaning on the fasces indicates that heroic law was a law
of force but subject to religion, which alone can keep force and arms in their
place where judiciary laws do not yet exist or are no longer recognized. This
law is precisely that of Achilles, the hero sung by Homer to the Greeks as an
example of heroic virtue, who made arms the arbiter of right. Here is revealed
the origin of duels; which, as they were certainly celebrated in the last barbarian
times, so they are found to have been practiced in the first barbarian times when
the mighty were not yet so tamed as to avenge offenses and injuries by appeal to
judiciary laws. The duels they practiced were appeals to certain divine judgments. They called on God as witness and made God judge of the offense, and

accepted with such reverence the decision that was given by the fortune of
the combat that even if the outraged party fell vanquished he was considered
guilty. This was a lofty counsel of divine providence, to the end that, in fierce
and barbarous times in which law was not understood, it might be measured
by God's favor or disfavor, so that such private wars might not sow the seeds
of [greater] wars which would have ended in the extinction of the human
race. This natural barbarian sense can only be grounded in the innate concept
which men have of that divine providence in which they must acquiesce when
they see the good oppressed and the wicked prospering. For all these reasons
the duel was thought to be a kind of divine purgation, and in barbarian times
the belief in its necessity was quite as firm as the prohibition of it in the humanity
of our day with its civil and criminal courts. In such duels or private wars is
found the origin of public wars which are waged by civil powers subject to no
one but God, in order that God may settle them by the fortune of victory; so
that the human race may rest on the certainty of civil states. This is the principle of the external justice, as it is called, of wars.

28   The purse resting against the fasces shows that commerce carried
on by means of money began late, after the civil empires were founded, so
that we read of no coined money in either of the two poems of Homer. This
same hieroglyph indicates the origin of such coined money, which is found
to have been the same as that of family coats-of-arms. The latter (as we have
intimated above in connection with the first fields-of-arms) are discovered to
have signified rights and titles of nobility belonging to one family rather than
to another. Thence came the origin of public emblems, or ensigns of the people,
which were then raised as military ensigns used as a mute language by military
discipline; and finally among all peoples they gave their imprint to coins. Here
are given new principles to numismatics, and thereby also to the science of
blazonry as it is called; which is one of the three topics on which we find ourselves satisfied with the first edition of the *New Science*.

29   The balance next to the purse is meant to indicate that, after the
aristocratic governments, which were heroic governments, there came human
governments, at first popular in character. The people had finally come to
understand that the rational nature (which is the true human nature) is equal
in all men. From this natural equality (by occasions conceived in the ideal
eternal history and encountered exactly in Roman history) they gradually
brought the heroes to civil equality in popular commonwealths. This civil
equality is symbolized by the balance, because, as the Greeks said, in the popular
commonwealths everything goes by lot or by balance. But finally, as the free
peoples could not by means of laws maintain themselves in civil equality because of the factions of the powerful, but were being driven to ruin by civil
wars, it came about naturally that, obeying a natural royal law or rather natural
custom of human peoples, they sought protection under monarchies, which constitute the other type of human government. (This natural royal law is com-

mon to all peoples in all times in popular states which have grown corrupt, but the civil royal law, which is said to have been commanded by the Roman people to legitimize the Roman monarchy in the person of Augustus, is shown in our *Principles of Universal Law* to have been a fable. Our demonstration of this, and of the legendary nature of the story that the Law of the Twelve Tables came from Athens, are two passages which permit us to believe that we did not write that work in vain.) In the humanity of our day, there are alternations of these last two forms of government, both human, but neither of the two passes by nature into an aristocratic state where only the nobles command and all the others obey. Hence the commonwealths of nobles now left in the world are few and far between: Nuremberg in Germany; Ragusa in Dalmatia; Venice, Genoa and Lucca in Italy. These, then, are the three types of states that divine providence, through the natural customs of the nations, has caused to come into the world, and they succeed one another in this natural order. Since other types, arising by human providence as mixtures of these three, are not supported by the nature of nations, they were characterized by Tacitus (who saw only the effects of the causes we here point out and later treat more fully) as "more laudable than susceptible of attainment, and if by chance any do occur they are not at all lasting." By this discovery new principles are given to political theory, not merely different from but contrary to those which have been imagined hitherto.

30 The caduceus is the last of the hieroglyphs, to tell us that the first peoples, in their heroic times when the natural law of force reigned supreme, looked upon each other as perpetual enemies, and pillage and piracy were continual because, as war was eternal between them, there was no need of declarations. (Indeed, as in the first barbarian times the heroes considered it a title of honor to be called thieves, so in the returned barbarian times the powerful rejoiced to be called pirates.) But when human governments had been established, whether popular or monarchical, by the law of human peoples heralds were introduced to give warning of wars, and periods of hostility began to be terminated by treaties of peace. And this by a high counsel of divine providence, to the end that nations in their period of barbarism, when they were new in the world and needed to take root, should remain circumscribed within their boundaries and not, fierce and untamed as they were, cross them to exterminate each other in wars; but after they had grown up and at the same time become familiar with each other and hence tolerant of each other's customs, it should then be easy for conquering peoples to spare the lives of the conquered by the just laws of victory.

31 So this New Science or metaphysic, pondering the common nature of nations in the light of divine providence, having discovered such origins of divine and human things among the gentile nations, establishes thence a system of the natural law of nations, which proceeds with the greatest equality and constancy through the three ages which the Egyptians handed down to us as

the three periods through which the world had passed up to their time. These
are: (1) The age of the gods, in which the gentiles believed they lived under
divine governments, and everything was commanded them by auspices and
oracles, which are the oldest things in profane history. (2) The age of the
heroes, in which they reigned everywhere in aristocratic commonwealths, on account of a certain superiority of nature which they held themselves to have over
the plebs. (3) The age of men, in which all men recognized themselves as equal
in human nature, and therefore there were established first the popular commonwealths and then the monarchies, both of which are forms of human government, as we observed a short while ago [29].

32   In harmony with these three kinds of nature and government, three
kinds of language were spoken which compose the vocabulary of this Science:
(1) That of the time of the families when gentile men were newly received into
humanity. This, we shall find, was a mute language of signs and physical objects
having natural relations to the ideas they wished to express. (2) That spoken by
means of heroic emblems, or similitudes, comparisons, images, metaphors, and
natural descriptions, which make up the great body of the heroic language
which was spoken at the time the heroes reigned. (3) Human language using
words agreed upon by the people, a language of which they are absolute lords,
and which is proper to the popular commonwealths and monarchical states;
a language whereby the people may fix the meaning of the laws by which the
nobles as well as the plebs are bound. Hence, among all nations, once the laws
had been put into the vulgar tongue, the science of laws passed from the control
of the nobles. Hitherto, among all nations, the nobles had kept the laws in a
secret language as a sacred thing, for it will be found that everywhere the nobles
were also priests. That is the natural reason for the secrecy of the laws among
the Roman patricians until popular liberty arose. Now these are the same three
languages that the Egyptians claimed had been spoken before in their world,
corresponding exactly both in number and in sequence to the three ages that had
run their course before them. (1) The hieroglyphic or sacred or secret language, by means of mute acts. This is suited to the uses of religion, which it
is more important to attend to than to talk about. (2) The symbolic, by means
of similitudes, such as we have just seen the heroic language to have been. (3)
The epistolary or vulgar, which served the common uses of life. These three
types of language are found among the Chaldeans, Scythians, Egyptians, Germans, and all the other ancient gentile nations; although hieroglyphic writing
was best preserved among the Egyptians, because for a longer time than the
other peoples they were closed to all foreign nations (it is for the same reason
that it has been found to exist still among the Chinese), and hence we have
a proof of the vanity of their imagined remote antiquity.

33   We here bring to light the beginnings not only of languages but also
of letters, which philology has hitherto despaired of finding. We shall give a
specimen [430] of the extravagant and monstrous opinions that have been held

up to now. We shall observe that the unhappy cause of this effect is that philologists have believed that among the nations languages first came into being and then letters; whereas (to give here a brief indication of what will be fully proved in this volume) letters and languages were born twins and proceeded apace through all their three stages. These beginnings are precisely exhibited in the causes of the Latin language, as set forth in the first edition of the *New Science* (which is the second of the three passages on whose account we do not regret that book). By the reasoning out of these causes many discoveries have been made in ancient Roman history, government and law, as you will observe a thousand times, O reader, in this volume. From this example, scholars of oriental languages, of Greek, and, among the modern languages, particularly of German, which is a mother language, will be enabled to make discoveries of antiquities far beyond their expectations and ours.

34 We find that the principle of these origins both of languages and of letters lies in the fact that the early gentile peoples, by a demonstrated necessity of nature, were poets who spoke in poetic characters. This discovery, which is the master key of this Science, has cost us the persistent research of almost all our literary life, because with our civilized natures we cannot at all imagine and can only understand by great toil the poetic nature of these first men. The [poetic] characters of which we speak are found to have been certain imaginative genera (images for the most part of animate beings, of gods or heroes, formed by their imagination) to which they reduced all the species or all the particulars appertaining to each genus; exactly as the fables of human times, such as those of late comedy, are intelligible genera reasoned out by moral philosophy, from which the comic poets form imaginative genera (for the perfected ideas of the various human types are nothing but that) which are the persons of the comedies. Hence such divine or heroic characters are found to have been true fables or stories, and their allegories are discovered to contain meanings not analogical but univocal, not philosophical but historical, of the peoples of Greece of those times. Furthermore, since these genera (for that is what the fables in essence are) were formed by most vigorous imaginations, as in men of the feeblest reasoning powers, we discover in them true poetic sentences, which must be sentiments clothed in the greatest passions and therefore full of sublimity and arousing wonder. Furthermore the sources of all poetic locution are found to be two: poverty of language and necessity to explain and make oneself understood. Hence it is evident that heroic speech followed immediately on the mute language of acts and objects that had natural relations to the ideas they were meant to signify, which was used in the divine times. And finally, through the necessary natural course of human things, language among the Assyrians, Syrians, Phoenicians, Egyptians, Greeks and Latins will be found to have begun with heroic verses, thence to have passed to iambics and finally to have settled into prose. This gives certainty to the history of the ancient poets and explains why in the German language, par-

ticularly in Silesia, a province of peasants, there are many natural versifiers, and in the Spanish, French and Italian languages the first authors wrote in verse.

35   From these three languages is formed the mental dictionary by which to interpret properly all the various articulated languages, and we make use of it here wherever it is needed. In the first edition of the *New Science* we gave a full particular example of it, in which this idea was presented: that from the eternal properties of the fathers, which we in virtue of this Science considered them to have had in the state of the families and of the first heroic cities in the time when the languages were formed, we find proper meanings [of terms] in fifteen different languages, both dead and living, by which they were diversely called, sometimes from one property and sometimes from another. (This is the third passage in which we take satisfaction in that edition of our book.) Such a lexicon is necessary for learning the language spoken by the ideal eternal history traversed in time by the histories of all nations, and for scientifically adducing authorities to confirm what is discussed in the natural law of nations and hence in every particular jurisprudence.

36   Along with these three languages—proper to the three ages in which three forms of government prevailed, conforming to three types of civil natures, which succeed one another as the nations run their course—we find there went also in the same order a jurisprudence suited to each in its time.

37   Of these [three types of jurisprudence] the first was a mystic theology, which prevailed in the period when the gentiles were commanded by the gods. Its wise men were the theological poets (who are said to have founded gentile humanity) who interpreted the mysteries of the oracles, which among all nations gave their responses in verse. Thus we find that the mysteries of this vulgar wisdom were hidden in the fables. In this connection we inquire into the reasons why the philosophers later had such a desire to recover the wisdom of the ancients, as well as into the occasions the fables provided them for bestirring themselves to meditate lofty things in philosophy, and into the opportunities they had for reading their own hidden wisdom into the fables.

38   The second was the heroic jurisprudence, all verbal scrupulosity (in which Ulysses was manifestly expert). This jurisprudence looked to what the Roman jurisconsults called civil equity and we call reason of state. With their limited ideas, the heroes thought they had a natural right to precisely what, how much and of what sort had been set forth in words; as even now we may observe in peasants and other crude men, who in conflicts between words and meanings obstinately say that their right stands for them in the words. And this by counsel of divine providence to the end that the gentiles, not yet being capable of universals, which good laws must be, might be led by this very particularity of their words to observe the laws universally. And if, as a consequence of this [civil] equity, the laws turned out in a given case to be not only harsh but actually cruel, they naturally bore it because they thought their law was naturally such. Furthermore they were led to observe their laws by their

own highest interest, with which, we find, the heroes identified that of their fatherlands, of which they were the only citizens. Hence they did not hesitate, for the safety of their various fatherlands, to consecrate themselves and their families to the will of the laws, which by maintaining the common security of the fatherland kept secure for each of them a certain private monarchical reign over his family. Moreover it was this great private interest, in conjunction with the supreme arrogance characteristic of barbarous times, which formed their heroic nature, whence came so many heroic actions in defense of their fatherlands. To these heroic deeds we must add intolerable pride, profound avarice and the pitiless cruelty with which the ancient Roman patricians treated the unhappy plebeians, as is clearly seen in Roman history precisely during that period which Livy himself describes as having been the age of Roman virtue and of the most flourishing popular liberty yet dreamed of in Rome. It will be found that such public virtue was nothing but a good use which providence made of such grievous, ugly and cruel private vices, in order that the cities might be preserved during a period when the minds of men, intent on particulars, could not naturally understand a common good. Thence are derived new principles by which to demonstrate the argument of St. Augustine's discussion of the virtue of the Romans [*City of God,* V, 12]; and the opinion hitherto held by the learned concerning the heroism of primitive peoples is put to rout. Civil equity of this sort we find naturally observed by the heroic nations in peace as well as in war (shining examples are adduced from the history of the first barbarian times as well as from that of the last); and it was practiced privately by the Romans as long as theirs was an aristocratic commonwealth, that is to say down to the times of the Publilian and Petelian laws, until which time everything was based on the Law of the Twelve Tables.

39   The last type of jurisprudence was that of natural equity, which reigns naturally in the free commonwealths, where the peoples, each for its particular good (without understanding that it is the same for all), are led to command universal laws. They naturally desire these laws to bend benignly to the least details of matters calling for equal utility. This is the *aequum bonum,* subject of the latest Roman jurisprudence, which from the times of Cicero had begun to be transformed by the edict of the Roman praetor. This type is also and perhaps even more connatural with monarchies, in which the monarchs have accustomed their subjects to attend to their own private interests, while they themselves have taken charge of all public affairs, and desire all nations subject to them to be made equal by the laws, in order that all may be equally interested in the state. Wherefore the emperor Hadrian reformed the entire heroic natural law of Rome with the aid of the human natural law of the provinces, and commanded that jurisprudence should be based on the Perpetual Edict which Salvius Julianus composed almost entirely from the provincial edicts.

40   We may now recapitulate all the prime elements of this world of na-

tions by reference to the hieroglyphs which stand for them. The lituus, water
and fire on the altar, the cinerary urn within the forest, the plough leaning
against the altar, and the rudder prostrate at the foot of the altar signify divination, sacrifices, the first families including sons only, the practice of burial, the
cultivation of the fields and their division, the asylums, the later families including *famuli,* the first agrarian conflicts and hence the first heroic inland
colonies and, when these failed, the overseas colonies and with these the first
transmigrations of peoples. All these came within the Egyptian age of the
gods, which Varro through ignorance or negligence called "the obscure period,"
as we have seen above. The fasces signify the first heroic commonwealths, the
distinction of the three domains (natural, civil and eminent), the first civil empires, the first unequal alliances accorded under the first agrarian law by which
these first cities were founded on rustic fiefs of the plebeians, which in turn
were subfiefs of the noble fiefs of the heroes, who, though themselves sovereigns, became subjects of the higher sovereignty of the reigning heroic orders.
The sword leaning on the fasces signifies the public wars that were waged by
these cities, beginning with raids and rapine. (Duels, or private wars, must have
started much earlier, as we shall show, within the state of the families.) The
purse signifies devices of nobility or family coats-of-arms carried over onto
medals, the first ensigns of the peoples, which later became military ensigns and
finally coins, which here stand for the extension of trade to movable goods by
means of money. (Trade in real estate, with natural prices in produce or work,
had begun before in divine times with the first agrarian law, on the basis of
which the commonwealths were born.) The balance signifies the laws of
equality, which are laws properly speaking. Finally the caduceus signifies
formally declared public wars, terminated by formal peace. All the hieroglyphs
of this second group are far from the altar because they all stand for civil things
of the times in which the false religions were slowly disappearing, beginning
with the heroic agrarian conflicts, which gave the name to the Egyptian age of
heroes, called by Varro the "fabulous period." The tablet with the alphabets is
put between the divine and human symbols because with letters, from which
philosophies had their beginning, the false religions began to disappear; in contrast with the true, which is our Christian religion, which indeed is humanly
confirmed to us by the most sublime philosophies, the Platonic and the Peri-
patetic (insofar as it conforms to the Platonic).

41   The whole idea of this work may be summed up as follows. The
darkness in the background of the picture is the material of this Science, uncertain, unformed, obscure, which is set forth in the Chronological Table and
in the Notes upon it. The ray with which divine providence lights up the
breast of metaphysic represents the Axioms, Definitions and Postulates that
this Science takes as Elements from which to deduce the Principles on which
it is based and the Method by which it proceeds. All these things are contained
in the first book. The ray that is reflected from the breast of metaphysic onto

the statue of Homer is the proper light which is given to poetic wisdom in the second book, and by which the true Homer is elucidated in the third book. By "The Discovery of the True Homer" everything that makes up this world of nations is clarified, proceeding from their origins according to the order in which the hieroglyphs come forth into the light of the true Homer. This is the Course of Nations considered in the fourth book. And having arrived finally at the foot of the statue of Homer, they begin a Recurrence in the same order. Of this we treat in the fifth and last book.

42   Last of all, to state the idea of the book in the briefest summary, the entire engraving represents the three worlds in the order in which the human minds of the gentiles have been raised from earth to heaven. All the hieroglyphs visible on the ground denote the world of nations to which men applied themselves before anything else. The globe in the middle represents the world of nature which the physicists later observed. The hieroglyphs above signify the world of minds and of God which the metaphysicians finally contemplated.

BOOK ONE

ESTABLISHMENT OF PRINCIPLES

[SECTION I]

NOTES ON THE CHRONOLOGICAL TABLE,
IN WHICH THE MATERIALS ARE SET IN ORDER

I

[Chronological table, based on the three temporal epochs of the Egyptians, who said all the world before them had passed through three ages: that of the gods, that of the heroes, and that of men.]

43   This Chronological Table sets forth in outline the world of the ancient nations, starting from the universal flood and passing from the Hebrews through the Chaldeans, Scythians, Phoenicians, Egyptians, Greeks and Romans down to the Second Punic War. On it there appear men and deeds of the greatest renown, assigned to certain times and places by the community of scholars. These men and deeds either did not have their being at the times or in the places to which they have been commonly assigned, or never existed at all. On the other hand, from the long dark shadows where they have lain buried, notable men and most pertinent facts emerge, through whom and by which the decisive changes in human affairs have come about. All this is set forth in these Notes, to show how uncertain, unseemly, defective, or vain are the beginnings of the nations.

44   Moreover this Table takes a position quite opposed to that of the Chronological Canon [*Canon chronicon, aegyptiacus, hebraicus, graecus*] of John Marsham, in which he tries to prove that the Egyptians preceded all the nations of the world in government and religion, and that their sacred rites and civil ordinances, transported to other peoples, were received with some emendation by the Hebrews. In this opinion he was followed by [John] Spencer in his dissertation *De Urim et Tummim,* in which he expresses the opinion that the Israelites had taken from the Egyptians all their science of divine things by means of the sacred Cabala. Finally Marsham was acclaimed by van Heurn in his *Antiquitates philosophiae barbaricae,* in which, in the part entitled *Chaldaicus,* he writes that Moses, instructed in the knowledge of them by the Egyptians, had brought divine things to the Hebrews in his laws. Against this line of argument arose Hermann Wits in his *Aegyptiaca.* He thinks that the first gentile author to give us reliable information about the Egyptians was Dion

Cassius, who flourished under the philosopher Marcus Aurelius. But on this point he may be confuted by the *Annals* of Tacitus, in which we are told that Germanicus, having gone into the East, proceeded thence to Egypt to see the famous antiquities of Thebes, and had one of the priests there interpret to him the hieroglyphs inscribed on some of the monuments. The priest, talking foolishly, told him that those characters preserved the memory of the boundless power that their king Ramses had held in Africa, in the East and even in Asia Minor, equal to the power of the Romans in their own time, which was very great. But this passage, perhaps because it was contrary to his position, Wits said nothing about.

45   But certainly such boundless antiquity did not yield much recondite wisdom to the inland Egyptians. For in the time of Clement of Alexandria, as he recounts in his Miscellanies [*Stromata*], their so-called "priestly" books were in circulation to the number of forty-two, and they contained the greatest errors in philosophy and astronomy, for which Chaeremon, teacher of St. Dionysius the Areopagite, is often scoffed at by Strabo. Their ideas about medicine are found by Galen in his discussion of Hermetic medicine to be obvious nonsense and mere quackery. Their morality was dissolute, for it not only tolerated or permitted harlots but made them respectable. Their theology was full of superstition, magic and witchcraft. And the magnificence of their pyramids and other monuments might well have sprung from barbarism, which accords well with hugeness. Egyptian sculpture and casting are regarded even today as extremely crude. For delicacy is the fruit of philosophy, wherefore Greece alone, which was the nation of philosophers, shone with all the fine arts that human genius has ever discovered: painting, sculpture, casting, and the arts of engraving, which are most delicate because they are compelled to abstract the surfaces of the bodies they represent.

46   This ancient wisdom of the Egyptians was raised to the stars by Alexandria, founded on the sea by Alexander the Great. Uniting African acuteness with Greek delicacy, it produced distinguished philosophers in divinity, through whom the city gained such renown for high divine wisdom that the Alexandrian Museum was later as much celebrated as the Academy, the Lyceum, the Stoa and the Cynosarges all together had been in Athens. Alexandria was called on this account "the mother of the sciences." Such was its excellence that the Greeks called it simply *Polis*, "The City," as Athens was called *Astu* and Rome *Urbs*. Thence came Manetho, the Egyptian high priest, who turned all Egyptian history into a sublime natural theology, just as the Greek philosophers had previously done with their fables, which will here be found to have been their most ancient histories. This explains why the same thing happened to the Greek fables as to the Egyptian hieroglyphs.

47   With such a show of high wisdom, the nation, arrogant by nature (and hence mockingly called "animals of glory"), in a city which was a great emporium of the Mediterranean and, through the Red Sea, of the Ocean and

the Indies (a city among whose abominable customs was that related by Tacitus in a golden passage, that it was "avid of new religions"), believed that the false gods which were scattered abroad in the world (as they learned from the nations which met there for maritime trade) must all have originated in their Egypt, and that their Jove Ammon was the oldest of all Joves (of which every gentile nation had one), and that the Herculeses of all the other nations (Varro enumerated as many as forty) must have taken their names from their Egyptian Hercules. These [pretensions], both reported to us by Tacitus, were due in part to the prejudiced opinion of their exceptional antiquity, which they vainly boasted over all other nations of the world, adding that in ancient times they had lorded it over a great part of the world. They were due in part also to their not knowing the way in which uniform ideas of gods and heroes were born among the gentile peoples without their having any knowledge of each other, as we shall fully demonstrate later on. Now for all the too flattering judgments with which Diodorus Siculus (who lived in the times of Augustus) adorns the Egyptians, he does not accord them more than two thousand years of antiquity, and his judgments are overthrown by Jacques Cappel in his *Historia sacra et exotica,* who puts them in the same class with those which Xenophon had ascribed to Cyrus (and we may add those which Plato often feigns of the Persians). Finally all this concerning the vanity of the high ancient wisdom of the Egyptians is confirmed by the hoax of the *Poimander,* palmed off as Hermetic doctrine. Saumaise considered this fragment a disordered and badly composed collection of things, and Casaubon found that it contained no doctrine more ancient than that which the Platonists set forth in the same phraseology.

48   This false opinion of their great antiquity was caused among the Egyptians by a property of the human mind—that of being indefinite—by which it is often led to believe that the things it does not know are vastly greater than in fact they are. The Egyptians were in this respect like the Chinese, who grew up into such a great nation cut off from all foreign nations, for the Egyptians were similarly cut off until Psammeticus, and the Scythians until Idanthyrsus. The latter indeed, according to a vulgar tradition, surpassed the Egyptians in antiquity. This vulgar tradition must have taken its start from [the legendary episode] with which profane universal history begins. It sets up, in Justin's version, as two pre-beginnings antedating the monarchy of the Assyrians, two powerful kings, Tanaus the Scythian and Sesostris the Egyptian, who have until now made the world seem older than it really is. [The story goes] that Tanaus had moved first through the East with a great army to subdue Egypt, which is by nature very difficult to penetrate with an army, and that then Sesostris with an equally great host had moved to subdue Scythia. Yet Scythia lived unknown to the Persians themselves (who had extended their monarchy over that of the Medes, their neighbors) down to the time of Darius called the Great, who declared war on Idanthyrsus, king of the Scythians; and this king was

so barbarous even in the days of a most civilized Persia that he answered him with five real words in the form of five objects, since he did not even know how to write with hieroglyphs. And we are to believe that these two great and mighty kings crossed Asia with two great hosts without making it a province either of Scythia or Egypt, but leaving it in such liberty that there later grew up there the first of the four most famous monarchies in the world, that of Assyria!

49   For the same reason, perhaps, the Chaldeans did not fail to enter the lists in this contest of antiquity. They too were an inland people and, as we shall show, more ancient than the other two, who vainly boasted that they had preserved the astronomical observations of a good twenty-eight thousand years. This was perhaps the reason that Flavius Josephus the Jew erroneously regarded as antediluvian the observations described on the two columns, one of marble and one of brick, raised against the two floods, and thought that he himself had seen the marble one in Syria. So important was it to the ancient nations to preserve astronomical records, whereas this sense was quite dead among the nations that followed them! Wherefore this column finds its proper place in the museum of credulity.

50   But the Chinese are found writing in hieroglyphs just as the ancient Egyptians did (to say nothing of the Scythians, who did not even know how to put their hieroglyphs in writing). For many thousands of years they had no commerce with other nations by whom they might have been informed concerning the real antiquity of the world. Just as a man confined while asleep in a very small dark room, in horror of darkness [on waking] believes it certainly much larger than groping with his hands will show it to be, so, in the darkness of their chronology, the Chinese and the Egyptians have done, and the Chaldeans likewise. It is true that Father Michele Ruggieri, a Jesuit, declares that he has himself read books printed before the coming of Jesus Christ. It is true further that Father Martini, another Jesuit, in his *Sinica historia* ascribes a great antiquity to Confucius, which has led many into atheism, as we are informed by Martin Schoock in his *Diluvium Noachi universale,* in which he says that Isaac de la Peyrère, author of the *Preadamitae,* perhaps for that reason abandoned the Catholic faith and then wrote that the flood spread over the lands of the Hebrews only. Nevertheless Nicolas Trigault, better informed than Ruggieri or Martini, writes in his *De christiana expeditione apud Sinas* that printing was in use in China not more than two centuries earlier than in Europe, and that Confucius flourished not more than five hundred years before Christ. And the Confucian philosophy, like the priestly books of the Egyptians, in its few references to physical nature is crude and clumsy, and it turns almost entirely on a vulgar moral code, that is to say on morals commanded to the people by laws.

51   Premising such reflections on the vain opinion of their own antiquity held by these gentile nations and above all by the Egyptians, we should begin our study of gentile learning [*tutto lo scibile gentilesco*] by scientifically ascer-

taining this important starting-point—where and when that learning had its first beginnings in the world—and by adducing human reasons thereby in support of Christian faith [*tutto il credibile cristiano*], which takes its start from the fact that the first people of the world were the Hebrews, whose prince was Adam, created by the true God at the time of the creation of the world. It follows that the first science to be learned should be mythology or the interpretation of fables; for, as we shall see, all the histories of the gentiles have their beginnings in fables, which were the first histories of the gentile nations. By such a method the beginnings of the sciences as well as of the nations are to be discovered, for they sprang from the nations and from no other source. It will be shown throughout this work that they had their beginnings in the public needs or utilities of the peoples and that they were later perfected as acute individuals applied their reflection to them. This is the proper starting-point for universal history, which all scholars say is defective in its beginnings.

52 In this undertaking we shall be greatly helped by the antiquity of the Egyptians, for they have preserved for us two great fragments not less marvelous than their pyramids, namely these two great philological verities. The first is narrated by Herodotus: that the Egyptians reduced all the preceding time of the world to three ages, the first that of the gods, the second that of the heroes, the third that of men. The other (as related in Scheffer's *De natura et constitutione philosophiae italicae seu pythagoricae*) is that, with corresponding number and sequence, through all that period three languages had been spoken: the first hieroglyphic, with sacred characters; the second symbolic, with heroic characters; the third epistolary, with characters agreed on by the people. This division of time was not followed by Marcus Terentius Varro; we must not say because he did not know of it, for, with his boundless erudition, he deserved the honor bestowed on him in the title "most learned of the Romans" in their most enlightened period, the age of Cicero; but rather because he did not choose to; perhaps because he applied [only] to Roman history what by our principles will be found true of all the ancient nations, namely that all Roman things, divine and human, were native to Latium. He therefore studied to give them all Latin origins in his great work on things divine and human [*Antiquitates*], of which the injustice of time has deprived us (yet Varro believed in the legendary bringing of the law of the Twelve Tables from Athens to Rome!). He divided the times of the world into three: a dark age, corresponding to the Egyptian age of the gods; a fabulous age, corresponding to their age of the heroes; and a historic age, corresponding to their age of men.

53 Furthermore the antiquity of the Egyptians will help us with two pretentious memories, examples of that national self-conceit by which, as Diodorus Siculus observed, every nation barbarian or civilized has considered itself to be the oldest and to have preserved its records from the beginning of the world; a privilege, as we shall see, of the Hebrews alone. These two pretentious

memories we have observed to be, first, the legend that their Jove Ammon was
the oldest of all the Joves in the world, and second, that the Herculeses of all
the other nations had taken their name from the Egyptian Hercules. That is,
that all nations had passed first through the age of gods, the king of whom was
by all these nations held to be Jove; and then through the age of heroes, who
were considered sons of the gods, and of whom Hercules was believed to be
the greatest.

II
[The Hebrews]

54   The first column is dedicated to the Hebrews, who, on the most reliable authority of Flavius Josephus, the Jew, and Lactantius Firmianus, to be
cited later, lived unknown to all the gentile nations. And yet they reckoned
rightly the account of the times passed through by the world, now accepted as
true by the severest critics, according to the calculation of Philo the Jew. If
his estimate varies from that of Eusebius, the deviation is one of a mere fifteen
hundred years, which is a very short period of time compared with the variations among the calculations made by the Chaldeans, Scythians, Egyptians,
and in our own day by the Chinese. And this should be an invincible proof that
the Hebrews were the first people in our world and that in the sacred history
they have accurately preserved their memories from the very beginning of the
world.

III
[The Chaldeans]

55   The second column is devoted to the Chaldeans, both because in
geography it is clear that the most inland monarchy of all the habitable world
must have been in Assyria, and because in this work it is shown that the inland
nations were populated first, and then the maritime nations. And certainly
the Chaldeans were the first gentile sages, and the common opinion of philologians regards Zoroaster the Chaldean as their prince. And without question
universal history takes its beginning from the monarchy of the Assyrians, which
must have begun to take shape among the Chaldean people; from whom, when
it had grown to great size, it must have passed to the nation of the Assyrians
under Ninus, who must have founded that monarchy not with people brought
in from outside but with those born within Chaldea itself, whereupon he did
away with the Chaldean name and brought forward the Assyrian in its stead. It
must have been the plebeians of that nation through whose support Ninus made
himself king. It will be shown in this work that such was the political custom
in almost all nations, as we know certainly it was of the Roman. Now the same
[universal] history tells us that Zoroaster was slain by Ninus. We shall see that
this was said, in heroic language, in the sense that the kingdom of the Chaldeans which had been aristocratic (and of which Zoroaster had been the heroic
character) was overthrown by means of the popular liberty of the plebeians of

that people. We shall see that in heroic times these plebeians were a different nation from the nobles, and that with the aid of this nation Ninus established himself as monarch. Otherwise, if things are not as we have stated them, this monster of chronology would emerge in Assyrian history: that within the life-time of one man, Zoroaster, Chaldea had grown from [a land of] lawless vaga-bonds to such greatness of empire that Ninus was able to found on it a mighty monarchy. For lack of these principles, Ninus, taken as the initiator of universal history, has hitherto made the monarchy of Assyria seem to have been born all at once, as a frog is born in a summer shower.

IV
[The Scythians]

56   The third column is set up for the Scythians, who surpassed the Egyptians in antiquity, as we learned not far back [48] from a vulgar tradi-tion.

V
[The Phoenicians]

57   The fourth column is assigned to the Phoenicians rather than to the Egyptians, to whom the Phoenicians brought from the Chaldeans the use of the quadrant and the knowledge of the elevation of the pole. Of so much there is a vulgar tradition. We shall show later that they brought also vulgar [alphabetic] characters.

VI
[The Egyptians]

58   For all the reasons discussed above, the Egyptians, to whom Marsham in his *Canon* accords the distinction of being the most ancient of all the na-tions, merit the fifth place in our Chronological Table.

VII
[Zoroaster, or the kingdom of the Chaldeans. Year of the world 1756.]

59   Zoroaster is shown in this work to have been a poetic character of founders of peoples in the East. There are as many of these founders scattered through that great part of the world as there are Herculeses scattered through the opposite part, the West. And perhaps the Herculeses whom Varro observed to exist in the likeness of the western ones even in Asia, such as the Tyrian or Phoenician, must have been considered by the easterners as so many Zoroasters. But the vanity of scholars, who will have it that whatever they know is as an-cient as the world, has made of them one individual man brimming with the highest esoteric wisdom, and has attached to him the oracles of philosophy, which do nothing but palm off as ancient a very modern doctrine, namely that of the Pythagoreans and the Platonists. But this vanity of the scholars did not stop here, for it swelled even further by deriving from him the scholastic suc-

cession among the nations. According to them, Zoroaster taught Berosus for
Chaldea; Berosus, Hermes Trismegistus for Egypt; Hermes Trismegistus, Atlas
for Ethiopia; Atlas, Orpheus for Thrace; and finally Orpheus founded his school
in Greece. But we shall see shortly how [far from] easy these long journeys were
for the ancient nations, who, because of their recent savage origin, lived everywhere unknown even to their nearest neighbors, and came to know each other
only by occasion of war or by reason of trade.

  60   But concerning the Chaldeans the philologians themselves, confused
by the various vulgar traditions which they have themselves collected, do not
know whether they were individual men or entire families or a whole people
or nation. All these doubts will be resolved by the following principles. They
were first individuals, then entire families, later a whole people and finally a
great nation on which the monarchy of Assyria was founded. Their wisdom was
at first in vulgar divinity, by means of which they divined the future from the
path of falling stars at night, and then in judicial astrology. Thus among the
Latins a judicial astrologer was still called a Chaldean.

VIII

[Iapetus, from whom spring the giants. Year of the world 1856.]

  61   Giants, as we shall show by physical histories found in the Greek
fables and by proofs both physical and moral drawn from civil histories, existed
in nature among all the first gentile nations.

IX

[Nimrod, or the confusion of tongues. Year of the world 1856.]

  62   The confusion of tongues came about in a miraculous way so that
on the instant many different languages were formed. The Fathers will have it
that through this confusion of tongues the purity of the sacred antediluvian language was gradually lost. This should be understood as referring to the languages of the Eastern peoples among whom Shem propagated the human race.
It must have been otherwise in the case of the nations of all the rest of the
world; for the races of Ham and Japheth were destined to be scattered through
the great forest of this earth in a savage migration of two hundred years. Wandering and alone, they were to bring forth their children, with a savage education, destitute of any human custom and deprived of any human speech, and
so in a state of wild animals. It was necessary that just so much time should pass
before the earth, having at last dried off from the wetness of the universal flood,
could send off dry exhalations of the sort wherein lightning could be generated,
which stunned and terrified men into abandoning themselves to the false religions of so many Joves that Varro was able to count forty of them, and the
Egyptians claimed their Jove Ammon to be the oldest of all. They turned to a
kind of divination which consisted in divining the future from the thunder and
lightning and from the flights of eagles which they held to be birds of Jove.
But among the Easterners there was born a more refined divination from the

observation of the movements of the planets and the aspects of the stars. Thus Zoroaster is honored as the first wise man among the gentiles. Bochart gives him the title "contemplator of the stars." Just as the first vulgar wisdom was born among the Easterners, so also among them arose the first monarchy, that of Assyria.

63   This chain of reasoning disposes of all those recent etymologists who attempt to trace all the languages of the world back to the origins of the eastern tongues. The fact is that all the nations sprung from Ham and Japheth first developed their native languages inland, and [only] then, having descended to the sea, began to deal with the Phoenicians, who were famous for navigation and colonies along the shores of the Mediterranean and of the Ocean. We have shown in the first edition of our New Science that this is true of the origins of the Latin language and that, by analogy with the Latin, it must hold for all the others as well.

X

[One of these giants, Prometheus, steals fire from the sun. Year of the world 1856.]

64   From this fable we perceive that Heaven reigned on earth, when it was believed to be no higher than the mountain tops, according to the vulgar tradition that also tells that it left great and numerous benefits to the human race.

XI

[Deucalion]

65   In those times Themis, or divine justice, had a temple on Mount Parnassus, and she judged on earth the affairs of mortals.

XII

[Hermes Trismegistus the elder, or the Egyptian age of the gods.]

66   This is the Hermes who, on the authority of Cicero, *On the Nature of the Gods,* was called by the Egyptians [Thoth or] Theuth (from which the Greeks are said to have derived *theos*), and who brought the Egyptians letters and laws. They in turn (according to Marsham) taught them to the other nations of the world. But the Greeks did not write their laws with hieroglyphs but with vulgar letters, which up to now Cadmus has commonly been thought to have brought to them from Phoenicia, though, as we shall see, they made no use of them for seven hundred years and more thereafter. For within this period there came Homer, who in none of his poems so much as mentions *nomos* (as Feith observed in his *Antiquitates homericae*), and who left his poems to the memory of his rhapsodes because in his time vulgar letters had not yet been discovered, as Flavius Josephus the Jew resolutely maintains against Apion, the Greek grammarian. Moreover, after Homer, Greek letters turned out so different from Phoenician!

67   But these are minor difficulties by comparison with the following:

how can there be nations already founded and yet without laws? and how within Egypt itself, before this Hermes, had the dynasties been founded? As if letters were essential to laws, and as if the laws of Sparta were thus not laws, where a law of Lycurgus himself forbade the knowledge of letters! As if the following order were impossible in civil nature: to devise laws orally and orally to publish them! As if we did not in fact find in Homer two sorts of assembly: one, called the *boulê,* secret, where the heroes met to consult by word of mouth about the laws; and another called the *agora,* public, in which, also by word of mouth, the laws were published! And as if, finally, providence had not made provision for this human necessity: so that, lacking letters, all nations in their barbarian period were first founded on customs, and [only] later, having become civilized, were governed by [statutory] laws! Just as in the second barbarian period the first laws of the new nations of Europe were born in customs, of which the feudal are the most ancient. This should be remembered because of what we shall have to say later: that fiefs were the first origins of all the laws that grew up later among all nations both ancient and modern, and hence the natural law of nations was established not with [statutory] laws but with these same human customs.

68   Now as to what touches on that great theme of the Christian religion —that Moses did not learn from the Egyptians the sublime theology of the Hebrews—there seems to be one great obstacle, chronology, which places Moses after Hermes Trismegistus. But this difficulty, besides being met by the reasons set forth above, is completely overcome by means of the principles expressed in a really golden passage of Iamblichus, *De mysteriis aegyptiorum,* where he says that the Egyptians ascribed to this same Hermes all they discovered that was necessary or useful to human civil life. He must therefore have been, not an individual man rich in esoteric wisdom who was subsequently made a god, but a poetic character of the first men of Egypt who were wise in vulgar wisdom and who founded there first the families and then the peoples that finally went to make up this great nation. From this same passage just cited from Iamblichus it follows that, if the Egyptian division stands of the three ages of gods, heroes and men, and their Trismegistus was a god, then the life of this Hermes must embrace the entire Egyptian age of the gods.

XIII
[The golden age, or the Greek age of the gods]

69   Legendary history acquaints us with one of the peculiarities of this age, namely that the gods associated with men on earth. To give certainty to the principles of chronology, we shall consider in this work a natural theogony or generation of the gods, formed naturally in the imaginations of the Greeks on certain occasions of human need or utility, in which they felt they had received help or comfort in the early childhood of the world, when it was overwhelmed by most frightful religions. For whatever men saw or imagined, or

even did themselves, they took to be divinity. Now by making twelve short epochs of the twelve famous gentile gods who were called greater, that is the gods consecrated by men in the time of the families, a rational chronology of poetic history leads us to assign to the age of the gods a duration of nine hundred years. This gives us the beginnings of universal profane history.

XIV

[Hellen—son of Deucalion, grandson of Prometheus, great grandson of Iapetus—through his three sons, spreads three dialects in Greece. Year of the world 2082.]

70 From this Hellen the native Greeks were called Hellenes; but the Greeks of Italy were called Graii and their land Graikia, whence they were called Graeci by the Latins. So well did the Greeks of Italy know the name of the mother country beyond the sea, whence they had come as colonists into Italy! For no such word as Graikia is found in any Greek writer, as Jacques Le Paulmier observes in his *Graeciae antiquae descriptio*.

XV

[Cecrops the Egyptian brings twelve colonies into Attica, of which Theseus later makes up Athens.]

71 When Strabo judges on the contrary that Attica, because of its rocky soil, could not attract foreigners to come and live there, he does so in order to support the further assertion that the Attic dialect is one of the first among the native dialects of Greece.

XVI

[Cadmus the Phoenician founds Thebes in Boeotia and introduces vulgar letters into Greece. Year of the world 2491.]

72 Since he introduced the Phoenician alphabet there, Boeotia should have been from its literate beginnings the most ingenious of all the nations of Greece; but it produced men of such doltish minds that "Boeotian" became a proverbial term for a man of slow wit.

XVII

[Saturn, or the Latin age of the gods. Year of the world 2491.]

73 This is the age of the gods beginning among the nations of Latium and corresponding in character to the golden age of the Greeks, among whom our [science of] mythology will show that the first gold was grain, by the harvests of which for many centuries the first nations counted their years. Saturn was so called by the Latins from *sati,* "sown" [fields], and is called Chronos by the Greeks, among whom *chronos* means "time," whence comes the word chronology.

XVIII

[Hermes Trismegistus the younger, or the Egyptian age of the heroes. Year of the world 2553.]

74 This Hermes the younger must be a poetic character of the age of the heroes in Egypt. This age in Greece comes only after an age of the gods

lasting nine hundred years; but among the Egyptians the age of the gods lasts only through the time of a father, son and grandson. Corresponding to this anachronism in Egyptian history we have already noticed a similar one in Assyrian history, the case of Zoroaster.

XIX

[Danaus the Egyptian drives the Inachids out of the kingdom of Argos. Year of the world 2553.]

75 These royal successions are great canons of chronology: thus Danaus occupies the kingdom of Argos, which had previously been ruled by nine kings of the house of Inachus, during whose time there must have passed three hundred years (according to the rule of the chronologers), as there must have passed nearly five hundred years during the time of the fourteen Latin kings who reigned in Alba.

76 But Thucydides says that in heroic times the kings drove one another off the throne almost daily; as Amulius drives Numitor from the kingdom of Alba and Romulus then dethrones Amulius and restores Numitor. This came about through the savagery of those times, and also because the heroic cities were without walls, nor were fortresses then in use. We shall see later that this was true also of the second barbarian period.

XX

[The Heraclids, spread abroad through Greece, bring in the age of the heroes there. Curetes in Crete, in Saturnia or Italy, and in Asia, bring in the kingdoms of priests. Year of the world 2682.]

77 These two great fragments of antiquity, as Denis Petau observes, fall in Greek history before the heroic age of the Greeks. The Heraclids or sons of Hercules are scattered abroad through Greece more than a hundred years before the coming of Hercules their father, whereas, in order to propagate so many descendants, he would have had to be born many centuries earlier.

XXI

[Dido of Tyre goes to found Carthage.]

78 We place her at the end of the heroic age of the Phoenicians, and thus [conceive her to have been] driven out of Tyre because she had been conquered in a heroic contest, as she professes to have left the city on account of the hatred of her brother-in-law. This multitude of Tyrian men was called in heroic diction a woman because it was made up of the weak and vanquished.

XXII

[Orpheus, and with him the age of the theological poets.]

79 This Orpheus, who reduces the wild beasts of Greece to humanity, is evidently a vast den of a thousand monsters. He comes from Thrace, a country of fierce warriors [Marti, Marses], not of humane philosophers, for the Thracians were through all later time so barbarous that Androtion the philos-

opher removed Orpheus from the number of sages simply because he had been born in Thrace. And [yet] in her beginnings he came forth so skilled in the Greek language that he composed in it verses of marvellous poetry, with which he tamed the barbarians through their ears; for though already organized in nations they were not restrained by their eyes from setting fire to cities full of marvels. And he finds the Greeks still wild beasts [though] Deucalion a thousand years before had taught them piety by his reverence and fear of divine justice. On Mount Parnassus, in front of the temple raised to divine justice (which was later the dwelling of the Muses and Apollo, the god and the arts of humanity), Deucalion with Pyrrha his wife, both with veiled heads (that is, with the modesty of human cohabitation, meaning marriage), seize the stones that lie before their feet (that is, the stupid brutes of the former savage times) and make them into men by throwing them over their shoulders, (that is, by the discipline of household economy in the state of the families). Hellen too, seven hundred years before, had brought [the Greeks] together by means of language and had sown the three dialects among them by means of his three sons. And the house of Inachus could show that it had founded its kingdoms three centuries before and had continued the royal successions through that period. Finally comes Orpheus to teach the Greeks humanity; and, from the savage condition in which he finds it, he brings Greece into such splendor as a nation that he is a companion of Jason on the naval enterprise of the Golden Fleece (naval enterprises and navigation being the last discoveries of peoples), and he is accompanied on this expedition by Castor and Pollux, the brothers of Helen, for whose sake the famous Trojan war was fought. So, in the life of one man, so many civil things [are] accomplished, for which the extent of a thousand years would hardly suffice! Such a monstrosity of Greek chronology in the person of Orpheus is like the other two we have observed above: one in Assyrian history in the person of Zoroaster, and another in Egyptian history in the two Hermeses. It was perhaps because of all this that Cicero in his *On the Nature of the Gods* suspected that such a person as Orpheus never existed in the world.

80   To these great chronological difficulties may be added others no less serious of a moral and political nature. For Orpheus then founds the humanity of Greece on the examples of an adulterous Jove, a Juno who is the mortal enemy of the virtues of the Herculeses, a chaste Diana who solicits the sleeping Endymions at night, an Apollo who gives oracular responses and pursues to the point of death modest maiden Daphnes, a Mars who, as if it were not enough for the gods to commit adultery on earth, carries it even into the sea with Venus. Nor is this unrestrained licentiousness of the gods satisfied by forbidden intercourse with women: Jove burns with wicked love for Ganymede; indeed this lust reaches the point of bestiality and Jove, transformed into a swan, lies with Leda. This licentiousness, practiced on men and beasts, was precisely the in-

famous evil of the outlaw world. Many of the gods and goddesses in heaven do
not contract matrimony at all. One marriage there is, that of Jove and Juno,
and it is sterile; and not only sterile but full of atrocious wrangling. Jove indeed
fixes in the air his chaste and jealous wife and he himself gives birth to Minerva,
who springs from his head. And finally Saturn, if he begets children, devours
them. Such examples, powerful divine examples as they are (though such
fables may contain all the recondite wisdom desired by Plato and in our time
by Bacon of Verulam in his *Wisdom of the Ancients* [*De sapientia veterum*]),
if taken at face value would corrupt the most civilized peoples and would incite
them to become as bestial as the very beasts of Orpheus; so apt and efficacious
they are to transform men from the state of beasts to that of humanity! In view
of these things it is a very slight reproof that Saint Augustine makes of the
gods of the gentiles in his *City of God,* apropos of the scene in the *Eunuch* of
Terence in which Chaerea, tempted by a painting of Jove lying with Danae in
a shower of gold, summons up the hardihood, which he had lacked, to violate
the slave girl with whom he was so madly and violently in love.

81   But these treacherous reefs of mythology will be avoided by the principles of this Science, which will show that such fables in their beginnings were
all true and severe and worthy of the founders of nations, and only later (when
the long passage of years had obscured their meanings, and customs had
changed from austere to dissolute, and because men to console their consciences
wanted to sin with the authority of the gods) came to have the obscene meanings with which they have come down to us. As for the rough chronological
tempests, they will be cleared up for us by the discovery of poetic characters,
one of whom was Orpheus, considered as a poet theologian, who through the
fables, in their first meaning, first founded and then confirmed the humanity
of Greece. This character stood out more clearly than ever in the heroic contests with the plebeians of the Greek cities. That was the age in which the poet
theologians distinguished themselves, as for example Orpheus himself, Linus,
Musaeus, and Amphion. The last of these, with self-moving stones (i.e. the
doltish plebeians) erected the walls of Thebes, which Cadmus had founded three
hundred years before; just as Appius, grandson of the decemvir, about as long
after the foundation of Rome, fortifies the heroic state for the Romans by singing to the plebs the strength of the gods in the auspices, the knowledge of which
was held by the patricians. From such heroic contests the heroic age got its
name.

XXIII
[Hercules, with whom the heroic time of Greece reaches its climax]

82   The same difficulties recur for Hercules if we take him for a real
man, the companion of Jason in the expedition to Colchis, and not, as we shall
find him to be in respect of his labors, a heroic character of the founder of
peoples.

XXIV
[Sancuniates writes histories in vulgar letters. Year of the world 2800.]

83 Called also Sanchuniathon and entitled "the historian of truth" (on the authority of Clement of Alexandria in his *Stromata*). He wrote the history of Phoenicia in vulgar characters, while the Egyptians and the Scythians, as we have seen, wrote in hieroglyphs, as the Chinese have been found to do down to our own days. The latter, like the Scythians and the Egyptians, boasted a monstrous antiquity because in the darkness of their isolation, having no dealings with other nations, they had no true idea of time. And Sancuniates wrote in vulgar Phoenician characters at a time when vulgar letters had not yet come into use among the Greeks, as we have said above.

XXV
[Trojan war. Year of the world 2820.]

84 This war, as it is recounted by Homer, is thought by circumspect critics never to have taken place; and authors like Dictys of Crete and Dares of Phrygia, who as historians of their time gave prose accounts of it, are by these same critics relegated to the library of impostur.

XXVI
[Sesostris reigns in Thebes. Year of the world 2949.]

85 This king brought under his empire the three other dynasties of Egypt, and is evidently the king Ramses of whom the Egyptian priest tells Germanicus in Tacitus.

XXVII
[Greek colonies in Asia, in Sicily, in Italy. Year of the world 2949.]

86 This is one of the very few things in which we do not follow the authority of chronology. Constrained by an overpowering reason, we put the colonies brought by the Greeks into Italy and Sicily about a hundred years after the Trojan War, and thus three hundred years before the time at which the chronologists place them; that is, about the time where the chronologists place the wanderings of the heroes such as Menelaus, Aeneas, Antenor, Diomed and Ulysses. Nor should this cause surprise when they [the chronologists] themselves vary as much as four hundred and sixty years in dating Homer, the author nearest to these affairs of the Greeks. [Our reason is that] in magnificence and delicacy Syracuse at the time of the Punic wars had nothing to envy Athens itself, and luxury and splendor of customs reach the islands later than the continents. The Croton of Livy's time calls forth his compassion because of its small number of inhabitants, when it had once had a population of several million.

XXVIII

[Olympic games, first founded by Hercules, then suspended, and restored by Isiphilus. Year of the world 3223.]

87   Since it is found that the years were numbered by Hercules from harvest to harvest, but from Isiphilus [i.e. Iphitus] on by the course of the sun through the signs of the zodiac, exact chronology among the Greeks begins with Isiphilus.

XXIX

[Founding of Rome. Year of Rome 1.]

88   But just as the clouds are dispersed by the sun, so all the magnificent opinions that have been held up to now concerning the beginnings of Rome and of all the other cities that have been capitals of famous nations, are dispersed by this golden passage of Varro (quoted by St. Augustine in his *City of God*): that Rome under the kings, who reigned there for two hundred and fifty years, subdued more than twenty peoples and did not extend her empire more than twenty miles.

XXX

[Homer, who came at a time when vulgar letters had not yet been invented, and who never saw Egypt. Year of the world 3290, of Rome 35.]

89   Regarding this first light of Greece we have been left in the dark by Greek history in both its chief aspects, geography and chronology, for nothing certain has come down to us regarding either his fatherland or the age in which he lived. In our third book we shall find him quite different from what he has been thought up to now. But, whoever he was, he certainly never saw Egypt; for he says in the *Odyssey* that the island on which there now stands the pharos of Alexandria was as far from the mainland as an unloaded boat with a north wind in the poop could sail in an entire day. Nor did he see Phoenicia; for he says that the island of Calypso, Ogygia, was so far away that Mercury, a god —and a winged god—could get there only with great difficulty, as if it were as far from Greece (where the gods reside on Mt. Olympus, as he himself sings in the *Iliad*) as America is from our world. So, if the Greeks in the times of Homer had had dealings with Egypt and Phoenicia, he would have lost credit in both his poems.

XXXI

[Psammeticus opens Egypt, but only to the Ionian and Carian Greeks. Year of the world 3334.]

90   It is from the time of Psammeticus that Herodotus begins to relate better ascertained facts about the Egyptians. This confirms our opinion that Homer did not see Egypt; and the various items of information that he narrates about Egypt and other countries of the world are either things and deeds that took place within Greece, as we shall show in our [section on] Poetic Geography, or they are traditions, altered by the passage of a long time, of the

Phoenicians, Egyptians and Phrygians who had colonized among the Greeks; or they are tales of Phoenician travelers who traded on Greek shores long before the time of Homer.

XXXII

[Aesop, vulgar moral philosopher. Year of the world 3334.]

91   In the [section on] Poetic Logic it will be found that Aesop was not an individual man in nature, but an imaginative type or poetic character of the *socii* or *famuli* of the heroes, who certainly came before the Seven Sages of Greece.

XXXIII

[Seven Sages of Greece: of whom one, Solon, ordains popular liberty in Athens; another, Thales the Milesian, gives a beginning to philosophy with physics. Year of the world 3406.]

92   Thales began with too simple a principle: water; perhaps because he had seen gourds grow on water.

XXXIV

[Pythagoras, of whom, according to Livy, not so much as the name can have been known at Rome during his lifetime. Year of the world 3468, of Rome 225.]

93   Livy puts him in the time of Servius Tullius (so firmly did he believe that Pythagoras had been the teacher of Numa in divinity!); and in these very times of Servius Tullius, almost two hundred years after Numa, he says that it was impossible, because of the barbarous character of inland Italy in that era, not merely for Pythagoras himself but even for his name to reach Rome from Croton, passing through so many peoples of varying languages and customs. It may thence be inferred how quick and easy were the really long journeys of Pythagoras to visit the disciples of Orpheus in Thrace, the mages in Persia, the Chaldeans in Babylonia, the gymnosophists in India; then, on his return, the priests of Egypt and, after crossing Africa at its widest, the disciples of Atlas in Mauritania; then, crossing the sea, the Druids in Gaul! Thence he is supposed to have returned to his fatherland, rich in what van Heurn calls barbarian wisdom from those barbarous nations to which, long years before, Hercules the Theban, slaying monsters and tyrants, had gone on his civilizing mission about the world; nations to whom the Greeks bragged, a long time after, that they had taught culture, but not to such profit that they did not remain barbarous. So sound and weighty is the succession of the schools of barbarian philosophy related by the aforesaid van Heurn, which the vanity of scholars has so much applauded!

94   Need we go so far as to appeal here to the authority of Lactantius, who firmly denies that Pythagoras was the disciple of Isaiah? This authority is strongly supported by a passage in the *Jewish Antiquities* [XII, 2, 14] of Josephus the Jew, which proves that the Hebrews in the times of Homer and Pythagoras lived unknown to their nearest inland neighbors, to say nothing of remote nations overseas. For when Ptolemy Philadelphus expressed surprise that no poet

or historian had ever made any mention of the Mosaic laws, Demetrius the Jew answered that some who had attempted to tell the gentiles about them had been miraculously punished by God; Theopompus for example had lost his mind and Theodectes his sight. Josephus himself [*Against Apion* I, 12] freely admits their obscurity and gives these reasons for it: "We do not live," he says, "on the seashore, nor do we delight in trading or in having dealings with foreigners for the sake of trade." Lactantius reflects that this custom was a counsel of divine providence, so that the religion of the true God might not be profaned by trafficking with gentiles. In this opinion Lactantius is followed by Peter van der Kuhn in his *De republica hebraeorum.* It is all confirmed by public confession of the Hebrews themselves, who, in expiation of the Septuagint, held a solemn fast each year on the eighth day of Tebet, which is our December; because when it was finished there were three days of darkness over all the world, according to the rabbinical books referred to by Casaubon (*Exercitationes in Baronium*), Buxtorf (*Synagoga iudaica*) and Hottinger (*Thesaurus philologicus*). And because the Grecizing Jews called Hellenists, among them Aristeas, who is said to have been in charge of it, claimed divine authority for this translation, the Jews of Jerusalem mortally hated them.

95   But by the nature of these civil things [it is to be considered impossible] that over confines [such as those] whose trespass was forbidden even by the highly civilized Egyptians (who were so inhospitable to the Greeks that even a long time after they had opened Egypt to them it was forbidden to use a Greek pot, spit, or knife, or even [to eat] meat cut by a Greek knife), over harsh and forbidding paths, without any language in common, and among the Hebrews of whom it was proverbially said by the gentiles that they would not so much as point out a fountain to a thirsty foreigner, the prophets should have profaned their sacred doctrine by making it accessible to foreigners, new men unknown to them; for in all nations of the world the priests kept such doctrine secret even from their own plebs, whence indeed it was everywhere called "sacred" doctrine, for sacred is as much as to say "secret." And from this there emerges a most luminous proof of the truth of the Christian religion: that Pythagoras and Plato, by grace of a most sublime human science, had exalted themselves to some extent to the knowledge of the divine truths which the Hebrews had been taught by the true God; and on the other hand there arises a weighty confutation of the errors of recent mythologists, who believe that the fables are sacred stories corrupted by the gentile nations and especially by the Greeks. And although the Egyptians had dealings with the Hebrews in their captivity, yet, by a custom common to primitive peoples, as we shall show later, namely that of holding the conquered to be men without gods, they rather mocked than heeded the Hebrew religion and history. Often, as the sacred book of Genesis narrates, they scornfully asked the Hebrews why the God they adored did not come to liberate them from their hands.

XXXV
[Servius Tullius king. Year of the world 3468, of Rome 225.]

96   By a common error it has hitherto been believed that this king set up the census in Rome as a basis of popular liberty, whereas we shall see [619 ff.] that the census was a basis of patrician liberty. And this error is in accord with that other one according to which it has been believed up to now that, in those times in which the sick debtor had to appear on an ass or in a cart before the praetor, Tarquinius Priscus ordained the insignia, togas, devices, and chairs of ivory (made of the tusks of elephants, which, because the Romans had first seen them in Lucania in the war with Pyrrhus, they called "Lucanian oxen") and finally the triumphal golden chariot, in which splendid equipage the Roman majesty shone brightest in the times of the popular commonwealth.

XXXVI
[Hesiod. Year of the world 3500.]

97   By the proofs we shall advance concerning the time when vulgar writing was introduced among the Greeks, we put Hesiod about the time of Herodotus or a little before. The chronologists with too much boldness put him thirty years before Homer, on whose period the authorities vary by as much as 460 years. Besides, Porphyry (according to Suidas) and Velleius Paterculus state that Homer preceded Hesiod by a great length of time. As for the tripod that Hesiod consecrated to Apollo on Helicon, with the inscription that he had surpassed Homer in song, although Varro accepts it (according to Aulus Gellius), it is to be kept in the museum of imposture, for it is a hoax similar to those perpetrated in our day by the falsifiers of medals who seek by such deceit to reap a rich profit.

XXXVII
[Herodotus, Hippocrates. Year of the world 3500.]

98   Hippocrates is placed by the chronologists in the time of the Seven Sages of Greece. But, partly because his life is too much tinged with fable (he is said to be the son of Aesculapius and grandson of Apollo), and partly because he is known to be the author of works written in prose with vulgar characters, he is here placed near the time of Herodotus, who likewise wrote prose with vulgar characters and wove his history almost entirely out of fables.

XXXVIII
[Idanthyrsus king of Scythia. Year of the world 3530.]

99   This king answered Darius the Great, who had threatened to make war on him, with five real words (which, as we shall later show, the first peoples must have used before they came to vocal words and finally to written ones). These real words were a frog, a mouse, a bird, a ploughshare, and a bow for shooting arrows. Further on we shall show the natural and proper meaning of

these objects. It would be tedious to report what St. Cyril of Alexandria relates of the council that Darius held to discuss the meaning of this reply, for
the interpretations his counselors put upon it are obviously ridiculous. And this
Idanthyrsus was the king of those Scythians who surpassed the Egyptians in
point of antiquity, and yet at that late epoch did not even know how to write
with hieroglyphs! Idanthyrsus must have been like one of the Chinese kings
who, up to a few centuries ago cut off from the rest of the world, vainly boast an
antiquity greater than that of the world, and, after so long a time, are still found
writing with hieroglyphs, and, although on account of the great mildness of the
climate they have most refined talents and make so many marvelously delicate
things, do not yet know how to make shadows in painting, against which high-
lights can stand out; whence, since it has neither relief nor depth, their painting is most crude. And as for the statuettes of porcelain which come from
there, they show the Chinese to be just as unskilled as the Egyptians were in casting; whence it may be inferred that the Egyptians were as unskilled in painting
as the Chinese are now.

100   To these Scythians belongs Anacharsis, author of the Scythian
oracles, as Zoroaster was of the Chaldean. They must first have been oracles of
soothsayers, which later, by the vanity of the learned, were turned into oracles
of philosophers. From the Hyperboreans of Scythia (either this one or another
born anciently within Greece itself) there came to Greece the two most famous
oracles of the gentiles, the Delphic and the Dodonian; so Herodotus believed,
and after him Pindar and Pherenicus, who are followed by Cicero in his *On
the Nature of the Gods*. This may explain why Anacharsis was proclaimed a
famous author of oracles and numbered among the most ancient soothsaying
gods, as we shall see in the [section on] Poetic Geography. Meanwhile, to show
how learned Scythia was in esoteric wisdom, let it suffice that the Scythians
would stick a knife in the ground and adore it as a god, in order to justify the
killings they were about to perform. From this wild religion emerged all the
civil and moral virtues narrated by Diodorus Siculus, Justin, Pliny, and lauded
to the skies by Horace. Thence Abaris [i.e. Anacharsis], wishing to order
Scythia by the laws of Greece, was killed by Caduidas his brother. Such was his
profit from the 'barbarian philosophy' of van Heurn that he did not discern by
himself the laws needed to bring a barbarian people to a humane civilization,
but had to learn them from the Greeks! For the very same thing is true of the
Greeks in relation to the Scythians which we have said of them a while ago
[90] in relation to the Egyptians: that by their vanity in giving to their knowledge high-sounding origins of foreign antiquity, they truly deserved the reproof
they represented the Egyptian priest as giving to Solon (as related by Critias in
the first or second *Alcibiades* of Plato): namely that the Greeks had always
been children. And so it must be said that by this vanity the Greeks, in relation both to the Scythians and to the Egyptians, lost as much in real merit as
they gained in vain glory.

XXXIX

[Peloponnesian war. Thucydides, who writes that up to his father's day the Greeks knew nothing of their own antiquities, therefore set himself to write of this war. Year of the world 3530.]

101   Thucydides was a young man at the time when Herodotus, who might have been his father, was already old. He lived in the most glorious age of Greece, which was that of the Peloponnesian war, and since he was a contemporary of this struggle he wrote its history in order to write of true things. By him it was said that down to his father's time, which was also that of Herodotus, the Greeks knew nothing of their own antiquities. What then can we think of the things they wrote of the barbarians? And we know of ancient barbarian history only what they tell us. And what must we think of the antiquities of the Romans, up to the time of the Carthaginian wars, in view of the fact that until then they had been concerned only with agriculture and military affairs, when Thucydides establishes this truth about his own Greeks, who so promptly came forth as philosophers? Unless, perhaps, we are willing to say that the Romans had had some particular privilege from God.

XL

[Socrates originates rational moral philosophy. Plato flourishes in metaphysics. Athens is resplendent with all the arts of the most cultivated humanity. Law of the Twelve Tables. Year of the world 3553, of Rome 303.]

102   At this time there is brought from Athens to Rome the Law of the Twelve Tables, just as crude, inhuman, cruel, uncivilized and monstrous as it is shown to be in our *Principles of Universal Law.*

XLI

[Xenophon, carrying the Greek arms into the heart of Persia, is the first to learn of Persian things with any certainty. Year of the world 3583, of Rome 333.]

103   Thus St. Jerome observes in his Commentary on Daniel. Just as the Greeks had begun under Psammeticus to learn something of Egypt by way of commerce (so that Herodotus's more reliable information about the Egyptians begins with that period), so now, starting from Xenophon, they began through the exigencies of war to learn more reliable things about the Persians. Even Aristotle, who accompanied Alexander the Great into Persia, writes that before that time the Greeks had but told fables about them, as we have indicated in this Chronological Table. In this way the Greeks began to have some real knowledge of the affairs of other peoples.

XLII

[Publilian Law. Year of the world 3658, of Rome 416.]

104   This law was put into effect in the 416th year of Rome, and contains a most important point of Roman history, for by this law the Roman commonwealth declared its change from an aristocratic to a popular form of government; whence Publilius Philo, who was its author, was called the "people's dictator." This has not been noticed because the language of the law has not been properly understood. We shall later make evident that this was the fact. Here it will suffice to give a hypothetical idea of it.

105 This law and the subsequent Petelian Law, which is of equal importance, remained unknown because of these three words which are not defined: "people," "kingdom," and "liberty." Because of these words it has been commonly but erroneously believed that the Roman people from the time of Romulus had been composed of citizens both noble and plebeian, that the Roman kingdom had been monarchical, and that the liberty set up by Brutus had been a popular liberty. And these three words, not properly defined, have led into error all the critics, historians, political theorists and jurists, because from none of these words could they get a clear idea of the heroic commonwealths, which were of a most severely aristocratic form and therefore entirely different from those of our time.

106 In an asylum opened in the forest, Romulus founded Rome on the clientships or protectorships under which the fathers of families maintained as day laborers in the fields those who had fled to this asylum. These fugitives had no privilege of citizenship and thus no share of civil liberty. Since they had taken refuge with the fathers to save their lives, the fathers protected their natural liberty by setting them separately to the cultivation of their several fields. The public domain of the Roman territory must have been made up of these fields, just as Romulus constituted the senate from the fathers themselves.

107 Later, Servius Tullius granted the workers bonitary ownership of the fields that were the property of the fathers and imposed the census [tax] upon them. They were to do their own cultivating under the burden of the census, and with the obligation of serving the fathers in war at their own expense; as in fact the plebeians did serve the patricians under what has hitherto been mistaken for popular liberty. This law of Servius Tullius was the first agrarian law of the world, and it set up the census as the basis of the heroic commonwealths, that is to say of the most ancient aristocracies of all the nations.

108 Subsequently, Junius Brutus, casting out the Tarquin tyrants, restored the Roman commonwealth to its original form, and, by setting up the consuls, as it were an annual pair of aristocratic kings (as Cicero calls them in his *Laws*) in place of one king for life, reëstablished the liberty of the patricians as against their tyrants, but not indeed the liberty of the people from the patricians. But, since the nobles did not keep faith with the plebeians under the agrarian law of Servius Tullius, the plebs brought about the creation of the plebeian tribunes and had them accepted under oath by the nobility. The tribunes were to protect for the people that degree of natural liberty represented by bonitary ownership of the fields. Thus, when the plebeians were wanting to secure civil ownership from the nobles, the plebeian tribunes drove from Rome Marcius Coriolanus because he had said that the plebeians should go and till the soil; that is, since they were not content with the agrarian law of Servius but wanted a fuller and stronger one, they should be reduced again to the day laborers they had been under Romulus. For if this be not a true picture of things, how [can we explain] the foolish pride of the plebs in disdaining agriculture, since we know that even the patricians deemed it honorable work? And would [such] a slight pretext have occasioned such a cruel war? For Marcius, to avenge his exile, would have brought about the ruin of Rome had it not been for the piteous tears of his mother and his wife which turned him aside from his impious enterprise.

109   In consequence of all this, the nobles proceeding to take back the fields from the plebs after they had cultivated them, and the latter having no civil action for laying claim to them, the plebeian tribunes now appealed to a Law of the Twelve Tables (by which, as is demonstrated in the *Principles of Universal Law,* no other affair but this was settled). By this law the nobles conceded to the plebs the quiritary ownership of the fields. This civil ownership is permitted to foreigners by the natural law of nations. And this was the second agrarian law of the ancient nations.

110   Now when the plebeians saw [on the one hand] that they could not transmit the fields intestate to their kin, because they had no *sui heredes,* agnates or gentiles (to which relations legitimate succession was then confined), since their marriages were not solemnized; and [on the other hand] that they could not even dispose of their fields by testament because they did not have the rights of citizens; they demanded for themselves the *connubium* of the nobles, that is the right to solemnized marriages (for such is the meaning of *connubium*). The most solemn part of the marriage service was the auspices, which were the property of the nobles. (These auspices indeed were the great source of all Roman law, private and public.) And thus the right of contracting marriages was communicated to the plebeians by the fathers. Since marriage is, by the definition of the jurisconsult Modestinus, "the sharing of every divine and human right" (*omnis divini et humani iuris communicatio*), and since citizenship itself is naught else, the fathers thereby gave the plebeians the rights of citizenship. Then, in the [natural] course of human desires, the plebeians secured from the fathers the communication of all those rights of private law which depended upon the auspices: as *patria potestas, sui heredes,* agnation and clan membership, and, in consequence of these rights, the further rights of legitimate succession, the making of testaments and guardianship. Then they claimed those dependent rights of public law, securing the communication first of the *imperium* by the opening to them of the consulship, and finally of the science of the laws, by the opening to them of priesthood and pontificate.

111   In this way the tribunes of the plebs, by pursuing the function for which they were created, that of protecting the natural liberty of the plebeians, were gradually led to secure for them the whole range of civil liberty as well. And the census ordered by Servius Tullius—with the subsequent provision that payment should no longer be made to the nobles privately but to the public treasury so that the treasury might supply to the plebeians the expenses of war —developed naturally from a basis of liberty for the lords into a basis of popular liberty. Further on we shall see the way in which this came about.

112   By a parallel development, these same tribunes progressed in the power of making laws. For the Horatian and Hortensian laws could not grant to the plebs that their plebiscites should be binding upon all the people except in two special emergencies. In the first of these the plebs had retired to the Aventine in the 304th year of Rome, at which time, as we state here by way of hypothesis and shall later show as a fact, the plebeians were not yet citizens. In the second they retired to the Janiculum in the 367th year of Rome, at which time the plebs were still struggling with the nobility for the sharing of the consulate. But on the basis of the two aforesaid laws, the plebs finally reached the point where they could make universal laws [binding on the nobles as well as on themselves]. To bring this about required factional movements and revolts at Rome, with the result that it was necessary to make Publilius Philo dictator, an office never created save in times of greatest danger to the commonwealth, such as this was. For it had fallen into such great disorder as to nourish within itself two supreme legislative powers without any distinction of time, scope or territory, with the result that the commonwealth was on the point of collapse. Wherefore Philo, to cure the ills of the state, ordained that whatever the plebs commanded by plebiscites in the assembly by tribes (*comitia tributa*) "should be binding on all the Quirites" (*omnes quirites teneret*), i.e. should be binding on all the people in the assembly by hundreds (*comitia centuriata*) in which "all the Quirites" (*omnes quirites*) met. (For the Romans called themselves Quirites only in public assembly, and Quiris in the singular is never found in common Latin speech.) By this formula Philo meant to signify that laws could not be enacted contrary to the plebiscites. The plebs had already been made in all respects equal to the nobles by laws to which the latter had agreed. By this most recent move, to which the nobles could offer no opposition without bringing the commonwealth to ruin, the plebs had become superior to the nobles, for without ratification by the senate the plebs could enact general laws for all the people. Thus the Roman commonwealth had now naturally become free and popular. Philo accordingly proclaimed it such by this law, and hence was called the people's dictator.

113   In conformity with this change in its nature, he gave the commonwealth two ordinances, which are contained in the other two sections of the Publilian Law. In the first this dictator ordained that authorization by the senate, which had been an authorization by the lords whereby what had first been decided by the people "the fathers had afterwards to ratify" (*deinde patres fierent auctores*)—so that the election of the consuls and the enacting of the laws, being determined in advance by the people, had been [respectively] public testimonials of merit and public demands of right—should thenceforth be given by the fathers to the people, who were now sovereign and free, prior to

the deliberations of the assembly (*in incertum comitiorum eventum*), as [if they, the fathers, were but] the guardians of the people, who were the real lords and masters of the Roman *imperium*. The people, if they wished to enact laws, were to do so according to the formula presented to them by the senate. If not, they could make use of their sovereign right and "antiquate" the [proposed] laws; that is, declare they wanted no innovation. Thus everything the senate should henceforth ordain concerning public affairs should be [regarded as] instructions given by it to the people or commissions given to it by the people. Finally there remained the census, for, since the treasury had hitherto been the property of the nobles, they alone had been created censors of it. Since, however, by this law the treasury became the property of the people as a whole, Philo ordered in the third place that the censorship, the only magistracy in which the plebs had as yet no share, should also be extended to them.

114   If we read further into the history of Rome in the light of this hypothesis, we shall find by a thousand proofs that it provides a foundation for all the things therein narrated, which have lacked a common foundation and a proper and particular connection among themselves because the three aforesaid words were undefined; wherefore this hypothesis should be accepted as true. However, if properly considered, this is not so much a hypothesis as a truth meditated in idea which later will be authoritatively shown to be the fact. And —granted Livy's generalization that the asylums were "an old counsel of founders of cities" (*vetus urbes condentium consilium*), as Romulus founded the city of Rome within the asylum opened in the forest—this hypothesis gives us also the history of all the other cities of the world in times we have so far despaired of knowing. This then is an instance of an ideal eternal history (which will later be meditated and discovered) whose course is run in time by the histories of all nations.

XLIII
[Petelian Law. Year of the world 3661, of Rome 419.]

115   This second law, called "on slavery for debt" (*de nexu*), was enacted in the year of Rome 419 (and thus three years after the Publilian law) by the consuls Caius Poetelius and Lucius Papirius Mugillanus. It contains another most important point in [the study of] Roman affairs, for by this law the plebeians were released from the feudal liability of becoming liege vassals of the nobles on account of debts, for which the nobles used to compel the plebeians to work for them, often for life, in their private prisons. But the senate retained the sovereign power it had over the lands of the Roman *imperium,* though the *imperium* itself had already passed to the people. And under the provisions of the *senatus consultum* which was called "the last," the senate kept this power for itself by force of arms as long as the Roman commonwealth remained free. Thus whenever the people wanted to dispose of these lands under the agrarian laws of the Gracchi, the senate armed the consuls, who proscribed as rebels and executed the tribunes of the plebs who had been the authors of these laws. This great effect could only be brought about by a system of sovereign fiefs subject to a higher sovereignty. This system is confirmed by a passage in one of the Catilinarian orations of Cicero where he affirms that Tiberius Gracchus by his agrarian law was destroying the form of government of the commonwealth, and had hence been rightfully put to death by Publius Scipio Nasica on the ground set forth in the formula by which the consul armed the people against the authors of the aforesaid law: "Whoever is for the safety of the commonwealth, let him follow the consul" (*Qui rempublicam salvam velit consulem sequatur*).

XLIV

[War with Tarentum wherein the Latins and the Greeks begin to know each other. Year of the world 3708, of Rome 489.]

116 The reason for this war was the maltreatment accorded by the Tarentines to the Roman ships which landed on their coasts, and likewise to the Roman ambassadors. Their excuse, as phrased by Florus, was that "they did not know who the Romans were or whence they came" (*qui essent aut unde venirent ignorabant*). So well acquainted were the first peoples, even when they were not separated by water and were not far apart by land!

XLV

[Second Carthaginian war, with which begins the period of Roman history known with some certainty by Livy, though he professes to be ignorant of three important circumstances. Year of the world 3849, of Rome 552.]

117 Livy professed to write the history of Rome with more certainty from the period of the second Carthaginian war, and promised to describe the most memorable of all wars fought by the Romans. And because of its incomparable greatness the chronicles he writes of it should have the greater certainty that belongs to things of greater fame. Yet he did not know, and openly admits he did not know, three most important circumstances. The first, in whose consulship Hannibal, after the capture of Saguntum, had started on his march from Spain to Italy. The second, over which Alps he had come, the Cottian or the Pennine. And the third, what strength he had with him. On this last matter there was in the ancient annals such a wide diversity of opinion that some had written 6,000 cavalry and 20,000 infantry, others 20,000 cavalry and 80,000 infantry.

[Conclusion]

118 It can be seen by our reasoning in these Notes that all that has come down to us from the ancient gentile nations for the times covered by this Table is most uncertain. So that in all this we have entered as it were into a no man's land where the rule of law obtains that "the [first] occupant acquires title" (*occupanti conceduntur*). For this reason we trust that we shall offend no man's right if we often reason differently and at times in direct opposition to the opinions which have been held up to now concerning the beginnings of the humanity of the nations. By so doing we shall reduce these beginnings to scientific principles, by which the facts of certain history may be assigned their first origins, on which they rest and by which they are reconciled. For up to now they do not seem to have had any common foundation nor any continuous sequence nor any coherence among themselves.

[SECTION II]

ELEMENTS

119 In order to give form to the materials hereinbefore set in order in the Chronological Table, we now propose the following axioms, both philosophical and philological, including a few reasonable and proper postulates and some clarified definitions. And just as the blood does in animate bodies, so will these elements course through our Science and animate it in all its reasonings about the common nature of nations.

I

120 Because of the indefinite nature of the human mind, wherever it is lost in ignorance, man makes himself the measure of all things.

121 This axiom explains those two common human traits, on the one hand that rumor grows in its course (*fama crescit eundo*), on the other that rumor is deflated by the presence [of the thing itself] (*minuit praesentia famam*). In the long course that rumor has run from the beginning of the world it has been the perennial source of all the exaggerated opinions which have hitherto been held concerning remote antiquities unknown to us, by virtue of that property of the human mind noted by Tacitus in his *Life of Agricola,* where he says that everything unknown is taken for something great (*omne ignotum pro magnifico est*).

II

122 It is another property of the human mind that whenever men can form no idea of distant and unknown things, they judge them by what is familiar and at hand.

123 This axiom points to the inexhaustible source of all the errors about the beginnings of humanity that have been adopted by entire nations and by all the scholars. For when the former began to take notice of them and the latter to investigate them, it was on the basis of their own enlightened, cultivated and magnificent times that they judged the origins of humanity, which must nevertheless by the nature of things have been small, crude and quite obscure.

124 Under this head are to be recalled two types of conceit we have mentioned above, one of the nations and the other of the scholars.

III

125 As for the conceit of the nations, we have heard that golden saying of Diodorus Siculus. Every nation, according to him, whether Greek or barbarian, has had the same conceit that it before all other nations invented the comforts of human life and that its remembered history goes back to the very beginning of the world.

126 This axiom disposes at once of the proud claims of the Chaldeans, Scythians, Egyptians, Chinese, to have been the first founders of the humanity of the ancient world. But Flavius Josephus the Jew purges his nation [of this vain boast] by that magnanimous confession that we have heard above: namely, that the Hebrews had lived cut off from all the gentiles. And sacred history assures us that the world is almost young in contrast to the antiquity with which it was credited by the Chaldeans, Scythians, Egyptians, and in our own day by the Chinese. This is a great proof of the truth of sacred history.

IV

127 To this conceit of the nations there may be added that of the scholars, who will have it that whatever they know is as old as the world.

128 This axiom disposes of all the opinions of the scholars concerning the matchless wisdom of the ancients. It convicts of fraud the oracles of Zoroaster the Chaldean, of Anacharsis the Scythian, which have not come down to us, the *Poimander* of Hermes Trismegistus, the *Orphics* (or verses of Orpheus), and the Golden Verses of Pythagoras, as all the more discerning critics agree. It further condemns as impertinent all the mystic meanings with which the Egyptian hieroglyphs are endowed by the scholars, and the philosophical allegories which they have read into the Greek fables.

V

129 To be useful to the human race, philosophy must raise and direct weak and fallen man, not rend his nature or abandon him in his corruption.

130 This axiom dismisses from the school of our Science the Stoics who seek to mortify the senses and the Epicureans who make them the criterion. For both deny providence, the former chaining themselves to fate, the latter abandoning themselves to chance. The latter moreover affirm that the human soul dies with the body. Both should be called monastic or solitary philosophers. On the other hand [this axiom] admits to our school the political philosophers, and first of all the Platonists, who agree with all the lawgivers on these three main points: that there is divine providence, that human passions should be moderated and made into human virtues, and that the human soul is immortal. Thus from this axiom are derived the three principles of this Science.

VI

131   Philosophy considers man as he should be and so can be of service to but very few, who wish to live in the Republic of Plato, not to fall back into the dregs of Romulus.

VII

132   Legislation considers man as he is in order to turn him to good uses in human society. Out of ferocity, avarice and ambition, the three vices which run throughout the human race, it creates the military, merchant and governing classes, and thus the strength, riches and wisdom of commonwealths. Out of these three great vices, which could certainly destroy all mankind on the face of the earth, it makes civil happiness.

133   This axiom proves that there is divine providence and further that it is a divine legislative mind. For out of the passions of men each bent on his private advantage, for the sake of which they would live like wild beasts in the wilderness, it has made the civil orders by which they may live in human society.

VIII

134   Things do not settle or endure out of their natural order.

135   In view of the fact that the human race, as far back as memory of the world goes, has lived and still lives conformably in society, this axiom alone decides the great dispute still waged by the best philosophers and moral theologians against Carneades the skeptic and Epicurus—a dispute to which not even Grotius could put an end—namely, whether law exists by nature, or whether man is naturally sociable, which comes to the same thing.

136   This same axiom, together with the seventh and its corollary, proves that man has free choice, however weak, to make virtues of his passions; but that he is aided by God, naturally by divine providence, and supernaturally by divine grace.

IX

137   Men who do not know the truth of things try to reach certainty about them, so that, if they cannot satisfy their intellects by science, their wills at least may rest on conscience.

X

138   Philosophy contemplates reason, whence comes knowledge of the true; philology observes the authority of human choice, whence comes consciousness of the certain.

139   This axiom by its second part defines as philologians all the grammarians, historians, critics, who have occupied themselves with the study of the languages and deeds of peoples: both their domestic affairs, such as customs and laws, and their external affairs, such as wars, peaces, alliances, travels and commerce.

140   This same axiom shows how the philosophers failed by half in not giving certainty to their reasonings by appeal to the authority of the philologians, and likewise how the latter failed by half in not taking care to give their authority the sanction of truth by appeal to the reasoning of the philosophers. If they had both done this they would have been more useful to their commonwealths and they would have anticipated us in conceiving this Science.

XI

141   Human choice, by its nature most uncertain, is made certain and determined by the common sense of men with respect to human needs or utilities, which are the two origins of the natural law of nations.

XII

142   Common sense is judgment without reflection, shared by an entire class, an entire people, an entire nation, or the whole human race.

143   This axiom, with the following definition, will provide a new art of criticism concerning the founders of nations, who must have preceded by more than a thousand years the writers with whom criticism has so far been occupied.

XIII

144   Uniform ideas originating among entire peoples unknown to each other must have a common ground of truth.

145   This axiom is a great principle which establishes the common sense of the human race as the criterion taught to the nations by divine providence to define what is certain in the natural law of nations. And the nations reach this certainty by recognizing the underlying agreements which, despite variations of detail, obtain among them all in respect of this law. Thence issues the mental dictionary for assigning origins to all the divers articulated languages. By means of this dictionary is conceived the ideal eternal history which determines the histories in time of all the nations. The axioms proper to this dictionary and to this history will shortly be proposed.

146   This same axiom does away with all the ideas hitherto held concerning the natural law of nations, which has been thought to have originated in one nation and been passed on to others. This error was encouraged by the bad example of the Egyptians and Greeks in vainly boasting that they had spread civilization throughout the world. It was this error that gave rise to the fiction that the Law of the Twelve Tables came to Rome from Greece. If that had been the case, it would have been a civil law communicated to other peoples by human provision, and not a law which divine providence ordained naturally in all nations along with human customs themselves. Indeed it will be one of our constant labors throughout this book to demonstrate that the natural law of nations originated separately among the various peoples, each in ignorance of the others, and that subsequently, as a result of wars, embassies, alliances and commerce, it came to be recognized as common to the entire human race.

XIV

147   The nature of things is nothing but their coming into being (*nascimento*) at certain times and in certain fashions. Whenever the time and fashion is thus and so, such and not otherwise are the things that come into being.

XV

148   The inseparable properties of things must be due to the mode or fashion in which they are born. By these properties we may therefore tell that the nature or birth (*natura o nascimento*) was thus and not otherwise.

XVI

149   Vulgar traditions must have had public grounds of truth, by virtue of which they came into being and were preserved by entire peoples over long periods of time.

150   It will be another great labor of this Science to recover these grounds of truth—truth which, in the passage of years and the changes in languages and customs, has come down to us enveloped in falsehood.

XVII

151   The vulgar tongues should be the most weighty witnesses concerning those ancient customs of the peoples that were observed at the time when the languages were being formed.

XVIII

152   A language of an ancient nation, which has maintained itself as the dominant tongue throughout its development, should be a great witness to the customs of the early days of the world.

153   This axiom assures us that the weightiest philological proofs of the natural law of nations (in the understanding of which the Romans were unquestionably preëminent) can be drawn from Latin speech. For the same reason scholars of the German language can do the like, since it retains this same property possessed by the ancient Roman language.

XIX

154   If the Laws of the Twelve Tables were customs of the peoples of Latium, originating in the age of Saturn, remaining unwritten elsewhere [in Latium] but set down by the Romans in bronze and guarded with religious care by Roman jurisprudence, then this Law is a great witness of the ancient natural law of the nations of Latium.

155   That this was true in fact, we showed many years ago in our *Principles of Universal Law,* and the present work will throw further light upon it.

XX

156   If the poems of Homer are civil histories of ancient Greek customs, they will be two great treasure houses of the natural law of the nations of Greece.

157   For the present this axiom is merely assumed; later its truth will be demonstrated.

XXI

158   The Greek philosophers hastened the natural course which their nation was to undergo, for when they appeared the Greeks were still in a crude state of barbarism, from which they advanced immediately to one of the highest refinement while at the same time preserving intact their fables both of gods and of heroes. The Romans, on the other hand, proceeding at an even pace in [the development of] their customs, quite lost sight of the history of their gods (whence the age of the gods, as the Egyptians named it, is called by Varro the obscure period of the Romans), but preserved in vulgar speech their heroic history, which extends from the time of Romulus to the Publilian and Petelian laws, and which will be found to be a continuous historic mythology of the Greek age of the heroes.

159   [That] this [is the] nature of human civil affairs is confirmed by the example of the French nation. For in the midst of the barbarism of the twelfth century there was opened the famous Parisian school where Peter Lombard, the celebrated master of the Sentences, began to lecture on the subtlest scholastic theology. And like a Homeric poem there still lived on the history of Bishop Turpin of Paris, full of all those fables of the heroes of France called paladins which were later to fill so many romances and poems. And because of this premature passage from barbarism to the subtlest sciences, French remained a language of the greatest refinement. So much so indeed that of all living languages it seems most to have restored to our times the atticism of the Greeks, and it is the best of all languages for scientific reasoning, as the Greek was. Yet French preserves, as Greek did, many diphthongs, which are natural to a barbarous tongue still stiff and inept at combining consonants with vowels. In confirmation of what we have said of both these languages, we may here add an observation in regard to young people at an age when memory is tenacious, imagination vivid, and wit nimble. At this age they may profitably occupy themselves with languages and plane geometry, without thereby subduing that acerbity of minds still bound to the body which may be called the barbarism of the intellect. But if they pass on while yet in this immature stage to the highly subtle studies of metaphysical criticism or algebra, they become overfine for life in their way of thinking and are rendered incapable of any great work.

160 But as we further meditated this work we came upon another cause for the effect in question, and this cause is perhaps more apposite. Romulus founded Rome in the midst of the other more ancient cities of Latium, and founded it by opening there the asylum which Livy defines generally as "an old counsel of founders of cities" (*vetus urbes condentium consilium*); for since violence still reigned he naturally established the city of Rome on the same basis on which the oldest cities of the world had been founded. And so it came about, since Roman customs were developing from such beginnings at a time when the vulgar tongues of Latium were already well advanced, that Roman civil affairs, the like of which the Greeks had set forth in heroic speech, were set forth by the Romans in vulgar speech. Thus ancient Roman history will be found to be a continuous mythology of the heroic history of the Greeks. And this must be the reason why the Romans were the heroes of the world. For Rome subdued the other cities of Latium, then Italy and finally the whole world, because heroism was still young among the Romans, whereas among the other peoples of Latium, from whose conquest all the greatness of Rome sprang, it must already have begun to decay.

XXII

161 There must in the nature of human things be a mental language common to all nations, which uniformly grasps the substance of things feasible in human social life, and expresses it with as many diverse modifications as these same things may have diverse aspects. A proof of this is afforded by proverbs or maxims of vulgar wisdom, in which substantially the same meanings find as many diverse expressions as there are nations ancient and modern.

162 This common mental language is proper to our Science, by whose light linguistic scholars will be enabled to construct a mental vocabulary common to all the various articulate languages living and dead. We gave a particular example of this in the first edition of the *New Science*. There we proved that the names of the first family fathers, in a great number of living and dead languages, were given them because of the various properties which they had in the state of the families and of the first commonwealths, at the time when the nations were forming their languages. As far as our small erudition will permit, we shall make use of this vocabulary in all the matters we discuss.

163 Of all the aforesaid propositions, the first, second, third and fourth give us the basis for refuting all opinions hitherto held about the beginnings of humanity. The refutations turn on the improbabilities, absurdities, contradictions and impossibilities of these opinions. The subsequent propositions, from the fifth to the fifteenth, which give us the basis of truth, will serve for considering this world of nations in its eternal idea, by that property of every science, noted by Aristotle, that "science has to do with what is universal and eternal" (*scientia debet esse de universalibus et aeternis*). The last propositions, from the fifteenth to the twenty-second, will give us the basis of certitude. By their use we shall be able to see in fact this world of nations which we have studied in idea, following the method of philosophizing made most certain by Francis Bacon, Lord of Verulam, but carrying it over from the things of nature, on which he composed his book *Cogitata [et] visa,* to the civil affairs of mankind.

164 The propositions set forth above are general and are the basis of our Science throughout; those which follow are particular and provide more specific bases for the various matters it treats of.

XXIII

165 Sacred history is more ancient than all the most ancient profane histories that have come down to us, for it narrates in great detail and over a period of more than eight hundred years the state of nature under the patriarchs; that is, the state of the families, out of which, by general agreement of political theorists, the peoples and cities later arose. Of this family state profane history has told us nothing or little, and that little quite confused.

166 This axiom proves the truth of sacred history as against the national conceit pointed out to us by Diodorus Siculus, for the Hebrews have preserved their memories in full detail from the very beginning of the world.

XXIV

167 The Hebrew religion was founded by the true God on the prohibition of the divination on which all the gentile nations arose.

168 This axiom is one of the principal reasons for the division of the entire world of the ancient nations into Hebrews and gentiles.

XXV

169 That the flood was worldwide is proved not indeed by the philological evidence of Martin Schoock, for it is far too slight, nor by the astrological evidence of Cardinal Pierre D'Ailly, followed by Giovanni Pico della Mirandola. For this latter evidence is too uncertain, indeed quite false, relying as it does on the *Alphonsine Tables,* which were refuted by the Jews and are now refuted by the Christians, who, having rejected the calculations of Eusebius and Bede, now follow those of Philo the Jew. But our demonstration will be drawn from physical histories discerned in the fables, as will be seen from the following axioms.

XXVI

170 The giants were by nature of enormous build, like those monstrous and fierce creatures which travelers claim to have seen at the foot of America, in the country of the so-called "Patagones" [= Big Feet]. And, putting aside the vain, abortive and false reasons adduced for these creatures by the philosophers, as collected and followed by Chassagnon in his *De gigantibus,* we shall adduce the causes, partly physical and partly moral, observed by Julius Caesar and Cornelius Tacitus in speaking of the gigantic stature of the ancient Germans. In our view, these causes are to be traced to the savage education of their children.

XXVII

171　　Greek history, from which we get all we know about the history of all other ancient gentile nations except the Roman, starts with the flood and the giants.

172　　These two axioms make it evident that the entire original human race was divided into two species: the one of giants, the other of men of normal stature; the former gentiles, the latter Hebrews. Also that this difference can only have come about as the result of the savage education of the former and the human education of the latter. Hence that the Hebrews had a different origin from that of the gentiles.

XXVIII

173　　Two great remnants of Egyptian antiquity have come down to us, as we have noted above [53]. One of them is the fact that the Egyptians reduced all preceding world time to three ages, namely, the age of the gods, the age of the heroes, and the age of men. The other is that during these three ages three languages had been spoken, corresponding in order to the three aforesaid ages; namely, the hieroglyphic or sacred language, the symbolic or figurative (which is the heroic) language, and the epistolary or vulgar language of men employing conventional signs for communicating the common needs of their life.

XXIX

174　　Homer, in five passages from his two poems to be cited later, mentions a language more ancient than his own (which was certainly a heroic language) and calls it "the language of the gods."

XXX

175　　Varro had the diligence to assemble thirty thousand names of gods —for the Greeks counted that many. These were related to as many needs of physical, moral, economic or civil life of the earliest times.

176　　These three axioms establish the fact that the world of peoples began everywhere with religion. This will be the first of the three principles of this science.

XXXI

177　　Wherever a people has grown savage in arms so that human laws have no longer any place among it, the only powerful means of reducing it is religion.

178　　This axiom establishes the fact that divine providence initiated the process by which the fierce and violent were brought from their outlaw state to humanity and entered upon national life. It did so by awaking in them a confused idea of divinity, which they in their ignorance attributed to that to which it did not belong. Thus through the terror of this imagined divinity, they began to put themselves in some order.

179 Such an [initiating] principle of things Thomas Hobbes failed to see among his own "fierce and violent men," because he went afield in search of principles and fell into error with the "chance" of his Epicurus. He thought to enrich Greek philosophy by adding a great part which it certainly had lacked (as George Pasch observes in his *De eruditis huius saeculi inventis*): the study of man in the whole society of the human race. But the result was as unhappy as the effort was noble. Nor would Hobbes have conceived this project if the Christian religion had not given him the inspiration for it. For it demands of all mankind not merely justice but charity. From this point begins the refutation of the false dictum of Polybius that if the world had philosophers there would be no need of religions. For if there were in the world no commonwealths, which cannot arise without religions, it would have no philosophers.

XXXII

180 When men are ignorant of the natural causes producing things, and cannot even explain them by analogy with similar things, they attribute their own nature to them. The vulgar, for example, say the magnet loves the iron.

181 This axiom is embraced by the first: namely, that the human mind, because of its indefinite nature, wherever it is lost in ignorance makes itself the rule of the universe in respect of everything it does not know.

XXXIII

182 The physics of the ignorant is a vulgar metaphysics by which they refer the causes of the things they do not know to the will of God without considering the means by which the divine will operates.

XXXIV

183 That is a true property of the human mind which Tacitus points out where he says "minds once cowed are prone to superstition" (*mobiles ad superstitionem perculsae semel mentes*). Once men are seized by a frightful superstition, they refer to it all they imagine, see, or even do.

XXXV

184 Wonder is the daughter of ignorance; and the greater the object of wonder, the more the wonder grows.

XXXVI

185 Imagination is more robust in proportion as reasoning power is weak.

XXXVII

186   The most sublime labor of poetry is to give sense and passion to insensate things; and it is characteristic of children to take inanimate things in their hands and talk to them in play as if they were living persons.

187   This philologico-philosophical axiom proves to us that in the world's childhood men were by nature sublime poets.

XXXVIII

188   That is a golden passage in Lactantius Firmianus where he considers the origins of idolatry, saying: "Rude men at first called [them, i.e. the king and his family] gods either for their wonderful excellence (wonderful it seemed to men still rude and simple), or, as commonly happens, in admiration of present power, or on account of the benefits by which they had been conducted to civilization."

XXXIX

189   Curiosity—that inborn property of man, daughter of ignorance and mother of knowledge—when wonder wakens our minds, has the habit, wherever it sees some extraordinary phenomenon of nature, a comet for example, a sun-dog, or a midday star, of asking straightway what it means.

XL

190   Witches, who are full of frightful superstitions, are also exceedingly savage and cruel. Indeed, if it is necessary for the solemnizing of their witchcraft, they do not shrink from killing and dismembering tender innocent children.

191   All these propositions from the twenty-eighth to the thirty-eighth reveal to us the beginnings of divine poetry or poetic theology. From the thirty-first on they give us the beginnings of idolatry; from the thirty-ninth, the beginnings of divination; and the fortieth finally gives us the beginnings of sacrifice in connection with bloodthirsty religions. These sacrifices began among the first crude savage men with votive offerings and human victims. The latter, as we learn from Plautus, were by the Latins vulgarly called "Saturn's victims" (*Saturni hostiae*). They were the sacrifices to Moloch among the Phoenicians, who passed through fire the children consecrated to that false divinity. Some of these consecrations were preserved in the Law of the Twelve Tables. These things give the right sense to that saying, "Fear first created gods in the world" (*Primos in orbe deos fecit timor*): false religions were born not of imposture but of credulity. Likewise the unhappy vow and sacrifice that Agamemnon made of his pious daughter Iphigenia, at which Lucretius impiously exclaims, "So great were the evils religion could prompt" (*Tantum religio potuit suadere malorum*), derive from the counsel of divine providence. For all this was necessary to tame the sons of the cyclopes and reduce them to the humanity of an Aristides, a Socrates, a Laelius and a Scipio Africanus.

XLI

192 We postulate, and the postulate is reasonable, that for several hundred years the earth, soaked by the water of the universal flood, sent forth no dry exhalations or matter capable of igniting in the air to produce lightning.

XLII

193 Jove hurls his bolts and fells the giants, and every gentile nation had its Jove.

194 This axiom contains the physical history that the fables have preserved for us: that the universal deluge covered the whole earth.

195 This same axiom with its preceding postulate should make it clear to us that for a long period of time the impious races of the three children of Noah had wandered in a wild state, and in their feral wandering had become scattered and dispersed through the great forest of the earth, and that with their wild education giants had sprung up and existed among them at the time when the heavens thundered for the first time after the flood.

XLIII

196 Every gentile nation had its Hercules, who was the son of Jove; and Varro, the most learned of antiquarians, numbered as many as forty of them.

197 This axiom marks the beginning of heroism among the first peoples, which was born of the false opinion that the heroes were of divine origin.

198 This same axiom and the preceding one, giving us so many Joves and then so many Herculeses among the gentile nations, together show us that these nations could not have been founded without religion and could not grow without courage. Moreover, since in their beginnings these nations were forest-bred and shut off from any knowledge of each other, and since by axiom XIII "uniform ideas, born among peoples unknown to each other, must have a common ground of truth," these axioms give us this great principle as well: that the first fables must have contained civil truths, and must therefore have been the histories of the first peoples.

XLIV

199 The first sages of the Greek world were the theological poets, who certainly flourished before the heroic poets, just as Jove was the father of Hercules.

200 This and the two preceding axioms establish the fact that all the gentile nations, inasmuch as they all had their Joves and their Herculeses, were poetic in their beginnings; and that divine poetry was born first among them, and later heroic poetry.

XLV

201 Men are naturally impelled to preserve the memories of the laws and orders that bind them in their societies.

XLVI

202 All barbarian histories have fabulous beginnings.

203 All these axioms from the forty-second on give us the beginning of our historical mythology.

XLVII

204 The human mind is naturally impelled to take delight in uniformity.

205 This axiom, as applied to the fables, is confirmed by the habit the vulgar have when making up fables of men famous for this or that, in these or those circumstances, of making the fable fit the character and occasion. These fables are ideal truths conforming to the merits of those of whom the vulgar tell them; and such falseness in fact as they now and then contain consists simply in failure to give their subjects their due. So that, if we consider the matter well, poetic truth is metaphysical truth, and physical truth which is not in conformity with it should be considered false. Thence springs this important consideration in poetic theory: the true war chief, for example, is the Godfrey that Torquato Tasso imagines; and all the chiefs who do not conform throughout to Godfrey are not true chiefs of war.

XLVIII

206 The nature of children is such that by the ideas and names associated with the first men, women and things they have known, they afterwards apprehend and name all the men, women and things which have any resemblance or relation to the first.

XLIX

207 A truly golden passage is that above cited from Iamblichus *On the Mysteries of the Egyptians* to the effect that the Egyptians attributed to Hermes Trismegistus all discoveries useful or necessary to human life.

208 This statement, supported by the preceding axiom, will turn back to this divine philosopher all the senses of sublime natural theology that he himself attributed to the mysteries of the Egyptians.

209 These three axioms [XLVII–XLIX] give us the origin of the poetic characters that constitute the essence of the fables. The first of the three shows the natural inclination of the vulgar to invent them, and to invent them appropriately. The second shows that the first men, the children as it were of the human race, not being able to form intelligible class-concepts of things, had a natural need to create poetic characters, that is, imaginative class-concepts or universals, by reducing to them as to certain models or ideal portraits all the particular species which resembled them. Because of the resemblance, the ancient fables could not but be created appropriately. Just so the Egyptians reduced to the genus "civil sage" all their inventions useful or necessary to the human race which are particular effects of civil wisdom, and because they could not abstract the intelligible genus "civil sage," much less the form of the civil wisdom in which these Egyptians were sages, they imaged it forth as Hermes Trismegistus. So far were the Egyptians, at the time when they were enriching the world with discoveries useful or necessary to the human race, from being philosophers and understanding universals or intelligible class-concepts!

210   This last axiom, following on those preceding, is the principle of the true poetic allegories which gave the fables univocal rather than analogous meanings for various particulars comprised under their poetic genera. They were therefore called *diversiloquia,* that is, expressions comprising in one general concept various species of men, deeds, or things.

L

211   In children memory is most vigorous, and imagination is therefore excessively vivid, for imagination is nothing but extended or compounded memory.

212   This axiom is the explanation of the vividness of the poetic images the world had to form in its first childhood.

LI

213   In every pursuit men without natural aptitude succeed by obstinate study of technique, but in poetry he who lacks native ability cannot succeed by technique.

214   This axiom shows that, since poetry founded gentile humanity, from which alone the arts were to spring, the first poets were such by nature.

LII

215   Children excel in imitation; we observe them generally amuse themselves by imitating what they are able to understand.

216   This axiom shows that the world in its infancy was composed of poetic nations, for poetry is nothing but imitation.

217   This axiom will explain the fact that all the arts of things necessary, useful, convenient, and even in large part those of human pleasure, were invented in the poetic centuries before the philosophers came; for the arts are nothing but imitations of nature, poems in a certain way made of things.

LIII

218   Men at first feel without observing, then they observe with a troubled and agitated spirit, finally they reflect with a clear mind.

219   This axiom is the principle of the poetic sentences, which are formed

with senses of passions and affections, in contrast with philosophic sentences, which are formed by reflection and reasoning. The more the latter rise toward universals, the closer they approach the truth; the more the former take hold of particulars, the more certain they become.

LIV

220 Whatever appertains to men but is doubtful or obscure, they naturally interpret according to their own natures and the passions and habits springing from them.

221 This axiom is a great canon of our mythology. According to it the fables originating among the first savage and crude men were very severe, as befitted the founding of nations emerging from a state of fierce bestial freedom. Then, with the long passage of years and change of customs, they were impropriated, altered and obscured in the dissolute and corrupt times even before Homer. Because religion was important to the men of Greece, and they feared to have the gods opposed to their desires as they were to their customs, they attributed their customs to the gods and gave improper, ugly and obscene meanings to the fables.

LV

222 That is a golden passage of Eusebius (from his account of the wisdom of the Egyptians as exalted above that of all other gentiles) in which he says: "The first theology of the Egyptians was simply a history interspersed with fables, to which later generations, growing ashamed of them, gradually attached mystical interpretations." That is what was done, for instance, by Manethos, or Manetho, the high priest of the Egyptians, when he translated all Egyptian history into a sublime natural theology, as has been said above [46].

223 These two axioms are two great proofs of our historic mythology, and they are at the same time two great whirlwinds to confound any notion of the matchless wisdom of the ancients, and two great foundations of the truth of the Christian religion, whose sacred history narrates nothing to be ashamed of.

LVI

224 The first authors among the Easterners, Egyptians, Greeks and Latins, and, in the second barbarism, the first writers in the modern languages of Europe, were poets.

LVII

225 Mutes make themselves understood by gestures or objects that have natural relations with the ideas they wish to signify.

226 This axiom is the principle of the hieroglyphs by which all nations spoke in the time of their first barbarism.

227 It is also the principle of the natural speech which Plato (in the *Cratylus*) and after him Iamblichus (*On the Mysteries of the Egyptians*) guessed to have been spoken in the world at one time. Their view was shared by the Stoics and by Origen (*Against Celsus*); but, since it was but a guess, it was opposed by Aristotle (in his *On Interpretation*) and by Galen (in his *Doctrines of Hippocrates and Plato*). The dispute is discussed by Publius Nigidius in Aulus Gellius. This natural speech must have been succeeded by the poetic discourse of images, similes, comparisons and natural properties.

LVIII

228 Mutes utter formless sounds by singing, and stammerers by singing teach their tongues to pronounce.

LIX

229 Men vent great passions by breaking into song, as we observe in the most grief-stricken and the most joyful.

230 These two axioms—supposing that the founders of the gentile nations had wandered about in the wild state of dumb beasts and that, being therefore sluggish, they were inexpressive save under the impulse of violent passions—[lead to the conjecture that] their first languages must have been formed in singing.

LX

231 Languages must have begun with monosyllables, for [even] in the present abundance of articulated [i.e. polysyllabic] words into which children are now born they begin with monosyllables in spite of the fact that in them the fibers of the organ necessary to articulate speech are very flexible.

LXI

232 Heroic verse is the oldest of all, and spondaic the slowest; and farther on we shall see that heroic verse was originally spondaic.

LXII

233 Iambic verse is the closest to prose, and the iamb is a "swift foot," as Horace puts it.

234 These last two axioms lead us to conjecture that ideas and language developed at equal pace.

235 All these axioms from the forty-seventh on, together with those previously set forth as principles for all the rest [I–XXII], cover the divisions of poetic theory: namely, fable [or plot], custom [or character] and its appropriateness, sentence [or thought], style [or diction] and its clarity, allegory, song and finally verse. The last seven axioms [LVI–LXII] establish the fact that among all nations speech in verse preceded speech in prose.

LXIII

236 The human mind is naturally inclined by the senses to see itself externally in the body, and only with great difficulty does it come to attend to itself by means of reflection.

237 This axiom gives us the universal principle of etymology in all languages: words are carried over from bodies and from the properties of bodies to express the things of the mind and spirit.

LXIV

238 The order of ideas must follow the order of things.

LXV

239 This was the order of human things: first the forests, after that the huts, thence the villages, next the cities and finally the academies.

240 This axiom is a great principle of etymology, for this sequence of human things sets the pattern for the histories of words in the various native languages. Thus we observe in the Latin language that almost the whole corpus of its words had sylvan or rustic origins. For example, *lex*. First it must have meant "collection of acorns." Thence we believe is derived *ilex*, as it were *illex*, "the oak" (as certainly *aquilex* is the "collector of waters"); for the oak produces the acorns by which the swine are drawn together. *Lex* was next "a collection of vegetables," from which the latter were called *legumina*. Later on, at a time when vulgar letters had not yet been invented for writing down the laws, *lex* by a necessity of civil nature must have meant "a collection of citizens" or the public parliament; so that the presence of the people was the law that solemnized the wills that were made *calatis comitiis,* in the presence of the assembled *comitia*. Finally collecting letters, and making as it were a sheaf of them in each word, was called *legere,* "reading."

LXVI

241 Men first feel necessity, then look for utility, next attend to comfort, still later amuse themselves with pleasure, thence grow dissolute in luxury, and finally go mad and waste their substance.

LXVII

242 The nature of peoples is first crude, then severe, then benign, then delicate, finally dissolute.

LXVIII

243 In the human race first appear the huge and grotesque, like the cyclopes; then the proud and magnanimous, like Achilles; then the valorous and just, like Aristides and Scipio Africanus; nearer to us, imposing figures with great semblances of virtue accompanied by great vices, who among the vulgar

win a name for true glory, like Alexander and Caesar; still later, the melancholy and reflective, like Tiberius; finally the dissolute and shameless madmen, like Caligula, Nero, and Domitian.

244 This axiom shows that the first sort were necessary in order to make one man obey another in the family-state and prepare him to be law-abiding in the city-state that was to come; the second sort, who naturally did not yield to their peers, were necessary to establish the aristocratic commonwealths on the basis of the families; the third sort to open the way for popular liberty; the fourth to bring in the monarchies; the fifth to establish them; the sixth to overthrow them.

245 This with the preceding axioms [LXV–LXVII] gives a part of the principles of the ideal eternal history traversed in time by every nation in its rise, development, maturity, decline and fall.

LXIX

246 Governments must conform to the nature of the men governed.

247 This axiom shows that in the nature of human civil things the public school of princes is the morality of the peoples.

LXX

248 Let that be granted which is not repugnant to nature and which we shall later find to be true in fact: that from the nefarious state of the outlaw world some few of the sturdiest first withdrew and established families, with whom and by whom they brought the fields under cultivation; and a long while later the many others also withdrew and took refuge on the lands cultivated by these fathers.

LXXI

249 Native customs, and above all that of natural liberty, do not change all at once but by degrees and over a long period of time.

LXXII

250 Since all nations began with the cult of some divinity, in the family state the fathers must have been the sages in auspicial divinity, the priests who sacrificed to take the auspices or to make sure of their meaning, and the kings who brought the divine laws to their families.

LXXIII

251 It is a vulgar tradition that the first to govern the world were kings.

LXXIV

252 It is another vulgar tradition that those were created the first kings who were the worthiest.

LXXV

253   It is yet another vulgar tradition that the first kings were sages, wherefore Plato expressed the vain wish for those ancient times in which philosophers reigned or kings were philosophers.

254   All these axioms show that in the persons of the first fathers there were united wisdom, priesthood and kingship, and the kingship and priesthood depended on the wisdom, not indeed the esoteric wisdom of philosophers but the vulgar wisdom of lawgivers. And therefore thenceforward in all nations the priests wore crowns.

LXXVI

255   It is a vulgar tradition that the first form of government in the world was the monarchical.

LXXVII

256   But the sixty-seventh axiom with the others following, and in particular with the corollary of the sixty-ninth, show us that in the family state the fathers must have exercised a monarchical power, subject only to God, over both the persons and the property of their children and to a much greater extent over those of the *famuli* who had taken refuge on their lands. So they were the first monarchs of the world, of whom sacred history must be understood to speak when it calls them patriarchs or father-princes. This monarchical right was preserved to them for the entire period of the Roman Republic by the Law of the Twelve Tables: "The family father shall have power of life and death over his children" (*Patrifamilias ius vitae et necis in liberos esto*); from which it follows that "Whatever the son acquires, he acquires for his father" (*Quicquid filius acquirit, patri acquirit*).

LXXVIII

257   The families cannot have taken their name, in keeping with their origin, from anything but these *famuli* of the fathers in the then state of nature.

LXXIX

258   The first *socii*, who are properly companions associated for mutual advantage, cannot be imagined or understood to have existed in the world previous to these fugitives who sought to save their lives by taking refuge with the aforesaid first fathers and who, having been received for their lives, were obliged to sustain them by cultivating the fields of the fathers.

259   These were the true *socii* of the heroes. Later they were the plebeians of the heroic cities and finally the provincials of sovereign peoples.

LXXX

260 Men come naturally to the feudal system [*ragione de' benefizi*] wherever they see a possibility of retaining in it or gaining from it a good and great share of utility, for such are the benefits [*benefizi*] which may be hoped for in civil life.

LXXXI

261 It is characteristic of the strong not to relinquish through laziness what they have acquired by courage. Rather do they yield, from necessity or for utility, as little as they can and bit by bit.

262 From these two axioms spring the perennial sources of fiefs, which are called, with Roman elegance, benefices (*beneficia*).

LXXXII

263 In all ancient nations we find everywhere clients and clienteles, which are best understood as vassals and fiefs. Nor can learned writers on feudal law find apter Latin terms [for the latter] than *clientes* and *clientelae*.

264 These last three axioms with the preceding twelve, beginning with the seventieth, reveal to us the principles of the commonwealths, born of a great necessity (which we shall later determine) imposed upon the family fathers by the *famuli;* a necessity such that the commonwealths naturally took the aristocratic form. For the fathers united themselves in orders to resist the *famuli* who had rebelled against them; and, once thus united, to satisfy these *famuli* and reduce them to obedience, they conceded to them a sort of rustic fiefs. The fathers in turn found their own sovereign family powers (which can only be understood on the analogy of noble fiefs) subjected to the sovereign civil authority of the ruling orders [in which they were now united]. The chiefs of the orders were called kings; it was their function, as the most courageous, to lead the fathers in times of revolt among the *famuli*. If such an origin of cities were offered as a hypothesis (which later we find to be the fact), it would command acceptance by its naturalness and simplicity and for the infinite number of civil effects which depend upon it as their proper cause. In no other way can we understand how civil power emerged from family power, and the public patrimony from private patrimonies, or how the commonwealths had their elements prepared in the form of an order of few to command and a multitude of plebeians to obey them. These are the two parts which make up the subject matter of politics. It will later be shown that civil states could not thus have been formed from families containing children only [and not *famuli*].

LXXXIII

265 This law concerning the fields is established as the first agrarian law of the world, and it would be hard to imagine or conceive one more restricted in nature.

266　This agrarian law distinguished the three types of ownership [or domain (*dominium*)] which can obtain in civil nature, attached to three classes of persons: the bonitary, to the plebeians; the quiritary, maintained by arms and consequently noble, to the fathers; and the eminent, to the order itself, which is the Seigniory or sovereign power in aristocratic commonwealths.

LXXXIV

267　There is a golden passage in Aristotle's *Politics* where, in his classification of commonwealths, he includes the heroic kingdoms in which the kings administered the laws at home, conducted wars abroad, and were heads of the state religion.

268　This axiom fits exactly the two heroic kingdoms of Theseus and Romulus, as we may see of the former in Plutarch's *Life* of him, and of the latter in Roman history; supplementing Greek history with Roman, where Tullus Hostilius administers the law in the accusation against Horatius. And the Roman kings were kings also of sacred things under the name of *reges sacrorum;* so that when the kings were driven from Rome, for the sake of certainty in the divine ceremonies an officer was created to be called *rex sacrorum*, who was the head of the *fetiales* or heralds.

LXXXV

269　There is another golden passage in the *Politics* where Aristotle states that the ancient commonwealths had no laws to punish private offenses or to right private wrongs, and he says that such are the mores of barbarous peoples, for peoples are in their origins barbarous precisely because they are not yet tamed by laws.

270　This axiom shows the necessity of duels and reprisals in barbarous times because in such times judicial laws are lacking.

LXXXVI

271　Golden too is that passage in the *Politics* where Aristotle says that in the ancient commonwealths the nobles swore to be eternal enemies of the plebs.

272　This axiom explains the cause of the haughty, avaricious and cruel practices of the nobles toward the plebeians, which we see clearly portrayed in Roman history. For, within the bounds of what has hitherto been mistaken for popular liberty, for a long time they compelled the plebeians at the latter's expense to serve them in war, and drowned them in a sea of usury. Then, as the wretched plebeians could not meet their claims, they confined them for life in private prisons to make them pay off their debts by work and toil, and tyrannically beat them with rods on their bare shoulders as if they were the most abject slaves.

LXXXVII

273   The aristocratic commonwealths are most cautious about going to war lest they make warriors of the multitude of plebeians.

274   This axiom is the principle of the justice of the Roman arms up to the Punic wars.

LXXXVIII

275   The aristocratic commonwealths keep the wealth within the order of the nobility, for wealth adds to the power of this order.

276   This axiom is the principle of Roman clemency in victory; for they deprived the vanquished only of their arms, and left them in bonitary ownership of everything [else they had], subject to a tolerable tribute. Here too is the reason why the [Roman] fathers constantly resisted the agrarian laws of the Gracchi, because they did not wish to enrich the plebs.

LXXXIX

277   Honor is the noblest stimulus to military valor.

XC

278   Peoples are likely to conduct themselves heroically in war if in peace they compete among themselves for honors, some to retain them, others to win the merit of attaining them.

279   This axiom is a principle of Roman heroism from the time of the expulsion of the tyrants down to the Punic wars. Within this period the nobles naturally dedicated themselves to such a safeguarding of their country as kept all civil honors safe within their own order, and the plebs undertook the most noteworthy enterprises to show that they were worthy of the honors held by the nobles.

XCI

280   The contests waged by the orders in the cities for equality of rights are the most powerful means of making the commonwealths great.

281   This is another principle of Roman heroism, implemented by three public virtues: the magnanimity of the plebs in wanting to share the civil rights and laws of the fathers; the strength of the fathers in keeping them within their own order; and the wisdom of the jurisconsults in interpreting them and extending their utility little by little as new cases demanded adjudication. These are the three proper reasons for the distinction which Roman law attained in the world.

282   All these axioms, beginning with the eighty-fourth, set ancient Roman history forth in its proper aspect; the following three serve in part the same purpose.

XCII

283   The weak want laws; the powerful withhold them; the ambitious, in order to win a following, advocate them; princes, in order to equalize the strong with the weak, protect them.

284   This axiom, by its first and second clauses, is the torch of the heroic contests in the aristocratic commonwealths, in which the nobles want to keep the laws a secret monopoly of their order, so that they may depend on their will and that they may administer them with a royal hand. These are the three causes adduced by Pomponius the jurisconsult where he relates that the Roman people desire the Law of the Twelve Tables, complaining against the burdensomeness of "secret, uncertain law and regal power" (*ius latens, incertum et manus regia*). And it is the cause of the reluctance of the fathers to give [these Tables] to the people, insisting that "the customs of the fathers must be preserved" (*mores patrios servandos*) and "the laws must not be published" (*leges ferri non oportere*), as Dionysius of Halicarnassus states. He was better informed on Roman matters than Livy, for he wrote of them under the guidance of Marcus Terentius Varro, who was acclaimed "the most learned of the Romans." On this particular matter he is diametrically opposed to Livy, who in his account of it says that the nobles (to use his words) "did not spurn the petitions of the plebs" (*desideria plebis non aspernari*). Because of this and other greater contradictions observed in our *Principles of Universal Law,* there being such opposition between the first authors who wrote of this fable almost five hundred years afterwards, it will be better not to believe either of the two. The more so since in the same period it was believed neither by Varro himself, who in his great work on things divine and human [*Antiquitates*] gave purely Latin origins to all the institutions divine and human of the Romans, nor by Cicero, who makes the orator Marcus [i.e. Lucius Licinius] Crassus say in the presence of Quintus Mucius Scaevola, the prince of jurisconsults of his day, that the wisdom of the decemvirs surpassed by a great deal that of Draco and Solon, who gave laws to the Athenians, and that of Lycurgus who gave them to the Spartans: which is as much as to say that the Laws of the Twelve Tables did not come to Rome from Athens or Sparta. Here we believe we are getting at the truth. In Cicero's day the fable was too generally accepted among scholars, born as it was of the conceit of the learned in giving wisest origins to the wisdom they profess. This is the point of the words spoken by Crassus himself: "Though all of you grumble, I shall say what I think" (*Fremant omnes, dicam quod sentio*). Cicero's reason, therefore, for having Quintus Mucius present on that first day only, was to remove any objection to his having an orator speak of the history of Roman law, the field of knowledge proper to the jurisconsults. (These were two distinct professions at that time.) For if Crassus had said anything false on the subject, Mucius would certainly have reproved him for it, as, according to Pomponius, he reproved Servius Sulpicius (who is present at this same dis-

cussion), saying to him that "it was a disgrace for a nobleman not to know the law which was his profession" (*turpe esse patricio viro ius, in quo versaretur, ignorare*).

285   But, more than Cicero and Varro, Polybius gives us an unanswerable reason for not believing either Dionysius or Livy. And Polybius without doubt knew more of politics than these two and lived some two hundred years nearer the age of the decemvirs than they did. He sets himself (in the sixth book and the fourth and many following sections in the edition of Jakob Gronov) to examine carefully the constitutions of the most famous free commonwealths of his time, and he observes that the Roman constitution is quite different from that of Athens or Sparta. He finds it to differ from that of Athens even more than from that of Sparta, though those who compare Attic with Roman law will have it that it was from Athens rather than from Sparta that the laws came to order the popular liberty already founded by Brutus. But Polybius observes, on the other hand, a great similarity between the Roman and the Carthaginian constitutions. Yet no one has ever dreamed that the freedom of the latter was ordered by the laws of Greece; indeed, so far is this from being true that there was a law in Carthage expressly forbidding the Carthaginians to learn Greek. And how is it that such a learned writer on commonwealths does not investigate the reason of this difference and does not raise on this point the very natural and obvious question: How can the Roman and Athenian commonwealths be different and yet ordered by the same laws, and the Roman and Carthaginian commonwealths be similar but ordered by different laws? To absolve him of so flagrant an oversight, we are compelled to say that in the time of Polybius there had not yet been born at Rome this fable that the Greek laws had been brought there from Athens to order free popular government.

286   This same axiom, by its third clause, opens the way for the ambitious in the popular commonwealths to make themselves monarchs by seconding a natural desire of the plebs, who, not understanding universals, want a law for every particular case. Thus Sulla, the head of the party of the nobles, when he had defeated Marius, the head of the party of the plebs, and was reorganizing the popular state with an aristocratic government, remedied the multitude of laws by the *quaestiones perpetuae* [a permanent tribunal for criminal investigation].

287   And this same axiom, by its last clause, is the hidden reason why, beginning with Augustus, the Roman emperors made innumerable laws for private cases, and why the sovereigns and powers all over Europe received into their kingdoms and free commonwealths the Corpus of Roman Civil Law and that of Canon Law.

XCIII

288   Since the door of honors in the popular commonwealths is wide open by law to the greedy multitude which is in command, in times of peace nothing

remains but to struggle for power, not by law but by arms, and use the power to make laws for one's own enrichment. Such were the agrarian laws of the Gracchi at Rome. The result is civil wars at home and unjust wars abroad at the same time.

289   In this axiom Roman heroism is confirmed by contrast for the entire period before the Gracchi.

XCIV

290   Natural liberty is fiercer in proportion as property attaches more closely to the persons of its owners; and civil servitude is clapped on with goods of fortune not essential to life.

291   The first part of this axiom is another principle of the natural heroism of the first peoples; the second part is the natural principle of monarchies.

XCV

292   At first men desire to be free of subjection and attain equality; witness the plebs in the aristocratic commonwealths, which finally turn popular. Then they attempt to surpass their equals; witness the plebs in the popular commonwealths, later corrupted into commonwealths of the powerful. Finally they wish to put themselves above the laws; witness the anarchies or unlimited popular commonwealths, than which there is no greater tyranny, for in them there are as many tyrants as there are bold and dissolute men in the cities. At this juncture the plebs, warned by the ills they suffer, and casting about for a remedy, seek shelter under monarchies. This is the natural royal law by which Tacitus legitimizes the Roman monarchy under Augustus, "who, when the world was wearied by civil strife, subjected it to empire under the title of Prince" (*qui cuncta, bellis civilibus fessa, nomine "principis" sub imperium accepit*).

XCVI

293   When the first cities were established on the basis of the families, the nobles, by reason of their native lawless liberty, were opposd to checks and burdens; witness the aristocratic commonwealths in which the nobles are lords. Later they are forced by the plebs, greatly increased in numbers and trained in war, to submit to laws and burdens equally with their plebeians; witness the nobles in the popular commonwealths. Finally, in order to preserve their comfortable existence, they are naturally inclined to accept the supremacy of one ruler; witness the nobles under the monarchies.

294   These two axioms with the others preceding, from the sixty-sixth on, are the principles of the ideal eternal history above referred to.

XCVII

295   Let it be granted, as a postulate not repugnant to reason, that after the flood men lived first on the mountains, somewhat later came down to the plains, and finally after long ages dared to approach the shores of the sea.

XCVIII

296 In Strabo [XIII, 1, 25] there is a golden passage of Plato [*Laws* III, 677 ff.] saying that, after the local Ogygian and Deucalionian floods, men dwelt in caves in the mountains; and he identifies these first men with the cyclopes, in whom elsewhere he recognizes the first family fathers of the world. Later they dwelt on the mountain sides, and he sees them represented by Dardanus, the builder of Pergamum which later became the citadel of Troy. Finally they came down to the plains; this he sees represented by Ilus, by whom Troy was moved onto the plain near the sea, and from whom it took the name of Ilium.

XCIX

297 It is also an ancient tradition that Tyre was founded first inland and later was moved onto the coast of the Phoenician sea; as it is certain history that it was transported from the shore onto a close-lying island, from which Alexander the Great reattached it to the mainland [by a causeway].

298 These two axioms and the preceding postulate show us that the inland nations were founded first and later the maritime. And they give us a great argument to prove the antiquity of the Hebrew people, which was founded by Noah in Mesopotamia, the country farthest inland of the first habitable world; so it must have been the most ancient of all nations. And this is confirmed by the fact that the first monarchy was founded there, that of the Assyrians over the Chaldean people, from whom came the first wise men of the world, their prince being Zoroaster.

C

299 Only by extreme necessities of life are men led to abandon their own lands, which are naturally dear to those native to them. Nor do they leave them temporarily, except from greed to get rich by trade, or from anxiety to keep what they have acquired.

300 This axiom is the principle of the transmigrations of peoples. It is an induction from the heroic maritime colonies, the inundations of the barbarians (of which alone Wolfgang Latius wrote), the latest known Roman colonies, and the colonies of Europeans in the Indies.

301 And this same axiom shows us that the lost races of the three sons of Noah must be supposed to have gone off into bestial wandering, fleeing from beasts (of which the great forest of the earth must have held an unhappy abundance), pursuing the shy and indocile women (for in such a savage state they must have been extremely indocile and shy), and then later seeking pastureland and water, in order to account for their being scattered over the whole earth by the time when the heavens first thundered after the flood. It was thus that every gentile nation began with its own Jove. For if these lost races had persisted in humanity as the people of God did, they would likewise have remained in Asia. For both because of the vastness of that great part of the world

and because of the paucity of men in those days, there was no compelling reason for their abandoning it, since it is not a natural custom to abandon one's native land through caprice.

CI

302   The Phoenicians were the first navigators of the ancient world.

CII

303   Nations in their barbarous condition are impenetrable; they must either be broken into from outside by war or voluntarily opened to strangers for the advantages of trade. Thus Psammeticus opened Egypt to the Ionian and Carian Greeks, whose renown for maritime traffic must have been second to that of the Phoenicians. So great was their wealth that the temple of Samian Juno was founded in Ionia, and the mausoleum of Artemisia was built in Caria; and these were two of the seven wonders of the world. The glory of this trade was inherited by the Rhodians; in the mouth of their port they erected the great Colossus of the Sun, which was also counted among the above-mentioned wonders. So too the Chinese, with a view to the advantages of trade, have recently opened their country to us Europeans.

304   These three axioms give us the principle of a new etymologicon for words of certainly foreign origin, different from that mentioned above [240] for native words. It can also give us the history of nations carried one after another into foreign lands by colonization. Thus Naples was first called Sirena (siren), a Syriac word; which is evidence that the Syrians, that is the Phoenicians, had been the first to establish a colony there, for commercial purposes. Later it was called Parthenope, in heroic Greek, and finally Neapolis, in vulgar Greek; names which prove that the Greeks had afterwards settled there to establish trading posts. From this succession there was sure to emerge a mixed language of Phoenician and Greek, in which it is said that the emperor Tiberius took greater pleasure than in pure Greek. Thus also on the gulf of Tarentum there was a Syrian colony called Siris, whose inhabitants were called Sirites. It was later called by the Greeks Polieion, whence the appellation Polias was given to Minerva, who had a temple there.

305   This axiom moreover gives a scientific foundation to the thesis of Giambullari that the Etruscan language is of Syriac origin. Such a language could have come only from the most ancient Phoenicians, who, by the axiom above laid down [302] were the first navigators of the ancient world. For later this glory belonged to the Carian and Ionian Greeks, and finally to the Rhodians.

CIII

306   The postulate must needs be granted that on the shore of Latium some Greek colony had been set up, which, after conquest and destruction by the Romans, remained buried in the darkness of antiquity.

307   If this is not granted, anyone who reflects systematically upon antiq-
uities must be baffled by Roman history when it speaks of Hercules and
Evander, Arcadians and Phrygians, within the boundaries of Latium, and of
Servius Tullius as a Greek, Tarquinius Priscus as the son of Demaratus the
Corinthian, and Aeneas as the founder of the Roman people. Tacitus [*Annals*
XI, 14] certainly speaks of the resemblance between Roman and Greek letters;
yet at the time of Servius Tullius, in the opinion of Livy, the Romans never even
heard of the famous name of Pythagoras, who was teaching in his most celebrated school at Croton, and they did not make the acquaintance of the Greeks
in Italy until the occasion of the war with Tarentum [116], which led to the
later war with Pyrrhus and the Greeks across the sea.

CIV

308   The remark of Dion Cassius [i.e. Chrysostom] is worthy of consideration, that custom is like a king and law like a tyrant; which we must
understand as referring to reasonable custom and to law not animated by natural
reason.

309   This axiom decides by implication the great dispute "whether law
resides in nature or in the opinion of men," which comes to the same thing
as that propounded in the corollary of the eighth axiom [135], "whether man is
naturally sociable." In the first place, the natural law of nations was ordained by
custom (which Dion says commands us by pleasure like a king) and not by
law (which Dion says commands us by force like a tyrant). For it began in
human customs springing from the common nature of all nations (which is the
proper subject of our Science) and it preserves human society. Moreover, there
is nothing more natural (for there is nothing more pleasant) than observing natural customs. For all these reasons, human nature, in which such customs have
had their origin, is perforce sociable.

310   This axiom, with the eighth and its corollary, shows that man is
unjust not by nature in the absolute sense, but by nature fallen and weak. Consequently it demonstrates the first principle of the Christian religion, which is
Adam before the fall, in the ideal perfection in which he must have been created
by God. And therefore it demonstrates the Catholic principles of grace: that it
operates in the man who has privation and not negation of good works and who
thus has an inefficacious power for them, and that grace is efficacious therefore
[to supply this lack]; that for that reason it cannot exist without the principle
of free will, which God naturally aids by His providence (as has been said
above in the second corollary of the same eighth axiom [136]), with regard to
which the Christian religion is in accord with all others. This is what Grotius,
Selden and Pufendorf should have founded their systems upon before everything
else, in agreement with the Roman jurisconsults who define "the natural law of
nations as having been ordained by divine providence."

CV

311 The natural law of nations is coeval with the customs of the nations, conforming one with another in virtue of a common human sense, without any reflection and without one nation following the example of another.

312 This axiom, with the saying of Dion quoted in the preceding axiom, proves that providence, being sovereign over the affairs of men, is the ordainer of the natural law of nations.

313 This same axiom establishes the difference between the natural law of the Hebrews, the natural law of nations, and the natural law of the philosophers. For whereas the gentile nations had only the ordinary help of providence, the Hebrews had extraordinary help from the true God; on this account the latter divided the whole world of nations into Hebrews and gentiles. The philosophers reason it out more completely than the gentiles are wont to, for they did not appear until some two thousand years after the gentile nations were founded. On account of their failure to observe these differences between the three [natural laws], the three systems of Grotius, Selden and Pufendorf must fall.

CVI

314 Doctrines must take their beginning from that of the matters of which they treat.

315 This axiom, placed here for [its application to] the particular matter of the natural law of nations, is universally used in all the matters which are herein discussed. It might have been laid down among the general axioms; but it has been placed here because in this more than any other particular matter its truth and the importance of using it are apparent.

CVII

316 The [first] *gentes* began before the cities; they were called by the Latins *gentes maiores* or ancient noble houses like those of the Roman fathers of whom Romulus constituted the senate, and, with the senate, the city of Rome. On the other hand they called *gentes minores* the new noble houses founded after the cities; those for example with whose fathers Junius Brutus, after the expulsion of the kings, replenished the senate when it had been depleted by the deaths of the senators executed by order of Tarquinius Superbus.

CVIII

317 There was a corresponding twofold division of the gods. First there were those of the *gentes maiores,* that is, gods who were consecrated by the families before the time of the cities. Among the Greeks and Latins these were certainly twelve in number. We shall show that such was also the case among the first Assyrians, Chaldeans, Phoenicians and Egyptians. Among the

Greeks their number was so well known that they were called simply "the twelve." These gods are brought confusedly together in a Latin distich quoted in our *Principles of Universal Law*. Here, however, in Book Two, following a natural theogony or generation of the gods framed naturally in the minds of the Greeks, they will be set forth in this order: Jove, Juno; Diana, Apollo; Vulcan, Saturn, Vesta; Mars, Venus; Minerva, Mercury; Neptune. Secondly, there were the gods of the *gentes minores,* that is to say those consecrated later by the peoples; for example Romulus, whom after his death the Roman people called the god Quirinus.

318   By these three axioms the three systems of Grotius, Selden and Pufendorf are found wanting in their beginnings. For they begin with nations reciprocally related in the society of the entire human race. Whereas, among all the first nations, as we shall show here, the race began in the time of the families, under the gods of the so-called *gentes maiores.*

CIX

319   Men of limited ideas take for law what the words expressly say.

CX

320   Golden is the definition which Ulpian [D.48.4.1.1] assigns to civil equity: "a kind of probable judgment, not naturally known to all men" (as natural equity is) "but to those few who, being eminently endowed with prudence, experience, or learning, have come to know what things are necessary for the conservation of human society" (*probabilis quaedam ratio, non omnibus hominibus naturaliter cognita, sed paucis tantum, qui, prudentia, usu, doctrina praediti, didicerunt quae ad societatis humanae conservationem sunt necessaria*). This is what is nowadays called "reason of state."

CXI

321   The certitude of the laws is an obscurity of judgment backed only by authority, so that we find them harsh in application, yet are obliged to apply them by their certitude. In good Latin *certum* means "particularized," or, as the schools say, "individuated"; so that, in overelegant Latin, *certum* and *commune* are opposed to each other.

322   This axiom [319] and the two following definitions [320, 321] constitute the principle of strict law. Its rule is civil equity, by whose certitude, that is to say by the determinate particularity of whose words, the barbarians, [men] of particular [not universal] ideas, are naturally satisfied, and such is the law they think is their due. So that what Ulpian says in such cases, "the law is harsh, but so it is written" (*lex dura est, sed scripta est*), may be put in finer Latin and with greater legal elegance, "the law is harsh, but it is certain" (*lex dura est, sed certa est*).

CXII

323 Intelligent men take for law whatever impartial utility dictates in each case.

CXIII

324 The truth of the laws is a certain light and splendor with which natural reason illuminates them; so that jurisconsults are often in the habit of saying *verum est* for *aequum est*.

325 This definition and the 111th [321] are particular propositions whose purpose is to apply to the particular matter of the natural law of nations the two general definitions [137, 138] which treat of the true and the certain in general with a view to conclusions in all the matters that are herein treated.

CXIV

326 The natural equity of fully developed human law is a practice of wisdom in affairs of utility, since wisdom in its broad sense is nothing but the science of making such use of things as their nature dictates.

327 This axiom [323] and the two following definitions [324, 326] constitute the principle of mild law. Its rule is the natural equity which is connatural with civilized nations. This is the public school from which, as we shall show, the philosophers emerged.

328 All these last six propositions [319, 320, 321, 323, 324, 326] establish the fact that the natural law of nations was ordained by providence. In order that the nations might be preserved, and since they had to live for centuries incapable of truth and natural equity (the latter of which the philosophers later clarified), providence permitted them to cleave to certitude and civil equity, which guards scrupulously the words of decrees and laws, and to be led by the words to observe them generally, even in cases where they proved harsh.

329 Now the fact that the three princes of the doctrine of the natural law of nations knew nothing of these six propositions caused all three of them to err in concert in establishing their systems. For they believed that natural equity in its perfect form had been understood by the gentile nations from their first beginnings; they did not reflect that it took some two thousand years for philosophers to appear in any of them; and they took no account of the particular assistance which a single people received from the true God.

[SECTION III]

PRINCIPLES

330 Now, in order to make trial whether the propositions hitherto enumerated as elements of this Science can give form to the materials prepared in the Chronological Table at the beginning, we beg the reader to consider whatever has been written concerning the principles of any subject in the whole of gentile knowledge, human and divine. Let him then see if it is inconsistent with these propositions, whether with all or some or one. For inconsistency with one would amount to inconsistency with all, since each accords with all. Certainly on making such a comparison he will perceive that it is a tissue of confused memories, of the fancies of a disordered imagination; that none of it is begotten of intelligence, which has been rendered useless by the two conceits enumerated in the Axioms [125, 127]. For on the one hand the conceit of the nations, each believing itself to have been the first in the world, leaves us no hope of getting the principles of our Science from the philologians. And on the other hand the conceit of the scholars, who will have it that what they know must have been eminently understood from the beginning of the world, makes us despair of getting them from the philosophers. So, for purposes of this inquiry, we must reckon as if there were no books in the world.

331 But in the night of thick darkness enveloping the earliest antiquity, so remote from ourselves, there shines the eternal and never-failing light of a truth beyond all question: that the world of civil society has certainly been made by men, and that its principles are therefore to be found within the modifications of our own human mind. Whoever reflects on this cannot but marvel that the philosophers should have bent all their energies to the study of the world of nature, which, since God made it, He alone knows; and that they should have neglected the study of the world of nations or civil world, which, since men had made it, men could hope to know. This aberration was a consequence of that infirmity of the human mind, noted in the Axioms [236], by which, immersed and buried in the body, it naturally inclines to take notice of bodily things, and finds the effort to attend to itself too laborious; just as the bodily eye sees all objects outside itself but needs a mirror to see itself.

332   Now since this world of nations has been made by men, let us see in what things all men agree and always have agreed. For these things will be able to give us the universal and eternal principles (such as every science must have) on which all nations were founded and still preserve themselves.

333   We observe that all nations, barbarous as well as civilized, though separately founded because remote from each other in time and space, keep these three human customs: all have some religion, all contract solemn marriages, all bury their dead. And in no nation, however savage and crude, are any human activities celebrated with more elaborate ceremonies and more sacred solemnity than religion, marriage and burial. For, by the axiom [144] that "uniform ideas, born among peoples unknown to each other, must have a common ground of truth," it must have been dictated to all nations that from these three institutions humanity began among them all, and therefore they must be most devoutly observed by them all, so that the world should not again become a bestial wilderness. For this reason we have taken these three eternal and universal customs as three first principles of this Science.

334   Let not our first principle be accused of falsehood by the modern travelers who narrate that peoples of Brazil, South Africa and other nations of the new world live in society without any knowledge of God, as Antoine Arnauld believes to be the case also of the inhabitants of the islands called Antilles. Persuaded perhaps by them, Bayle affirms in his treatise on comets that peoples can live in justice without the light of God. This is a bolder statement than Polybius ventured in the dictum for which he has been acclaimed [179], that if the world had philosophers, living in justice by reason and not by laws, it would have no need of religions. These are travelers' tales, to promote the sale of their books by the narration of portents. Certainly Andreas Rüdiger in his *Physics,* pretentiously entitled *divine* [*Physica divina*] and purporting to show the only middle path between atheism and superstition, is gravely reproved for this opinion by the censors of the University of Geneva. They charge that "he states it with too much assurance," which is the same as saying with not a little boldness. (Yet in the Republic of Geneva, as being free and popular, there would be considerable freedom in writing.) For all nations believe in a provident divinity, yet through all the length of years and all the breadth of this civil world it has been possible to find only four primary religions. The first is that of the Hebrews, whence came that of the Christians, both believing in the divinity of an infinite free mind. The third is that of the gentiles, who believe in the divinity of a plurality of gods, each imagined as composed of body and of free mind. Hence, when they wish to signify the divinity that rules and preserves the world, they speak of *deos immortales*. The fourth and last is that of the Mohammedans, who believe in the divinity of one god, an infinite free mind in an infinite body, for they look forward to pleasures of the senses as rewards in the other life.

335   No nation has believed in a god all body or in a god all mind but

not free. And so neither the Epicureans who attribute to God body alone, and chance together with body, nor the Stoics who (in this respect the Spinozists of their day) make God an infinite mind, subject to fate, in an infinite body, could reason of commonwealths or laws; and Benedict Spinoza speaks of the commonwealth as of a society of shopkeepers. Cicero was indeed right when he told the Epicurean Atticus that he could not discuss laws with him unless he first granted the existence of divine providence. Such is the compatibility of these two sects, the Stoic and the Epicurean, with Roman jurisprudence, which takes divine providence for its first principle!

336   In the second place, the opinion that the sexual unions which certainly take place between free men and free women without solemn matrimony are free of natural wickedness [i.e. do not offend the law of nature], all the nations of the world have branded as false by the human customs with which they all religiously celebrate marriages, thereby determining that this sin is bestial, though in venial degree. And for this reason: such parents, since they are held together by no necessary bond of law, are bound to abandon their natural children. Since their parents may separate at any time, if they are abandoned by both, the children must lie exposed to be devoured by dogs. If humanity, public or private, does not bring them up, they will have to grow up with no one to teach them religion, language, or any other human custom. So that, as for them, they are bound to cause this world of nations, enriched and adorned by so many beautiful arts of humanity, to revert to the great ancient forest through which in their nefarious feral wanderings once roamed the foul beasts of Orpheus, among whom bestial venery was practiced by sons with mothers and by fathers with daughters. This is the infamous *nefas* of the outlaw world, which Socrates by rather inappropriate physical reasons tried to prove was forbidden by nature, whereas it is human nature that forbids it; for such relationships are abhorred naturally by all nations, nor were they ever practiced by any save in their last stage of corruption, as among the Persians.

337   Finally, [to realize] what a great principle of humanity burial is, imagine a feral state in which human bodies remain unburied on the surface of the earth as food for crows and dogs. Certainly this bestial custom will be accompanied by uncultivated fields and uninhabited cities. Men will go about like swine eating the acorns found amidst the putrefaction of their dead. And so with good reason burials were characterized by the sublime phrase "compacts of the human race" (*foedera generis humani*), and with less grandeur were described by Tacitus as "fellowships of humanity" (*humanitatis commercia*). Furthermore, it is an opinion in which all gentile nations have certainly concurred, that the souls of the unburied remain restless on the earth and go wandering about their bodies, and consequently that they do not die with their bodies but are immortal. That such was the consensus of the ancient barbarous nations may be inferred from what we are told of the [present] peoples of Guinea by Hugo van Linschooten; of those of Peru and Mexico, by Acosta;

of the inhabitants of Virginia, by Thomas Harriot; of those of New England, by Richard Whitbourne; of those of the kingdom of Siam, by Joost Schouten. Thus Seneca [*Ep.* cxvii, 5–6] concludes: "When we discuss immortality, we are influenced in no small degree by the general opinion of mankind, who either fear or worship the spirits of the lower world. I make the most of this general belief." (*Quum de immortalitate loquimur, non leve momentum apud nos habet consensus hominum aut timentium inferos aut colentium: hac persuasione publica utor.*)

[SECTION IV]

METHOD

338   To complete the establishment of the principles which have been adopted for this Science, it remains in this first book to discuss the method which it should follow. It must begin where its subject matter began, as we said in the Axioms [314]. We must therefore go back with the philologians and fetch it from the stones of Deucalion and Pyrrha, from the rocks of Amphion, from the men who sprang from the furrows of Cadmus or the hard oak of Vergil. With the philosophers we must fetch it from the frogs of Epicurus, from the cicadas of Hobbes, from the simpletons of Grotius; from the men cast into this world without care or aid of God, of whom Pufendorf speaks, as clumsy and wild as the so-called Patagonian giants, who are said to be found near the strait of Magellan; which is as much as to say from the cyclopes of Homer in whom Plato recognizes the first fathers in the state of the families. (This is the science the philologians and philosophers have given us of the beginnings of humanity!) Our treatment of it must take its start from the time these creatures began to think humanly. In their monstrous savagery and unbridled bestial freedom there was no means to tame the former or bridle the latter but the frightful thought of some divinity, the fear of whom, as we said in the Axioms [177], is the only powerful means of reducing to duty a liberty gone wild. To discover the way in which this first human thinking arose in the gentile world, we encountered exasperating difficulties which have cost us the research of a good twenty years. [We had] to descend from these human and refined natures of ours to those quite wild and savage natures, which we cannot at all imagine and can apprehend only with great effort.

339   By reason of all this, we must start from some notion of God such as even the most savage, wild and monstrous men do not lack. That notion we show to be this: that man, fallen into despair of all the succors of nature, desires something superior to save him. But something superior to nature is God, and this is the light that God has shed on all men. Confirmation may be found in a common human custom, that libertines grown old, feeling their natural forces fail, turn naturally to religion.

340   But these first men, who later became the princes of the gentile nations, must have done their thinking under the strong impulsion of violent passions, as beasts do. We must therefore proceed from a vulgar metaphysics, such as we have mentioned in the Axioms [182] and such as we shall find the theology of the poets to have been, and seek by its aid that frightful thought of some divinity which imposed form and measure on the bestial passions of these lost men and thus transformed them into human passions. From this thought must have sprung the impulse proper to the human will, to hold in check the motions impressed on the mind by the body, so as either to quiet them alto-gether, as becomes the sage, or at least to direct them to better use, as becomes the civil man. This control over the motion of their bodies is certainly an effect of the freedom of the human will, and thus of free will, which is the home and seat of all the virtues, and among the others of justice. When informed by justice, the will is the fount of all that is just and of all the laws dictated by justice. But to endow bodies with impulse amounts to giving them freedom to regulate their motions, whereas all bodies are by nature necessary agents. And what the theorists of mechanics call powers, forces, impulses, are insensible mo-tions of bodies, by which they approach their centers of gravity, as ancient mechanics had it, or depart from their centers of motion, as modern mechanics has it.

341   But men because of their corrupted nature are under the tyranny of self-love, which compels them to make private utility their chief guide. Seek-ing everything useful for themselves and nothing for their companions, they cannot bring their passions under control to direct them toward justice. We thereby establish the fact that man in the bestial state desires only his own wel-fare; having taken wife and begotten children, he desires his own welfare along with that of his family; having entered upon civil life, he desires his own wel-fare along with that of his city; when its rule is extended over several peoples, he desires his own welfare along with that of the nation; when the nations are united by wars, treaties of peace, alliances and commerce, he desires his own welfare along with that of the entire human race. In all these conditions man desires principally his own utility. Therefore it is only by divine providence that he can be held within these orders to practice justice as a member of the society of the family, the state, and finally of mankind. Unable to attain all the utilities he wishes, he is constrained by these orders to seek those which are his due; and this is called just. That which regulates all human justice is therefore divine justice, which is administered by divine providence to preserve human society.

342   In one of its principal aspects, this Science must therefore be a ra-tional civil theology of divine providence, which seems hitherto to have been lacking. For the philosophers have either been altogether ignorant of it, as the Stoics and the Epicureans were, the latter asserting that human affairs are agi-tated by a blind concourse of atoms, the former that they are drawn by a deaf [inexorable] chain of cause and effect; or they have considered it solely in the

order of natural things, giving the name of natural theology to the metaphysics in which they contemplate this attribute [i.e. the providence] of God, and in which they confirm it by the physical order observed in the motions of such bodies as the spheres and the elements and in the final cause observed in other and minor natural things. But they ought to have studied it in the economy of civil things, in keeping with the full meaning of applying to providence the term divinity, from *divinari,* to divine; that is, to understand what is hidden from men, the future, or what is hidden in them, their consciousness. It is this that makes up the first and principal part of the subject matter of jurisprudence, namely the divine things on which depend the human things which make up its other and complementary part. Our new Science must therefore be a demonstration, so to speak, of the historical fact of providence, for it must be a history of the forms of order which, without human discernment or intent, and often against the designs of men, providence has given to this great city of the human race. For though this world has been created in time and particular, the orders established therein by providence are universal and eternal.

343   In contemplation of this infinite and eternal providence our Science finds certain divine proofs by which it is confirmed and demonstrated. Since divine providence has omnipotence as minister, it develops its orders by means as easy as the natural customs of men. Since it has infinite wisdom as counselor, whatever it establishes is order. Since it has for its end its own immeasurable goodness, whatever it ordains must be directed to a good always superior to that which men have proposed to themselves.

344   In the deplorable obscurity of the beginnings of the nations and in the innumerable variety of their customs, for a divine argument which embraces all human things, no sublimer proofs can be desired than those provided by the aforesaid naturalness, order and end (the preservation of the human race). These proofs will become luminous and distinct when we reflect with what ease things are brought into being, by occasions arising far apart and sometimes quite contrary to the proposals of men, yet fitting together of themselves. Such proofs omnipotence affords. Compare the things with one another and observe the order by which those are now born in their proper times and places which ought now to be born, and others deferred for birth in theirs (and all the beauty of order, according to Horace, consists in this). Such proofs eternal wisdom provides. Consider, finally, if in these occasions, places and times we can conceive how other divine benefits could arise by which, in view of the particular needs and ills of men, human society could be better conducted or preserved. Such proofs the eternal goodness of God will give.

345   Thus the proper and consecutive proof here adduced will consist in comparing and reflecting whether our human mind, in the series of possibilities it is permitted to understand, and so far as it is permitted to do so, can conceive more or fewer or different causes than those from which issue the effects of this civil world. In doing this the reader will experience in his mortal

body a divine pleasure as he contemplates in the divine ideas this world of nations in all the extent of its places, times and varieties. And he will find that he
has in effect convinced the Epicureans that their chance cannot wander foolishly about and everywhere find a way out, and the Stoics that their eternal
chain of causes, to which they will have it the world is chained, itself hangs
upon the omnipotent, wise and beneficent will of the best and greatest God.

346   These sublime proofs of natural theology will be confirmed for us
by the following sorts of logical proofs. In reasoning of the origins of things
divine and human in the gentile world, we reach those first beginnings beyond
which it is vain curiosity to demand others earlier; and this is the defining
character of [first] principles. We explain the particular ways in which they
come into being, that is to say, their nature, the explanation of which is the distinguishing mark of science. And finally [these proofs] are confirmed by the
eternal properties [the things] preserve, which could not be what they are if
the things had not come into being just as they did, in those particular times,
places and fashions, which is to say with those particular natures, as we have
set forth in two axioms [147, 148].

347   In search of these natures of human things our Science proceeds by
a severe analysis of human thoughts about the human necessities or utilities of
social life, which are the two perennial springs of the natural law of nations,
as we have remarked in the Axioms [141]. In its second principal aspect, our
Science is therefore a history of human ideas, on which it seems the metaphysics
of the human mind must proceed. This queen of the sciences, by the axiom
[314] that "the sciences must begin where their subject matters began," took
its start when the first men began to think humanly, and not when the
philosophers began to reflect on human ideas (as in an erudite and scholarly little
book recently published [by Brucker] under the title *Historia philosophica doc-
trinae de ideis,* which comes down to the latest controversies between the two
foremost minds of our age, Leibniz and Newton).

348   To determine the times and places for such a history, that is, when
and where these human thoughts were born, and thus to give it certainty by
means of its own (so to speak) metaphysical chronology and geography, our
Science applies a likewise metaphysical art of criticism with regard to the
founders of these same nations, in which it took more than a thousand years for
those writers to come forward with whom philological criticism has hitherto
been occupied. And the criterion our criticism employs, in accordance with
an axiom above stated [142], is that taught by divine providence and common
to all nations, namely the common sense of the human race, determined by
the necessary harmony of human things, in which all the beauty of the civil
world consists. The decisive sort of proof in our Science is therefore this: that,
once these orders were established by divine providence, the course of the affairs
of the nations had to be, must now be and will have to be such as our Science

demonstrates, even if infinite worlds were produced from time to time through eternity, which is certainly not the case.

349   Our Science therefore comes to describe at the same time an ideal eternal history traversed in time by the history of every nation in its rise, progress, maturity, decline and fall. Indeed we go so far as to assert that whoever meditates this Science tells himself this ideal eternal history only so far as he makes it by that proof "it had, has, and will have to be." For the first indubitable principle above posited [331] is that this world of nations has certainly been made by men, and its guise must therefore be found within the modifications of our own human mind. And history cannot be more certain than when he who creates the things also describes them. Thus our Science proceeds exactly as does geometry, which, while it constructs out of its elements or contemplates the world of quantity, itself creates it; but with a reality greater in proportion to that of the orders having to do with human affairs, in which there are neither points, lines, surfaces, nor figures. And this very fact is an argument, O reader, that these proofs are of a kind divine, and should give thee a divine pleasure; since in God knowledge and creation are one and the same thing.

350   By the definitions of truth and certitude above proposed [138], men were for a long period incapable of truth and of reason, which is the fount of that inner justice by which the intellect is satisfied. This justice was practiced by the Hebrews, who, illuminated by the true God, were by his divine law forbidden even to have unjust thoughts, about which no mortal lawgiver ever troubled himself. (For the Hebrews believed in a God all mind who searches the hearts of men, and the gentiles believed in gods composed of bodies and mind who could not do so.) This same inner justice was later reasoned out by the philosophers, who did not arise until two thousand years after the nations were founded. In the meantime the nations were governed by the certitude of authority, that is, by the same criterion which is used by our metaphysical criticism; namely the common sense of the human race, which we have defined above in the elements [142], and on which the conscience of all nations reposes. So that, in this [third] principal regard, our Science comes to be a philosophy of authority, which is the fount of the outer justice of which the moral theologians speak. Of such authority account should have been taken by the three princes of the doctrine of the natural law of nations, and not of that drawn from passages in the writers. For the authority of which we speak reigned among the nations for more than a thousand years before writers could arise, and they could have taken no cognizance of it. For that reason Grotius, more learned and erudite than either of the others, combats the Roman jurisconsults in almost every particular detail of this doctrine; but all his blows fall short, for the jurisconsults established their principles of justice on the certitude of the authority of the human race, not on the authority of the learned.

351   These are the philosophic proofs our Science will use, and conse-

quently those which are absolutely necessary for pursuing it. The philological proofs must come last. They all reduce to the following kinds:

352   First, that our mythologies agree with the results of our meditations, not by force and distortion, but directly, easily and naturally; that they will be seen to be civil histories of the first peoples, who are everywhere found to have been naturally poets.

353   Second, that the heroic phrases, as here explained in the full truth of the sentiments and the full propriety of the expressions, also agree.

354   Third, that the etymologies of the native languages also agree, which tell us the histories of the things signified by the words, beginning with their original and proper meanings and pursuing the natural progress of their metaphors according to the order of the ideas, on which the history of languages must proceed, as we have premised in the Axioms [238–240].

355   Fourth, the mental vocabulary of human social things, which are the same in substance as felt by all nations but diversely expressed in language according to their diverse manifestations, is exhibited to be such as we conceived it in the Axioms [161].

356   Fifth, truth is sifted from falsehood in everything that has been preserved for us through long centuries by those vulgar traditions which, since they have been preserved for so long a time and by entire peoples, must by an axiom above stated [149] have had a public ground of truth.

357   Sixth, the great fragments of antiquity, hitherto useless to science because they lay neglected, broken and scattered, shed great light when cleaned, pieced together and set in place.

358   Seventh and last, to all these things, as to their necessary causes, are assigned all the effects narrated by certain history.

359   These philological proofs enable us to see in fact the things we have meditated in idea concerning this world of nations, in accordance with Bacon's method of philosophizing, which is "think [and] see" (*cogitare videre*). Thus it is that with the help of the preceding philosophical proofs, the philological proofs which follow both confirm their own authority by reason and at the same time confirm reason by their authority.

360   From all that has been set forth in general concerning the establishment of the principles of this Science, we conclude that, since its principles are divine providence, moderation of the passions by marriage, and immortality of human souls [witnessed] by burial, and since the criterion it uses is that what is felt to be just by all men or by the majority must be the rule of social life (and on these principles and this criterion there is agreement between the vulgar wisdom of all lawgivers and the esoteric wisdom of the philosophers of greatest repute), these must be the bounds of human reason. And let him who would transgress them beware lest he transgress all humanity.

BOOK TWO

POETIC WISDOM

[PROLEGOMENA]

INTRODUCTION

361 We have said above in the Axioms [202] that all the histories of the gentile nations have had fabulous beginnings, that among the Greeks (who have given us all we know of gentile antiquity) the first sages were the theological poets, and that the nature of everything born or made betrays the crudeness of its origin. It is thus and not otherwise that we must conceive the origins of poetic wisdom. And as for the great and sovereign esteem in which it has been handed down to us, this has its origin in the two conceits mentioned in the Axioms [125, 127], that of the nations on the one hand and that of the scholars on the other. And it springs even more from the latter than from the former. For just as Manetho, the Egyptian high priest, translated all the fabulous history of Egypt into a sublime natural theology, as we have said in the Axioms [222], so the Greek philosophers translated theirs into philosophy. And they did so not merely for the reason that, as we have seen above in the Axioms [221], to both alike the histories that had come down to them were disgusting, but for the following five reasons as well.

362 The first was reverence for religion, for the gentile nations were everywhere founded by fables on religion. The second was the grand effect thence derived of this civil world, so wisely ordered that it could only be the effect of a superhuman wisdom. The third was the occasions which, as we shall see, these fables, assisted by the veneration of religion and the credit of such great wisdom, gave the philosophers for instituting research and for meditating lofty things in philosophy. The fourth was the ease with which they were thus enabled, as we shall also show farther on, to explain their sublime philosophical meditations by means of the expressions happily left them by the poets. The fifth and last, which is the sum of them all, is the confirmation of their own meditations which the philosophers derived from the authority of religion and the wisdom of the poets. Of these five reasons, the first two and the last contain the praises of the divine wisdom which ordained this world of nations, and the witness the philosophers bore to it even in their errors. The third and fourth are deceptions permitted by divine providence, that thence there might arise philosophers to understand and recognize it for what it truly is, an attribute of the true God.

363   Throughout this book it will be shown that only so much as the poets had first sensed of vulgar wisdom did the philosophers later understand of esoteric wisdom; so that the former may be said to have been the sense and the latter the intellect of the human race. What Aristotle said of the individual man is therefore true of the race in general: *Nihil est in intellectu quin prius fuerit in sensu.* That is, the human mind does not understand anything of which it has had no previous impression (which our modern metaphysicians call "occasion") from the senses. Now the mind uses the intellect when, from something it senses, it gathers something which does not fall under the senses; and this is the proper meaning of the Latin verb *intelligere.*

[CHAPTER I]

WISDOM IN GENERAL

364   Now, before discussing poetic wisdom, it is necessary for us to see what wisdom in general is. Wisdom is the faculty which commands all the disciplines by which we acquire all the sciences and arts that make up humanity. Plato defines wisdom as "the perfecter of man." Man, in his proper being as man, consists of mind and spirit, or, if we prefer, of intellect and will. It is the function of wisdom to fulfill both these parts in man, the second by way of the first, to the end that by a mind illuminated by knowledge of the highest things the spirit may be led to choose the best. The highest things in the universe are those turned toward and conversant with God; the best are those which look to the good of all mankind. The former are called divine things, the latter human. True wisdom, then, should teach the knowledge of divine things in order to conduct human things to the highest good. We believe that this was the foundation on which Marcus Terentius Varro, who earned the title "most learned of the Romans," erected his great work on things divine and human [his *Antiquitates*], of which the injustice of time has unhappily bereft us. We shall treat of these things in the present book so far as the weakness of our education and the meagerness of our erudition permit.

365   Wisdom among the gentiles began with the Muse defined by Homer in a golden passage of the *Odyssey* [VIII, 63] as "knowledge of good and evil," and later called divination. It was on the natural prohibition of this practice, as something naturally denied to man, that God founded the true religion of the Hebrews, from which our Christian religion arose, as set forth in one of the Axioms [167]. The Muse must thus have been properly at first the science of

divining by auspices, and this, as stated in the Axioms [342], was the vulgar wisdom of all nations, of which we shall have more to say presently. It consisted in contemplating God under the attribute of his providence, whereby from *divinari* his essence came to be called divinity. We shall see presently that the theological poets, who certainly founded the humanity of Greece, were versed in this wisdom, and this explains why the Latins called the judicial astrologers "professors of wisdom." Wisdom was later attributed to men renowned for useful counsels given to mankind, as in the case of the Seven Sages of Greece. The attribution was afterwards extended to men who for the good of peoples and nations wisely ordered and governed commonwealths. Still later the word wisdom came to mean knowledge of natural divine things; that is, metaphysics, called for that reason divine science, which, seeking knowledge of man's mind in God, and recognizing God as the source of all truth, must recognize him as the regulator of all good. So that metaphysics must essentially work for the good of the human race, whose preservation depends on the universal belief in a provident divinity. It is perhaps for having demonstrated this providence that Plato deserved to be called divine; and that which denies to God this great attribute must be called stupidity rather than wisdom. Finally among the Hebrews, and thence among us Christians, wisdom was called the science of eternal things revealed by God; a science which, among the Tuscans, considered as knowledge of the true good and true evil, perhaps owed to that fact the first name they gave it, "science in divinity."

366 We must therefore distinguish more truly than Varro did the three kinds of theology. First, poetic theology, that of the theological poets, which was the civil theology of all the gentile nations. Second, natural theology, that of the metaphysicians. Third, our Christian theology, a mixture of civil and natural with the loftiest revealed theology; all three united in the contemplation of divine providence. (Our third kind takes the place of Varro's poetic theology, which among the gentiles was the same as civil theology, though he distinguished it from both civil and natural theology because, sharing the vulgar common error that the fables contained high mysteries of sublime philosophy, he believed it to be a mixture of both.) Divine providence has so conducted human affairs that, starting from the poetic theology which regulated them by certain sensible signs believed to be divine counsels sent to men by the gods, and by means of the natural theology which demonstrates providence by eternal reasons which do not fall under the senses, the nations were disposed to receive revealed theology in virtue of a supernatural faith, superior not only to the senses but to human reason itself.

[CHAPTER II]

EXPOSITION AND DIVISION OF POETIC WISDOM

367   But because metaphysics is the sublime science which distributes their determinate subject matters to all the so-called subaltern sciences; and because the wisdom of the ancients was that of the theological poets, who without doubt were the first sages of the gentile world, as we have established in the Axioms [199]; and because the origins of all things must by nature have been crude: for all these reasons we must trace the beginnings of poetic wisdom to a crude metaphysics. From this, as from a trunk, there branch out from one limb logic, morals, economics and politics, all poetic; and from another physics, the mother of their cosmography and hence of astronomy, which gives their certainty to its two daughters, chronology and geography, all likewise poetic. We shall show clearly and distinctly how the founders of gentile humanity by means of their natural theology (or metaphysics) imagined the gods; how by means of their logic they invented languages; by morals, created heroes; by economics, founded families, and by politics, cities; by their physics, established the beginnings of things as all divine; by the particular physics of man, in a certain sense created themselves; by their cosmography, fashioned for themselves a universe entirely of gods; by astronomy, carried the planets and constellations from earth to heaven; by chronology, gave a beginning to [measured] times; and how by geography the Greeks, for example, described the [whole] world within their own Greece.

368   Thus our Science comes to be at once a history of the ideas, the customs, and the deeds of mankind. From these three we shall derive the principles of the history of human nature, which we shall show to be the principles of universal history, which principles it seems hitherto to have lacked.

[CHAPTER III]

THE UNIVERSAL FLOOD AND THE GIANTS

369   The founders of gentile humanity must have been men of the races of Ham, Japheth and Shem, which gradually, one after the other, renounced that true religion of their common father Noah which alone in the family state had been able to hold them in human society by the bonds of matrimony

and hence of the families themselves. As a result of this renunciation, they dissolved their marriages and broke up their families by promiscuous intercourse, and began roving wild through the great forest of the earth. The race of Ham wandered through southern Asia, Egypt and the rest of Africa; that of Japheth through northern Asia or Scythia, and thence through Europe; and that of Shem through all middle Asia toward the east. By fleeing from the wild beasts with which the great forest must have abounded, and by pursuing women, who in that state must have been wild, indocile and shy, they became separated from each other in their search for food and water. Mothers abandoned their children, who in time must have come to grow up without ever hearing a human voice, much less learning any human custom, and thus descended to a state truly bestial and savage. Mothers, like beasts, must merely have nursed their babies, let them wallow naked in their own filth, and abandoned them for good as soon as they were weaned. And these children, who had to wallow in their own filth, whose nitrous salts richly fertilized the fields, and who had to exert themselves to penetrate the great forest, grown extremely dense from the flood, would flex and contract their muscles in these exertions, and thus absorb nitrous salts into their bodies in greater abundance. They would be quite without that fear of gods, fathers and teachers which chills and benumbs even the most exuberant in childhood. They must therefore have grown robust, vigorous, excessively big in brawn and bone, to the point of becoming giants. This upbringing of theirs was even more savage than that to which, as noted above in the Axioms [170], Caesar and Tacitus ascribe the gigantic stature of the ancient Germans; from which was derived that of the Goths whom Procopius mentions, and which was like that of the Patagonians supposed to exist today near the strait of Magellan. Philosophers in physics have spoken much nonsense on this subject, collected by Chassagnon, who wrote *De gigantibus.* Of such giants there have been found and are still being found, for the most part in the mountains (a circumstance with an important bearing on what we have to say below), great skulls and bones of an unnatural size which is further exaggerated by vulgar tradition for reasons of which we shall speak in their proper place.

370   Such giants were scattered over the earth after the flood. We have seen them in the fabulous history of the Greeks, and the Latin philologians, without being aware of it, have told us of their existence in the ancient history of Italy, where they say that the most ancient peoples of Italy, the so-called aborigines, claimed to be *autochthones,* which is as much as to say "sons of Earth," which among the Greeks and Latins meant nobles. And in the fables the Greeks quite properly called the sons of earth giants, and the Earth mother of giants. The Greek term *autochthones* should be rendered in Latin *indigenae,* that is, properly, those born of a land; thus the native gods of a people or nation were called *dii indigetes,* as if *inde geniti,* or, as we should say more shortly today, *ingeniti.* For the syllable *de* is one of the redundancies of the first languages of the peoples which we shall discuss later. Thus among the Latins we

find *induperator* for *imperator,* and in the Law of the Twelve Tables *endoiacito* for *iniicito,* whence perhaps it came that armistices were called *induciae,* as if *iniiciae,* because they must have been so called from *icere foedus,* to make a pact of peace. So, in the case in hand, from *indigeni* was derived *ingenui,* whose first and proper meaning was "noble" (whence the term *artes ingenuae,* "noble arts") but which finally came to mean "free" (though *artes liberales* kept the meaning "noble arts"). For nobles alone, as will shortly be demonstrated, composed the first cities, in which the plebeians were slaves or precursors of slaves.

371   The same Latin philologians observe that all the ancient peoples were called aborigines, and sacred history tells us of whole peoples called *emim* and *zomzommim,* which Hebrew scholars take to mean giants, one of whom was Nimrod; and the giants before the flood are described by Scripture as "brave, famous and powerful men of the age." The Hebrews, on account of their cleanly upbringing and their fear of God and of their fathers, continued to be of the proper stature in which God had created Adam and Noah had begotten his three sons; and it was perhaps in abomination of giantism that the Hebrews had so many ceremonial laws pertaining to bodily cleanliness. The Romans preserved a great vestige of these laws in the public sacrifice intended to purge the city of all the sins of the citizens, which was performed with water and fire. Their solemn nuptials were also celebrated with water and fire, and participation in these two things was even the mark of citizenship, the deprivation of which was called *interdictum aqua et igni.* The sacrifice with fire and water was called *lustrum,* which came to mean a period of five years because that was the interval between these sacrifices, much as among the Greeks an Olympiad meant a period of four years. But *lustrum* also meant a den of wild beasts, and the verb *lustrari,* "to seek out" or "to purge," must at first have meant to seek out these dens and purge them of the beasts lurking within; whence the water required for the sacrifice was called *aqua lustralis.* The Greeks began to count their years from the burning of the Nemean forest by Hercules to clear it for sowing grain, in commemoration of which, as we pointed out in the "Idea of the Work" [3] and as we shall see fully later, he founded the Olympiads. The Romans, with more discernment, began to count their years in *lustra* from the water of the sacred ablutions, because civilization began with water, the need of which was felt before that of fire, as appears from the formulas of marriage and the interdict, in which *aqua* comes before *igni.* This is the origin of the sacred ablutions which must precede sacrifices, a custom which was and is common to all nations. It was by becoming imbued with this cleanliness of body and this fear of gods and of fathers—in both cases a fear we shall find amounting to terror in the earliest times—that the giants diminished to our normal stature. It was perhaps for this reason that from *politeia,* which in Greek means "civil government," was derived the Latin *politus,* "clean" or "neat."

372   This diminution of stature must have continued down to the human period of the nations, as is demonstrated by the excessively large weapons of

the ancient heroes, which Augustus, according to Suetonius, preserved along with the bones and skulls of the ancient giants in his museum. Thus, as stated in the Axioms [172], the entire first world of men must be divided into two kinds: the first, men of normal size, which includes the Hebrews only; the second, giants, who were the founders of the gentile nations. Of the giants there were in turn two kinds: the first, the sons of Earth, or nobles, from whom, as being giants in the full sense of the term, the age of giants took its name, as we have said (and it is these whom sacred history defines as "strong, famous and powerful men of the age"); the second, less properly so called, those other giants who were subjugated [by the former].

373   The time at which the founders of the gentile nations reached this condition [of giantism] is fixed a century after the deluge for the race of Shem, and two centuries for those of Japheth and Ham, as postulated above [62]. Below, presently, will be given the physical history of this matter [387], which, though related to us in the Greek fables, has not hitherto been observed, and which at the same time will give us a new physical history of the universal flood [380].

[SECTION I]

[POETIC METAPHYSICS]

[CHAPTER I]

POETIC METAPHYSICS AS THE ORIGIN OF POETRY, IDOLATRY, DIVINATION AND SACRIFICES

374   From these first men, stupid, insensate and horrible beasts, all the philosophers and philologians should have begun their investigations of the wisdom of the ancient gentiles; that is, from the giants in the proper sense in which we have just taken them. (Father Boulduc in his *De ecclesia ante Legem* says the scriptural names of the giants signify "pious, venerable and illustrious men"; but this can be understood only of the noble giants who by divination founded the gentile religions and gave the age of giants its name.) And they should have begun with metaphysics, which seeks its proofs not in the external world but within the modifications of the mind of him who meditates it. For, as we have said above, since this world of nations has certainly been made by men, it is within these modifications that its principles should have been sought. And human nature, so far as it is like that of animals, carries with it this property, that the senses are its sole way of knowing things.

375   Hence poetic wisdom, the first wisdom of the gentile world, must have begun with a metaphysic not rational and abstract like that of learned men now, but felt and imagined as that of these first men must have been, who, without power of ratiocination, were all robust sense and vigorous imagination, as established in the Axioms [185]. This metaphysic was their poetry, a faculty born with them (for they were furnished by nature with these senses and imaginations); born of their ignorance of causes, for ignorance, the mother of wonder, made everything wonderful to men who were ignorant of everything, as noted in the Axioms [184]. Their poetry was at first divine, because they imagined the causes of the things they felt and wondered at to be gods, as we saw in the passage from Lactantius cited in the Axioms [188]. (This is now confirmed by the American Indians, who call gods all the things that surpass their

small understanding. We may add the ancient Germans dwelling about the Arctic Ocean, of whom Tacitus tells that they spoke of hearing the Sun pass at night from west to east through the sea, and affirmed that they saw the gods. These very rude and simple nations help us to a much better understanding of the founders of the gentile world with whom we are now concerned.) At the same time they gave the things they wondered at substantial being after their own ideas, just as children do, whom we see take inanimate things in their hands and play with them and talk to them as though they were living persons, as laid down in an axiom [186].

376   In such fashion the first men of the gentile nations, children of nascent mankind as we have styled them in the Axioms [209], created things according to their own ideas. But this creation was infinitely different from that of God. For God, in his purest intelligence, knows things, and, by knowing them, creates them; but they, in their robust ignorance, did it by virtue of a wholly corporeal imagination. And because it was quite corporeal, they did it with marvelous sublimity; a sublimity such and so great that it excessively perturbed the very persons who by feigning did the creating, for which they were called "poets," which is Greek for "makers." Now this is the threefold labor of great poetry: (1) to invent sublime fables suited to the popular understanding, (2) to perturb to excess, with a view to the end proposed: (3) to teach the vulgar to act virtuously, as the poets have taught themselves; as will presently be shown. Of this nature of human things there came an eternal property, expressed in a noble phrase of Tacitus: that frightened men vainly "no sooner feign than they believe" (*fingunt simul creduntque* [*Annals* V 10]).

377   Of such natures must have been the first founders of gentile humanity when at last the sky fearfully rolled with thunder and flashed with lightning, as could not but follow from the bursting upon the air for the first time of an impression so violent. As we have postulated [62, 195], this occurred a hundred years after the flood in Mesopotamia and two hundred after it throughout the rest of the world; for it took that much time to reduce the earth to such a state that, dry of the moisture of the universal flood, it could send up dry exhalations or matter igniting in the air to produce lightning. Thereupon a few giants, who must have been the most robust, and who were dispersed through the forests on the mountain heights where the strongest beasts have their dens, were frightened and astonished by the great effect whose cause they did not know, and raised their eyes and became aware of the sky. And because in such a case, as stated in the Axioms [180], the nature of the human mind leads it to attribute its own nature to the effect, and because in that state their nature was that of men all robust bodily strength, who expressed their very violent passions by shouting and grumbling, they pictured the sky to themselves as a great animated body, which in that aspect they called Jove, the first god of the so-called *gentes maiores,* who by the whistling of his bolts and the noise of his thunder was attempting to tell them something. And thus they began to

exercise that natural curiosity which is the daughter of ignorance and the mother of knowledge, and which, opening the mind of man, gives birth to wonder, as we have put it above in the Axioms [189]. This characteristic still persists in the vulgar, who, when they see a comet or sun-dog or some other extraordinary thing in nature, and particularly in the countenance of the sky, at once turn curious and anxiously inquire what it means, as we have it in an axiom [189]. When they wonder at the prodigious effects of the magnet on iron, even in this age of minds enlightened and made erudite by philosophy, they come out with this: that the magnet has an occult sympathy for the iron; and they make of all nature a vast animate body which feels passions and effects, as we have noted in the Axioms [180].

378   But the nature of our civilized minds is so detached from the senses, even in the vulgar, by abstractions corresponding to all the abstract terms our languages abound in, and so refined by the art of writing, and as it were spiritualized by the use of numbers, because even the vulgar know how to count and reckon, that it is naturally beyond our power to form the vast image of this mistress called "Sympathetic Nature." Men shape the phrase with their lips but have nothing in their minds; for what they have in mind is falsehood, which is nothing; and their imagination no longer avails to form a vast false image. It is equally beyond our power to enter into the vast imagination of those first men, whose minds were not in the least abstract, refined, or spiritualized, because they were entirely immersed in the senses, buffeted by the passions, buried in the body. That is why we said above [338] that we can scarcely understand, still less imagine, how those first men thought who founded gentile humanity.

379   In this fashion the first theological poets created the first divine fable, the greatest they ever created: that of Jove, king and father of men and gods, in the act of hurling the lightning bolt; an image so popular, disturbing and instructive that its creators themselves believed in it, and feared, revered and worshiped it in frightful religions which we shall shortly describe. And by that trait of the human mind we found noticed by Tacitus in the Axioms [183], these men attributed to Jove all they saw, imagined or even did themselves; and to all of the universe that came within their scope, to all its parts, they assigned the being of animate substance. This is the civil history of the expression "all things are full of Jove" (*Iovis omnia plena*), by which Plato understood the ether which penetrates and fills the universe. But for the theological poets, as will shortly be seen, Jove was no higher than the mountain peaks. The first men, who spoke by signs, naturally believed that lightning bolts and thunder claps were signs made to them by Jove; whence from *nuo,* to make a sign, came *numen,* the divine will, by an idea more than sublime and worthy to express the divine majesty. They believed that Jove commanded by signs, that such signs were real words, and that nature was the language of Jove. The science of this language the gentiles universally believed to be divination, which by the Greeks was called theology, meaning the science of the language of the

gods. Thus Jove acquired the fearful kingdom of the lightning and became the king of men and gods; and he acquired the two titles, that of best (*optimus*) in the sense of strongest (*fortissimus*) (as by a reverse process *fortis* meant in early Latin what *bonus* did in late), and that of greatest (*maximus*) from his vast body, the sky itself. For the first great mercy he showed mankind by not destroying it with his bolts, he received the title *Soter* or savior. (This is the first of the three principles we have taken for our Science.) And for having put an end to the feral wandering of these few giants, so that they became the princes of the *gentes,* he received the epithet *Stator,* stayer or establisher. The Latin philologians explain this epithet too narrowly from Jove, invoked by Romulus, having stopped the Romans in their flight from the battle with the Sabines.

380   Thus the many Joves the philologians wonder at are so many physical histories preserved for us by the fables, which prove the universality of the flood, as we premised in the Axioms [194]. For every gentile nation had its Jove, and the Egyptians had the conceit to say that their Jove Ammon was the most ancient of them all, as was said above in the Axioms [62].

381   Thus, in accordance with what has been said in the Axioms [209] about the principles of the poetic characters, Jove was born naturally in poetry as a divine character or imaginative universal, to which everything having to do with the auspices was referred by all the ancient gentile nations, which must therefore all have been poetic by nature. Their poetic wisdom began with this poetic metaphysics, which contemplated God by the attribute of his providence; and they were called theological poets, or sages who understood the language of the gods expressed in the auspices of Jove; and were properly called divine in the sense of diviners, from *divinari,* to "divine" or "predict." Their science was called Muse, defined above [365] by Homer as the knowledge of good and evil; that is, divination, on the prohibition of which God ordained his true religion for Adam, as was said in the Axioms [167]. Because they were versed in this mystic theology, the Greek poets, who explained the divine mysteries of the auspices and oracles, were called *mystae,* which Horace learnedly translates "interpreters of the gods." Every gentile nation had its own sybil versed in this science, and we find mention of twelve of them. Sybils and oracles are the most ancient things of the gentile world.

382   All the things here discussed agree with that golden passage of Eusebius [i.e. Lactantius] referred to in the Axioms [188], where he speaks of the origins of idolatry: that the first people, simple and rough, invented the gods "from terror of present power." Thus it was fear which created gods in the world; but, as was remarked in the Axioms [191], not fear awakened in men by other men, but fear awakened in men by themselves. Along with this origin of idolatry is demonstrated likewise the origin of divination, which was brought into the world at the same birth. The origins of these two were followed by that of the sacrifices made to procure or rightly understand the auspices.

383   That such was the origin of poetry is finally confirmed by this eternal property of it: that its proper material is the credible impossibility. It is impossible that bodies should be minds, yet it was believed that the thundering sky was Jove. And nothing is dearer to poets than singing the marvels wrought by sorceresses by means of incantations. All this is to be explained by a hidden sense the nations have of the omnipotence of God. From this sense springs another by which all peoples are naturally led to do infinite honors to divinity. In this manner the poets founded religions among the gentiles.

384   All that has been so far said here upsets all the theories of the origin of poetry from Plato and Aristotle down to Patrizzi, Scaliger and Castelvetro. For it has been shown that it was deficiency of human reasoning power that gave rise to poetry so sublime that the philosophies which came afterwards, the arts of poetry and of criticism, have produced none equal or better, and have even prevented its production. Hence it is Homer's privilege to be, of all the sublime, that is, the heroic poets, the first in the order of merit as well as in that of age. This discovery of the origins of poetry does away with the opinion of the matchless wisdom of the ancients, so ardently sought after from Plato to Bacon's *De sapientia veterum*. For the wisdom of the ancients was the vulgar wisdom of the lawgivers who founded the human race, not the esoteric wisdom of great and rare philosophers. Whence it will be found, as it has been in the case of Jove, that all the mystic meanings of lofty philosophy attributed by the learned to the Greek fables and the Egyptian hieroglyphics are as impertinent as the historical meanings they both must have had are natural.

[CHAPTER II]

COROLLARIES CONCERNING THE PRINCIPAL ASPECTS OF THIS SCIENCE

I

385   From what has been said up to this point it is concluded that divine providence, apprehended by such human sense as could have been possessed by rough, wild and savage men who in despair of nature's succors desired something superior to nature to save them (which is the first principle on which we established the method of this Science), permitted them to be deceived into fearing the false divinity of Jove because he could strike them with lightning. Thus, through the thick clouds of those first tempests, intermittently lit by those flashes, they made out this great truth: that divine providence watches over the welfare of all mankind. So that this Science becomes, in this principal aspect a rational civil theology of divine providence, which began in the vulgar

wisdom of the lawgivers who founded the nations by contemplating God under the attribute of providence, and which is completed by the esoteric wisdom of the philosophers who give a rational demonstration of it in their natural theology.

II

386   Here begins also a philosophy of authority, a second principal aspect of this Science, taking the word authority in its original meaning of property. The word is always used in this sense in the Law of the Twelve Tables, and the term *auctores* was accordingly applied to those from whom we derive title to property. *Auctor* certainly comes from *autos* (= *proprius* or *suus ipsius*); many scholars write *autor* and *autoritas,* leaving out the aspirate.

387   Authority was at first divine; the authority by which divinity appropriated to itself the few giants we have spoken of, by properly casting them into the depths and recesses of the caves under the mountains. This is the iron ring by which the giants, dispersed upon the mountains, were kept chained to the earth by fear of the sky and of Jove, wherever they happened to be when the sky first thundered. Such were Tityus and Prometheus, chained to a high rock with their hearts being devoured by an eagle, that is, by the religion of Jove's auspices. Their being rendered immobile by fear was expressed by the Latins in the heroic phrase *terrore defixi,* and the artists depict them chained hand and foot with such links upon the mountains. Of these links was formed the great chain which Dionysius Longinus admires as the highest sublimity in all the Homeric fables. Concerning this chain, Jove, to prove that he is king of men and gods, asserts that if all the gods and men were to take hold of one end, he alone at the other end would be able to drag them all. The Stoics would have the chain represent the eternal series of causes by which their Fate holds the world girdled and bound, but let them look out lest they be entangled in it themselves, because the dragging of men and gods by this chain depends on the will of Jove, yet they would have Jove subject to Fate.

388   Upon this divine authority followed human authority in the full philosophic sense of the term, that is, the property of human nature which not even God can take from man without destroying him. It is in this sense that Terence speaks of *voluptates proprias deorum,* meaning that the felicity of God does not depend on others; and Horace of *propriam virtutis laurum,* meaning that the triumph of virtue cannot be taken away by envy; and Caesar of *propriam victoriam,* which Denis Petau erroneously considers bad Latin, whereas it is exceedingly elegant Latin for a victory which could not be snatched from his hands by the enemy. This authority is the free use of the will, the intellect on the other hand being a passive power subject to truth. For from this first point of all human things, men began to exercise the freedom of the human will to hold in check the motions of the body, either to subdue them entirely or to give them better direction (this being the impulse proper to free agents, as we have said above in the Method [340]). Hence it was that the giants gave up the

bestial custom of wandering through the great forest of the earth and habituated themselves to the quite contrary custom of remaining settled and hidden for a long period in their caves.

389   This authority of human nature was followed by the authority of natural law; for, having occupied and remained settled for a long time in the places where they chanced to find themselves at the time of the first thunderbolts, they became lords of them by occupation and long possession, the source of all dominion in the world. These are those "few whom just Jupiter loved" (*pauci quos aequus amavit / Iupiter*) [Vergil, *Aeneid* VI 129 f.], whom the philosophers later metamorphosed into men favored by God with natural aptitudes for science and virtue. But the historical significance of this phrase is that in the recesses and depths [of the caves] they became the princes of the so-called *gentes maiores,* who counted Jove the first god, as noted in the Axioms [317]. As will be shown later, these were the ancient noble houses, branching out into many families, of which the first kingdoms and the first cities were composed. Their memory was preserved in those fine heroic Latin phrases: *condere gentes, condere regna, condere urbes; fundare gentes, fundare regna, fundare urbes.*

390   This philosophy of authority follows the rational civil theology of providence because by means of the former's theological proofs the latter with its philosophical ones makes clear and distinct the philological ones (all three kinds of proofs being enumerated in the Method); and with reference to the things of the most obscure antiquity of the nations it reduces to certitude the human will, which is by its nature most uncertain, as noted in the Axioms [141]. Which is as much as to say that it reduces philology to the form of a science.

III

391   The third principal aspect is a history of human ideas. These, as we have just seen, began with divine ideas by way of contemplation of the heavens with the bodily eyes. Thus in their science of augury the Romans used the verb *contemplari* for observing the parts of the sky whence the auguries came or the auspices were taken. These regions, marked out by the augurs with their wands, were called "temples of the sky" (*templa coeli*), whence must have come to the Greeks their first *theoremata* and *mathemata,* things divine or sublime to contemplate, which eventuated in metaphysical and mathematical abstractions. This is the civil history of the saying "From Jove the Muse began" (*A Iove principium musae* [Vergil, *Bucolica,* III 60]). For we have just seen that Jove's bolts produced the first muse, which Homer defines as "knowledge of good and evil." At this point it was all too easy for the philosophers later to intrude the dictum that the beginning of wisdom is piety. The first muse must have been Urania, who contemplated the heavens to take the auguries. Later she came to stand for astronomy, as will presently be shown. Just as poetic metaphysics was above divided into all its subordinate sciences, each sharing the poetic nature of their mother, so this history of ideas will present the rough origins both of the prac-

tical sciences in use among the nations and of the speculative sciences which, now refined, are celebrated by the learned.

IV

392 The fourth aspect is a philosophical criticism which grows out of the aforesaid history of ideas. Such a criticism will render true judgment upon the founders of the nations, which must have taken well over a thousand years to produce the writers who are the subjects of philological criticism. Beginning with Jove, our philosophical criticism will give us a natural theogony or generation of the gods as it took form naturally in the minds of the founders of the gentile world, who were by nature theological poets. The twelve gods of the so-called *gentes maiores,* the ideas of whom were imagined by them from time to time on certain occasions of human necessity or utility, are assigned to twelve short epochs, into which we divide the period in which the fables were born. Thus this natural theogony will give us a rational chronology of poetic history for at least nine hundred years before vulgar history (which came after the heroic period) had its first beginnings.

V

393 The fifth aspect is an ideal eternal history traversed in time by the histories of all nations. Wherever, emerging from savage, fierce and bestial times, men begin to domesticate themselves by religion, they begin, proceed and end by those stages which are investigated in this second book, to be encountered again in the fourth book, where we treat the course the nations run, and in the fifth, where we treat the recurrence of human things.

VI

394 The sixth is a system of the natural law of nations. The three princes of this doctrine, Hugo Grotius, John Selden and Samuel Pufendorf, should have taken their start, by one of the Axioms above laid down [314], from the beginnings of the nations, where their subject matter begins. But all three of them err together in this respect, by beginning in the middle; that is, with the latest times of the civilized nations (and thus of men enlightened by fully developed natural reason) from which the philosophers emerged and rose to meditation of a perfect idea of justice.

395 First Grotius, just because of the great love he bears the truth, sets aside divine providence and professes that his system will stand even if all knowledge of God be left out of account. Thus all the reproofs which in a great number of matters he brings against the Roman jurists, do not touch them at all, since they took divine providence for their first principle and proposed to treat of the natural law of nations, not that of the philosophers and moral theologians.

396 Then Selden assumes providence, but without paying any attention to the inhospitableness of the first peoples, or to the division the people of God

made of the whole world of nations at that time into Hebrews and gentiles. Or to the fact that, since the Hebrews had lost sight of their natural law during their slavery in Egypt, God himself must have reëstablished it for them by the law he gave Moses on Sinai. Or to the further fact that God in his law forbids even thoughts that are less than just, with which no mortal lawgiver has ever troubled himself. Or to the bestial origins here discussed of all the gentile nations. And although he pretends that the Jews presently taught their natural law to the gentiles, he is entirely unable to prove it, opposed as he is by the magnanimous confession of Josephus seconded by the grave reflection of Lactantius cited above, and by the hostility with which, as we have also observed above, the Jews have always regarded the gentiles, and which they preserve even now when dispersed among all the nations.

397   And finally Pufendorf begins with an Epicurean hypothesis, supposing man to have been cast into this world without any help or care from God. Reproved for this, he defends himself in a special dissertation, but, because he does not admit providence as his first principle, he cannot even begin to speak of law, as we have heard Cicero tell Atticus the Epicurean in his dialogue *De legibus.*

398   For all these reasons, we begin our treatment of law—the Latin for which is *ius,* contraction of the ancient *Ious*—at this most ancient point of all times, at the moment when the idea of Jove was born in the minds of the founders of the nations. To the Latin derivation of *ius* from *Ious* there is a striking parallel in Greek; for, as by a happy chance we find Plato observing in the *Cratylus,* the Greeks called law at first *diaïon.* This means "pervasive" or "enduring" by a philosophical etymology intruded by Plato himself, whose erudite mythology makes Jove the ether which penetrates and flows through all things. But the historical derivation of *diaïon* is from Jove, whom the Greeks called *Dios,* whence the Latin expression *sub dio,* which, equally with *sub Iove,* means "under the open sky." For the sake of euphony, *diaïon* came later to be pronounced *dikaion.* This then is our point of departure for the discussion of law, which was originally divine, in the proper sense expressed by divination, the science of Jove's auspices, which were the divine things by which the nations regulated all human things. These two classes of things taken together make up the adequate subject matter of jurisprudence. Thus our treatment of natural law begins with the idea of divine providence, in the same birth with which was born the idea of law. For law began naturally to be observed, in the manner examined above, by the founders of the *gentes* properly so called, those of the most ancient order, which were called *gentes maiores,* whose first god was Jove.

VII

399   The seventh and last of the principal aspects of this Science is that of the principles of universal history. It begins with this first moment of all

human things of the gentile world, with the first of the three ages of the world which the Egyptians said had elapsed before them; namely, the age of the gods, in which Heaven began to reign on earth and to bestow great benefits on men, as noted in the Axioms [64]. This is the golden age of the Greeks, in which the gods consorted with men on earth, as we have seen Jove begin to do. Starting with this first age of the world, the Greek poets in their fables have faithfully narrated the universal flood and the existence of giants in nature, and thus have truly narrated the beginnings of profane universal history. Yet [this history has hitherto lacked beginning for the following reasons.] Later men were unable to enter into the imaginations of the first men who founded the gentile world, which made them think they saw the gods. The verb *atterrare* was no longer understood in its proper sense, "to send underground." The giants who lived hidden in the caves under the mountains were metamorphosed in the later traditions of overcredulous peoples, and were supposed to have piled Olympus, Pelion and Ossa one on top of the other to drive the gods from heaven. Actually, the first impious giants not only did not fight the gods but were not even aware of them until Jove hurled his bolts. And whereas heaven was raised to an enormous height by the much more developed minds of later Greeks, to the first giants it was but the mountain summits, as we shall presently show. The fable above mentioned [of the giants storming heaven] must have been invented after Homer and fastened on him by interpolation in the *Odyssey* [XI 313 ff.]; for in his time merely to shake Olympus would have sufficed to dislodge the gods, since in the *Iliad* he always represents them as residing on the summit of Mount Olympus. For all these reasons profane universal history has hitherto lacked its beginning, and, for lack of the rational chronology of poetic history, it has lacked its continuity as well.

[SECTION II]

[POETIC LOGIC]

[CHAPTER I]

POETIC LOGIC

400 That which is metaphysics insofar as it contemplates things in all the forms of their being, is logic insofar as it considers things in all the forms by which they may be signified. Accordingly, as poetry has been considered by us above as a poetic metaphysics in which the theological poets imagined bodies to be for the most part divine substances, so now that same poetry is considered as poetic logic, by which it signifies them.

401 The word logic comes from *logos*, whose first and proper meaning was *fabula*, "fable," carried over into Italian as *favella*, "speech." In Greek the fable was also called *mythos*, "myth," whence comes the Latin *mutus*, "mute." For speech was born in mute times as mental [or sign] language, which Strabo in a golden passage says existed before vocal or articulate [language]; whence *logos* means both "word" and "idea." It was fitting that the matter should be so ordered by divine providence in religious times, for it is an eternal property of religions that they attach more importance to meditation than to speech. Thus, as stated in the Axioms [225], the first language in the first mute times of the nations must have begun with signs, whether gestures or physical objects, which had natural relations to the ideas [to be expressed]. For this reason *logos* or "word" meant also "deed" to the Hebrews and "thing" to the Greeks, as Thomas Gataker observes in his *De instrumenti stylo*. Similarly, *mythos* came to be defined for us as *vera narratio* or "true speech," the natural speech which first Plato and then Iamblichus said had been spoken in the world at one time. But this was mere conjecture on their part, as we saw in the Axioms [227], and Plato's effort to recover this speech in the *Cratylus* was therefore vain, and he was criticized for it by Aristotle and Galen. For that first language, spoken by the theological poets, was not a language in accord with the nature of the things it dealt with (as must have been the sacred language invented by Adam, to whom God granted divine onomathesia, the giving of names to things according to the nature of each), but was a fantastic speech making use of physical substances endowed with life and most of them imagined to be divine.

402   This is the way in which the theological poets apprehended Jove, Cybele or Berecynthia, and Neptune, for examples, and, at first mutely pointing, explained them as substances of the sky, the earth and the sea, which they imagined to be animate divinities and were therefore true to their senses in believing them to be gods. By means of these three divinities, in accordance with what we have said above concerning poetic characters, they explained everything appertaining to the sky, the earth and the sea. And similarly by means of the other divinities they signified the other kinds of things appertaining to each, denoting all flowers for instance by Flora, and all fruits by Pomona. We nowadays reverse this practice in respect of spiritual things, such as the faculties of the human mind, the passions, virtues, vices, sciences and arts; for the most part the ideas we form of them are so many feminine personifications, to which we refer all the causes, properties and effects that severally appertain to them. For when we wish to give utterance to our understanding of spiritual things, we must seek aid from our imagination to explain them and, like painters, form human images of them. But these theological poets, unable to make use of the understanding, did the opposite and more sublime thing: they attributed senses and passions, as we saw not long since, to bodies, and to bodies as vast as sky, sea and earth. Later, as these vast imaginations shrank and the power of abstraction grew, the same objects were apprehended by diminutive signs. Metonymy erected into dogma the prevailing ignorance of these origins of human things, which have remained buried until now. Jove becomes so small and light that he is flown about by an eagle. Neptune rides the waves in a fragile chariot. And Cybele rides seated on a lion.

403   Thus the mythologies, as their name indicates, must have been the proper languages of the fables; the fables being imaginative class-concepts, as we have shown, the mythologies must have been the allegories corresponding to them. Allegory, as observed in the Axioms [210], is defined as *diversiloquium* insofar as, by identity not of proportion but (to speak scholastically) of predicability, allegories signify the diverse species or the diverse individuals comprised under these genera. So that they must have a univocal signification connoting a quality common to all their species and individuals (as Achilles connotes an idea of valor common to all strong men, or Ulysses an idea of prudence common to all wise men); such that these allegories must be the etymologies of the poetic languages, which would make their origins all univocal, whereas those of the vulgar languages are more often analogous. We also have the definition of the word etymology itself as meaning *veriloquium,* just as fable was defined as *vera narratio.*

[CHAPTER II]

COROLLARIES CONCERNING POETIC TROPES,
MONSTERS AND METAMORPHOSES

I

404   All the first tropes are corollaries of this poetic logic. The most luminous and therefore the most necessary and frequent is metaphor. It is most praised when it gives sense and passion to insensate things, in accordance with the metaphysics above discussed, by which the first poets attributed to bodies the being of animate substances, with capacities measured by their own, namely sense and passion, and in this way made fables of them. Thus every metaphor so formed is a fable in brief. This gives a basis for judging the time when metaphors made their appearance in the languages. All the metaphors conveyed by likenesses taken from bodies to signify the operations of abstract minds must date from times when philosophies were taking shape. The proof of this is that in every language the terms needed for the refined arts and recondite sciences are of rustic origin.

405   It is noteworthy that in all languages the greater part of the expressions relating to inanimate things are formed by metaphor from the human body and its parts and from the human senses and passions. Thus, head for top or beginning; eyes for the looped heads of screws and for windows letting light into houses; mouth for any opening; lip for the rim of a vase or of anything else; the tooth of a plow, a rake, a saw, a comb; beard for rootlets; the mouth of a river; a neck of land; handful for a small number; heart for center (the Latins used *umbilicus,* "navel," in this sense); foot for end; the flesh of fruits; a vein of water, rock or mineral; the blood of grapes for wine; the bowels of the earth.[1] Heaven or the sea smiles; the wind whistles; the waves murmur; a body groans under a great weight. The farmers of Latium used to say the fields were thirsty, bore fruit, were swollen with grain; and our own rustics speak of plants making love, vines going mad, resinous trees weeping. Innumerable other examples could be collected from all languages. All of which is a consequence of our axiom [120] that man in his ignorance makes himself the rule of the universe, for in the examples cited he has made of himself an entire world. So that, as rational metaphysics teaches that man becomes all things by understanding them (*homo intelligendo fit omnia*), this imaginative metaphysics shows that man becomes all things by not understanding them (*homo non intelligendo fit*

---

[1] Several of Vico's examples for which there are no English equivalents are here omitted.

omnia); and perhaps the latter proposition is truer than the former, for when man understands he extends his mind and takes in the things, but when he does not understand he makes the things out of himself and becomes them by transforming himself into them.

II

406 In such a logic, sprung from such a metaphysics, the first poets must have given names to things from the most particular and the most sensible ideas. Such ideas are the sources, respectively, of synecdoche and metonymy. Metonymy of agent for act resulted from the fact that names for agents were commoner than names for acts. Metonymy of subject for form and accident was due to the fact that, as we have said in the Axioms [209], they did not know how to abstract forms and qualities from subjects. Certainly metonymy of cause for effect produced in each case a little fable, in which the cause was imagined as a woman clothed with her effects: ugly Poverty, sad Old Age, pale Death.

III

407 Synecdoche developed into metaphor as particulars were elevated into universals or parts united with the other parts together with which they make up their wholes. Thus the term "mortals" was originally and properly applied only to men, as the only beings whose mortality there was any occasion to notice. The use of "head' for man or person, so frequent in vulgar Latin, was due to the fact that in the forests only the head of a man could be seen from a distance. The word "man" itself is abstract, comprehending as in a philosophic genus the body and all its parts, the mind and all its faculties, the spirit and all its dispositions. In the same way, *tignum* and *culmen,* "log" and "top," came to be used with entire propriety when thatching was the practice for rafter and thatch; and later, with the adornment of cities, they signified all the materials and trim of a building. Again, *tectum,* "roof," came to mean a whole house because in the first times a covering sufficed for a house. Similarly, *puppis,* "poop," for a ship, because it was the highest part and therefore the first to be seen by those on shore; as in the returned barbarian times a ship was called a sail. Similarly, *mucro,* "point," for sword, because it is an abstract word and as in a genus comprehends pummel, hilt, edge and point; it was the point they felt which aroused their fear. Similarly, the material for the formed whole, as iron for sword, because they did not know how to abstract the form from the material. That bit of synecdoche and metonymy, *Tertia messis erat,* "it was the third harvest," was doubtless born of a natural necessity, for it took more than a thousand years for the astronomical term "year" to arise among the nations; and even now the Florentine peasantry say "we have reaped so many times" when they mean "so many years." And that knot of two synecdoches and a metonymy, *Post aliquot, mea regna videns, mirabor, aristas?* ("After a few harvests shall I wonder at seeing my kingdoms?"), betrays only too well the poverty of expres-

sion of the first rustic times, in which the phrase "so many ears of wheat"—even more particular than harvests—was used for "so many years." And because of the excessive poverty of the expression, the grammarians have assumed an excess of art behind it.

IV

408   Irony certainly could not have begun until the period of reflection, because it is fashioned of falsehood by dint of a reflection which wears the mask of truth. Here emerges a great principle of human things, confirming the origin of poetry disclosed in this work: that since the first men of the gentile world had the simplicity of children, who are truthful by nature, the first fables could not feign anything false; they must therefore have been, as they have been defined above, true narrations.

V

409   From all this it follows that all the tropes (and they are all reducible to the four types above discussed), which have hitherto been considered ingenious inventions of writers, were necessary modes of expression of all the first poetic nations, and had originally their full native propriety. But these expressions of the first nations later became figurative when, with the further development of the human mind, words were invented which signified abstract forms or genera comprising their species or relating parts with their wholes. And here begins the overthrow of two common errors of the grammarians: that prose speech is proper speech, and poetic speech improper; and that prose speech came first, and afterwards speech in verse.

VI

410   Poetic monsters and metamorphoses arose from a necessity of this first human nature, its inability, as shown in the Axioms [209], to abstract forms or properties from subjects. By their logic they had to put subjects together in order to put their forms together, or to destroy a subject in order to separate its primary form from the contrary form which had been imposed upon it. Such a putting together of ideas created the poetic monsters. In Roman law, as Antoine Favre observes in his *Iurisprudentiae papinianeae scientia,* children born of prostitutes are called monsters because they have the nature of men together with the bestial characteristic of having been born of vagabonds or of casual unions. Of such sort we shall find those monsters to have been (children born of noble women without benefit of solemn nuptials) whom the Law of the Twelve Tables commanded to be thrown into the Tiber.

VII

411   The distinguishing of ideas produced metamorphoses. Among other examples preserved by ancient jurisprudence is the heroic Latin phrase *fundum*

fieri, used in place of *autorem fieri;* the explanation being that, as the ground supports the farm or soil and that which is sown, planted or built thereon, so the approver supports the act, which without his approbation would fail; and he does this by quitting the form of a being moving at will, which he is, and taking on the contrary form of a stable thing.

[CHAPTER III]

COROLLARIES CONCERNING SPEECH BY POETIC CHARACTERS AMONG THE FIRST NATIONS

412   The poetic speech which our poetic logic has helped us to understand continued for a long time into the historic period, much as great and rapid rivers continue far into the sea, keeping sweet the waters borne on by the force of their flow. We have cited in the Axioms [207] the statement of Iamblichus that the Egyptians attributed to Hermes Trismegistus all their inventions useful to human life. And we confirmed this by another axiom [206]: that "children, by the ideas and names of the men, women and objects they have seen first, afterwards apprehend and name all the men, women and objects which have any resemblance or relation with the first." This we said was the great natural source of the poetic characters, with which the first peoples naturally thought and spoke. We also remarked in the Axioms [207–209] that, if Iamblichus had reflected upon this nature of human things, bringing into relation with it the habit of the ancient Egyptians which he himself reports, he would certainly not have injected into the mysteries of the vulgar wisdom of the Egyptians the sublime mysteries of his own Platonic wisdom.

413   Now in view of this characteristic of children and this habit of the first Egyptians, we assert that poetic speech, in virtue of the poetic characters it employs, can yield many important discoveries concerning antiquity.

I

414   Solon must have been a sage of vulgar wisdom, party leader of the plebs in the first times of the aristocratic commonwealth at Athens. This fact was indeed preserved by Greek history where it narrates that at first Athens was held by the optimates. In this work we shall show that such was universally the case in all the heroic commonwealths. The heroes or nobles, by a certain nature of theirs which they believed to be of divine origin, were led to say that the gods belonged to them, and consequently that the auspices of the gods were theirs also. By means of the auspices they kept within their own orders all the public and private rights of the heroic cities. To the plebeians, whom they be-

lieved to be of bestial origin and consequently men without gods and hence without auspices, they conceded only the use of natural liberty. (This is a great principle of things that are discussed through almost the whole of the present work.) Solon, however, had admonished the plebeians to reflect upon themselves and to realize that they were of like human nature with the nobles and should therefore be made equal with them in civil rights.—Unless, indeed, Solon was [a poetic character for] the Athenian plebeians themselves, considered under this aspect [of knowing themselves and demanding their rights].

415   The ancient Romans must also have had such a Solon among them. For the plebeians in the heroic struggles with the nobles, as ancient Roman history openly tells us, kept saying that the fathers of whom Romulus had composed the Senate (and from whom these patricians were descended) *non esse caelo demissos;* that is, that they did not have that divine origin of which they boasted, and that Jove was equal [just] to all. This is the civil history of the expression, *Iupiter omnibus aequus,* into which the learned later read the tenet that all minds are equal and that the differences they take on arise from differences in the organization of their bodies and in their civil education. By this reflection the Roman plebeians began to achieve equality with the patricians in civil liberty, until they entirely changed the Roman commonwealth from an aristocratic to a popular form. We proposed this as a hypothesis in the Notes on the Chronological Table [104], in a theoretical discussion of the Publilian law; and we shall show that it occurred in fact not only in the Roman but in all the other ancient commonwealths. Both by reasons and by authority we shall demonstrate that the plebeians of the peoples universally, beginning with Solon's reflection, changed the commonwealths from aristocratic to popular.

416   Hence Solon was made the author of that celebrated saying, "Know thyself," which, because of the great civil utility it had had for the Athenian people, was inscribed in all the public places of the city. Later the learned preferred to regard it as having been intended for what it is, a great counsel respecting metaphysical and moral things, and because of it Solon was reputed a sage in esoteric wisdom and made prince of the Seven Sages of Greece. In this way, because from this reflection there sprang up at Athens all the orders and laws that shape a democratic commonwealth, and because of the first peoples' habit of thinking in poetic characters, these orders and laws were all attributed by the Athenians to Solon, just as, by the Egyptians, all inventions useful to human civil life were attributed to Hermes Trismegistus.

II

417   In the same way all the laws concerning the orders must have been attributed to Romulus.

III

418   And to Numa, as many concerning sacred things and divine ceremonies, for which Roman religion was later conspicuous in its time of greatest pomp.

IV

419   To Tullus Hostilius, all the laws and orders of military discipline.

V

420   To Servius Tullius, the census [tax] which is the basis of democratic commonwealths, and other laws in great number having to do with popular liberty, so that he was acclaimed by Tacitus as *praecipuus sanctor legum*, "chief ordainer of laws." For, as we shall show, the census was the basis in aristocratic commonwealths on which the plebeians obtained from the nobles the bonitary ownership of the fields, which gave them occasion later for creating the tribunes of the plebs to defend for them this part of natural liberty, and the tribunes gradually led them to the attainment of full civil liberty. Thus the census of Servius Tullius, by affording the occasions and starting-points, developed into the census which was the basis of the Roman popular commonwealth. This was discussed by way of hypothesis in the notes on the Publilian law [111–113], and will later be shown to be true in fact.

VI

421   To Tarquinius Priscus, all the ensigns and devices with which the majesty of the Roman empire was later resplendent in the most illustrious times of Rome.

VII

422   In the same way there must have been interpolated in the Twelve Tables very many laws which will be shown to have been enacted in later times. And since (as was fully demonstrated in our *Principles of Universal Law*) the law of quiritary ownership when it was extended by the nobles to the plebeians was the first law to be inscribed on a public tablet (the sole purpose for which the decemvirs were created), all the laws making for equal liberty which were later inscribed on public tablets were attributed to the decemvirs because of their aspect of popular liberty. Take as a test case Greek luxury in the matter of funerals. Since the decemvirs would not have taught it to the Romans by prohibiting it, the prohibition must have come after the Romans had adopted it. But that cannot have been until after the wars with the Tarentines and with Pyrrhus, in which their acquaintance with the Greeks began. This explains the fact observed by Cicero that this law translated into Latin the very words in which it had been conceived in Athens.

VIII

423   It is the same with Draco, author of the laws written in blood at the time when, as noted above, Greek history tells us Athens was occupied by the optimates. This, as we shall presently see, was in the time of the heroic aristocracies, in which Greek history also tells us the Heraclids were scattered through all Greece, even into Attica (as we set forth above in the Chronological Table). They finally settled in the Peloponnesus and established their kingdom in Sparta, which will be shown to have been certainly an aristocratic commonwealth. Draco must have been one of the Gorgon's serpents nailed to the shield of Perseus, which will be found to signify the rule of the laws. This shield with the frightful penalties it bore turned to stone those who looked upon it; just as in sacred history similar laws were called *leges sanguinis,* laws of blood, because of the exemplary punishments they carried. Minerva, who was called Athena for reasons to be fully set forth below, armed herself with this shield. And among the Chinese, who write in hieroglyphics to this day, a dragon is the ensign of the civil power. It is something to wonder at that two nations so distant from each other in space and time should think and express themselves in the same poetic manner. For in all Greek history nothing else is told of this Draco.

IX

424   This discovery of the poetic characters confirms us in placing Aesop considerably earlier than the Seven Sages of Greece, as in the Notes to the Chronological Table [91] we promised to show in this place. For this philological truth is confirmed for us by the following history of human ideas. The seven sages were admired because they began to impart precepts of morality or of civil doctrine in the form of maxims like the famous "Know thyself" of Solon, who was their prince. We have seen above that this was a precept of civil doctrine, later carried over into metaphysics and morals. But Aesop had previously imparted such counsels in the form of comparisons, which the poets had still earlier used to express themselves. And the order of human ideas is to observe the similarities of things first to express itself and later for purposes of proof. Proof, in turn, is first by example, for which a single likeness suffices, and finally by induction, for which more are required. Socrates, father of all the sects of philosophers, introduced dialectic by induction, which Aristotle later perfected with the syllogism, which cannot proceed without a universal. But to undeveloped minds it suffices to present a single likeness in order to persuade them; as, by a single fable of the sort invented by Aesop, the worthy Menenius Agrippa reduced the rebellious Roman plebs to obedience.

425   That Aesop was a poetic character of the *socii* or *famuli* of the heroes, is revealed to us with prophetic insight by the urbane Phaedrus in one of the prologs of his *Fables:*

Attend me briefly while I now disclose
How art of fable telling first arose.
Unhappy slaves, in servitude confined,
Dared not to their harsh masters show their mind,
But under veiling of the fable's dress
Contrived their thoughts and feelings to express,
Escaping still their lords' affronted wrath.
So Aesop did; I widen out his path,[2]

as is clearly confirmed for us by his fable of the lion's share. For the plebeians, as noted in the Axioms [259], were called *socii* of the heroic cities, and shared the hardships and dangers of war but not the spoils and the conquests. Hence Aesop was called a slave, because the plebeians, as will presently be shown, were *famuli* of the heroes. And he was represented as ugly, because civil beauty was considered to come only from solemnized marriages, and only the heroes contracted such marriages, as will also be shown. For the same reason Thersites was ugly, for he must have been a character of the plebeians who served the heroes in the Trojan war. He was beaten by Ulysses with the scepter of Agamemnon, just as the ancient Roman plebeians were beaten by the nobles with rods over their bare shoulders—*regium in morem,* "in royal fashion," as Sallust puts it in St. Augustine's *City of God*—until the Porcian law freed Roman shoulders from the rod.

426   Such counsels, then, dictated by natural reason as useful to free civil life, must have been sentiments cherished by the plebs of the heroic cities. Aesop was made a poetic character of these plebs in this respect. Later, fables having to do with moral philosophy were ascribed to him, and he was turned into the first moral philosopher, just as Solon, who by his laws made Athens a free commonwealth, was turned into a sage. And because Aesop counseled in fables, he was supposed to have lived before Solon, who counseled in maxims. These fables must have been conceived originally in heroic verse. There is a tradition that they were later conceived in iambic verse (which we shall later find the Greek peoples to have spoken). This is intermediate between heroic verse and prose. They were finally written in prose and have reached us in that form.

X

427   In this way the later discoveries of esoteric wisdom were attributed to the first authors of vulgar wisdom; and [poetic characters like] Zoroaster in the East, Trismegistus in Egypt, Orpheus in Greece, Pythagoras in Italy,

---

[2] *Nunc fabularum cur sit inventum genus,*
Brevi docebo. Servitus obnoxia,
Quia, quae volebat, non audebat dicere,
Affectus proprios in fabellas transtulit.
Aesopi illius semita feci viam. . . .

originally lawgivers, were finally believed to have been philosophers, as Confucius is today in China. For certainly the Pythagoreans in Magna Graecia, as will later be shown, were so called in the sense of nobles who, having tried to reduce all their commonwealths from popular to aristocratic, were all slain. And the *Carmen aureum* of Pythagoras has been shown above [128] to have been an imposture, as were also the *Oracles* of Zoroaster, the *Poimander* of Trismegistus, and the *Orphics* or verses of Orpheus. There did not come down to the ancients any book on philosophy written by Pythagoras, and Philolaus was the first Pythagorean to write one, as Scheffer observes in his *De philosophia italica.*

[CHAPTER IV]

COROLLARIES CONCERNING THE ORIGINS OF LANGUAGES AND LETTERS; AND, THEREIN, THE ORIGINS OF HIEROGLYPHICS, LAWS, NAMES, FAMILY ARMS, MEDALS AND MONEY; AND HENCE OF THE FIRST LANGUAGE AND LITERATURE OF THE NATURAL LAW OF NATIONS

428   Now from the theology of the poets, or poetic metaphysics, by way of the poetic logic sprung from it, we go on to discover the origin of languages and letters. Concerning these there are as many opinions as there are scholars who have written on the subject. So that Gerard Jan Vossius says in his *Grammatica:* "With regard to the invention of letters, many authors have brought together many things, in such profusion and confusion that you go away from them more uncertain than you came." And Herman Hugo in his *De prima scribendi origine* observes: "There is no other subject on which more numerous or more conflicting opinions are to be found than in the discussion of the origin of letters and writing. How many conflicts of opinion! What is one to believe? What not believe?" Not without reason, therefore, did Bernard von Mallinckrodt, in his *De natura et usu literarum,* conclude from the impossibility of understanding how they arose that they were divine inventions; in which view he was followed by Ingewald Eling in his *Historia linguae graecae.*

429   But the difficulty as to the manner of their origin was created by the scholars themselves, all of whom regarded the origin of letters as a separate question from that of the origin of languages, whereas the two were by nature conjoined. And they should have made out as much from the words for grammar and for characters. From the former, because grammar is defined as the art of speaking, yet *grammata* are letters, so that grammar should have been defined as the art of writing. So, indeed, it was defined by Aristotle, and so in fact it originally was; for, as will here be shown, all nations began to speak by writing,

since all were originally mute. The word character, on the other hand, means idea, form, model, and certainly poetic characters came before those of articulate sounds. Josephus stoutly maintains, against the Greek grammarian Apion, that at the time of Homer the so-called vulgar letters had not yet been invented. Moreover, if these letters had been forms representing articulated sounds instead of being arbitrary signs, they would have been uniform among all nations, as the articulated sounds themselves are. But, giving up hope of knowing how languages and letters began, scholars have failed to learn that the first nations thought in poetic characters, spoke in fables, and wrote in hieroglyphics. These should have been the principles, which must by their nature be most certain, of philosophy in its study of human ideas and of philology in its study of human words.

430 Having now to enter upon a discussion of this matter, we shall give a brief sample of the opinions that have been held respecting it—opinions so uncertain, frivolous, inept, pretentious or ridiculous, and so numerous, that we need not relate them. By way of sample, then: because in the returned barbarian times Scandinavia by the conceit of the nations was called *vagina gentium* and was believed to be the mother of all other nations in the world, therefore by the conceit of the scholars Johannes and Olaus Magnus were of opinion that their Goths had preserved from the beginning of the world the letters divinely invented by Adam. This dream was laughed at by all the scholars, but this did not keep Johannes van Gorp from following suit and going one better by claiming that his own Dutch language, which is not much different from Saxon, has come down from the Earthly Paradise and is the mother of all other languages. This claim was ridiculed by Joseph Justus Scaliger, Philipp Camerarius, Christian Becman, and Martin Schoock. And yet this conceit swelled to the bursting point in the *Atlantica* of Olof Rudbeck, who will have it that the Greek letters came from the runes; that the Phoenician letters, to which Cadmus gave the order and values of those of the Hebrews, were inverted runes; and that the Greeks finally straightened them here and rounded them there by rule and compass. And because the inventor is called Merkurssman among the Scandinavians, he will have it that the Mercury who invented letters for the Egyptians was a Goth. Such license in rendering opinions concerning the origins of letters should prepare the reader to receive the things we shall say of them here not merely with impartial readiness to see what they bring forward that is new, but with diligence to meditate upon them and to accept them for what they must be: namely, principles of all the human and divine knowledge of the gentile world.

431 The philosophers and philologians should all have begun to treat of the origins of languages and letters from the following principles. (1) That the first men of the gentile world conceived ideas of things by imaginative characters of animate and mute substances. (2) That they expressed themselves by means of gestures or physical objects which had natural relations with the ideas; for example, three ears of grain, or acting as if swinging a scythe three

times, to signify three years. (3) That they thus expressed themselves by a language with natural significations. (Plato and Iamblichus said such a language had once been spoken in the world; it must have been the most ancient language of Atlantis, which scholars would have us believe expressed ideas by the nature of the things, that is, by their natural properties.) It is because the philosophers and philologians have treated separately these two things which, as we have said, are naturally conjoined [the origins of languages and letters], that the inquiry into the origins of letters has proved so difficult for them, involving equal difficulty with the inquiry into the origins of languages, with which they have been either not at all or very little concerned.

432   At the outset of our discussion, then, we posit as our first principle the philological axiom [173] that according to the Egyptians there had been spoken in their world in all preceding time three languages corresponding in number and order to the three ages that had elapsed in their world: the ages of gods, heroes, and men. The first language had been hieroglyphic, sacred or divine; the second, symbolic, by signs or by heroic devices; the third, epistolary, for men at a distance to communicate to each other the current needs of their lives. Concerning these three languages there are two golden passages in Homer's *Iliad,* from which it clearly appears that the Greeks agreed with the Egyptians in this matter. In the first it is told how Nestor lived through three generations of men speaking different languages. Nestor must therefore have been a heroic character of the chronology determined by the three languages corresponding to the three ages of the Egyptians; and the phrase "to live the years of Nestor" must have meant "to live the years of the world." The other passage is that in which Aeneas relates to Achilles that men of different language began to inhabit Ilium after Troy was moved to the seashore and Pergamum became its fortress. To this first principle we join the tradition, also Egyptian, that their Thoth or Mercury invented both laws and letters.

433   Around this truth we assemble the following others. Among the Greeks the words name and character had the same meaning, so that the Church Fathers used indiscriminately the two expressions *de divinis characteribus* and *de divinis nominibus*. Name and definition have also the same meaning; thus, in rhetoric, under the head of *quaestio nominis* we find a search for definition of the fact, and in medicine the nomenclature of diseases is the head under which their nature is defined. Among the Romans names meant originally and properly houses branching into many families. And that the first Greeks had also used names in this sense is shown by the patronymics or names of fathers, which are so often used by the poets and above all by Homer. (According to Livy, a tribune of the plebs defined the patricians as those *qui possunt nomine ciere patrem,* "who can use the surnames of their fathers.") These patronymics later disappeared in the popular liberty of all the rest of Greece, but were preserved by the Heraclids in the aristocratic commonwealth of Sparta. In Roman law *nomen* signifies right. Similarly in Greek *nomos* signifies law, and from *nomos*

comes *nomisma,* "money," as Aristotle notes; and according to etymologists *nomos* becomes in Latin *nummus.* In French, *loi* means "law," and *aloi* means "money"; and among the second barbarians the term canon was applied both to ecclesiastical law and to the annual rent paid by the feudal leaseholder to the lord of the land he held in fief. This uniformity of thinking perhaps explains why the Latins used the term *ius* both for law and for the fat of sacrificed animals, which was Jove's due; for Jove was originally called *Ious,* from which were later derived the genitives *Iovis* and *iuris* (as pointed out above). Among the Hebrews also, of the three parts into which they divided the animal sacrificed as a peace-offering, the fat was accounted God's due and was burnt on the altar. The Latin *praedia,* "estates" (a term which must have been applied to rustic earlier than to urban estates), were so called because, as we shall presently show, the first cultivated fields were the first booty (*praeda*) in the world. The first taming was of such fields, which were therefore in ancient Roman law called *manucaptae* (whence *manceps* for one under real-estate bond to the public treasury); and in Roman laws *iura praediorum* remained a term for the so-called real servitudes, which were attached to real estate. And lands referred to as *manucaptae* must at first have been called *mancipia;* and it is certainly in this sense that we must understand the article of the Law of the Twelve Tables, *Qui nexum faciet mancipiumque,* that is, "Whoever consigns the bond, consigns therewith the manor." The Italians, following the same line of thought as the ancient Romans, called the manors *poderi,* as having been acquired by force. Further evidence: The returned barbarism called the fields with their boundaries *presas terrarum.* The Spaniards call bold enterprises *prendas.* The Italians call family coats-of-arms *imprese,* and use *termini* in the sense of "words" (a usage surviving in scholastic dialectic). They also call family coats-of-arms *insegne,* from which is derived the verb *insegnare,* "to teach." So Homer, in whose time so-called vulgar letters had not yet been invented, says Proetus' letter to Eureia against Bellerophon was written in *sēmata,* "signs."

434   To crown all these things, let the following three incontrovertible truths be added. (1) Since it has been demonstrated that the first gentile nations were all mute in their beginnings, they must have expressed themselves by gestures or by physical objects having natural relations with their ideas. (2) They must have used signs to fix the boundaries of their estates and to have enduring witnesses of their rights. (3) They all made use of money. All these truths will give us the origins of languages and letters, and thereby of hieroglyphics, laws, names, family coats-of-arms, medals, money, and of the language and writing in which the first natural law of nations was spoken and written.

435   In order to establish more firmly the principles of all this, we must here uproot the false opinion held by some of the Egyptians that the hieroglyphics were invented by philosophers to conceal in them their mysteries of lofty esoteric wisdom. For it was by a common natural necessity that all the first nations spoke in hieroglyphics (concerning which an axiom [226] has been proposed

above). In Africa, to the case of Egypt already noted, we may add, following Heliodorus in his *Aethiopica,* the Ethiopians, who used as hieroglyphics the tools of all the mechanical arts. In the East the magic characters of the Chaldeans must have been hieroglyphics. In northern Asia, as we have seen above, Idanthyrsus king of the Scythians (quite late in their extremely long history, in which they had conquered even the Egyptians who boasted themselves the most ancient of all nations) used five real words to answer Darius the Great, who had declared war on him. These five were a frog, a mouse, a bird, a ploughshare, and a bow. The frog signified that he, Idanthyrsus, was born of the earth of Scythia, as frogs are born of the earth in summer rains, and so that he was a son of that land. The mouse signified that he, like a mouse, had made his home where he was born; that is, that he had established his nation there. The bird signified that in that place he had his auspices; that is, as we shall see, that he was subject to none but God. The ploughshare signified that he had reduced those lands to cultivation, and thus tamed and made them his own by force. And finally the bow signified that as supreme commander of the arms of Scythia he had the duty and might to defend her. This explanation, so natural and necessary, is to be set against the ridiculous ones worked out, according to St. Cyril, by the counselors of Darius. Add to the interpretation of the Scythian hieroglyphics by Darius's counselors the far-fetched, artificial and contorted interpretations by scholars of the Egyptian hieroglyphics, and it will be evident that in general the true and proper use made of hieroglyphics by the first peoples has hitherto not been understood. As for the Latins, Roman history has not left us without such a tradition; witness the mute heroic answer which Tarquinius Superbus sends to his son in Gabii, when in the presence of the messenger he cuts off the heads of poppies with the stick he has in his hands. In northern Europe, as Tacitus observes in describing their customs, the ancient Germans were not acquainted with the secrets of letters (*literarum secreta*); that is, that they did not know how to write their hieroglyphics. This must have remained the case down to the times of Frederick the Swabian, indeed to those of Rudolph of Hapsburg, when they began to write state papers in vulgar German script. In northern France there was a hieroglyphic speech called rebus of Picardy, which must have been, as in Germany, a speech by physical things; that is, by the hieroglyphics of Idanthyrsus. Even in Ultima Thule, in fact in its remotest part, namely Scotland, as Hector Boece relates in his history of that nation, they wrote in hieroglyphics in ancient times. In the West Indies the Mexicans were found to write in hieroglyphics, and Jan de Laet in his description of the new India describes the hieroglyphics of the Indians as divers heads of animals, plants, flowers and fruits, and notes that they distinguish families by their cippi; which is the same use that is made of family coats-of-arms in our world. In the East Indies the Chinese still write in hieroglyphics.

436   Thus is deflated the conceit of the scholars who came afterwards, a conceit to which that of the extremely conceited Egyptians dared not swell

itself: namely, that the other sages of the world had learned from the Egyptians how to conceal their esoteric wisdom under hieroglyphics.

437 Having posited these principles of poetic logic and dissipated this conceit of the scholars, we return to the three languages of the Egyptians. The first of these, that of the gods, is attested for the Greeks by Homer, who, in five passages of his two poems, as noted in the Axioms [174], makes mention of a language more ancient than his own, which is certainly heroic, and calls it "language of the gods." Three of the passages are in the *Iliad:* the first where he tells that the creature called Briareus by the gods was called Aegaeon by men; the second where he speaks of a bird called *chalkida* by the gods and *kumindin* by men; the third where he says the river of Troy is called Xanthus by the gods, Scamander by men. In the *Odyssey* there are two passages: one where he says what men call Scylla and Charybdis the gods call *planktas petras;* the other where Mercury gives Ulysses a secret remedy against the enchantments of Circe, an herb called moly by the gods, knowledge of which is denied to men. Plato has many things to say about these passages, but to no purpose; so that Dion Chrysostom later slanderously accuses Homer of pretending to understand the language of the gods, which naturally is denied to men. But we may question whether in these Homeric passages we should not read "heroes" in place of "gods"; for, as will presently be shown, the heroes took the name of gods over the plebeians of their cities, whom they called men (as in the returned barbarian times the vassals were called *homines,* to the great astonishment of Hotman), and the great lords (as in the returned barbarism) made a vaunt of possessing marvelous medical secrets. Thus the differences referred to may have been no more than differences between noble and vulgar speech. Be that as it may, there can be no doubt that among the Latins Varro occupied himself with the language of the gods, for he had the diligence to collect thirty thousand of their names, which would have sufficed for a copious divine vocabulary, with which the peoples of Latium might express all their human needs, which in those simple and frugal times must have been few indeed, being only the things that were necessary to life. The Greeks too had gods to the number of thirty thousand, as has also been noted in the Axioms [175]; for they made a deity of every stone, spring, brook, plant and off-shore rock. Such deities included the dryads, hamadryads, oreads and napeads. Just so the American Indians make a god of everything that exceeds their limited understanding. Thus the divine fables of the Greeks and Latins must have been the true first hieroglyphics, or sacred or divine characters, corresponding to those of the Egyptians.

438 The second kind of speech, corresponding to the age of heroes, was said by the Egyptians to have been spoken by symbols. To these may be reduced the heroic emblems, which must have been the mute comparisons which Homer calls *sēmata* (the signs in which the heroes wrote). In consequence they must have been metaphors, images, similitudes or comparisons, which, having passed into articulate speech, supplied all the resources of poetic expression. For

certainly Homer, if we accept the resolute denial of Josephus the Jew that there
has come down to us any writer more ancient than he, was the first author of the
Greek tongue; and, since we owe to the Greeks all that has reached us of the
gentile world, he was the first author of that entire world. Among the Latins
the earliest memorials of their tongue are the fragments of the Salian songs,
and the first writer of whom there is mention is Livius Andronicus the poet.
With the recurrence of barbarism in Europe, new languages were born. The first
language of the Spaniards was that which is called romance, and consequently
that of heroic poetry, for the romancers were the heroic poets of the returned
barbarian times. In France the first writer in vulgar French was Arnaut Daniel
Pacca, the first of all the Provençal poets, who flourished in the eleventh century. And finally the first writers in Italy were the Florentine and Sicilian
rhymers.

439   The epistolary speech of the Egyptians, suitable for expressing the
needs of common everyday life in communication from a distance, must have
been born of the lower classes of a dominant people in Egypt, which must have
been that of Thebes (whose king Ramses, as noted above, extended his rule over
all that great nation), because for the Egyptians that language corresponds to
the age of men, the term used for the plebeians of the heroic peoples to differentiate them from the heroes, as noted above. This language must be understood as having sprung up by their free consent, by this eternal property, that
vulgar speech and writing are a right of the people. When the emperor Claudius
found three additional letters necessary to the Latin language, the Roman people would not accept them; nor have the Italians accepted those devised by
Giorgio Trissino, though their lack is felt in Italian.

440   The epistolary or vulgar language of the Egyptians must have been
written with letters likewise vulgar. Since the vulgar letters of the Egyptians
resemble those of the Phoenicians, it is necessary to suppose that one of these
peoples borrowed from the other. Those who think that the Egyptians were
the first discoverers of all the things necessary or useful to human society, must
consequently hold that the Egyptians taught their letters to the Phoenicians. But
Clement the Alexandrian, who must have been better informed than any other
author in matters Egyptian, relates that Sanchuniathon or Sancuniates the
Phoenician (who in the Chronological Table is placed in the heroic age of
Greece) had written the history of Phoenicia in vulgar letters; and he therefore
proposes him as the first author of the gentile world to have written in vulgar
characters. In this connection it has to be said that the Phoenicians, certainly
the first merchant people of the world, having entered Egypt for trading purposes, may well have carried thither their vulgar letters. But, entirely apart from
argument or conjecture, vulgar tradition assures us that these same Phoenicians
brought their letters to Greece. Tacitus, examining this tradition, suggests that
they passed off as their own invention the letters invented by others, meaning
the Egyptian hieroglyphics. But, to allow the popular tradition some ground of

truth (as we have proved all such traditions must have [144]), let us say that the Phoenicians brought to Greece hieroglyphics received from others, and that these could only have been the mathematical characters or geometric figures which they had received from the Chaldeans. The latter were beyond question the first mathematicians and especially the first astronomers of the nations; whence Zoroaster the Chaldean (whose name means "observer of the stars" according to Bochart) was the first sage of the gentile world. The Phoenicians used these Chaldean characters as notations for numbers in their mercantile business, in pursuit of which long before Homer's time they frequented the shores of Greece. This is made evident by Homer's own poems, and especially the *Odyssey*. For in Homer's time, as Josephus vigorously maintains against the Greek grammarian Apion, vulgar letters had not yet been invented by the Greeks. But the latter, with supreme genius, in which they certainly surpassed all nations, took over these geometric forms to represent the various articulated sounds, and shaped them into vulgar characters of letters with consummate beauty. These were later adopted by the Latins, whose letters, as Tacitus himself observes, resembled the most ancient Greek ones. Weighty proof of this is the fact that the Greeks for a long period, and the Latins down to their latest times, used capital letters to represent numbers. It must have been these letters that were taught to the Latins by Demaratus the Corinthian and by Carmenta, the wife of Evander the Arcadian. We shall explain presently that in ancient times Greek colonies had been taken to Latium by sea and by land.

441 There is no worth in the contention of many scholars that, because the Hebrews and the Greeks give almost the same names to their vulgar letters, the Greeks must have got theirs from the Hebrews. It is more reasonable that the Hebrews should have imitated the Greek nomenclature than vice versa. For it is universally agreed that from the time that Alexander the Great conquered the empire of the East (which after his death was divided by his captains) Greek speech spread throughout Egypt and the East. And since it is also generally agreed that grammar was introduced quite late among the Hebrews, it follows necessarily that the Hebrew men of letters called their Hebrew letters by the Greek names. Moreover, since the elements [of anything] are very simple in nature, the Greeks must at first have called their letters by the simplest sounds [e.g. "ah" for *a*], and it must have been for that reason that the letters were called elements. The Latins, following suit, called them with the same gravity, and also kept the forms of the letters like the most ancient Greek ones. We must therefore conclude that calling the letters by complex names [e.g. "alpha" for *a*] was introduced late among the Greeks, and later still brought by the Greeks to the Hebrews in the East.

442 These arguments confute the opinion of those who would have it that Cecrops the Egyptian brought vulgar letters to the Greeks. Another opinion, that Cadmus the Phoenician must have brought them from Egypt into Greece because he founded a city there and named it Thebes after the capital of

the greatest Egyptian dynasty, will be refuted presently by the principles of Poetic Geography, by which it will appear that the Greeks who went to Egypt called the Egyptian capital Thebes because it bore a resemblance to their native city of that name. And finally we understand why cautious critics, cited by an anonymous English writer on the uncertainty of the sciences [Thomas Baker, *Reflections on Learning*], conclude from the too early date assigned to Sancuniates that he never existed. We, accordingly, not to put him out of the world entirely, judge that he must be set in a later age, certainly after Homer. And to allow the Phoenicians priority over the Greeks in the invention of the so-called vulgar letters (not failing, however, to take into account that the Greeks had more genius than the Phoenicians), it has to be said that Sancuniates must have lived a little before Herodotus, who was called the father of Greek history, which he wrote in the vulgar speech. For Sancuniates was called the historian of truth; that is, a writer of what Varro in his division of times calls the historical time. In that time, according to the Egyptian division of three languages corresponding to the three ages of the world that had elapsed before them, they spoke in the epistolary language written in vulgar characters.

443   Now, as the heroic or poetic language was founded by the heroes, so the vulgar languages were introduced by the common people, whom we shall find to have been the plebs of the heroic peoples. By the Latins these languages were properly called vernacular. They could not, however, have been introduced by those *vernae* defined by the grammarians as slaves born at home of enslaved prisoners of war, for these naturally learn the languages of their parents' peoples. But the first and properly so-called *vernae,* as will be shown, were the *famuli* of the heroes in the state of the families. These *famuli,* of whom the masses of the first plebs of the heroic cities were later composed, were precursors of the slaves later secured by the cities through war. All this is confirmed by the two languages of which Homer speaks: the one of the gods, the other of men, which above we interpreted as the heroic and the vulgar language, which we shall shortly explain more fully.

444   The philologians have all accepted with an excess of good faith the view that in the vulgar languages meanings were fixed by convention. On the contrary, because of their natural origins, they must have had natural significations. This is easy to observe in vulgar Latin (which is more heroic than vulgar Greek, and therefore as much more robust as the latter is more refined), which has formed almost all its words by metaphors drawn from natural objects according to their natural properties or sensible effects. And in general metaphor makes up the great body of the language among all nations. But the grammarians, encountering great numbers of words which give confused and indistinct ideas of things, and not knowing their origins, which had made them at first clear and distinct, have given peace to their ignorance by setting up the universal maxim that articulate human words have arbitrary significations. And

they have dragged in Aristotle, Galen and other philosophers, and armed them against Plato and Iamblichus, as we have said [227].

445   There remains, however, the very great difficulty: How is it that there are as many different vulgar tongues as there are peoples? To solve it, we must here establish this great truth: that, as the peoples have certainly by diversity of climates acquired different natures, from which have sprung as many different customs, so from their different natures and customs as many different languages have arisen. For by virtue of the aforesaid diversity of their natures they have regarded the same utilities or necessities of human life from different points of view, and there have thus arisen so many national customs, for the most part differing from one another and at times contrary to each other; so and not otherwise there have arisen as many different languages as there are nations. An evident confirmation of this is found in the proverbs, which are maxims of human life, the same in substance but expressed from as many points of view as there are or have been different nations, as has been noted in the Axioms [161]. Thus the same heroic origins, preserved in brief in the vulgar tongues, have given rise to the phenomenon so astonishing to biblical critics: that the names of the same kings appear in one form in sacred and in another in profane history. The reason is that the one perchance considers men with regard to their appearance or power, the other with regard to their customs, undertakings, or whatever else it may have been. In the same way we still find the cities of Hungary given one name by the Hungarians, another by the Greeks, another by the Germans, another by the Turks. The German language, which is a living heroic language, transforms almost all names from foreign languages into its own. We may conjecture that the Latins and Greeks did the same when we find them discussing so many barbarian matters with Greek and Latin elegance. This must be the cause of the obscurity encountered in ancient geography and in the natural history of fossils, plants and animals. And for this reason we excogitated, in the first edition of this work, an Idea of a Mental Dictionary for assigning meanings to all the different articulate languages, reducing them all to certain unities of ideas in substance, which, considered from various points of view, have come to be expressed by different words in each. We make continual use of this in working out the argument of our Science. And we gave a very full example of it in the fourth chapter [actually book III, chapter 41], where we showed that the fathers of families, considered from fifteen different points of view in the state of the families and of the first commonwealths, at the time when the languages must have been taking form, were called by an equal number of different names by fifteen nations ancient and modern. (And most weighty are those arguments concerning the things of that time which are taken from the original meanings of the words, as set forth in the Axioms [240].) This is one of the three passages on account of which we do not regret the publication of that book. The aforesaid Dictionary develops in a new way the argu-

ment presented by Thomas Hayne in his dissertation on the kinship of languages and in his others on languages in general and on the harmony of various languages. From all this we infer the following corollary: that languages are more beautiful in proportion as they are richer in these condensed heroic expressions; that they are more beautiful because they are more evident; and that because they are more evident they are truer and more faithful. And that on the contrary, in proportion as they are more crowded with words of unknown origin, they are less delightful, because obscure and confused, and therefore more likely to deceive and lead astray. The latter must be the case with languages formed by the mixture of many barbarous tongues, the history of whose original and metaphorical meanings has not come down to us.

446 To enter now upon the extremely difficult [question of the] way in which these three kinds of languages and letters were formed, we must establish this principle: that as gods, heroes and men began at the same time (for they were after all men who imagined the gods and believed their own heroic nature to be a mixture of the divine and human natures), so these three languages began at the same time, each having its letters, which developed along with it. They began, however, with these three very great differences: that the language of the gods was almost entirely mute, only very slightly articulate; the language of the heroes, an equal mixture of articulate and mute, and consequently of vulgar speech and of the heroic characters used in writing by the heroes, which Homer calls *sēmata;* the language of men, almost entirely articulate and only very slightly mute, there being no vulgar language so copious that there are not more things than it has words for. Thus necessarily the heroic language was in the beginning disordered in the extreme; and this is a great source of the obscurity of the fables. The fable of Cadmus will serve as a signal example. Cadmus slays the great serpent, sows its teeth, armed men spring up from the furrows, he throws a great rock among them, they fight to the death, and finally Cadmus himself changes into a serpent. So ingenious was this Cadmus, who brought letters to the Greeks, by whom this fable has been transmitted, that, as we shall explain presently, it contains several centuries of poetic history!

447 To follow up what has already been said: at the same time that the divine character of Jove took shape—the first human thought in the gentile world—articulate language began to develop by way of onomatopoeia, through which we still find children happily expressing themselves. By the Latins Jove was at first, from the roar of the thunder, called *Ious;* by the Greeks, from the whistle of the lightning, *Zeus;* by the Easterners, from the sound of burning fire, he must have been called *Ur,* whence came *Urim,* the power of fire; and from this same origin must have come the Greek *ouranos,* sky, and the Latin verb *uro,* to burn. From the whistle of the lightning must also have come the Latin *cel,* one of the monosyllables of Ausonius, pronounced however with the Spanish cedilla (*ç*), which is required to give point to Ausonius's own jesting line about Venus: *Nata salo, suscepta solo, patre edita caelo,* "Born of the sea,

adopted by the soil, raised by her father to the sky." With respect to these origins it is to be noted that the same sublimity of invention evinced in the fable of Jove, which we have observed above, marks the beginning of poetic locution in onomatopoeia, which Dionysius Longinus certainly includes among the sources of the sublime, and which he illustrates from Homer, citing the sizzling sound (*siz'*) emitted by the eye of Polyphemus when Ulysses pierces it with the fiery stake.

448   Human words were formed next from interjections, which are sounds articulated under the impetus of violent passions. In all languages these are monosyllables. Thus it is not beyond likelihood that, when wonder had been awakened in men by the first thunderbolts, these interjections of Jove should give birth to one produced by the human voice: "*pa!*"; and that this should then be doubled: "*pape!*" From this interjection of wonder was subsequently derived Jove's title of "father of men and gods," and thus it came about presently that all the gods were called fathers, and the goddesses, mothers; whence the Latin names *Iupiter, Diespiter, Marspiter, Iuno genitrix*. The fables certainly tell us that Juno was sterile; and we have observed above that many other gods and goddesses did not marry among their kind. (Venus was called the concubine, not the wife, of Mars.) None the less they were all called fathers. (On this point there are some verses of Lucilius which we have cited in the Notes to our *Universal Law*.) They were called fathers in the sense in which *patrare* originally meant to do or make, which is the prerogative of God. *Patrare* occurs thus even in Scripture, where, in the story of the creation of the world, it is said that on the seventh day God rested *ab opere quod patrarat*, "from the work which He had done." Thence must have been derived the verb *impetrare*, as if for *impatrare*. The form used in the science of augury was *impetrire*, "to obtain a good augury," concerning whose origin the Latin grammarians have written so much nonsense. This proves that the first interpretation (*interpretatio* as if for *interpatratio*) was the interpretation of the divine laws declared by the auspices.

449   The strong men in the family state, from a natural ambition of human pride, arrogated to themselves this divine title of "fathers" (a fact which may have been the ground for the vulgar tradition that the first strong men of the earth had caused themselves to be adored as gods); but, observing the piety they owed to the deities, they called the latter gods. Later, when the strong men of the first cities took the name of gods upon themselves, they were moved by the same piety to call the deities "immortal gods," to differentiate them from themselves, the "mortal gods." But in this may be observed the grossness of these giants, like that which travelers report of *los patacones* [170]. A fair trace of it has remained in the ancient Latin words *pipulum* and *pipare*, in the sense of "complaint" and "to complain," which must be derived from the interjection of lament, "*pi, pi*." *Pipulum* in this sense in Plautus is generally interpreted as synonymous with *obvagulatio* in the Twelve Tables, which must come from

vagire, which is properly the crying of children. A similar origin from the interjection of fear must be assigned to the Greek word *paian*, which begins with *pai*. Concerning this the Greeks have a very ancient golden tradition to the effect that when they were terrified by the great serpent called Python they invoked the aid of Apollo with the words *iō paiān*. Dazed with fear, they first pronounced them slowly three times, but then, when Apollo had slain the Python, they jubilantly pronounced them another three times quickly, dividing the omega into two omicrons and the diphthong *ai* into two syllables. Thus naturally was Greek heroic verse at first spondaic and then dactylic, and it has retained this eternal property, that it gives preference to the dactyl in every foot except the last. Song arose naturally, in the measure of heroic verse, under the impulse of most violent passions, even as we still observe men sing when moved by great passions, especially extreme happiness or grief, as has been said in the Axioms [229]. What has been said here will shortly be of much use when we discuss the origins of song and verse.

450   They went on to form pronouns; for interjections give vent to one's own passions, a thing which one can do even by oneself, but pronouns serve in sharing our ideas with others concerning things which we cannot name or whose names another may not understand. Pronouns are likewise in all languages for the greater part, if not quite all, monosyllables. The first of them, or at least among the first, must have been the one which occurs in that golden passage of Ennius: *Aspice hoc sublime cadens, quem omnes invocant Iovem,* "Behold this sublime overhanging, which all invoke as Jove," where *hoc* stands for *caelum*, the sky. It occurs also in vulgar Latin: *Luciscit hoc iam*, for *albescit caelum*, "the sky grows light." And articles from the time of their first appearance have this eternal property: that they go before the nouns to which they are attached.

451   Later were formed the particles, of which a great part are the prepositions, which also, in almost all languages, are monosyllables. These preserve in the name they bear this eternal property: that they go before the nouns which require them and the verbs with which they form compounds.

452   Gradually nouns were formed. In the chapter on the Origins of the Latin Language in the first edition of this work, we listed a great number of nouns which sprang up within Latium, beginning with the sylvan life of the Latins and continuing through their rural into their earliest city life; all of them formed as monosyllables, showing no trace of foreign origin, not even Greek, except for four words: *bous, sūs, mūs*, and *sēps*, the last of which means "hedge" in Latin and "serpent" in Greek. This is the second of the three passages in that work which we regard as adequate. It may serve as a model to scholars of other languages in investigating their origins to the great profit of the republic of letters. Certainly in the German language, for instance, which is a mother language (because foreign nations never entered that country to rule over it), the

roots are all monosyllabic. And that nouns sprang up before verbs is proved by this eternal property: that there is no significant discourse that does not begin with a noun, expressed or understood, which governs it.

453 Last of all the authors of the languages formed the verbs, as we observe children expressing nouns and particles but leaving the verbs to be understood. For nouns awaken ideas which leave firm traces; particles, signifying modifications, do the same; but verbs signify motions, which involve past and future, which are measured from the indivisible present, which even philosophers find very hard to understand. Our assertion may be supported by a medical observation. There is a good man living among us who, after a severe apoplectic stroke, utters nouns but has completely forgotten verbs. Even the verbs which are genera of all the others—as *sum* is of being, to which are reduced all essences, which is as much as to say all metaphysical things; *sto* of rest and *eo* of motion, to which are reduced all physical things; *do, dico* and *facio,* to which are reduced all matters of action, whether moral, economic or civil—these verbs must have begun as imperatives. For in the state of the families, which was extremely poor in language, the fathers alone must have spoken and given commands to their children and *famuli,* who, under the terrors of patriarchal rule, as we shall soon see, must have executed the commands in silence and with blind obsequiousness. These imperatives are all monosyllables, as they have remained: *es, sta, i, da, dic, fac,* "be," "stand," "go," "give," "say," "make."

454 This [theory of the] genesis of languages is in conformity with the principles of universal nature, by which the elements of all things, out of which they are composed and into which they are bound to be resolved, are indivisible; and also with the principles of human nature in particular, according to the axiom [231] that "children, even in the present copiousness of language into which they are born, and in spite of the extreme flexibility of the fibers of their organs for articulating words, begin with monosyllables." So much the more must we deem the first men of the nations to have done so, for their organs were extremely obdurate, and they had not yet heard a human voice. [Our theory] gives us, moreover, the order in which the parts of speech arose, and consequently the natural causes of syntax.

455 All this seems more reasonable than what Julius Caesar Scaliger and Francisco Sanchez have said with regard to the Latin language, reasoning from the principles of Aristotle, as if the peoples that invented the languages must first have gone to school to him!

[CHAPTER V]

COROLLARIES CONCERNING THE ORIGINS OF POETIC STYLE, EPISODE, INVERSION, RHYTHM, SONG AND VERSE

456   In this way the nations formed the poetic language, composed of divine and heroic characters, later expressed in vulgar speech, and finally written in vulgar characters. It was born entirely of poverty of language and need of expression. This is proved by the first lights of poetic style, which are vivid representations, images, similes, comparisons, metaphors, circumlocutions, phrases explaining things by their natural properties, descriptions gathered from their minuter or their more sensible effects, and, finally, their striking and even their trifling collateral circumstances.

457   Episodes were born of the grossness of the heroic minds, unable to confine themselves to those essential features of things that were to the purpose in hand, as we see to be naturally the case with the feeble-minded and above all with women.

458   Inversions arose from the difficulty of completing statements with their verbs, which, as we have seen, were the last part of speech to be invented. Thus the Greeks, who were more ingenious, used fewer inversions than the Latins, and the Latins fewer than the Germans.

459   Prose rhythm was understood late by the writers—in Greek by Gorgias of Leontini, and in Latin by Cicero—because earlier (according to Cicero himself) they had given a rhythmic character to their orations by using certain poetic measures. This fact will presently be very useful when we discuss the origins of song and verse.

460   From all this it appears to have been demonstrated that, by a necessity of human nature, poetic style arose before prose style; just as, by the same necessity, the fables, or imaginative universals, arose before the rational or philosophic universals which were formed through the medium of prose speech. For after the poets had formed poetic speech by associating particular ideas, as we have fully shown, the peoples went on to form prose speech by contracting into a single word, as into a genus, the parts which poetic speech had associated. Take for example the poetic phrase, "the blood boils in my heart," based on a property natural, eternal and common to all mankind. They took the blood, the boiling and the heart, and made of them a single word, as it were a genus, called in Greek *stomachos,* in Latin *ira* and in Italian *collera.* Following the same pattern, hieroglyphics and heroic letters were reduced to a few vulgar letters, as genera assimilating innumerable diverse articulate sounds; a feat requiring con-

ummate genius. By means of these vulgar genera, both of words and of letters,
he minds of the peoples grew quicker and developed powers of abstraction,
nd the way was thus prepared for the coming of the philosophers who formed
ntelligible genera. What has here been discussed is a small portion of the his-
ory of ideas. To such an extent has it been necessary, in seeking the origins of
etters, to deal in the same breath with those of languages!

461   Concerning song and verse we have proposed the axiom [228] that
ince men are shown to have been originally mute, they must have uttered
vowel sounds by singing, as mutes do; and later, like stammerers, they must
have uttered articulate consonantal sounds, still by singing. This first singing of
the peoples has left a great testimony in the diphthongs surviving in the languages. These must originally have been much more numerous, as the Greeks
and the French, who passed prematurely from the poetic to the vulgar age, have
left us a great many of them, as observed in the Axioms [159]. The reason for
this is that the vowels are easy to form and the consonants difficult, and, as has
been shown, the first dull-witted men were moved to utterance only by very
violent passions, which are naturally expressed in a very loud voice. And nature
brings it about that when man greatly raises his voice, he breaks into diphthongs
and song, as noted in the Axioms [229]. Thus, as shown a little above [449],
the first Greeks, in the time of their gods, formed the first spondaic heroic verse
with the diphthong *pai,* employing twice as many vowels as consonants.

462   Again, this first song of the peoples sprang naturally from the difficulty of the first utterances, which can be demonstrated both from cause and
from effect. From cause, since in these men the fibers of the organ for articulating
sounds were quite hard, and there were very few sounds they could make; as
on the other hand children, with very flexible fibers, born into our present plenty
of words, are observed to pronounce consonants only with the greatest difficulty
(as remarked in the Axioms [231]); and the Chinese, whose vulgar language has
no more than three hundred articulated words, which with various modifications
of pitch and tempo correspond to their one hundred and twenty thousand hieroglyphs, also speak by singing. And from effect, by the contraction of words, of
which innumerable examples are observed in Italian poetry (in our Origins of
the Latin Language we set forth a great number which must have begun short
and been lengthened in the course of time); and on the other hand by redundancies, because stutterers use a syllable which they can more readily utter singing in such a way as to compensate for those they find it difficult to pronounce
(as set forth in the Axioms [228]). Thus there was among us in my time an
excellent tenor with this speech defect, who, when he stumbled over a word,
would break into the sweetest song and so pronounce it. Certainly the Arabs
begin almost all their words with *al-;* and it is said the Huns were so called because they began all theirs with *hun-.* Finally, that languages began with song
is shown by what we have just said [459]: that prior to Gorgias and Cicero the
Greek and Latin prose writers used certain almost poetic rhythms, as in the

returned barbarian times the Fathers of the Roman Church did (and, it will be found, those of the Greek Church did too), so that their prose seems made for chanting.

463   The first verse must have sprung up (as we have recently shown it did) conformably to the language and time of the heroes; that is, it was heroic verse, the grandest of all, and the proper verse for heroic poetry; and it was born of the most violent passions of fear and joy, for heroic poetry has to do only with extremely perturbed passions. However, its spondaic origin was not from the great fear of the Python, as vulgar tradition relates; for such perturbation rather quickens ideas and words than retards them; whence in Latin *festinans* and *solicitus* connote fear. No, it was because of the slowness of mind and stiffness of tongue of the founders of the nations that heroic verse was born spondaic, as we have shown; and from that origin it retains the characteristic of never admitting anything but a spondee in the last foot. Later, as minds and tongues became quicker, the dactyl was introduced. Then, as both became still more practiced, there arose the iamb, the "quick" foot, as Horace calls it. Two axioms [232, 233] have been set forth with regard to these origins. Finally, when mind and tongue had reached the highest degree of celerity, there developed prose, which, as we recently saw, speaks as it were in intelligible genera. Iambic verse comes so near to prose that prose writers have often fallen into it inadvertently. Thus song went on growing swifter in its verse forms in proportion as ideas and tongues became quicker among the nations, as we have also noted in the Axioms [238, 239].

464   This philosophy is confirmed by history, which tells us of nothing more ancient than oracles and sybils, as set forth in the Axioms [381]. Thus, to signify that a thing was very old, there was the saying, "That is older than the sybil"; and the sybils, of whom a good dozen have come down to us, were scattered among all the first nations. There is a vulgar tradition to the effect that the sybils sang in heroic verse, and the oracles of all nations also gave their responses in heroic verse. For that reason the Greeks called this verse Pythian from their famous oracle of Pythian Apollo, who must have been so called from his slaying of the serpent called Python, which, in the account related above gave rise to the first spondaic verse. By the Latins heroic verse was called Saturnian, as Festus attests. It must have sprung up in Italy in the age of Saturn, which corresponds to the Golden Age of the Greeks, in which Apollo, like the other gods, had dealings on earth with men. And Ennius, again according to Festus, says that in this verse the fauns of Italy delivered their prophecies or oracles (which certainly among the Greeks, as we have said, were delivered in hexameters). But later the term Saturnian verses was applied to iambic senarii, perhaps because by then it was as natural to speak in these Saturnian iambic verses as it had previously been to speak in Saturnian heroic verses.

465   Hebraists today are divided in their opinions upon the question whether Hebrew poetry is metrical or merely rhythmical. However, Josephus,

Philo, Origen and Eusebius stand as favoring meter, and (what is most to our present purpose) St. Jerome holds that the Book of Job, which is older than the books of Moses, was composed in heroic verse from the beginning of the third chapter to the end of the forty-second.

466 The Arabs, ignorant of letters, as related by the anonymous author [Thomas Baker] of [a book on] the uncertainty of the sciences [442], preserved their language by memorizing their poems until they overran the eastern provinces of the Greek empire.

467 The Egyptians inscribed memorials of their dead in verse on columns called syringes from *sir,* which means song; whence the name of the Siren, a deity beyond doubt celebrated for her singing. Ovid says the nymph Syrinx was equally celebrated for beauty and for song. By the same token, the Syrians and Assyrians, whose names are likewise derived from *sir,* must have spoken at first in verse.

468 Certainly the founders of Greek humanity were the theological poets, and these were heroes and sang in heroic verse.

469 We have seen that the first authors of the Latin language were the Salii, who were sacred poets, from whom we have the fragments of the Salian verses, which have an air of heroic verse and are the oldest memorials of Latin speech. The conquering ancient Romans left memorials of their triumphs in a sort of heroic verse, like the *Duello magno dirimendo, regibus subigendis* of Lucius Aemilius Regillus, and the *Fundit, fugat, prosternit maximas legiones* of Acilius Glabrio, and others. In the fragments of the Law of the Twelve Tables, the articles seem upon careful reflection to end for the most part in Adonic verses, which are the concluding portions of heroic verses. Cicero must have imitated them in his laws [*De leg.* II, 8], which begin thus: *Deos caste adeunto; Pietatem adhibento.* Whence the Roman custom, also mentioned by Cicero, whereby the children learned the Law of the Twelve Tables by singing it *tanquam necessarium carmen,* "as an indispensable song," to use his words. The Cretan children, we are told by Aelian [*Var. Hist.* II, 39], did likewise [with the laws of their country]. Certainly Cicero, famous as the discoverer of prose rhythm among the Latins, as Gorgias of Leontini had been among the Greeks (a point reflected upon above), must have shunned in his prose—prose of such weighty argument—not merely verses so sonorous, but iambic verse as well, much as the latter resembles prose; and he guarded himself against it even in his familiar correspondence. Hence the vulgar traditions concerning this kind of verse must be true: the first, according to Plato, that the laws of the Egyptians were poems of the goddess Isis; the second, according to Plutarch, that Lycurgus gave his laws to the Spartans in verse, forbidding them in one particular law to acquire knowledge of letters; the third, according to Maximus of Tyre, that Jove had given the laws to Minos in verse; the fourth and last, cited by Suidas, that Draco, who by another vulgar tradition wrote his laws in blood, proclaimed them to the Athenians in verse.

470   We return now from laws to history. Tacitus in his account of the customs of the ancient Germans relates that they preserved in verse the beginnings of their history, and Lipsius in his notes on this passage says the same of the American Indians. The example of these two nations, of which the first was known only to the Romans, and to them very late, and the second discovered but two centuries ago by our Europeans, gives us a strong argument for conjecturing the same of all other barbarous nations, both ancient and modern; and, conjecture aside, the authorities tell us that the Persians among the ancient nations, and the Chinese among those discovered in modern times, wrote their first histories in verse. And here let this important observation be made: that, if the peoples were established by laws, and if among all these peoples the laws were given in verse, and if the first things of these peoples were likewise preserved in verse, it necessarily follows that all the first peoples were poets.

471   We resume now the subject under discussion, concerning the origins of verse. According to Festus, the wars with Carthage were described in heroic verse by Naevius even before Ennius's time; and Livius Andronicus, the first Latin writer, wrote the *Romanidae,* a heroic poem containing the annals of the ancient Romans. In the returned barbarian times the Latin historians were heroic poets, like Gunther, William of Apulia and others. We have seen that the first writers in the modern languages of Europe were versifiers; and in Silesia, a province almost entirely inhabited by peasants, the people are born poets. And generally the German language preserves its heroic origins intact— even to excess—and this is the reason, though Adam Rechenberg is unaware of it, for the fact he attests, that Greek compound words can be happily rendered in German, especially in poetry. Bernegger compiled a catalog of these words, and Georg Christoph Peisker has since been at pains to extend it in his *Index . . . pro graecae et germanicae linguae analogia.* The ancient Latin language has also left us many examples of compounds formed by combining whole words; and of these compounds, as of their right, the poets have continued to make use. For it must have been a common property of all the first languages that, as has been shown, they were furnished first with nouns and only later with verbs, and so they had supplied the lack of verbs by putting nouns together. These must be the informing principles of what [G. D.] Morhofen has written in his *Unterricht von der teutschen Sprache und Poesie.* Let this stand as a proof of the opinion which we stated in the Axioms [153]: that "if the scholars of the German language apply themselves to seeking its origins by these principles they will make marvelous discoveries."

472   All that has here been reasoned out seems clearly to confute the common error of the grammarians, who say that prose speech came first and speech in verse afterward. And within the origins of poetry, as they have here been disclosed, we have found the origins of languages and letters.

[CHAPTER VI]

THE OTHER COROLLARIES ANNOUNCED AT THE BEGINNING
[OF CHAPTER IV]

I

473   Along with this first birth of characters and languages was also
born law, which the Latins called *ious* and the ancient Greeks *diaïon*, which we
explained above [398] as derived from *Dios* and meaning celestial. Thence
came the Latin phrases *sub dio* and *sub Iove*, both meaning "under the sky."
Later, as Plato says in the *Cratylus*, by refinement of speech, *diaïon* became
dikaion. For the heavens were observed as the aspect of Jove by all the gentile
nations the world over, to receive therefrom their laws in the auspices which
they considered to be his divine admonishments or commands. And this shows
that all the nations were born in the persuasion of divine providence.

474   To enumerate: (1) For the Chaldeans the sky was Jove in that they
believed they could foretell the future by the aspects and movements of the
stars. The two sciences of these matters were called astronomy and astrology,
the former dealing with the laws of the stars and the latter (in the [restricted]
sense of judicial astrology) with their language. In the Roman laws, judicial
astrologers were still called Chaldeans.

475   (2) For the Persians too the sky was Jove, for it signified for them
things hidden from men. Those who were learned in the science of these things
were called mages, and the word magic was applied to two sciences, one the
legitimate natural science of the marvelous hidden forces of nature, the other
the illicit science of the supernatural; in the latter sense a mage was a wizard.
The mages used the rod (the *lituus* of the Roman augurs) to describe the circles
of the astronomers; later the wizards made use of the rod and circles in their
witchcraft. For the Persians the sky was the temple of Jove; and Cyrus, because
this was his religion, destroyed the temples built by the Greeks.

476   (3) For the Egyptians too, Jove was the sky, for they believed that
the heavens influenced sublunar affairs and announced future events. Hence
they believed they could direct celestial influences by casting their images at the
right time, and to this day they have preserved a vulgar art of divination.

477   (4) To the Greeks Jove was likewise the sky, for they considered
as of celestial origin the theorems and mathemata we have mentioned elsewhere
[391]. These they believed to be divine or sublime things to be contemplated by

the bodily eyes and to be observed (in the sense of obeyed) as laws of Jove. From mathemata comes the term mathematicians as applied in the Roman laws to the judicial astrologers.

478   (5) As for the Romans, the verse of Ennius quoted above [450] is well known: *Aspice hoc sublime cadens, quem omnes invocant Iovem.* The pronoun *hoc* should here be taken, as we have said, as standing for *coelum.* The Romans also used the phrase *templa coeli,* as we have said, for the regions of the sky marked out by the augurs for taking the auspices. Thus the Latin *templum* came to signify any place which is free on every side and has an unobstructed prospect. Hence *extemplo,* meaning "immediately." It is with this old sense in mind that Vergil calls the sea *neptunia templa.*

479   (6) The ancient Germans, as Tacitus narrates, worshiped their gods in holy places which he calls *luci et nemora.* These must have been clearings leveled in the midst of the forest. The Church had great trouble in weaning them from this practice, as we gather from the councils of Nantes and Braga in Burchard's collection of *Decreta;* and even today traces remain of it in Lapland and Livonia.

480   (7) The Peruvian Indians, it has been learned, called their god simply "the sublime," and their open-air temples were hills up which one climbed on either of two sides by very long stairways; and all their magnificence consists in their height. Thus everywhere the magnificence of temples is measured by their disproportionate height. The pediment of temples we find in Pausanias was called *aetos,* which is very much to our purpose, for it means "eagle." The forests were cleared to afford a prospect for observing whence came the auspices of the eagles, who fly higher than all other birds. Perhaps for that reason the pediments were called *pinnae templorum,* which must later have prompted the term *pinnae murorum,* because on the confines of these first temples of the world the walls of the first cities were erected, as we shall see later. And finally in architecture what we now call the merlons or battlements were called eagles.

481   But the Hebrews worshiped the true All Highest, who is above the heavens, in the enclosure of the tabernacle; and Moses, wherever the people of God extended their conquests, gave orders that the sacred groves inclosing the *luci* that Tacitus speaks of should be burned.

482   From the foregoing we gather that the first laws everywhere were the divine laws of Jove. So ancient in origin is the usage which has come down in the languages of many Christian nations of taking heaven for God. We Italians, for example, say *voglia il cielo,* "may heaven please," and *spero al cielo,* "I hope to heaven," meaning God in both expressions. The Spanish have the same usage. The French say *bleu* for "blue," and since blue is a term of sense perception they must have meant by *bleu* the sky; and, just as the gentile nations used "sky" for Jove, the French must have used *bleu* for God in that impious oath of theirs, *moure bleu!,* "God's death!"; and they still say *parbleu!,*

"by God!" And this may serve as an example of the Mental Dictionary proposed in the Axioms [162], which has been discussed above.

II

483 The need for certainty of ownership was a large part of the necessity for the invention of characters and names in the native sense of houses branching into many families, which, with perfect propriety, were called *gentes*. Thus [Hermes or] Mercury Trismegistus, a poetic character of the first founders of the Egyptians, as we have shown, was their inventor of laws and letters. From this Mercury, who was likewise held to be the god of trade, the Italians—by a wonderful parallel in thought and expression lasting to our own time—took the verb *mercare*, "to mark," in the sense of branding with letters or insignia the cattle or other merchandise they have for sale, to distinguish and identify the owners.

III

484 Such are the first origins of family coats-of-arms and hence of medals and coins. From these devices, employed first for private and later for public needs, came the learned emblems for pleasure's sake. These latter, by a sort of divination [on the part of the scholars], were called heroic; but they have to be explained by mottoes, for their meanings are [now merely] analogical; whereas the natural heroic emblems were such from lack of mottoes, and spoke forth in their very muteness. Hence they were in their own right the best emblems, for they carried their meaning in themselves. For example, three ears of grain, or three scythe-swinging motions, naturally signified three years. And so it came about that names and characters were interchangeable, and names and natures came to mean the same thing, as we have said above.

485 Now, beginning all over again with family arms, in the returned barbarian times the nations again became mute in vulgar speech. For this reason no notice has come down to us of the Spanish, French, Italian or other languages of those times, and Greek and Latin were known only by the priests, so that among the French *clerc* was used in the sense of a literate man, and on the other hand the Italians, as we see from a fine passage in Dante, used *laico*, "layman," for a man ignorant of letters. Indeed even among the clergy ignorance was so dense that we read documents signed by bishops with the simple sign of the cross because they did not know how to write their own names. And even the learned prelates could write but little, as is shown by the diligent Father Mabillon in his work *De re diplomatica*, with its copperplate facsimiles of the signatures of bishops and archbishops to the acts of the councils of those barbarous days. They can be seen to have been written with letters more misshapen and clumsy than those of the most untaught simpleton of today. Yet for the most part the chancellors of the realms of Europe were such prelates, as was the case with the three Chancellor Archbishops of the Empire, one each for German, French and Italian; and from these, because of the way they had of writing their letters with such irregular shapes, must have come the phrase "chancellor's script." Because of this scarcity of literate men an English law was decreed according to which a criminal under sentence of death who knew his letters would be spared as "excelling in art" [*excellens in arte non debet mori*]. Perhaps from this the term "lettered" came later to signify "learned."

486   Because of this same scarcity of men who could write, we do not find a single wall in ancient houses without some device carved upon it. Moreover, the barbarous Latins applied the term *terrae presa* to a farm with its boundaries, and the Italians called it *podere* with the same idea the Latins had in calling it *praedium,* for the lands brought under cultivation were the first booty [prey] of the world. In the Law of the Twelve Tables estates were called *mancipia,* and those under real-estate bond (principally to the public treasury) were called *praedes* or *mancipes,* and the so-called real servitudes were referred to as *iura praediorum.* The Spanish moreover used the word *prenda* for bold enterprises, because the first bold enterprises of the world were the taming and cultivation of the land, which we shall find to have been the greatest of all the labors of Hercules. Again, a coat-of-arms was called by the Italians an ensign in the sense of a thing signifying, whence the Italian verb *insegnare,* "to teach." They also call it *divisa,* "device," because the ensigns were used as signs of the first division of the fields, which had previously been used in common by all mankind. The originally real terms [boundary posts] of these fields later became the vocal terms of the scholastics; that is, significant words serving as terms of propositions. Among the American Indians, as we have seen above, the hieroglyphs for distinguishing their families have a similar use as terms.

487   The conclusion to be drawn from the foregoing is that in the time of mute nations the great need answered by ensigns was that for certainty of ownership. Later they became public ensigns in time of peace, and from these were derived the medals, which, with the introduction of warfare, were found suitable for military insignia. The latter have their primary use as hieroglyphs, inasmuch as wars are waged for the most part between nations differing in speech and hence mute in relation to each other. Striking confirmation of what has been so far reasoned out is to be found in the example of the eagle on the scepter; for this symbol was used alike by the Egyptians, the Etruscans, the Romans and the English, who still use it as an ornament of their royal arms. This by a uniformity of ideas, for in all these nations, divided though they are by immense tracts of land and sea, the symbol was meant to signify that the realms had their origins from the first divine kingdoms of Jove by virtue of his auspices. Finally, when commerce by means of coined money was introduced, it was found that these medals were suitable for use as coins, which indeed were for that reason called *monetae* from *monendo* by the Latins, just as *insegnare* came from *insegna* among the Italians. In like fashion from the Greek *nomos* came *nomisma,* as Aristotle tells us; and perhaps from it too came the

Latin *numus,* which the best authorities write thus with one *m.* In French too law is called *loi,* and the metal for coins, *aloi.* These terms can have had no other origin than the law or right signified by the hieroglyph, which is precisely the use of medals. All of which is strikingly confirmed by the following names of coins: ducat from *ducendo,* which is said of captains; soldo, whence soldier; and scudo, a defensive arm, which originally meant the escutcheon or field of family arms, which in the beginning was the tilled land of each father in the time of the families, as will be shown later. This will shed light on the many ancient medals on which we find an altar, a *lituus* (the augur's rod for taking the auspices, as noted above), or a tripod (from which the oracle spoke, as is indicated by the phrase *dictum ex tripode* for the word of the oracle).

488   To this sort of medals must have belonged the wings which the Greeks in their fables attached to all the physical objects signifying the heroic constitutions based on the auspices. Thus Idanthyrsus, among the real hieroglyphs with which he answered Darius, sent a bird. And the Roman patricians in all their heroic contests with the plebs (as clearly appears in Roman history) for the preservation of their heroic rights maintained as law that the auspices were theirs. Similarly in the returned barbarism we find noble arms bearing plumed helmets, and in the West Indies only the nobles are adorned with feathers.

IV

489   The name *Ious,* "Jove," when contracted to *ius,* must have meant first of all the fat of the victims owed to Jove, as we have said above. Similarly in the returned barbarism the term canon was applied both to ecclesiastical law and to the payment made by the fief-holder to his immediate master; perhaps because the first fiefs were introduced by the ecclesiastics, who, not being able to cultivate them themselves, gave the fields of the Church to others to till. These two observations are corroborated by the two above mentioned: the Greek usage by which *nomos* means law and *nomisma* means coin, and the French usage by which *loi* and *aloi* have the same meanings. Precisely in the same way that was called *Ious optimus,* for "Jove most strong," which by the force of the thunderbolt gave a beginning to divine authority in its primary sense, which was that of ownership, as we have said above, for all things were of Jove.

490   That truth of rational metaphysics concerning the omnipresence of God, which had been taken in the false sense of poetic metaphysics: . . . *Iovis omnia plena,* "all things are full of Jove," conferred human authority on those giants who had occupied the first empty lands of the world, in the same sense of ownership. In Roman law this was certainly called *ius optimum,* but its original meaning was quite different from that in which it was used in later times. For it had at first the sense defined by Cicero in a golden passage in his orations: "ownership of real estate subject to no encumbrance private or public."

This *ius* was called *optimum* in the same sense of "strongest," as not having been weakened by any extraneous encumbrance. For right was reckoned by strength in the first times of the world, as we shall see. This ownership must have belonged to the fathers in the family state, and was consequently the natural ownership which had to precede the civil. As cities were formed by uniting families based on this best ownership (called in Greek *dikaion ariston*), they were originally aristocratic, as we shall see later. Springing from the same origin among the Latins, the so-called commonwealths of the optimates were also called commonwealths of the few, because they were made up of those "few whom just Jupiter loved," *pauci quos aequus amavit Iupiter.* In their heroic contests with the plebs, the heroes maintained their heroic constitutions by means of the divine auspices. In mute times they signified their constitutions by the bird of Idanthyrsus, by the wings of the Greek fables; and finally in the articulate language of the Roman patricians, by declaring "the auspices are ours."

491 Jove with his bolts, from which the most important auspices were drawn, had struck down the first giants and driven them under the earth to live in the caves of the mountains. By striking them down in this fashion he had given them the opportunity of becoming lords of the fields of those lands where they found themselves settled in hiding, and thereby they became the lords in the first commonwealths; and because of this ownership, [when they approved or authorized anything] each of them was said to become its *fundus* in the sense of its *auctor.* From their private authority within the family came, with the union of the families, as we shall see, the civil or public authority of their ruling heroic senates, as set forth in the medal (of which there are so many examples among those of the Greek commonwealths reproduced in Goltz) depicting three human thighs united in the center with the soles of the feet on the circumference. This signifies the ownership of the fields of each region or territory or district of each commonwealth. This is now called eminent domain and is signified by the hieroglyph of the pome which today surmounts the crowns of civil powers, as will be set forth later. The [fact that the legs in the medal are] three [in number] lends particular strength to this interpretation, as the Greeks were accustomed to express the superlative by the number three, as the French now say *très* for "very." By the same figure of speech, Jove's thunderbolt was called three-furrowed because it furrowed the air most forcefully. (Thus the idea of furrowing was perhaps first applied to air, then earth and finally water.) Similarly Neptune's trident was so called because, as we shall see, it was a most powerful hook for biting or grappling ships; and Cerberus was called three-throated as having an enormous gullet.

492 What we have said here of family arms is to be preferred to our discussion of their origins in the first edition of this work, though that is the third passage in that edition on whose account we do not regret its publication.

V

493 It follows from all this that Grotius, Selden and Pufendorf, the three princes of the natural law of nations, should have begun their expositions from the letters and laws which Hermes Trismegistus devised for the Egyptians, from the characters and names of the Greeks, and from the names which signify both *gentes* and laws to the Romans. And they should have gone on to unfold it by a well-informed interpretation of the hieroglyphs and fables as the medals of the times in which the gentile nations were founded; and thus to ascertain their customs by a metaphysical criticism of the founders of the nations, which should have given the first light to the philological criticism of their writers, who did not come forth until more than a thousand years after the nations had been founded.

[CHAPTER VII]

FINAL COROLLARIES CONCERNING THE LOGIC OF THE LEARNED

I

494 The results so far reached by the aid of this poetic logic concerning the origins of languages do justice to their first creators. They were rightly regarded as sages in all subsequent times because they gave natural and proper names to things, so that, as we saw above, among the Greeks and Latins name and nature meant the same thing.

II

495 The first founders of humanity applied themselves to a sensory topics, by which they brought together those properties or qualities or relations of individuals and species which were so to speak concrete, and from these created their poetic genera.

III

496 So that we may truly say that the first age of the world occupied itself with the primary operation of the human mind.

IV

497 And first it began to hew out topics, which is an art of regulating well the primary operation of our mind by noting the commonplaces that must all be run over in order to know all there is in a thing that one desires to know well, that is, completely.

V

498 Providence gave good guidance to human affairs when it aroused human minds first to topics rather than to criticism, for acquaintance with things must come before judgment of them. Topics has the function of making minds inventive, as criticism has that of making them exact. And in those first times all things necessary to human life had to be invented, and invention is the property of genius. In fact, whoever gives the matter some thought will observe that not only the necessaries of life but the useful, comfortable, pleasing and even luxurious and superfluous, had already been invented in Greece before the advent of the philosophers, as we shall show later when we speak of the age of Homer. On this point we have set forth an axiom above [215]: namely, that "children are extraordinarily gifted in imitation," that "poetry is nothing but imitation," and that "the arts are only imitations of nature and consequently in a certain sense real poetry." Thus the first peoples, who were the children of the human race, founded first the world of the arts; then the philosophers, who came a long time afterwards and so may be regarded as the old men of the nations, founded the world of the sciences, thereby making humanity complete.

VI

499 This history of human ideas is strikingly confirmed by the history of philosophy itself. For the first kind of crude philosophy used by men was *autopsia* or the evidence of the senses. It was later made use of by Epicurus, for he, as a philosopher of the senses, was satisfied with the mere exhibition of things to the evidence of the senses. And the senses of the first poetic nations were extremely lively, as we have seen in our account of the origins of poetry. Then came Aesop, or the moral philosophers whom we would call vulgar. (As we have noted above, Aesop preceded the Seven Sages of Greece.) Aesop taught by example and, since he lived in what was still the poetic age, he took his examples from fictitious similitudes. (The good Menenius Agrippa used one such to reduce the rebellious Roman plebs to obedience.) An example of this sort, or better still a true one, is even now more persuasive to the ignorant crowd than the most impeccable reasoning from maxims. After Aesop came Socrates, who introduced dialectic, employing induction of several certain things related to the doubtful thing in question. Before Socrates, medicine, by induction of observations, had given us Hippocrates, prince of all doctors both in merit and in precedence, who earned the immortal eulogy: "He deceives no one nor is deceived by any" (*Nec fallit quenquam, nec falsus ab ullo est*). Mathematics by the unitive [inductive] method called synthetic had made, in Plato's time, its greatest progress in the Italian school of Pythagoras, as we can see from the *Timaeus*. Thus by virtue of this unitive method, Athens at the time of Socrates and Plato was resplendent in all the arts for which human genius can be admired—poetry, eloquence and history as well as music, casting in bronze, painting, sculpture and architecture. Then came Aristotle and Zeno. The former taught the syllogism, a method which displays the universals in their particulars rather than putting together the particulars to form universals. The latter taught the sorites, which, like the method of modern philosophers, makes minds subtle but not sharp. Neither of them yielded anything else of note to the advantage of the human race. Hence with great reason Bacon, great alike as philosopher and statesman, proposes, commends and illustrates the inductive method in his [*Novum*] *Organum,* and is still followed by the English with great profit in experimental philosophy.

VII

500   This history of human ideas clearly convicts of their common error all those who, under the influence of the mistaken popular belief in the superlative wisdom of the ancients, have held that Minos, the first lawgiver of the gentile nations, Theseus at Athens, Lycurgus at Sparta, and Romulus and other kings at Rome, established universal laws. For the most ancient laws, we observe, were conceived as commanding or forbidding one individual alone; only later were they given general application (so incapable of universals were the first peoples!); and furthermore they were not conceived at all before the acts occurred that made them necessary. The law of Tullus Hostilius in the case against Horatius is nothing else but the penalty decreed by the duumvirs, appointed for that purpose by the king, against the illustrious culprit. Livy calls it *lex horrendi carminis;* it is one of the laws which Draco wrote in blood, and sacred history calls them *leges sanguinis.* Livy's observation that the king did not wish to proclaim the law, in order not to be responsible for such a harsh and unpopular verdict, is quite ridiculous. For the king himself prescribed the formula of condemnation to the duumvirs, so that the latter could not have absolved Horatius even had they found him innocent. Livy is here not at all clear, for he did not understand that in the heroic senates, which were aristocratic as we shall see, the kings had no other power than that of creating duumvirs to act as commissioners to adjudicate public suits, and that the peoples of the heroic cities consisted of nobles only, to whom the condemned could appeal.

501   To return now to the point, that law of Tullus is in fact one of the so-called examples, in the sense of exemplary punishments, which must have been the first examples used by human reason. (This agrees with what we learned from Aristotle above in the Axioms [269]: that "in the heroic commonwealths there were no laws concerning private wrongs or injuries.") Thus first came real examples and later the reasoned ones of logic and rhetoric. But when intelligible universals had come to be understood, that essential property of law—that it must be universal—was recognized, and the maxim of jurisprudence was established that we must judge by the laws, not by examples (*legibus, non exemplis, est iudicandum*).

[SECTION III]

[POETIC MORALS]

[CHAPTER I]

POETIC MORALS AND THE ORIGINS OF THE VULGAR VIRTUES TAUGHT BY RELIGION THROUGH THE INSTITUTION OF MATRIMONY

502   The metaphysics of the philosophers, by means of the idea of God, fulfills its first task, that of clarifying the human mind, which needs logic so that with clear and distinct ideas it may form its conclusions, and descend therewith to cleanse the heart of man with morality. Just so the metaphysics of the poet giants, who had warred against heaven in their atheism, conquered them by the terror of Jove, whom they knew as the wielder of the thunderbolt. And it humbled not only their bodies but their minds as well, by creating in them this frightful idea of Jove. (The idea was of course not formed by reasoning, for they were not yet capable of that, but by the senses, which, however false in the matter, were true enough in form—which was the logic conformable to such natures as theirs.) This idea, by making them god-fearing, was the source of their poetic morality. From this nature of human things arose the eternal property that minds to make good use of the knowledge of God must humble themselves, just as on the other hand arrogance will lead them to atheism, for atheists become giants in spirit, ready to say with Horace: *Caelum ipsum petimus stultitia,* "heaven itself we assail in our folly."

503   Such god-fearing giants Plato certainly recognizes as represented by the Polyphemus of Homer. And we find support in what Homer himself tells of this same giant, in the passage where he makes him say that an augur who had lived at one time among the Cyclopes, had predicted the woes which he later suffered at the hands of Ulysses; for augurs certainly cannot live among atheists. Thus poetic morality began with piety, which was ordained by providence to found the nations, for among them all piety is proverbially held to be the mother of all the moral, economic and civil virtues. Religion alone has the power to make us practice virtue, as philosophy is fit rather for discussing it. And piety sprang from religion, which properly defined is the fear of divinity.

The heroic origin of the word religion was preserved among the Latins by those who derived it from *religando,* binding, with reference to those fetters with which Tityus and Prometheus were bound on the mountain crags to have their hearts and entrails devoured by the eagle, that is, by the frightful religion of the auspices of Jove. Hence came the eternal property among all nations, that piety is instilled in children by the fear of some divinity.

504   Moral virtue began, as it must, with effort. For the giants, confined under the mountains by the frightful religion of the thunderbolts, learned to restrain their bestial habit of wandering wild through the great forest of the earth, and acquired the contrary custom of remaining hidden and settled in their fields. Hence they later became the founders of the nations and the lords of the first commonwealths, as we have indicated above and as we shall set forth more fully further on. This has been preserved by vulgar tradition as one of the great benefits conferred on the human race by Heaven when it reigned on earth through the religion of the auspices. And hence came Jove's title of stayer or stablisher, as we have said above. And with this effort likewise the virtue of moderation began to show itself among them, restraining their bestial lust from finding its satisfaction in the sight of heaven, of which they had a mortal terror. So it came about that each of them would drag one woman into his cave and would keep her there in perpetual company for the duration of their lives. Thus the act of human love was performed under cover, in hiding, that is to say, in shame; and they began to feel that sense of shame which Socrates described as the color of virtue. And this, after religion, is the second bond that keeps nations united, even as shamelessness and impiety destroy them.

505   Such was the origin of marriage, which is a chaste carnal union consummated under the fear of some divinity. We made this the second principle of our Science, with its source in our first principle, which is divine providence. It arose accompanied by three solemnities.

506   The first of these solemnities was the auspices of Jove, taken from the thunderbolts by which the giants were induced to observe them. From this *sors* or lot [signified by the auspices], marriage was defined among the Romans as *omnis vitae consortium,* "a lifelong sharing of lot," and the husband and wife were called *consortes* or "lot-sharers." And to this day Italian girls when they marry are said to take up their lot, *prender sorte.* In this determinate way and in this first time of the world arose the law of nations that the wife follows the public religion of her husband. For husbands shared their first human ideas with their wives, beginning with the idea of a divinity of theirs which compelled them to drag their women into their caves; and thus even this vulgar metaphysics began to know the human mind in God. And from this first point of all human things gentile men began to praise the gods, in the ancient Roman legal sense of citing or calling them by name; whence the phrase *laudare auctores,* bidding men to cite the gods as authors of whatever they themselves did. Such must have been the praises which men owed to the gods.

507　From this most ancient origin of marriage came the custom by which women enter the families and houses of the men they marry. This natural custom of the gentile nations was preserved by the Romans, among whom women were regarded as daughters of their husbands and sisters of their children. Thus not merely must marriage have been from the beginning a union with one woman only, as it continued to be among the Romans (a custom Tacitus admires in the ancient Germans, who like the Romans kept intact the institutional origins of their nations, and who give us ground for conjecturing similar beginnings for all others), but it must also have been a union to last for life, as indeed remained the custom among a great many peoples. Hence among the Romans marriage was defined, with this property in view, as *individua vitae consuetudo,* "unbroken companionship of life" [*Inst.* 1.9.1]; and divorce was introduced very late among them.

508　Proceeding from the auspices thus taken from the thunderbolts of Jove, fabulous Greek history describes Hercules (a [poetic] character of founders of nations, as we saw above and as we shall observe more closely) as born of Alcmena by a thunderbolt of Jove. Another great hero of Greece is Bacchus, born of thunderstruck Semele. This was the first reason for which the heroes called themselves sons of Jove; the assertion was a truth of the senses for them, persuaded as they were that all things were the work of the gods, as we have reasoned above. And this is the meaning of that passage of Roman history in which, to the patricians who said in the heroic contests that the auspices were theirs, the plebs replied that the fathers of whom Romulus had composed the senate, and from whom the patricians traced their descent, *non esse caelo demissos,* "were not descended from heaven"; for if this does not mean that the fathers were not heroes, it is hard to see how the reply is appropriate. Hence, to signify that *connubium* or the right to contract solemn nuptials, whose chief solemnity was the auspices of Jove, was the prerogative of the heroes, they represented noble Love as winged and blindfolded in token of his modesty, and called him *Eros,* a name similar to *heros,* "hero," which was their own. And they created a winged Hymen too, the son of Urania, whose name is from *ouranos,* "heaven," and signifies "she who contemplates the heavens" to take thence the auspices. Urania must have been the first of the Muses; she was defined by Homer, as we have noted above, as "the science of good and evil"; and she too, like the rest, was conceived as winged because she belonged to the heroes, as we have set forth above. We have also explained above the historic sense of the saying about her: *A Iove principium musae.* She and the other Muses were held to be daughters of Jove (for religion gave birth to all the arts of humanity, of which Apollo, held to be principally the god of divination, is the presiding deity), and they "sing" in that sense of *canere* and *cantare* which means "foretell" to the Latins.

509　The second solemnity is the requirement that the women be veiled in token of that sense of shame that gave rise to the first marriages in the world. This custom has been preserved by all nations; among the Latins it is reflected in the very name "nuptials," for *nuptiae* is from *nubendo,* which means "to cover." And since the returned barbarian times maidens have been called virgins *in capillo,* "in [uncovered] hair," in distinction from married women who go about veiled.

510   The third solemnity—also preserved by the Romans—was a certain show of force in taking a wife, recalling the real violence with which the giants dragged the first wives into their caves. And by analogy with the first lands which the giants had occupied by taking physical possession of them, properly wedded wives were said to be *manucaptae,* "taken by force."

511   Out of solemnized marriages the theological poets fashioned another divine character, second to that of Jove; namely, Juno, the second divinity of the so-called *gentes maiores.* She is both wife and sister of Jove, because the first lawful or solemn marriages (called lawful from the solemnity of the auspices of Jove) must have taken place between brothers and sisters. She is queen of gods and men because the kingdoms were afterwards born of these legitimate marriages. And she is fully clothed, as we observe in statues and medals, to signify modesty.

512   The heroic Venus too, called *pronuba* in her character of patron goddess of solemn marriage, covers her private parts with the girdle, which effeminate poets later embroidered with all the incentives to lust. But later, when the austere history of the auspices had become corrupt, Venus was believed to have lain with men, even as Jove with women, and to have conceived Aeneas by Anchises, for Aeneas was born under the auspices of this Venus. And to this Venus are attributed the swans—shared by her with Apollo—who sing in that sense of *canere* or *cantare* which means *divinari,* "to foretell." Taking the shape of one of these swans Jove lies with Leda, signifying that under the auspices of Jove Leda conceives the egg-born Castor, Pollux and Helen.

513   Juno is called *jugalis,* "of the yoke," with reference to the yoke of solemn matrimony for which it was called *conjugium* and the married pair *conjuges.* She is also known as Lucina, who brings the offspring into the light; not natural light, for that is shared by the offspring of slaves, but the civil light by reason of which the nobles are called illustrious. And she is jealous with a political jealousy, that from which the Romans down to the 309th year of Rome excluded the plebs from *connubium* or lawful marriage. By the Greeks however she was called Hera, whence the name the heroes gave themselves, for they were born of solemn nuptials, of which Juno was the goddess, and hence generated in noble love (which is the meaning of Eros), which was identical with Hymen. And the heroes must have been so called in the sense of "lords of the families" in distinction from the *famuli,* who as we shall see were in effect slaves. *Heri* had this same meaning in Latin, whence *hereditas* for "inheritance," for which the native Latin word had been *familia.* With such an origin, *hereditas* must have meant a despotic sovereignty, and by the law of the Twelve Tables there was reserved to the family fathers a sovereign power of testamentary disposition, in the article [5.3]: *Uti paterfamilias super pecunia tutelave suae rei legassit, ita ius esto,* "As the family father has disposed concerning his property and the guardianship of his estate, so let it be binding." The disposing was generally called *legare,* which is a prerogative of sovereigns; thus the heir becomes a "legate" [legatee] who in inheriting represents the defunct paterfamilias, and the children no less than the slaves were included in the words *rei suae* and *pecunia.* All of which proves only too conclusively the monarchic power that the fathers had had over their families in the state of nature. This they were bound to retain—and we shall see later that they did in fact retain it—in the state of the heroic cities. These must in origin have been aristocratic commonwealths, that is, commonwealths of lords, in origin, for the fathers still retained their power even in the popular commonwealths. All these matters will later be discussed at length.

514   The goddess Juno imposes great labors on the Theban, that is the Greek, Hercules. (For every ancient gentile nation had a Hercules as its founder, as we have said above in the Axioms [196].) This signifies that piety and marriage form the school wherein are learned the first rudiments of all the great virtues. And Hercules, with the favor of Jove under whose auspices he was begotten, surmounts all the difficulties. He was therefore called Heracles, that is *Heras kleos,* the glory of [Hera or] Juno. And if glory be properly esteemed, as Cicero defines it, as "widespread fame for meritorious acts on behalf of the human race," how great a glory must it have been for the Herculeses to have founded the nations by their labors! But when these severe significations had been obscured by time and customs had become effeminate, Juno's sterility was taken as natural and she was held to be jealous only of an adulterous Jove. Hercules was then made a bastard son of Jove, who by Jove's favor and in despite of Juno had carried out all his labors. Thus he became not Juno's glory but her complete disgrace (by a[n interpretation of his] name quite contrary to the facts), and Juno was made a mortal enemy of virtue. [Originally] the hieroglyph or fable of Juno hanging in the air with a rope around her neck and her hands tied by another rope and with two heavy stones tied to her feet, had signified the sanctity of marriage. (Juno was in the air to signify the auspices essential to solemn nuptials, and for the same reason Iris was made her handmaiden and the peacock with its rainbow tail was assigned to her. She had a rope about her neck to recall the violence used by the giants on the first wives. Her hands were bound in token of the subjection of wives to their husbands, later represented among all nations by the more refined symbol of the wedding ring. The heavy stones tied to her feet denoted the stability of marriage, for which Vergil calls solemn matrimony *conjugium stabile.*) But now this fable was taken as representing a cruel punishment inflicted by an adulterous Jove, and, with the unworthy interpretations bestowed upon it by later times with corrupted customs, it has greatly exercised the mythologists ever since.

515   For these very reasons Plato interpreted the Greek fables as Manetho

had the Egyptian hieroglyphs, observing on the one hand the incongruity of gods having such customs, and on the other the congruity [of the fables] with his own ideas. Into the fable of Jove he intruded the idea of his ether which flows and penetrates everywhere, on the strength of the phrase "all things are full of Jove" (*Iovis omnia plena*), as we have said above. But the Jove of the theological poets dwelt no higher than the mountains and the region of the air in which lightning is generated. Into the fable of Juno he intruded the idea of breathable air; but Juno has no offspring by Jove, whereas ether and air produce everything. (So far were the theological poets from understanding by this fable that truth of physics which teaches that the universe is filled with ether, or that truth of metaphysics which demonstrates the omnipresence attributed to God by the natural theologians!) Above poetic heroism Plato raised his own philosophic heroism, placing the hero above man as well as beast; for the beast is the slave of his passions, and man, in the middle of the scale, struggles with his passions, while the hero at will commands his passions; and thus the heroic nature is midway between the human and the divine. And Plato held that the noble Love of the poets (called Eros from the same root as *heros,* "hero") was fittingly imagined as winged and blindfolded, and plebeian Love as without wings or blindfold, to set forth the two loves, divine and bestial; the one blind to the things of the senses, the other intent upon them; the one rising on wings to the contemplation of intelligible things, the other, for lack of wings, falling back upon sensible things. Ganymede, borne off to heaven by an eagle of Jove, and thus signifying to the austere poets the contemplator of Jove's auspices, became in corrupt times an ignoble pleasure of Jove; but Plato by a fine conceit took him for the metaphysical contemplative, who through contemplation of supreme being by the method he calls unitive has achieved union with Jove.

516   In this way, piety and religion made the first men naturally (1) prudent, by taking counsel from the auspices of Jove; (2) just both in that first justice toward Jove (who, as we have seen, gave his name to the just) and in that toward men, by not meddling in one another's affairs, as Polyphemus tells Ulysses of the giants scattered among the caves of Sicily (which, though it appears to be justice, was in fact savagery); and moreover (3) temperate, content with one woman for their lifetime. And, as we shall see later, piety and religion likewise made them (4) strong, industrious, and magnanimous. Such were the virtues of the golden age, which was not, as effeminate poets later pictured it, an age in which pleasure was law. For in the golden age of the theological poets, men insensible to every refinement of wearisome reflection took pleasure only in what was lawful and [regarded as lawful only what was] useful, as is still the case, we observe, with peasants. (The heroic origin of the Latin verb *iuvare* is preserved in the expression *iuvat* ["it helps"] for "it is pleasant.") Nor were the philosophers right in imagining it as an age in which men read the eternal laws of justice in the bosom of Jove, for at first they read in the aspect of the sky the laws dictated to them by the thunderbolts. In conclusion, the vir-

tues of that first time were such as we found [100] admired by the Scythians, who would fix a knife in the ground and adore it as a god, and thus justify their killings; that is, they were virtues of the senses, with an admixture of religion and savage cruelty, whose affinity may still be observed among witches, as we noted in the Axioms [190].

517 From this early morality of the superstitious and cruel gentile world came the custom of sacrificing human victims to the gods. This we have from the most ancient Phoenicians, among whom, when some great calamity was imminent, such as war, famine or pestilence, the kings sacrificed their own children to placate the wrath of heaven, as Philo of Byblus narrates. Such sacrifices of children were regularly offered to Saturn, according to Quintus Curtius. Justin says the custom was continued by the Carthaginians, a people undoubtedly of Phoenician origin (as we shall observe), and was practiced by them down to their latest times. This is confirmed by Ennius in the verse: *Et Poinei solitei sos sacruficare puellos,* "and the Phoenicians [i.e. Carthaginians] were accustomed to sacrifice their own children." After their defeat at the hands of Agathocles, they sacrificed two hundred children to placate their gods. The Greeks fell in with this impiously pious custom of the Phoenicians and Carthaginians in the votive sacrifice Agamemnon made of his daughter Iphigenia. This should cause no surprise to anyone who reflects upon the cyclopean paternal power of the first fathers of the gentile world; a power exercised by the most learned nation, the Greeks, and by the wisest, the Romans. In both these nations down to the times of their most cultivated humanity, fathers had the right to kill their newborn children. This consideration will certainly lessen the repugnance our modern mildness makes us feel for the action of Brutus in decapitating his two sons who had plotted to restore the tyrant Tarquinius to the rule of Rome; and for that of Manlius, called the Imperious, in cutting off the head of his brave son who had fought and won a battle against his father's orders. Caesar reports that the Gauls also offered sacrifices of human victims, and Tacitus in the *Annals* relates of the Britons that the divine science of the Druids (who, according to the conceit of the scholars, were rich in esoteric wisdom) divined the future from the entrails of human victims. This cruel and frightful religion was prohibited by Augustus to Romans living in Gaul, and it was forbidden to the Gauls themselves by Claudius, according to Suetonius in his life of that emperor. Students of oriental languages thus hold that the Phoenicians had spread through the rest of the world the sacrifices of Moloch (identified with Saturn by Mornay, van der Driesche and Selden), to whom they offered a man burnt alive. Such was the humanity which the Phoenicians, who brought letters to Greece, went about inculcating in the first nations of the most barbarous gentiles! It is said that Hercules had purged Latium of a like fearful custom, that of throwing living men into the Tiber as sacrifices, and that he had introduced instead the practice of throwing in men of straw. But Tacitus tells of solemn human sacrifices among the ancient Germans, who certainly throughout all remembered time

were cut off from all foreign nations, so that the Romans with all the strength in the world could not penetrate among them. The Spaniards too found such rites in America, which until two centuries ago was hidden from all the rest of the world. The barbarians there feasted on human flesh (according to Lescarbot, *Histoire de la nouvelle France*), which must have been that of men who had been consecrated and killed by them. (Such sacrifices are described by Oviedo, *Hystoria . . . de las Indias*.) So that, while the ancient Germans were behold-ing the gods on earth, and the American Indians likewise (as we have noted of both above), and while the most ancient Scythians were rich in so many golden virtues as we have heard them praised for by the writers—in these same times they were practicing such inhuman humanity! All these [human sacrifices] were those called in Plautus *Saturni hostiae*, Saturn's victims, at a time that writers call the golden age of Latium. Such a mild, benign, sober, decent and well-behaved time it was!

518   We may conclude from all this how empty has been the conceit of the learned concerning the innocence of the golden age observed in the first gentile nations. In fact it was a fanaticism of superstition which kept the first men of the gentiles, savage, proud and most cruel as they were, in some sort of restraint by main terror of a divinity they had imagined. Reflecting on this superstition, Plutarch poses the problem whether it was a lesser evil thus im-piously to venerate the gods than not to believe in them at all. But he is not just in weighing this cruel superstition against atheism, for from the former arose the most enlightened nations while no nation in the world was ever founded on atheism, as we have shown above in the Principles [334].

519   So much may be said of the divine morality of the first peoples of the lost human race. The heroic morality we shall discuss in its place.

[SECTION IV]

[POETIC ECONOMY]

[CHAPTER I]

OF POETIC ECONOMY, AND HERE OF THE FAMILIES WHICH AT
FIRST INCLUDED ONLY CHILDREN [AND NOT *Famuli*]

520 The heroes apprehended with human senses those two truths which
make up the whole of economic doctrine, and which were preserved in the two
Latin verbs *educere* and *educare*. In the prevailing best usage the first of these
applies to the education of the spirit and the second to that of the body. The
first, by a learned metaphor, was transferred by the natural philosophers to the
bringing forth of forms from matter. For heroic education began to bring forth
in a certain way the form of the human soul which had been completely submerged in the vast bodies of the giants, and began likewise to bring forth the
form of the human body itself in its just dimensions from the disproportionate
giant bodies.

521 As regards the first part, the heroic fathers, as we noted in the
Axioms [250], must have been, in the state called that of nature, the wise men
in the wisdom of the auspices or vulgar wisdom, and consequently they must
have been the priests who, as being more worthy, had the duty of making
sacrifices in order to take or understand well the auspices. And finally they must
also have been the kings who had the duty of carrying the laws from the gods
to their own families; that is, they were legislators in the proper sense of the
word, "bearers of laws," as were later the first kings in the heroic cities. For these
carried the laws from the reigning senates to the people, as we have observed
above in the Notes on the Chronological Table [67], in the two kinds of heroic
assemblies described by Homer, the Boulê and the Agora. In the former the
heroes decreed the laws orally and in the latter they published them also orally,
for letters had not yet been invented. The kings bore the laws from the reigning
senates in the persons of the duumvirs whom they had appointed to announce
the laws, as Tullus Hostilius did in the case against Horatius. The duumvirs

thus came to be living and speaking laws. It is this which Livy does not understand, and hence he does not make himself clear in his account of the sentence of Horatius, as we observed above.

522   This vulgar tradition together with the false belief in the matchless wisdom of the ancients tempted Plato to a vain longing for those times in which philosophers reigned or kings were philosophers. And certainly the fathers, as noted in the Axioms [256], must have been monarchic family kings, superior to all other members of their families and subject only to God. Their authority was fortified by frightful religions and sanctioned by dreadful punishments, as must have been that of the Cyclopes, in whom Plato recognizes the first family-fathers of the world. This tradition, misunderstood, gave rise to that common error of all political theorists, that the first form of civil government in the world was monarchic. They are thus given over to those false principles of evil politics: that civil governments were born either of open violence or of fraud which later broke out into violence. But [the truth is that] in those times, full of arrogance and savagery because of the fresh emergence from bestial liberty (on which we have set forth an axiom [290] above), in the extreme simplicity and crudeness of a life content with the spontaneous fruits of nature, satisfied to drink the water of the springs and to sleep in the caves, in the natural equality of a state in which each of the fathers was sovereign in his own family, one cannot conceive of either fraud or violence by which one man could subject all the others to a civil monarchy. Further proof of this will be set forth later on.

523   Here, however, we may be permitted to reflect how much it took for the men of the gentile world to be tamed from their feral native liberty through a long period of cyclopean family discipline to the point of obeying naturally the laws in the civil states which were to come later. Hence there remained the eternal property that happier than the commonwealth conceived by Plato are those where the fathers teach only religion and where they are admired by their sons as their sages, revered as their priests, and feared as their kings. Such and so much divine force was needed to reduce these giants, as savage as they were crude, to human duties. Since they were unable to express this force abstractly, they represented it in concrete physical form as a cord, called *chorda* in Greek and in Latin at first *fides,* whose original and proper meaning appears in the phrase *fides deorum,* "force of the gods." From this cord (for the lyre must have begun with the monochord) they fashioned the lyre of Orpheus, to the accompaniment of which, singing to them the force of the gods in the auspices, he reduced the beasts of Greece to humanity. And Amphion raised the walls of Thebes with stones that moved themselves. These were the stones which Deucalion and Pyrrha, standing before the temple of Themis (that is, in the fear of divine justice) with veiled heads (the modesty of marriage) found lying before their feet (for men were at first stupid and *lapis,* "stone," remained Latin for a stupid person) and threw over their shoulders (introducing family orders by means of household discipline), thus making

men of them, as this fable was explained in the [Notes to the] Chronological Table [79].

524   As for the other part of household discipline, the education of bodies, the fathers with their frightful religions, their cyclopean authority and their sacred ablutions began to educe or bring forth from the giant bodies of their sons the proper human form, in accordance with what we have said above. And herein is providence above all to be admired, for it ordained that until such time as domestic education should supervene, the lost men should become giants in order that in their feral wanderings they might better endure with their robust constitutions the inclemency of the heavens and the seasons, and that they might with their disproportionate strength penetrate the great forest of the earth (which must have been very dense as a result of the recent flood), so that, fleeing from wild beasts and pursuing reluctant women and thus becoming lost from each other, they might be scattered through it in search of food and water until it should be found in due time fully populated; while after they began to remain in one place with their women, first in caves, then in huts near perennial springs (as we shall presently relate), and in the fields which, brought under cultivation, gave them sustenance, providence ordained that, from the causes we are now setting forth, they should shrink to the present proper stature of mankind.

525   In the very birth of [domestic] economy, they fulfilled it in its best idea, which is that the fathers by labor and industry should leave a patrimony to their sons, so that they may have an easy and comfortable and secure subsistence, even if foreign commerce should fail, or even all the fruits of civil life, or even the cities themselves, so that in such last emergencies the families at least may be preserved, from which there is hope that the nations may rise again. And the patrimony they leave should include places with good air, with their own perennial water supply, in situations of natural strength whither withdrawal is possible in case the cities have to be abandoned, and in fields with wide bottom lands on which to maintain the poor peasants taking refuge with them on the downfall of the cities, by whose labor they can maintain themselves as lords. Such were the orders that providence established for the state of the families, not like a tyrant laying down laws but like the queen it is of human affairs working through customs, according to the saying of Dion which we cited in the Axioms [308]. For the strong men were found with their lands on the mountain heights, in air stirred by the wind and hence healthful, and in sites naturally strong, which were the first *arces* in the world, later fortified by the devices of military architecture (as in Italian steep rugged mountains were called *rocce,* whence later the term *rocche* for fortresses), and finally they were found near perennial springs, which for the most part rise in the mountains. Near such springs the birds of prey make their nests, and consequently in their vicinity hunters set their snares. Perhaps for this reason all birds of prey were called *aquilae* by the Latins, as if for *aquilegae,* for certainly *aquilex* retained the

sense of finder or conductor of water. For doubtless those birds whose auspices Romulus observed to fix the site of the new city were vultures as history tells us, but later became eagles and the protecting deities of all the Roman armies. Thus simple and uncouth men, following the eagles which they believed to be birds of Jove because they flew high in the heavens, discovered the perennial springs and hence venerated this other great benefit which Heaven had bestowed upon them when it reigned on earth. And after the auspices of the lightning, the most august were those of the eagle's flight. These were called by Messala and Corvinus major or public auspices, and it was to them that the Roman patricians referred when in the heroic contests they answered the plebs that the auspices were theirs (*auspicia esse sua*). All this, ordained by providence to give a beginning to gentile humanity, was regarded by Plato as the result of wise human measures on the part of the first founders of the cities. But in the returned barbarism which destroyed cities everywhere, it was in just this way that the families were preserved whence sprang the new nations of Europe. And all the new seigniories which then arose were called *castella* by the Italians, for we may observe generally that the most ancient cities and almost all the capitals of peoples were placed on the crests of mountains, while the villages on the other hand lie scattered on the plains. Such must be the origin of the Latin phrases *summo loco, illustri loco nati* to signify "nobles," and *imo loco, obscuro loco nati* for "plebeians"; for, as we shall see later, the heroes dwelt in the cities, the *famuli* in the plains.

526   However, above all else, it was with reference to these perennial springs that political theorists asserted that the sharing of water was the occasion for families being brought together in their vicinity. Hence the first communities were called *phratriai* by the Greeks as the first lands were called *pagi* by the Latins from the Dorian Greek for "spring," *paga;* that is, water, the first of the two principal solemnities of marriage. For the Romans celebrated marriage *aqua et igni* because the first marriages were naturally contracted between men and women sharing the same water and fire, that is, of the same family; whence, as we have said above, marriage must have begun between brothers and sisters. And the lar of each house was the god of the fire aforesaid; hence *focus laris* for the hearth where the family father sacrificed to the household gods. In the Law of the Twelve Tables, in the article on parricide, according to the reading of Jacobus Raevardus, these gods are called *deivei parentum*. A similar expression is frequently found in Holy Scripture: *Deus parentum nostrorum,* the God of our fathers, or, more explicitly, *Deus Abraham, Deus Isac, Deus Iacob,* the God of Abraham, Isaac and Jacob. On this matter there is also the law proposed by Cicero, *Sacra familiaria perpetua manento,* "let sacred family rites be perpetually maintained"; whence the phrase of such frequent occurrence in Roman laws by which a son of a family is said to be *in sacris paternis,* and the paternal power itself is called *sacra patria,* for in the first times, as this work demonstrates, all its judgments were believed to be sacred. It must be added that a like custom

was observed by the barbarians who came in after; for in Florence in Giovanni Boccaccio's time (as he attests in his *Genealogies of the Gods*) it was the custom for the father of a family at the beginning of each year to sit at the hearth and throw incense and sprinkle wine on the end of a log to which he had set fire. And among the lower classes of our own Naples the Christmas Eve custom is observed which calls for the father of the house solemnly to set fire to such a log in the hearth. Indeed in the Kingdom of Naples families are counted by hearthfires. When cities were later founded the custom became universal of contracting marriages between those of the same city; and there finally remained the rule that when marriages are contracted between those of different cities or countries they should at least have religion in common.

527   To return now from fire to water, the Styx, by which the gods swore, was the source of the springs; hence the gods must have been the nobles of the heroic cities (as noted above), for the sharing of the water had given them dominion over men. Hence down to the 309th year of Rome the patricians excluded the plebs from *connubium,* as we have said above and as we shall set forth at greater length farther on. For all these reasons we often read in Holy Writ of the "well of the oath" or the "oath of the well." Thus the city of Pozzuoli preserves in its name an indication of its great antiquity, for it was called *Puteoli* on account of the number of small wells it contained. And it is a reasonable conjecture, based on the Mental Dictionary of which we have spoken, that the many cities with plural names scattered through the ancient nations received their names from the things signified by the singulars of the same names in the several articulate languages.

528   From this source imagination conceived the third major deity, Diana, representing the first human need which made itself felt among the giants when they had settled on definite lands and united in marriage with particular women. The theological poets have described the history of these things in two fables of Diana. The first, signifying the modesty of marriage, tells of Diana silently lying with the sleeping Endymion under the darkness of night; so that Diana is chaste with that chastity referred to in a law proposed by Cicero, *Deos caste adeunto,* that one should go to the sacrifice only after making the sacred ablutions. The other tells us of the fearful religion of the water-springs, to which was attached the perpetual epithet of sacred. It is the tale of Actaeon, who, seeing Diana naked (the living spring) and being sprinkled with water by the goddess (to signify that the goddess cast over him the great awe of her divinity), was changed into a stag (the most timid of animals) and torn to pieces by his dogs (the remorse of his own conscience for the violation of religion). Hence *lymphati* (properly, sprinkled with *lympha* or pure water) must have been originally a term applied to the Actaeons who had been maddened by superstitious terror. This poetic history was preserved by the Latins in their word *latices* (evidently from *latendo*), to which is always added the epithet *puri,* and which means the water gushing from a spring. The *latices* of the Latins

must have been identical with the Greek nymphs, handmaidens of Diana, for *nymphai* in Greek meant the same as *lymphae* [in Latin]. The nymphs were so named at a time when all things were apprehended as animate and for the most part human substances, as we have set forth above in the [Poetic] Metaphysics.

529   Afterwards, the god-fearing giants, those settled in the mountains, must have become sensible of the stench from the corpses of their dead rotting on the ground near by, and must have begun to bury them; for enormous skulls and bones have been found and are still found, generally on mountain tops, which is a strong indication that the bodies of the impious giants who were scattered everywhere through the valleys and the plains must have rotted unburied and their skulls and bones must have been swept into the sea by the rivers or completely worn away by the rains. And they surrounded these sepulchers with so much religion, or divine terror, that burial grounds were called by the Latins religious places par excellence. Hence emerged the universal belief in the immortality of human souls, which we established above in the Principles as the third of those on which our Science is based. [The souls of the departed] were called *dii manes,* and in the Law of the Twelve Tables in the article on parricide they are spoken of as *deivei parentum.* Furthermore, they must have fixed a stake as a burial marker upon or near the mound, which originally can have been nothing but a slight rounding over of the earth. (The ancient Germans, according to Tacitus, believed that they should not cover the dead with overmuch earth, whence the prayer for the dead, *Sit tibi terra levis,* "May the earth lie light upon thee!" And this German practice permits us to conjecture that the same custom must have prevailed among all the other first barbarous nations.) The grave marker was called by the Greeks the *phylax* or guardian, because these simple people believed that the post would guard the grave. *Cippus,* the Latin name for the post, came to mean sepulcher, and *ceppo* in Italian means the trunk of a genealogical tree. *Phylax* must accordingly have been the origin of the Greek *phylē,* a tribe. And the Romans set forth their genealogies by placing the statues of their ancestors in rows along the halls of their houses, and these rows were called *stemmata.* (This term must have been derived from *temen,* "thread"; whence *subtemen* for the thread that is carried under as weft in weaving cloth.) The jurisconsults later called these genealogical rows *lineae* or "lines," and down to our time *stemmata* has kept the meaning of family arms. Thus it is highly probable that the first lands with such buried bodies were the first shields of the families, and the phrase of the Spartan mother, presenting the shield to her son as he goes to war, *aut cum hoc, aut in hoc,* must be understood as meaning, "return with this or on a bier." Even to this day in Naples the bier is called a shield (*scudo*). And since the sepulchers were at the lower end of the fields, which were at first fields for planting, the shield is defined in the science of heraldry as the base of the field, later called the base of the arms.

530   From the same origin must have come the word *filius*, which, qualified by the name or house of the father, signified noble, precisely as we saw above that the Roman patrician was defined as one *qui potest nomine ciere patrem*, "who can name his father." And we saw above that the names of the Romans were really patronymics, which were so often used by the first Greeks; Homer, for example, calling the heroes *filii Achivorum*, "sons of the Achaeans"; and in like fashion in Holy Scripture *filii Israel* is used of the nobles of the Hebrew people. Hence necessarily, if the tribes were originally composed of nobles, the cities must at first have been made up of nobles alone, as we shall show later.

531   Thus by the graves of their buried dead the giants showed their dominion over their lands, and Roman law called for burial of the dead in a proper place to make it religious. With truth they could pronounce those heroic phrases: we are sons of this earth, we are born from these oaks. Indeed the heads of families among the Latins called themselves *stirpes* and *stipites*, "stems" or "stocks," and their progeny were called *propagines*, "slips" or "shoots." In Italian such families were called *legnaggi*, "lineages." And the most noble houses of Europe and almost all its reigning families take their names from the lands over which they rule. Thus in Latin and Greek alike son of the earth means the same thing as noble; and in Latin *ingenui*, "the indigenous ones," as if for *indegeniti* or the shorter form *ingeniti*, meant the nobles; as certainly *indigenae* retained the meaning of natives of a country. *Dii indigetes* was the term used for the native gods, who must have been the nobles of the heroic cities, for they were called gods, as we have said above, and the Earth was their great mother. Hence from the beginning *ingenuus* and *patricius* meant noble, for the first cities were of nobles only; and these *ingenui* must have been the aborigines, styled as it were "without origin" or self-born, to which correspond exactly the Greek *autochthones*. And the aborigines were giants, and the term giants properly signifies sons of Earth. Thus, as the fables faithfully tell us, Earth was the mother of gods and giants.

532   These matters have already been set forth above, but here in their proper place we have repeated them to show that Livy [I.8] misattributed the heroic phrase to Romulus and the fathers who were his companions when he made them say to those who had taken refuge in the asylum opened in the clearing that they were sons of that land; and he makes that become in their mouths a barefaced lie which in [the case of] the founders of the first peoples had been a heroic truth. For on the one hand Romulus was recognized as of the royal family of Alba, and on the other hand their mother [earth] had been so unjust to them as to give birth only to men, so that they had to carry off the Sabine maidens to be their wives. We must therefore say that, in the manner the first peoples had of thinking in terms of poetic characters, Romulus, regarded as the founder of a city, was invested with the properties of the founders of the first cities of Latium, in the midst of a great number of which Romulus founded

Rome. Linked with the aforesaid error of Livy is the definition he gives of the asylum, that it was *vetus urbes condentium consilium,* "an old counsel of founders of cities"; for in the first founders of cities, who were simple men, it was not counsel but nature that was employed by providence.

533　Imagination here created the fourth divinity of the so-called *gentes maiores;* namely, Apollo, apprehended as god of civil light. Thus the heroes were called *kleitoi,* "resplendent," by the Greeks, from *kleos,* "glory," and they were called *inclyti* by the Latins from *cluer,* "the splendor of arms," and consequently from that light into which Juno Lucina brought noble offspring. So here, after Urania—whom we noted above to be the Muse defined by Homer as the science of good and evil, or of divination, in virtue of which Apollo is the god of poetic wisdom or divination—they must have conceived the second of the Muses, Clio, the narrator of heroic history. The first history of this sort must have begun with the genealogies of the heroes, just as sacred history begins with the descendants of the patriarchs. Apollo begins this history by pursuing Daphne, a vagabond maiden wandering through the forests (in the nefarious life); and she, by the aid she besought of the gods (whose auspices were necessary for solemn nuptials), on standing still is changed to a laurel (a plant which is ever green in its certainly known offspring), in the same sense in which the Latins use *stipites* for the stocks of families; and the returned barbarism brought back the same heroic phraseology, for they call genealogies trees, and the founders they call stocks or stems, and the descendants branches, and the families lineages. Hence the pursuit of Apollo was the act of a god, and the flight of Daphne that of an animal; but later, when the language of this austere history had been forgotten, it came about that the pursuit of Apollo was viewed as the act of a libertine, and the flight of Daphne as the reaction of a woman.

534　Further, Apollo is the brother of Diana, for the perennial springs made possible the founding of the first nations on the mountain tops; wherefore Apollo has his seat on Mount Parnassus where dwell the Muses (the arts of humanity), near the fount of Hippocrene, whose waters give drink to the swans, birds that sing in that sense in which the Latin verbs *canere* and *cantare* mean "to predict." Under the auspices of one of these swans, as we have said above, Leda conceives two eggs and from one of them gives birth to Helen and from the other to the twins Castor and Pollux.

535　And Apollo and Diana are children of Latona, so called from *latere,* "to hide" (the sense which *condere* originally had in the phrases *condere gentes, condere regna, condere urbes*), whence in Italy the name of Latium. And Latona brought forth her children near the waters of the perennial springs we have mentioned; and at their birth men became frogs, which in summer rains are born from the earth, called mother of giants, for these are properly sons of Earth. One of these frogs was sent by Idanthyrsus to Darius, and it must be three frogs and not three toads that appear in the royal arms of France, later changed to golden lilies. And since the number three was used for the superlative—a usage which persisted in the French *très*—the three frogs mean one great frog, which is to say a great son, and therefore lord, of the earth.

536 Apollo and Diana are both hunters, slaying beasts with uprooted trees, one of which is the club of Hercules. They do this first in defense of themselves and their families (since they are no longer permitted to save themselves by flight as the vagabonds of the lawless life had done), and later to provide food. Thus Vergil makes the heroes feast on such game; and with like purpose, according to Tacitus, the ancient Germans and their wives hunted down the beasts.

537 Apollo is also the founding god of humanity and of its arts, which we have just seen to be the Muses. These arts the Latins call *liberales* in the sense of noble. One of them is the art of riding, whence Pegasus soars over Mount Parnassus armed with wings because he pertains to the nobility. And in the returned barbarism the nobles were called cavaliers by the Spaniards because only they could don armor [for fighting] on horseback. This humanity had its origin in *humare*, "to bury" (which is the reason we took the practice of burial as the third principle of our Science), and the Athenians, who were the most human of all the nations, were, according to Cicero, the first to bury their dead.

538 Lastly, Apollo is always young (just as the life of Daphne, changed to a laurel, is always verdant), for Apollo, through the names of the great houses, makes men eternal in their families. And he wears his hair long as a sign of nobility. The custom of wearing the hair long was preserved by the nobility of many nations, and we read that one of the punishments of nobles among both the Persians and the American Indians was to pull one or several hairs from their heads. And perhaps *Gallia comata*, Long-haired [Transalpine] Gaul, was so called from the nobles who founded that nation; as certainly the slaves in all nations have their heads shaved.

539 Now, however, when the heroes had settled within circumscribed lands and when with the increase of their families the spontaneous fruits of nature were no longer sufficient, while yet they feared to seek for abundance beyond the confines they had set for themselves by those chains of religion by which the giants were chained under the mountains, and having been taught by that same religion to set fire to the forests in order to have a prospect of the open sky whence came the auspices, they then set about the long, arduous, and heavy task of bringing their lands under cultivation and sowing them with grain, which, roasted among the thorns and briers, they had perhaps discovered to be useful for human nourishment. Hereupon, by a fine natural and necessary metaphor, they called the ears of grain golden apples, transferring the idea of the apples which are fruits of nature gathered in summer, to the ears of grain which human industry gathers likewise in summer.

540 From this labor, the greatest and most glorious of all, the [poetic]

character of Hercules sprang up, reflecting great glory on Juno who set this task for the nourishment of the families. And, in other metaphors both beautiful and necessary, they imagined the earth in the aspect of a great dragon, covered with scales and spines (the thorns and briers), bearing wings (for the lands belonged to the heroes), always awake and vigilant (thickly grown in every direction). This dragon they made the guardian of the golden apples in the garden of the Hesperides. Because of the wetness from the waters of the flood, the dragon was later believed to have been born in the water. Under another aspect they imagined [the earth as] a hydra (also from *hydōr,* "water"), which, when any of its heads were cut off, always grew others in their place. It was of three alternating colors: black (the burnt-over land), green (the leaf), and gold (the ripe grain). These are the three colors of the serpent's skin, which, when it grows old, is sloughed off for a fresh one. Finally, under the aspect of its fierceness in resisting cultivation, the earth was also imagined as a most powerful beast, the Nemean lion (whence later the name lion was given to the most powerful of the animals); which philologists hold to have been a monstrous serpent. All these beasts vomit forth fire, which is the fire set to the forests by Hercules.

541 These three different stories, from three different parts of Greece, signify the same thing in substance. In another part of Greece another story grew up, telling of the child Hercules slaying the serpents while yet in his cradle; that is, in the infancy of the heroic age. In yet another, Bellerophon slays the monster called the Chimaera, having the tail of a serpent, the body of a goat (to signify the enforested earth), and the head of a lion belching flames. In Thebes it is Cadmus who slays the great dragon and sows his teeth. (By a fine metaphor they gave the name of serpent's teeth to the curved pieces of hard wood which must have been used to plough the earth before the use of iron was discovered.) Cadmus himself becomes a serpent (the ancient Romans would have said Cadmus *fundus factus est*), as we have indicated above and as we shall explain more fully later on, when we shall see that the serpents of Medusa's head and Mercury's staff signified the dominion of the lands. Hence land rent was called *ōpheleia* from *ophis,* "serpent," and was also called the tithe of Hercules. It is in this sense that we read in Homer of the soothsayer Calchas interpreting the action of the serpent in devouring the eight swallows and their mother as meaning that the land of Troy would fall under the dominion of the Greeks at the end of nine years; so that the Greeks, while fighting the Trojans, when a serpent is slain by an eagle in the air and falls among them in the midst of the battle, take it for a good augury in conformity with the soothsaying science of Calchas. Hence Proserpine, who was the same as Ceres, is depicted in sculpture as being borne off in a chariot drawn by serpents, and hence serpents so often appear on the coins of the Greek commonwealths.

542 Thus, in illustration of the Mental Dictionary (and it is a matter worthy of reflection), the kings of the American Indians, as Fracastoro sings in his *Syphilis,* were found to carry a dried snakeskin in place of a scepter. The Chinese too charge their royal arms with a dragon and bear a dragon as the emblem of the civil power. Such must have been the Dragon [Draco] who wrote the Athenian laws in blood; and we remarked above that this Dragon was one of the serpents of the Gorgon, nailed by Perseus to his shield, which later became the shield of Minerva, goddess of the Athenians, and its aspect turned to stone whoever gazed upon it; and this will be found to have been a hieroglyph of the civil power of Athens. Holy Scripture too, in the book of Ezekiel, bestows on the king of Egypt the title of the great dragon lying in the midst of his rivers, just as the dragons noted above were born in the water and the Hydra took its name from that element. The emperor of Japan has created an order of knights who bear the dragon as their device. And in the returned barbarian times the histories tell us that the house of the Visconti because of its great nobility was called to the duchy of Milan, and this house bears on its arms a dragon devouring a child, which is none other than the Python which devoured the men of Greece and was slain by Apollo, the god of nobility as we have seen. This blazoning may well cause astonishment at the uniformity between the heroic mode of thought of the men of this second barbarism and that of the ancients of the first. Such must be the two winged dragons wearing the necklace of flints by which the fire they vomit forth was kindled; the two guardians, that is, of the Golden Fleece, whose significance Chiflet, who wrote the history of that illustrious order, could not understand, so that Pietrasanta avows its history obscure.

543   As in some parts of Greece it was Hercules who killed the serpents, the lion, the Hydra, or the dragon, and in another it was Bellerophon who slew the Chimaera, so in yet another it is Bacchus who tames the tigers, which must have been the lands clothed in colors as varied as their skin, and hence the name tiger passed to the animals of this powerful species. The story of Bacchus taming the tigers with wine is a physical history far from the thought of the rustic heroes who founded the nations, nor was it ever related in those times that Bacchus went to Africa or to Hyrcania to tame them, for the Greeks, as we shall show in our Poetic Geography, could not then have known if there was a Hyrcania in the world, much less an Africa, to say nothing of tigers in the forests of Hyrcania or the deserts of Africa.

544   Further, when they called the ears of grain golden apples, these must have been the only gold in the world. For at that time metallic gold was still unmined, and they did not know how to extract it in crude masses, to say nothing of shining and burnishing it; nor indeed, when men still drank the water of springs, could the use of gold have been at all prized. It was only later, from the metal's resemblance in color to the most highly prized food of those times, that it was metaphorically called gold. Hence Plautus was obliged to say *thesaurum auri* to distinguish a hoard of gold from a granary. Certainly Job, among the great things from which he had fallen, mentions that he had been

wont to eat bread made of grain. And in the country districts of our most remote provinces, in place of the juleps of powdered pearls used in cities, they give bread made from grain to the sick, and they say the sick man is eating grain bread when they mean that he is at the point of death.

545 Later, by a further extension of the idea of prizing and cherishing, they must have applied the term golden to fine wool. Hence in Homer Atreus complains that Thyestes has stolen his golden sheep, and the Argonauts stole from Pontus the Golden Fleece. For this reason Homer gives his kings and heroes the fixed epithet *polymēlos,* "rich in flocks"; as the ancient Latins, by uniformity of ideas, called the patrimony *pecunia,* which the Latin grammarians derive from *pecus,* "herd" or "flock." Among the ancient Germans, in Tacitus's account, the flocks and herds are their most highly prized, indeed their only wealth (*solae et gratissimae opes sunt*). This custom must also have prevailed among the ancient Romans, whose patrimony was *pecunia,* as the Law of the Twelve Tables attests in the article on testaments. And *mēlon* means both apple and sheep to the Greeks, who, perhaps also under the aspect of precious fruit, called honey *meli;* and the Italians call apples *mele.*

546 These ears of grain must then have been the golden apples which Hercules was the first to bring back (or harvest) from Hesperia. The Gallic Hercules, with chains of this gold issuing from his mouth, binds men by the ears; this too we shall find later is a history of the cultivation of the fields. Hence Hercules was a propitious deity in the search for treasures, of which Dis was the god. Dis is the same as Pluto, who carries Proserpine, who is the same as Ceres (that is, grain), into the underworld of which the poets tell us. According to them there were three underworlds: the first by the Styx, the second where the dead lay, and the third at the bottom of the furrow, as we shall show in its proper place. From this god Dis the rich are called *dites,* and the rich were the nobles. The Spaniards call their nobles rich men (*ricos hombres*) and among us the nobles were formerly called *benestanti,* "well off." The ancient Latins called *dicio* what we now call the domain of a state, for the cultivated fields make up the true wealth of states; and in like fashion the Latins called the area of a domain *ager,* which is properly land which has been put to the plough (*aratro agitur*). So it must be true that the Nile was called *Chrysorrhoas,* "flowing with gold," because it overflows the wide fields of Egypt and its inundations are the source of the great abundance of the harvests. So too the Pactolus, the Ganges, the Hydaspes and the Tagus are called rivers of gold because they make fertile the fields of grain. Vergil must have had these golden apples in mind when, learned in heroic antiquities as he was, he extended the metaphor and created the golden bough that Aeneas carries into the lower world. This fable we shall explain later in its more proper place. For the rest, metallic gold was not more highly prized than iron in heroic times. Etearchus, for example, king of Ethiopia, replying to the ambassadors of Cambyses who had presented him with many golden vessels in the name of their king, said that he could see no use for them and

much less any need, thus refusing them with a magnanimity that was quite natural. Tacitus relates the same of the ancient Germans, who in his time were just such ancient heroes as those of whom we are now speaking: "You may see among them vessels of silver, which have been presented to their envoys and chieftains, held as cheap as those of clay." So in Homer we find the armories of the heroes stocked with arms of iron or gold indifferently, for the first world must have abounded in these minerals (as America was found to do at its discovery), which were later to be exhausted by human avarice.

547   From all of which we derive this great corollary: that the division of the four ages of the world—that is, the ages of gold, silver, copper and iron —was invented by the poets of degenerate times. For it was this poetic gold, namely, grain, that among the Greeks lent its name to the golden age, whose innocence was but the extreme savagery of the Cyclopes (in whom, as we have said several times above, Plato recognizes the first fathers of families), who lived separately and alone in their caves with their wives and children, never concerning themselves with one another's affairs, as Polyphemus tells Ulysses in Homer.

548   In confirmation of all we have so far said of the poetic gold, it may be useful to cite two customs which are still observed and the causes of which can be explained only on these principles. The first is the custom of putting a golden globe [pomo, "apple"] in the hands of the king in the midst of the solemnities of his coronation. This is evidently the same [pome or globe] that they bear in their royal arms, surmounting their crowns. This custom can have no other origin than the golden apples of grain we are here discussing. For here too the apples will be found to be a hieroglyph of the dominion of the heroes over their lands (which perhaps the Egyptians too signified by an apple, if it is not an egg, in the mouth of their [god Knuphis or] Knef, of whom we shall speak later on). And this hieroglyph, we shall find, was carried by the barbarians who invaded all the nations subject to the Roman Empire. The other custom is that of the gold coins which kings give their queen consorts among the other solemnities of their nuptials. These too must go back to the poetic gold or grain of which we are speaking (for the gold coins signify the heroic nuptials of the ancient Romans coëmptione et farre, "by mutual mock sale and bread offering"), in conformity with the heroic practice related by Homer of buying their wives with a wedding gift. It was in a shower of this gold that Jove must have appeared to Danaë locked in her tower (which must have been the granary), to signify the abundance of this solemnity. In striking agreement is the Hebrew phrase "and abundance in thy towers" (et abundantia in turribus tuis [Ps. 122:7]). The conjecture is confirmed by the custom of the ancient Britons, among whom grooms, as a part of the wedding ceremony, gave their brides cakes.

549   At the birth of these human things, three other deities of the gentes maiores sprang forth in the imaginations of the Greeks, with this order of ideas, corresponding to the order of the things themselves. First Vulcan, then

Saturn (so called from *sati,* "sown fields," whence the age of Saturn among the Latins corresponds to the golden age of the Greeks), and thirdly Cybele or Berecynthia, the cultivated land. Cybele is depicted as seated on a lion (the enforested earth which the heroes reduced to tillage, as explained above), and is called the great mother of the gods and also the mother of the giants (who were properly so called in the sense of sons of Earth, as noted above). Hence she is the mother of the gods (that is, of the giants, who in the time of the first cities arrogated to themselves the name of gods, as we have also noted before), and the pine is sacred to her (as a sign of the stability of the founders of peoples, who, remaining settled on the first lands, founded the cities, of which Cybele is the goddess). She was called Vesta, goddess of divine ceremonies among the Romans, for the lands ploughed at that time were the first altars of the world (as we shall see in the Poetic Geography). Here the goddess Vesta, armed with a fierce religion, watched over fire and spelt, which was the grain of the ancient Romans. Hence too among the Romans nuptials were celebrated *aqua et igni,* "with water and fire," and also with spelt (*far*), and were then called *nuptiae confarreatae.* This ceremony was later confined to priests, for the first families had been all of priests (as has been found to be the case in the kingdoms of the bonzes in the East Indies). And water, fire and spelt were the elements used in the Roman divine ceremonies. On these first lands Vesta sacrificed to Jove the impious [practicers] of the infamous sharing [of women and things], who violated the first altars (which we have said above were the first fields of grain, as we shall explain later). These were the first *hostiae,* the first victims of the gentile religions. Plautus called them *Saturni hostiae,* "Saturn's victims," as we have observed above; and they were called *victimae* from *victi,* as being weak because alone (the Latin *victus* has preserved this meaning of weakness), and they were called *hostes* because such impious men were rightly held to be enemies of the whole human race. And among the Romans it remained the custom to cover with spelt the brow and the horns of sacrificial victims. From the name of Vesta the Romans called Vestal virgins those who guarded the eternal fire, which if extinguished by mishap had to be relighted from the sun, for from the sun, as we shall see later, Prometheus stole the first fire and brought it to the Greeks on earth, who therewith set fire to the forests and began to cultivate the land. On this account Vesta is the goddess of divine ceremonies among the Romans, for the first *colere* or cultivating in the world of the gentiles was the cultivation of the land, and the first cult was raising these altars, setting this first fire to them, and sacrificing upon them the impious men of whom we have just spoken.

550   In this way the boundaries of the fields were fixed and maintained. This division, too generally set forth by Hermogenianus the jurisconsult, has been imagined as taking place by deliberate agreement of men, and carried out with justice and respected in good faith, at a time when there was as yet no armed public force and consequently no civil authority of law. But it cannot be

understood save as taking place among men of extreme wildness, observing a frightful religion which had fixed and circumscribed them within certain lands, and whose bloody ceremonies had consecrated their first walls. For even the philologists say the walls were traced by the founders of the cities with the plough, the moldboard of which, by the origins of language above discovered, must have been first called *urbs,* whence the ancient *urbum,* "curved." Perhaps *orbis* is from the same origin, so that at first *orbis terrae* must have meant any fence made in this way, so low that Remus jumped over it to be killed by Romulus and thus, as Latin historians narrate, to consecrate with his blood the first walls of Rome. Such a fence must evidently have been a hedge (*siepe*) (and among the Greeks *sēps* signifies "serpent" in its heroic meaning of "cultivated land"), from which origin must come *munere viam,* "to build a road," which is done by strengthening the hedges around the fields. Hence walls are called *moenia,* as if for *munia,* and certainly *munire* kept the sense of "fortifying." The hedges must have been of those plants the Latins called *sagmina,* blood-wort or elder, whose use and name still survive. The name *sagmina* was preserved in the sense of the herbs with which the altars were adorned; it must have come from the blood (*sanguis*) of the slain, who, like Remus, had transgressed them. Hence the so-called sanctity of walls, and also of heralds, who, as we shall see later, crowned themselves with these herbs, as certainly the ancient Roman ambassadors did with those plucked on the Capitoline. And hence finally the sanctity of the laws of war and peace of which the heralds were bearers, whence that part of a law which imposes penalties on its transgressors is called its sanction. And here begins what we are demonstrating in this work: that the natural law of nations was by divine providence ordained separately for each people, and only when they became acquainted did they recognize it as common to all. For if the Roman heralds consecrated with these herbs were inviolate among the other peoples of Latium, it could only have been because the latter, without knowing anything of Roman usage, observed the same custom.

551   So the family fathers provided a subsistence for their heroic families through religion, and through religion it had to be maintained. Hence it was the perpetual custom of the nobles to be religious, as Julius Scaliger observes in his *Poetica.* It must then be a strong indication of the decline of a nation when the nobles scorn their native religion.

552   Philologians and philosophers have commonly supposed that the families in the so-called state of nature included children only; whereas in fact they included *famuli* and that was the original reason for their being called families. On this defective economy a false politics has been erected, as we have noted above and shall show fully later on. Wherefore from this matter of the *famuli,* which pertains to economic theory, we shall proceed to discourse of politics.

[CHAPTER II]

THE FAMILIES WITH THEIR *Famuli,* WHICH PRECEDED THE CITIES, AND WITHOUT WHICH THE CITIES COULD NOT HAVE BEEN BORN

553   Among the impious giants who had continued the infamous sharing of property and women, the quarrels produced by the sharing finally brought it about, at the end of a long period of time, that (to borrow the language of the jurists) Grotius's simpletons and Pufendorf's abandoned men had recourse to the altars of the strong to save themselves from Hobbes's violent men, even as beasts driven by intense cold will sometimes seek salvation in inhabited places. Thereupon the strong, with a fierceness born of their union in the society of families, slew the violent who had violated their lands, and took under their protection the miserable creatures who had fled from them. And above the heroism of nature which was theirs as having been born of Jove or engendered under his auspices, there now shone forth preëminently in them the heroism of virtue. In this heroism the Romans excelled all other peoples of the earth, practicing precisely these two aspects of it, sparing the submissive and vanquishing the proud: *Parcere subiectis et debellare superbos.*

554   And here it is worth reflecting how men in the feral state, fierce and untamed as they were, came to pass from their bestial liberty into human society. For in order that the first of them should reach that first kind of society which is matrimony, they had need of the sharp stimulus of bestial lust, and to keep them in it the stern restraints of frightful religions were necessary, as we have shown above. Thus marriage emerged as the first kind of friendship in the world; whence Homer, to indicate that Jove and Juno lay together, says with heroic gravity that "they celebrated their friendship." The Greek word for friendship, *philia,* is from the same root as *phileō,* "to love"; and from it is derived the Latin *filius,* "son." *Philios* in Ionic Greek means "friend," and mutation to a letter of similar sound yielded the Greek *phylē,* "tribe." We have already seen above that *stemmata* was the word for the genealogical threads called *lineae* by the jurisconsults. From this nature of human things there remained the eternal property that the true natural friendship is matrimony, in which are realized the three final goods: the honorable, the useful and the pleasant. Husband and wife by nature share the same lot in all the prosperities and adversities of life, just as by choice friends have all things in common (*amicorum omnia*

sunt communia), and Modestinus therefore defines matrimony as a life-long lot-sharing (*omnis vitae consortium*).

555   The second comers came into this second society (which had that name by a certain excellence, as we shall shortly show) only for the ultimate necessities of life. And here again is a matter worthy of reflection. For the first comers to human society were driven thereto by religion and the natural instinct to propagate the human race (the former a pious motive, the latter in the strict sense a gentle one), and thus gave a beginning to noble and lordly friendship. The second comers, since they came out of a necessity of saving their lives, gave a beginning to society in the proper sense, with a view principally to utility, and consequently base and servile. These refugees were received by the heroes under the just law of protection, by which they preserved their natural lives under the obligation of serving the heroes as day laborers. So from the fame (*fama*) of the heroes (primarily acquired through the practice of the aforesaid two parts of the heroism of virtue) and from the worldly renown which is the *kleos* or "glory" of the Greeks (called *fama* by the Latins and *phēmē* too by the Greeks), the refugees were called *famuli,* and it was principally from these *famuli* that the families took their name. It is certainly from this fame that sacred history, speaking of the giants before the flood, calls them famous men. Vergil too similarly describes *Fama* as seated on a high tower (the high-lying lands of the heroes) with her head in the sky (whose vault rises from the mountain tops), having wings (as pertaining to the heroes, whence on the battlefield before Troy Fame flies amid the ranks of the Greek heroes and not amid the masses of their plebeians), and with a trumpet (which must be the trumpet of Clio, that is, heroic history) celebrating the names of the great (the founders of nations).

556   In these families before the time of the cities, the *famuli* lived in a state of slavery. (They were the forerunners of the slaves who were captured in the wars which began after the founding of cities. These latter slaves were called *vernae* by the Latins; with them came the languages called *vernaculae,* as we have explained above.) To distinguish the sons of the heroes from those of the *famuli,* the former were called *liberi,* "free." But it was a distinction without a difference. For Tacitus tells us of the ancient Germans (and we may thence conjecture the same custom among all the first barbarous peoples) that the master is not distinguished from the slave by being brought up with greater delicacy (*dominum ac servum nullis educationis deliciis dignoscas*); and certainly among the ancient Romans the family fathers had a sovereign power of life and death over their children and a despotic dominion over the property they acquired, so that down to imperial times there was no difference between sons and slaves in respect of their property. But originally the word *liberi* meant also "noble," so that *artes liberales* are noble arts, and *liberalis* kept the meaning "well-born," and *liberalitas* that of "gentility." From the same ancient origin the noble houses of the Latins were called *gentes,* for, as we shall see, the first *gentes* were made up of nobles alone, and only nobles were free in the first cities. Furthermore, the

famuli were called *clientes,* originally *cluentes* from the ancient verb *cluere,* "to shine in the light of arms" (whose splendor was called *cluer*), for they reflected the light of the arms borne by their respective heroes. The latter were called first *incluti* and later *inclyti* from the same root. If not thus resplendent they were not noticed, as if they had no place among men, as will be explained later.

557 Thus began the clienteles and the first intimations of the fiefs of which we shall have much to say later. In ancient history we read of such clienteles and clients scattered through all nations, as is set forth in the Axioms [263]. But Thucydides relates that in Egypt, even in his time, the dynasties of Tanis were all divided among family fathers, the shepherd princes of such families; and Homer calls each hero of whom he sings a king, and describes them as shepherds of the peoples, who must have appeared before the shepherds of the flocks, as we shall show later. They are still found in great numbers in Arabia, as they once were in Egypt; and in the West Indies the greater part were found in this state of nature to be governed by such families, surrounded by slaves in such numbers as to cause Charles V, king of Spain, to consider imposing restrictive measures. It must have been with a family such as these that Abraham made war against the gentile kings; and his servants, who aided him, are called by a name much to our purpose which Hebrew scholars translate *vernaculos,* according well with the *vernae* discussed above.

558 With the beginning of these things came the true origin of the famous Herculean knot by which clients were said to be *nexi* or tied to the lands they had to cultivate for the nobles. Later this became a figurative knot, as we shall see, in the Law of the Twelve Tables, which gave form to the civil mancipation by which all the *actus legitimi* of the Romans were solemnized. Now at this point, because one cannot conceive an association more restricted from the side of those having abundance of goods nor more necessary for those who need them, the first *socii* in the world must have had their beginning. As we have noted in the Axioms [258], these were the *socii* of the heroes, received for life, as they had placed their lives in the hands of the heroes. This explains how Ulysses is on the point of cutting off the head of Antinous [i.e Eurylochus], the chief of his *socii,* just for a word which, though well meant, does not please him; and the pious Aeneas kills his *socius* Misenus when it is needful for a sacrifice. This episode was preserved in a vulgar tradition, but Vergil, since in the mild days of the Roman people it was too harsh a thing to tell of Aeneas, whom the poet himself celebrates for his piety, discreetly pretends that Misenus was killed by Triton for presuming to rival him on the trumpet. At the same time he gives clear hints for the right understanding of the story by placing the death of Misenus among the solemnities prescribed to Aeneas by the Sybil. For one of them was that he must bury Misenus before he could make his descent to the lower world; and this is an open acknowledgment that the Sybil had predicted his death.

559 Thus the *socii* shared only the labors of the heroes, not their winnings,

and still less their glory. With this last only the heroes shone, and they were therefore called *kleitoi* or "illustrious" by the Greeks and *inclyti* by the Latins. (There was a similar relationship between the Romans and the provinces they called associate.) Aesop complains of this state of affairs in his fable of the lion's partnership, as we have said above [425]. Among the ancient Germans, certainly, as Tacitus tells us (thereby justifying a like conjecture for all other barbarous peoples), the principal oath of these *famuli* or clients or vassals was to guard and defend each his own prince and to assign to his prince's glory his own deeds of valor (*suum principem defendere et tueri, sua quoque fortia facta gloriae eius adsignare, praecipuum iuramentum est*); which is one of the most impressive characteristics of our own feudalism. Thus and not otherwise must it have come about that under the person or head (which, as we shall later see, meant the same as "mask") and under the name (or as we would now say "device") of a Roman paterfamilias were counted, in law, all his children and all his slaves. Hence the Romans called *clypea* or shields the half-busts representing the images of their ancestors, set in the hollow niches of their courtyard walls. And in modern architecture, quite in line with what we have been saying about the origins of medals, these shields are called medallions. And thus in the heroic times of the Greeks Homer could say with perfect truth that Ajax was "the tower of the Greeks," as alone he battles with whole battalions of Trojans; as in the heroic times of the Romans Horatius alone on the bridge stands off an army of Etruscans; for Ajax and Horatius are alone with their vassals. Just so in the history of the returned barbarism forty Norman heroes returning from the Holy Land scatter an army of Saracens besieging Salerno. Whence it must be said that these first ancient examples of protection extended by the heroes over those who had taken refuge on their lands marked the beginning of fiefs in the world. The first were personal rustic fiefs, and the vassals must have been the first *vades* or "implements," obliged to follow their heroes in person wherever they led them to till their fields (whence the term *vades* was later applied to defendants obliged to appear with their attorneys in court). And just as the vassal was called *vas* in Latin and *bas* in Greek, he continued to be called *was* and *wassus* by the barbarian writers on feudal law. Later the real rustic fiefs must have developed, under which the vassals must have been the first *praedes* or *mancipes,* under real-estate bond; and *mancipes* remained the proper term for those under bond to the treasury, of whom we shall have more to say later.

560   Here likewise must have been the origin of the first heroic colonies which we call inland to differentiate them from the maritime colonies which came later. The latter we shall see were simply bands of refugees who took to the sea and found safety in other lands (as noted in the Axioms [300]). For the term colony properly signifies merely a crowd of workers who till the soil (as they still do) for their daily sustenance. The histories of these two kinds of colonies are contained in two fables. (1) For the inland colonies, the famous

Gallic Hercules who, with the chains of poetic gold (that is, grain) issuing from his mouth, chains by the ears great multitudes of men and leads them after him whither he will. This has hitherto been taken as a symbol of eloquence, but the fable was born at a time when the heroes had as yet no articulate speech, as has been fully shown above. (2) For the maritime colonies, the fable of the net with which heroic Vulcan drags plebeian Venus and Mars from the sea (a distinction of which a general explanation will be given later), so that the Sun discovers them completely naked (that is, not clothed in the civil light with which the heroes shone, as we have just stated), and the gods (the nobles of the heroic cities, as explained above) laugh them to scorn (as the patricians ridiculed the poor plebs of ancient Rome).

561   And lastly the asylums had here their first origin. Thus Cadmus founds Thebes, the most ancient city of Greece, as an asylum. Theseus founds Athens on the altar of the unhappy, for such was the appropriate epithet for the impious vagabonds who were without all the divine and human blessings that human society had afforded the pious. Romulus founds Rome by opening an asylum in the grove, in the way in which the ancient cities of Latium had arisen; for Livy defines it generally as an ancient counsel of founders of cities; wherefore he is wrong, as we have seen above, in attributing to Romulus the saying that he and his comrades were sons of that land. Yet Livy's phrase is to our purpose in that it shows that the asylums were the origins of the cities, whose eternal property it is that men live secure from violence in them. In this way, from the multitude of impious vagabonds who everywhere repaired to the lands of the pious and strong and found safety there, came Jove's gracious title, the hospitable. For these asylums were the first hospices in the world, and those who were there received were the first guests or strangers of the first cities, as we shall later see. And among the many labors of Hercules poetic Greek history preserved these two: how he went about the world slaying monsters, men in aspect but beasts in their habits, and how he cleansed the filthy Augean stables.

562   In this connection gentile poetic imagination created two other major divinities, Mars and Venus. The former was a [poetic] character of the heroes as first and properly fighting for their altars and hearths, *pro aris et focis*. This sort of fighting was always heroic, for it was fighting for their own religion, upon which mankind falls back when all natural help is despaired of. Whence the wars of religion are most sanguinary. Libertines, too, as they grow older, turn to religion, for they feel nature failing them. It was for these reasons that we took religion for the first principle of our Science. Now Mars fought on truly real fields and behind truly real shields, which, from *cluer,* were called by the Romans first *clupei* and later *clypei;* just as from the time of the returned barbarism pastures and enclosed woods have been called defenses. And these shields were charged with true arms, which at first, before there were arms of iron, were simply poles with their ends burnt and then tapered to a point and given sharp edges to make them suitable for inflicting wounds. Such were the simple spears,

without iron tips, which were given as military prizes to the Roman soldiers
for heroic conduct in war. Hence among the Greeks the spear is borne by
Minerva, Bellona and Pallas [Athena]. And among the Latins, from *quiris,*
"spear," Juno is called Quirina and Mars Quirinus; and Romulus, because in
life he excelled with the spear, was called Quirinus after his death. Similarly the
Roman people, who were armed with javelins (as the Spartans, the heroic people
of Greece, were armed with spears), were called Quirites in solemn assembly. But
the barbarian nations, Roman history tells us, used to fight with the primitive
spears we are speaking of, and it describes them for us as *praeustas sudes,* "burnt-
tip spears," similar to those the American Indians were found to wield. And in
our own times the nobles are armed with spears in the tournaments, as they
formerly used them in war. The invention of this sort of weapon proceeded from
a just idea of strength, as it were elongating the arm and thus using the body to
ward off harm from the body: whereas the arms that are held close to the body
belong rather to beasts.

563   We learned above that the lower ends of the fields where the dead
were buried were the first shields in the world, whence in the science of heraldry
the shield is the ground or escutcheon of the arms. The colors of the fields were
true colors. The black came from the burnt fields to which Hercules had set
fire. The green from the fields of grain in leaf. And it was by an error that the
gold was taken as a metal, for it was the yellowing of the standing grain as it
ripened that made the third color of the earth, as we have said before. Thus the
Romans, among their heroic military prizes, charged with grain the shields of
soldiers who had distinguished themselves in battle, and military glory was
called *adorea* from *ador,* the parched grain which was their primitive food. The
ancient Latins called it *adur,* from *uro,* "to burn," so that perhaps the first adora-
tion in religious times was the burning of grain. Blue was the color of the sky
with which these clearings were covered, which is why *bleu* is French for "blue,"
"sky," and "God," as we have said above. Red was from the blood of the impious thieves slain by the heroes when found in their fields. The noble arms
which have come down to us from the returned barbarism are observed to be
charged with many lions, black, green, gold, blue, and finally red. These, according to what we have seen above of the fields of grain that later became fields
of arms, must be the cultivated lands, viewed under the aspect, set forth above,
of the lion overcome by Hercules, with their above enumerated colors. Many
charged with vairs, which must be the furrows whence sprang the armed men
of Cadmus, sprouting from the dragon's teeth he had sown after slaying the
monster. Many are charged with pales, which must be the spears with which the
first heroes waged war. And finally many are charged with rakes, which are
clearly agricultural implements. From all this we must conclude that agriculture
was the first foundation of nobility not only in the first barbarian times, as we
ascertain from the Romans, but also in the second.

564   The shields of the ancients were covered with leather, as we learn

from the poets that the old heroes dressed in leather, that is, in the hides of the beasts they hunted and killed. On this there is a fine passage in Pausanias where he says that leather clothing was invented by Pelasgus (an ancient hero of Greece after whom the people of that nation were first called Pelasgians, and whom Apollodorus in his *De origine deorum* calls autochthonous or son of earth, or, in a word, a giant). And there is a striking correspondence between the first and second barbarian times, for Dante, speaking of the grand old personages of the second, says they were clothed in leather and bone, and Boccaccio too relates that they went about wrapped in leather. This must have been the reason for covering the family arms with leather, and the curling into scrolls of the skin of head and feet is an appropriate finishing touch. The shields were round because the cleared and cultivated lands were the first *orbes terrarum,* as above noted; and this characteristic survived among the Romans, whose clypeus was round, in distinction from their scutum, which had corners. Every clearing was called a *lucus* in the sense of an eye, as even today we call eyes the openings through which light enters houses. The true heroic phrase that "every giant had his *lucus*" [clearing or eye] was altered and corrupted when its meaning was lost, and had already been falsified when it reached Homer, for it was then taken to mean that every giant had one eye in the middle of his forehead. With these one-eyed giants came Vulcan to work in the first forges—that is, the forests to which Vulcan had set fire and where he had fashioned the first arms, which as we have seen were the spears with burnt tips—and, by an extension of the idea of arms, to forge bolts for Jove. For Vulcan had set fire to the forests in order to observe in the open sky the direction from which Jove sent his bolts.

565   The other divinity born among these most ancient human things was Venus, a [poetic] character of civil beauty, whence *honestas* had the meanings of nobility, beauty and virtue. For this is the order in which these three ideas must have been born. The first to be understood was the civil beauty which appertained to the heroes. Then the natural beauty which is apprehended by the human senses, but only by those of men of perception and comprehension, who know how to discern the parts and grasp their harmony in the body as a whole, in which beauty essentially consists. This is why peasants and men of the squalid plebs understand little or nothing of beauty (which shows the error of the philologians who say that in these simple and stupid times of which we are speaking kings were chosen for their handsome and well-proportioned bodies; for this tradition is to be understood as referring to civil beauty, which was the nobility of the heroes, as we shall shortly state). And lastly the beauty of virtue, which is called *honestas* and is understood only by philosophers. Hence it must have been the civil beauty that was possessed by Apollo, Bacchus, Ganymede, Bellerophon, Theseus and other heroes, and perhaps on their account Venus was imagined as male [androgynous].

566   The idea of civil beauty must have been engendered in the minds of the theological poets when they saw that the impious creatures who had

taken refuge on their lands were men in aspect but brute beasts in their habits. It was this civil beauty and no other that was cherished by the Spartans, the heroes of Greece, who cast down from Mt. Taygetus the ugly and deformed offspring, that is, those borne by noble women but without benefit of solemn nuptials. Such too must have been the monsters condemned by the Law of the Twelve Tables to be thrown into the Tiber. For it is not at all likely that the decemvirs, in that parsimony of laws proper to the first commonwealths, would have given any thought to natural monsters, because of whose extreme rarity anything rare in nature is called monstrous, when even in the abundance of laws with which we are now afflicted, legislators leave to the discretion of judges those cases that seldom present themselves. Such then must have been the monsters which were first and properly called civil. (It is one of these that Pamphilus had in mind when, under the false suspicion that the maiden Philumena was pregnant, he says: *Aliquid monstri alunt,* "Something monstrous is a-breeding.") And so they continued to be called in the Roman laws, which must have spoken with all propriety, as Antoine Favre observes in his *Iurisprudentiae papinianeae scientia,* and as we have already remarked above in another connection.

567   This must be what Livy has in mind when, with as much good faith as ignorance of the Roman antiquities of which he writes, he says that if the nobles shared *connubium* with the plebeians the resulting offspring would be *secum ipsa discors,* which is as much as to say a monster of mixed and twofold nature, the one heroic, of the nobles, the other feral, of the plebeians who "practiced marriages like those of wild animals" (*agitabant connubia more ferarum*). This phrase [*secum ipsa discors*] Livy took from some ancient writer of annals and used it ignorantly, for he quotes it as if it meant "if the nobles intermarried with the plebeians." But the plebeians in their miserable state of quasi slavery could not ask any such thing of the nobles. What they demanded was the right of contracting solemn nuptials (for such is the meaning of *connubium*), which right was at that time confined to the nobles. But among animals no species has intercourse with another. We must therefore say that [*secum ipsa discors*] was a phrase of insult applied by the nobles to the plebeians in that heroic contest. For inasmuch as the latter did not possess the public auspices, whose solemnities were required to make marriages legitimate, none of them had an ascertained father (by the well-known definition in Roman law that *nuptiae demonstrant patrem,* "the marriage ceremony identifies the father"), and with reference to this uncertainty the plebeians were said by the nobles to have intercourse with their mothers and daughters as beasts do.

568   To the plebeian Venus, however, were attributed the doves, not to signify passionate love but because they are, as Horace describes them, *degeneres,* base birds in comparison with eagles, which Horace calls *feroces;* and thus to signify that the plebeians had private or minor auspices as contrasted with those of the eagles and thunderbolts possessed by the nobles and called by Varro and

Messala major or public auspices. On the latter depended all the heroic rights of the nobles, as Roman history plainly confirms. To the heroic Venus or Venus *pronuba,* on the other hand, were attributed the swans which appertain also to Apollo (who, as we saw above, was the god of the nobility), and under the auspices of one of which Leda conceives the eggs by Jove, as set forth above.

569   The plebeian Venus was depicted as naked, whereas Venus *pronuba* wore the girdle, as stated above. And here we may see how ideas concerning these poetic antiquities have been distorted. For that [nakedness] was later taken as an incentive to lust which in truth had been invented to signify the natural modesty or the punctuality of good faith with which natural obligations were fulfilled among the plebeians. For as we shall see shortly in the Poetic Politics the plebeians had no part of citizenship in the heroic cities, and thus did not contract obligations sanctioned by any bond of civil law to make their fulfilment necessary. Hence to Venus were attributed the Graces, likewise nude; and among the Latins *caussa* and *gratia* meant the same thing, so that the Graces must have signified to the poets the *pacta nuda* or simple agreements which involve only natural obligation. And thus those pacts which the Roman jurisconsults called *pacta stipulata* were later described by the medieval interpreters as "vested." For, understanding by nude pacts those not stipulated, they did not derive *stipulatio* from *stipes* (for such an origin would have yielded *stipatio*), in the forced sense of "that which sustains the pacts," but from *stipula* as used by the peasants of Latium for the blade which "clothes the grain." On the other hand, the "vested pacts" of the early writers on feudal law were so called from the same origin from which came the "investiture" of the fiefs, from which certainly comes *exfestucare,* "to divest of [legal] standing." For the reasons set forth, therefore, *gratia* and *caussa* were understood by the poetic Latins as having the same meaning with respect to the contracts observed by the plebeians of the heroic cities. Similarly, with the later introduction of contracts *de iure naturali gentium,* "by the natural law of nations" (to which Ulpian adds *humanarum,* "human" [nations]), *caussa* and *negocium* signified the same thing, for in such kinds of contracts the transactions themselves are almost always *caussae* or *cavissae* or *cautelae* which serve as stipulations to give security to the pacts.

[CHAPTER III]

COROLLARIES CONCERNING CONTRACTS SEALED BY
SIMPLE CONSENT

570   The heroic peoples were concerned only with the necessities of life. The only fruits they gathered were natural fruits, as they did not yet understand

the use of money. They were so to speak all body. Hence the most ancient law of the heroic nations could certainly take no cognizance of the contracts which nowadays are said to be sealed by simple consent. They were extremely crude people and therefore suspicious, for crudeness is born of ignorance and it is a property of human nature that he who does not know is ever doubtful. For all these reasons they did not recognize good faith, and they made sure of all obligations by a real or fictitious physical transfer. Moreover, the transfer was made certain by solemn stipulations in the course of the transaction. Hence the celebrated article in the Law of the Twelve Tables: *Si quis nexum faciet mancipiumque, uti lingua nuncupassit, ita ius esto,* "if anyone executes a bond or conveyance, as he has declared with his tongue, so let it be binding." And from this nature of human civil things the following truths emerge.

I

571   It is [rightly] said that the most ancient buying and selling was barter. In the case of real estate, however, the barter must have been of the kind which in the returned barbarism was called *libellus* or feudal leasehold. Its utility was apparent from the fact that one man had more than enough fields yielding an abundance of fruits which another man lacked, and vice versa.

II

572   The letting of houses could not be practiced as long as cities were quite small and dwellings simple. Landlords must therefore have let out their lands for others to build on; and thus the only rental was ground rent.

III

573   The letting of land must have been by emphyteusis, which the Latins called *clientela;* whence the grammarians, by an inspired guess, said the *clientes* had been so called as being *colentes,* "tillers."

IV

574   This must be the reason why, for the returned barbarism, the only contracts we find in the old archives are leases for dwellings or farms, in perpetuity or for limited periods of time.

V

575   This is perhaps the reason why emphyteusis is a contract *de iure civili,* that is, by our principles, *de iure heroico romanorum.* To this Ulpian opposes the *ius naturale gentium humanarum,* the natural law of human nations as distinguished from that of the barbarous nations that had preceded them, not from that of the barbarous nations outside the Roman empire in his own day, for their law was of no importance to Roman jurisconsults.

VI

576   Partnerships were unknown, by that cyclopean custom whereby each family father cared only for his own affairs and did not trouble himself with those of others, as, above, Homer gave us to understand by what he has Polyphemus tell Ulysses.

VII

577   For the same reason mandates or contracts of agency were unknown. The rule of ancient civil law was: *Per extraneam personam acquiri nemini,* "no one may acquire by a person not under his power."

VIII

578   But when the heroic law was succeeded by what Ulpian defines as that of the human nations, there was a revolutionary change. The contract of purchase and sale, which in ancient times did not guarantee recovery unless double recovery was stipulated in the contract, now became the queen of those contracts called *bonae fidei,* "of good faith," and the right of recovery obtained naturally even without stipulation.

[CHAPTER IV]

MYTHOLOGICAL CANON

579   Returning now to the three [poetic] characters, Vulcan, Mars and Venus, it must be noted here (and this must be considered an important canon of our mythology) that there were three divine characters signifying the heroes, distinguished from three others signifying the plebeians. Vulcan splits Jove's head with a hatchet to give birth to Minerva, attempts to interfere in a quarrel between Jove and Juno, is kicked out of heaven by Jove, and is left lame. Mars, in a stern reproof reported by Homer, is called by Jove "the vilest of all the gods," and Minerva in the battle of the gods related by the same poet hurls a stone at him and wounds him. (This Vulcan and this Mars must be the plebeians who served the heroes in war.) And Venus (signifying the natural wives of the plebeians) along with the plebeian Mars is trapped in the net of the heroic Vulcan; and, being discovered naked by the Sun, they are made the butt of the other gods. Hence Venus was erroneously believed to be the wife of Vulcan, but we saw above that there was no marriage in heaven save that between Jove and Juno, and that was sterile. And it was not said that Mars had committed adultery

with Venus but that she was his concubine, because among the plebeians there were only natural marriages, as we shall show later, and these were called by the Latins concubinages.

580   As we have explained these three characters here, so we shall explain others in their proper places. Among them we shall find the plebeian Tantalus who cannot reach the apples (which rise beyond his grasp) nor the water (which sinks beneath the reach of his lips); the plebeian Midas dying of hunger because all he touches turns to gold; and the plebeian Linus who contends in song with Apollo and is vanquished and slain by the god.

581   Such double fables or characters must have been necessary in the heroic state in which the plebeians, having no names of their own, bore those of their heroes, as we have said above. To say nothing of the extreme poverty of speech that must have obtained in the first times, when even in the abundance of our present languages the same word often signifies different and sometimes contrary things.

[SECTION V]

[POETIC POLITICS]

[CHAPTER I]

POETIC POLITICS, UNDER WHICH THE FIRST COMMONWEALTHS
IN THE WORLD WERE BORN IN A MOST SEVERELY
ARISTOCRATIC FORM

582   In this fashion, then, the families were founded with the *famuli*
taken by the heroes under their faith, power, or protection. And these *famuli*
were the first *socii* in the world, as we have seen above. Their lives were in the
hands of their lords, and consequently their acquisitions likewise. The heroes,
with their cyclopean paternal authority, had the right of life and death over
their own children, and, in consequence of this right over their persons, had
also a despotic right over all their acquisitions. This was Aristotle's meaning
when he defined the children of a family as "animate instruments of their
fathers." And the Law of the Twelve Tables, even into the period of the most
unbounded popular liberty, preserved to the Roman family fathers both these
monarchical rights of power over the persons and dominion over the acquisitions [of their children]. Indeed, until imperial times, sons, like slaves, had
only one kind of *peculium* or private property, namely *peculium profecticium*
[that acquired by their father's consent]. In the earliest times the fathers must
have had the power of really selling their children as many as three times; for
later, with the progressive softening of human times, they made three pretended
sales when they wished to free their children from their paternal power. The
Gauls and the Celts, however, retained an equal power over slaves and children;
and the custom of fathers really selling their children was found in the West
Indies, and in Europe they are sold up to four times by the Muscovites and Tartars. So true is it, forsooth, that other barbarous nations do not have paternal
authority *talem qualem habent cives romani,* such as Roman citizens have [*Inst.*
1.9.2]! This evident falsehood springs from the common vulgar error of which
the scholars have been guilty in interpreting this statement; for it was made by

the jurisconsults with reference to the nations conquered by the Roman people. For such nations, as we shall later show at greater length, having lost all their civil rights by the law of war, had left to them only natural paternal powers and, consequently, natural blood ties called those of cognation; and similarly only the natural property rights called bonitary; and hence on both these accounts only the natural obligations said to be *de iure naturali gentium,* which Ulpian further specified as *humanarum.* But the civil rights these subject nations had lost must all have been possessed by the peoples outside the Roman empire, precisely as the Romans themselves had them.

583   To return to our argument: when the sons of the families were freed by their fathers' death from this private monarchical rule, each son took it up entire for himself, so that every Roman citizen when free of paternal power is called a *paterfamilias* in Roman law. The *famuli* on the other hand went on living in that servile state. After a long period of time they must naturally have chafed under it, by the axiom set forth above [292] that "subject man naturally aspires to free himself from servitude." Such must have been the Tantalus above called plebeian, striving in vain to reach the fruit (the golden apples of the grain raised on the lands of the heroes, as above explained), and unable to slake his burning thirst with so much as a mouthful of the water which rises to his lips only to sink away again. Such also were Ixion, forever turning the wheel, and Sisyphus pushing the rock uphill. (Like the dragon's teeth sown by Cadmus, this rock was the hard earth, and its rolling back when it reached the top was preserved in the Latin phrases *vertere terram* for cultivating it and *saxum volvere* for painfully performing a long and arduous task.) For all these reasons the *famuli* must have revolted against the heroes. And this is that "necessity" which we conjectured generally in the Axioms [261] to have been imposed by the *famuli* upon the heroic fathers in the state of the families, as a result of which the commonwealths were born.

584   For at this point, under pressure of the emergency, the heroes must naturally have been moved to unite themselves in orders so as to resist the multitudes of rebellious *famuli.* And they must have chosen as their head a father fiercer than the rest and with greater presence of spirit. Such men were called *reges,* "kings," from *regere,* which properly means "to sustain" or "direct." In this fashion, to use the well-known phrase of the jurisconsult Pomponius, "things themselves dictating it, kingdoms were founded" (*rebus ipsis dictantibus, regna condita*); a phrase in keeping with the doctrine of Roman law which declares that the natural law of nations was established by divine providence (*ius naturale gentium divina providentia constitutum*). Such was the generation of the heroic kingdoms. And since the fathers were sovereign kings of their families, the equality of their state and the fierce nature of the Cyclopes being such that no one of them naturally would yield to another, there sprang up of themselves the reigning senates, made up of so many family kings. These, without any human discernment or counsel, were found to have united their private interests in a

common interest called *patria,* which, the word *res* being understood, means "the interest of the fathers." The nobles were accordingly called patricians, and the nobles must have been the only citizens of the first *patriae* or fatherlands. In this sense we may regard as truthful the tradition that has come down to us which says that in the earliest times kings were chosen by nature. On this point there are two golden passages in Tacitus's *Germania* [ch. 7], which give us ground for conjecturing the same custom for all the other first barbarous peoples. The first is that "their squadrons or battalions, instead of being formed by chance or by a fortuitous gathering, are composed of families and clans." And the second is that "their chiefs do more by example than by authority; if they are energetic, if they are conspicuous, if they fight in the front, they lead because they are admired."

585 Evidence that the first kings on earth were of this nature is afforded by the fact that the heroic poets imagined Jove in heaven to have just such kingship over men and gods, as is shown by that golden passage in Homer where Jove explains to Thetis that he can do nothing contrary to what the gods have once determined in their great celestial council. Here speaks a true aristocratic king. On this episode the Stoics later erected their dogma of a Jove subject to fate, but in fact Jove and the other gods held council concerning the affairs of men and freely determined them. And the passage we have cited explains two others in Homer which political theorists have erroneously interpreted as Homeric references to monarchy. In one of them Agamemnon reproves the stubborn Achilles. In the other Ulysses persuades the Greeks, mutinous and desirous of returning home, to continue the siege of Troy. In both passages it is said that "one alone is king." But both passages refer to warfare, in which there is but one commander-in-chief, by the maxim quoted by Tacitus [*Annals* I, 6] "the condition of bearing rule is that an account cannot be balanced unless it is rendered to one person" (*eam esse imperandi conditionem, ut non aliter ratio constet quam si uni reddatur*). Moreover, Homer himself, as often as he mentions the heroes by name in his two poems, adds the fixed epithet "king." In striking harmony with this is a golden passage in Genesis in which Moses, enumerating the descendants of Esau, calls them all kings, or rather, as the Vulgate has it, *duces,* "captains." Likewise the ambassadors of Pyrrhus report having seen in Rome a senate of so many kings. And in fact one cannot conceive in civil nature any reason why the fathers, in such a change of forms of government, should have altered anything of what they had had in the state of nature, save to subject their sovereign family powers to these reigning orders of theirs. For the nature of the strong, as we have set forth above in the Axioms [261], is to surrender as little as possible of what they have acquired by valor, and only so much as is necessary to preserve their acquisitions. Hence we read so often in Roman history of that heroic disdain of the strong which will not suffer an ignominious surrender of what has been won by valor (*virtute parta per flagitium amittere*). And among all human possibilities, once we have seen that

civil governments were not born either of fraud or of the violence of a single man (as we have already shown and shall show more fully later), one cannot imagine any way but the one we have described by which civil power could emerge from family authority, or the eminent domain of civil states from the paternal natural domains (which, as we have indicated above, were *ex iure optimo* in the sense of being free of every private or public encumbrance).

586   This development which we have established by reason is strikingly confirmed by the origins of the words relating to it. For on this *dominium optimum* or unencumbered domain of the fathers (called *dikaion ariston* by the Greeks) were erected the commonwealths which (as noted above) were called aristocratic by the Greeks, and by the Romans commonwealths of the optimates, so called from Ops, goddess of power. Perhaps for this reason Ops was called Jove's wife (from whom he must have been called *optimus,* for he is *aristos* to the Greeks and hence *optimus* to the Latins), the wife, that is, of the reigning order of those heroes who, as noted above, had arrogated to themselves the name of gods. (For Juno by the law of the auspices was the wife of Jove understood as the thundering sky.) The mother of these gods, as said above, was Cybele, also called mother of the giants properly so called in the sense of nobles, and she was later taken, as we shall see in the Poetic Cosmography, for the queen of cities. From Ops, then, came the term optimates, for all such commonwealths are ordained to preserve the power of the nobles, and to preserve it they retain as eternal properties two principal custodies, one of the orders, the other of the frontiers. Under the custody of the orders came first the custody of the families, by which the Romans down to the 309th year of the city excluded the plebs from *connubium.* Then the custody of the magistracies, by which the patricians so strongly contested the claim of the plebs to the consulship. Then the custody of the priesthoods, and finally, by its means, the custody of the laws, which all the first nations regarded as sacred. Whence down to the Law of the Twelve Tables the nobles governed Rome by custom, as we were assured by Dionysius of Halicarnassus in the Axioms [284], and for a century afterwards the interpretation of that Law was kept within the college of pontiffs, according to the jurisconsult Pomponius, because until then that college was open only to nobles. The other principal custody is that of the frontiers, in which connection the Romans, until their destruction of Corinth, had observed an incomparable justice in war in order not to militarize the plebeians, and an extreme clemency in victory in order not to enrich them. On this we have set forth two axioms above [273–276].

587   This great and important tract of poetic history is all contained in the fable of Saturn seeking to devour the infant Jove, and the priests of Cybele concealing him and by the clash of their arms preventing his infant cries from being heard. Here Saturn must be a character of the *famuli,* who as day laborers till the fields of their masters, the heroic fathers, and with ardent longing seek fields from the fathers on which they may find sustenance for themselves. And

this Saturn is the father of Jove because from this Saturn, as its occasion, was born the civil government of the fathers which, as we said before, was set forth in the character of that Jove whose wife was Ops. For Jove taken as the god of the auspices, of which the most solemn were the thunderbolt and the eagle—the Jove whose wife was Juno—is the father of the gods, that is, of the heroes. For they believed themselves sons of Jove, as having been engendered under his auspices in solemn nuptials, of which Juno is the goddess, and so they took the name of gods, whose mother is Earth, that is, Ops, the wife of this Jove, as has all been said above. And this same Jove was called king of men, that is of the *famuli* in the state of the families and of the plebeians in that of the heroic cities. These two divine titles [father and king], through ignorance of this poetic history, have been confused, as if Jove were also the father of men. But men [*famuli* and plebeians] down into the days of the ancient Roman republic could not name their fathers (*non poterant nomine ciere patrem*), as Livy says, because they were born of natural marriages and not of solemn nuptials; whence jurisprudence retained the maxim: *Nuptiae demonstrant patrem,* "The marriage ceremony identifies the father."

588   The fable goes on to relate that the priests of Cybele or Ops (for the first kingdoms were everywhere priestly, as we have said above and shall show more fully later) conceal Jove. (From this concealment Latin philologians guess the name Latium must have come, and the Latin language preserved the history in its phrase *condere regna,* as we said before, for the fathers formed a closed order against the mutinous *famuli,* and the secrecy of this order was the source of what political theorists called *arcana imperii.*) And by the clash of their arms they prevent Saturn from hearing the wailing of Jove (newly born to the union of that order), and thus they save him. In this way the same thing is distinctly narrated that Plato stated so obscurely, that "the commonwealths were born on the basis of arms." To this may be added what Aristotle told us above in the Axioms [271], that in the heroic commonwealths the nobles swore eternal enmity against the plebs. And there remained from all this the eternal property expressed in the saying that servants are the paid enemies of their masters. The Greeks preserve this history for us in the etymology of *polemos,* "war," from *polis,* "city."

589   In this connection the Greek nations imagined the tenth divinity of the *gentes maiores,* namely Minerva. And her birth was fancied in this wild and uncouth fashion: Vulcan, it was said, split with an axe the forehead of Jove, whence sprang Minerva. By this they meant to signify that the multitude of *famuli* practicing servile arts (which, as we have said, came under the poetic genus of the plebeian Vulcan) broke (in the sense of weakening or diminishing) the rule of Jove. (The Latins used for this the expression *minuere caput,* "to split the head," because, not being able to express rule as an abstraction, they used the concrete word for "head.") For Jove's rule in the state of the families had been monarchic, and they changed it to aristocratic in the state of the cities.

Hence it is not an unlikely conjecture that Minerva's name was derived from *minuere,* nor that from this most ancient poetic antiquity came the phrase in Roman law, *capitis deminutio,* in the sense of change of form of government, as Minerva changed the state of the families into that of the cities.

590   To this fable the philosophers later attached the most sublime of their metaphysical meditations: that the eternal idea in God is generated by God himself, while created ideas are produced in us by God. But the theological poets contemplated Minerva under the idea of civil order, whence order was the Latin term par excellence for the senate (which perhaps led the philosophers to consider it an eternal idea of God, who is naught else than eternal order); and thence there remained the eternal property that the order of the best is the wisdom of cities. However Minerva in Homer is always distinguished by the fixed epithets warlike and predatory, and only twice do we recall having found her called counselor. And the owl and the olive were sacred to her not because she spends the night in meditation and reads and writes by the light of the lamp, but rather to signify the dark night of the hiding places in which, as we have said above, humanity had its beginnings, and perhaps more properly to signify that the heroic senates that composed the cities conceived their laws in secret. Certainly it remained the custom of the Areopagites to give their votes under cover of darkness in the senate of Athens, the city of Minerva, whom the Greeks called Athena. From this heroic custom came the Latin phrase *condere leges,* so that *legum conditores* properly signified the senates that commanded the laws, and *legum latores* those who carried the laws from the senates to the plebs of the various peoples, as we have noted above in the case of Horatius. How far the theological poets were from considering Minerva the goddess of wisdom appears from the statues and medals in which she is always shown as armed, and from the fact that the same goddess was Minerva in the curia, Pallas in the plebeian assemblies (for example in Homer it is Pallas who leads Telemachus, about to depart in search of his father Ulysses, into the assembly of the plebs, whom he calls the "other people"), and lastly Bellona in warfare.

591   It must be said that the erroneous belief that Minerva was understood as wisdom by the theological poets is of a piece with the other error that the curia was so called from *curanda respublica* at a time when the nations were confused and stupid. The word must rather have been derived by the most ancient Greeks from *cheir,* "hand," in the form *kyria,* whence *curia* in Latin. We may infer as much from one of the two great fragments of antiquity (entered in the Chronological Table and mentioned in the Notes upon it [77]) which, to our good fortune, Denis Petau found embedded in Greek history before the heroic age of Greece and consequently in what the Egyptians called the age of the gods, which we are here investigating.

592   One of these fragments relates that the Heraclids or descendants of Hercules had been scattered through the whole of Greece, even in Attica where Athens was, and had later retired to the Peloponnesus where Sparta was,

an aristocratic commonwealth or kingdom under two kings of the race of Hercules, called Heraclids or nobles, who administered laws and conducted wars
under the supervision of the ephors. The latter were guardians not of popular
but of aristocratic liberty. They had king Agis strangled because he had tried to
bring to the people a law wiping out debts, which Livy [XXXII, 38] calls "a
firebrand for inflaming the plebs against the optimates" (*facem ad accendendum
adversus optimates plebem*), and another concerning testaments which would
have diverted inheritances outside the order of the nobles, within which they
had previously been kept by the law of legitimate succession; for only the nobles
had had *sui heredes,* agnates, or gentiles [110]. There had been similar
attempts at Rome before the Law of the Twelve Tables, as will be shown later.
And just as men like [Spurius] Cassius, [Manlius] Capitolinus, the Gracchi and
other leading citizens of Rome were declared traitors and executed by the
senate for attempting with like laws to raise up somewhat the poor oppressed
plebs of Rome, so Agis was strangled by the ephors. So far were the ephors of
Sparta from being, as Polybius represents them, guardians of the popular liberty
of Lacedaemon. Thus Athens (named for Minerva, whom they called Athena)
must have had in its earliest times an aristocratic form of government; and Greek
history has faithfully recounted as much, telling us (as noted above) that Draco
reigned in Athens at the time when it was occupied by the optimates. And this
is confirmed by Thucydides [i.e. Isocrates], who tells us that as long as the city
was governed by the severe Areopagites it shone with the finest heroic virtues
and carried out the worthiest enterprises, just as Rome did in the time when, as
we shall see later, it was an aristocratic commonwealth. (Juvenal renders their
name "judges of Mars" in the sense of armed judges, though *Arēs,* Mars, +
pēgē, in Latin *pagus,* a country or its people, might better have been rendered
"the people of Mars," as the Roman people were called; for at their birth the
peoples were composed only of nobles, who alone had the right to bear arms.)
But Athens was cast down from this lofty state by Pericles and Aristides in
favor of popular liberty, and Rome suffered a like fate beginning with Sextius
and Canuleius, tribunes of the plebs.

593   The other great fragment tells how the Greeks traveling abroad observed the Curetes or priests of Cybele scattered through Saturnia or ancient
Italy, through Crete, and through Asia; so that everywhere among the first
barbarous nations there must have prevailed kingdoms of Curetes, corresponding to the kingdoms of the Heraclids scattered through ancient Greece. These
Curetes were the armed priests who by the clashing of their arms muffled the
cries of the infant Jove whom Saturn sought to devour in the fable we were just
explaining.

594   It follows from our entire argument that the first *comitia curiata*
must have had their origin at this most ancient point of time and in this way.
They are the oldest *comitia* we read of in Roman history. They had to be held
under arms, and they were continued for the purpose of dealing with sacred

things, for in the earliest times all profane matters were seen under this aspect. Livy wonders that such assemblies were held in Gaul at the time when Hannibal passed through. But Tacitus in his *Germania* tells us that they were also held by priests, who dealt out penalties in the midst of arms as if in the presence of their gods. This showed a just sense of the fitness of things, for the heroic assemblies were armed for dealing out penalties because the supreme authority of the laws follows the supreme authority of arms. And speaking generally Tacitus tells us that the Germans conducted all their public affairs under arms and presided over by priests, as we have just said. Hence among the ancient Germans, whose custom allows us to assume the like for all the first barbarous peoples, we find the kingdom of the Egyptian priests; we find the kingdoms of the Curetes or armed priests which prevailed, as we have seen, among the Greeks of Saturnia or ancient Italy, of Crete and of Asia; we find the Quirites of ancient Latium.

595   In view of what has been set forth, the law of the Quirites must have been the natural law of the heroic peoples of Italy, which, to distinguish it from that of the other peoples, was called *ius Quiritium Romanorum*. This did not come about through any pact made between the Sabines and the Romans that they should be called Quirites from Cures, the capital city of the Sabines, for in that case they would have been called Curetes, the name used by the Greeks of Saturnia. And if the capital of the Sabines had been called Ceres (as the Latin grammarians will have it), they should rather have been called (and note the distortion of ideas!) Cerites, a name applied to those Roman citizens who were condemned by the censors to bear the burdens while having no part of civil honors, just as were the plebs who were composed of the *famuli,* as we shall presently see, at the birth of the heroic cities. It was with the mass of the plebs that the Sabines must have been merged in those barbarous times when conquered cities were destroyed and the survivors scattered over the plains and forced to till the fields for the conquering peoples—a fate that the Romans did not spare even the mother city of Alba. Such [conquered neighbor cities] were the first provinces, so called as if for *prope victae* "near conquered" (for example, Corioli, for the conquest of which Marcius was called Coriolanus), as on the other hand the last or farthest provinces were so called as being *procul victae,* "far conquered." And in such plains were settled the first inland colonies, called in all propriety *coloniae deductae,* that is, bands of peasant day laborers led down from above; whereas in the case of the last or farthest colonies *deductae* meant just the opposite, for, from the low and cramped quarters of Rome where the poor plebeians must have dwelt, they were led to high and strong places in the provinces, to keep them in order, to be lords therein, and to change the existing lords of the fields into poor laborers. In this way, according to Livy who saw only the effects, Rome grows on the ruins of Alba, and the Sabines bring to their Roman sons-in-law the wealth of Ceres as the dowry of their abducted daughters, as Florus vainly remarks. And these are the colonies before those which

came after the agrarian laws of the Gracchi. Livy says the Roman plebs, in the
heroic contests they carried on with the nobility, disdained, or rather resented,
these first colonies because they were not of the same kind as the last; and because they did nothing to raise up the Roman plebs, and Livy finds that they
even added fuel to the contests, he offers these vain reflections upon them.

596   Finally, that Minerva had signified armed aristocratic orders is attested by Homer where he tells of Minerva wounding Mars with a stone in the
course of their contest. (Mars, as we saw above, was the [poetic] character of
the plebeians who served the heroes in war.) And again where he tells of
Minerva attempting a conspiracy against Jove, which is after the manner of
aristocracies, in which the lords by secret counsels overthrow their chiefs when
the latter affect tyranny. It is only in this time that we read of statues being
erected to the slayers of tyrants; whereas if the latter had been monarchical
kings, as commonly supposed, their slayers would have been accounted traitors.

597   Thus the first cities were made up solely of nobles, who were in command. But because they had need of others to serve them, by a common sense of
utility the heroes were constrained to satisfy the multitude of their aroused
clients; hence they sent to them the first embassies, which by the law of nations
are sent by sovereigns. And they sent them with the first agrarian law in the
world, under which, as the strong do, they conceded to the clients the least they
could, which was bonitary ownership of the fields the heroes might choose to
assign to them. Thus it may be true that Ceres discovered both grain and laws.
This law was dictated by the following natural law of nations: since ownership
follows power, and since the lives of the *famuli* were dependent on the heroes
who had saved them by granting them asylum, it was lawful and right that they
should have a similarly precarious ownership, which they might enjoy as long
as it suited the heroes to maintain them in possession of the fields they had
assigned to them. Thus the *famuli* merged to form the first plebs of the heroic
cities, in which they had none of the privileges of citizenship. It is just like one
of these that Achilles declares he has been treated by Agamemnon when the
latter wrongfully takes Briseis from him, for he says he has suffered an outrage
which would not have been committed against a laborer without any rights of
citizenship.

598   Such were the Roman plebeians down to the struggle over *connubium*. For when, by the second agrarian law, conceded to them by the nobles
in the Law of the Twelve Tables, they had gained quiritary ownership of the
fields, as we showed many years ago in our *Principles of Universal Law* (in one
of the two passages on whose account we do not regret the publication of that
book), yet, because by the law of nations strangers were not capable of civil
ownership, and the plebeians were not yet citizens, they were still unable to leave
their fields intestate to their kin, because they did not have *sui heredes,* agnates,
or cognates, which relations were all dependent on solemn nuptials. Nor
could they even dispose of their fields by testament, for they were not citizens.

Hence the lands assigned to them soon returned to the nobles, from whom they had had the title to their ownership. When they had become aware of this, within three short years they demanded the right of *connubium*. In the condition of miserable slaves that Roman history clearly relates that of the plebeians to have been, they did not demand the right of intermarrying with the nobles, for in that case the Latin would have read *connubia cum patribus*. What they did ask was the right to contract solemn nuptials just as the fathers did, and so they demanded *connubia patrum,* the principal solemnity of which was the public auspices called by Varro and Messala major auspices, those meant by the fathers when they said the auspices were theirs. The plebeians, in making this demand, were in effect asking for Roman citizenship, whose natural principle was solemn nuptials, which were therefore defined by the jurisconsult Modestinus as the sharing of every divine and human right (*omnis divini et humani iuris communicatio*), than which no more proper definition can be given of citizenship itself.

[CHAPTER II]

ALL COMMONWEALTHS ARE BORN FROM CERTAIN ETERNAL PRINCIPLES OF FIEFS

599   In such fashion, in part from the nature of the strong to preserve their acquisitions, and in part from the nature of the benefits which can be looked for in civil life, on which two natures of human things we said in the Axioms [260–262] the eternal principles of fiefs were founded, the commonwealths were born in the world with three kinds of ownership for three kinds of fiefs, which were held by three kinds of persons over three kinds of things.

600   The first was bonitary ownership of rustic or human fiefs, which the "men" (those whom Hotman is surprised to find called vassals in the feudal laws of the returned barbarism), that is, the plebeians, had of the fruits on the farms of their heroes.

601   The second was quiritary ownership of noble, heroic or armed fiefs, nowadays called military; for the heroes, when they united themselves in armed orders, kept their sovereignty over their farms. This was what had been in the state of nature the best ownership, which Cicero, as we said before, recognizes in his *De aruspicum responsis* as held over a few houses still remaining in the Rome of his day, and which he defines as "ownership of real estate free of any real encumbrance whether private or public." On this there is a golden passage in the Pentateuch, where Moses relates that in the time of Joseph the priests of Egypt did not pay the king tribute on their fields. And we have pointed out not

far back that all the heroic kingdoms were priestly, and we shall demonstrate shortly that at first the Roman patricians did not pay the treasury any tribute on their fields. When the heroic commonwealths were formed, these sovereign private fiefs naturally became subject to the higher sovereignty of the reigning heroic orders (each community of which was called a *patria* with *res* understood, meaning "interest of the fathers"), which was to be defended and maintained because it had preserved their sovereign family powers on a basis of mutual equality; and this is the sole mark of aristocratic liberty.

602   The third, with full propriety called civil ownership [= eminent domain], was that which the heroic cities, composed in the beginning of heroes only, had over the lands by certain divine fiefs which the family fathers had previously received from the provident divinity, as we have shown above (in virtue of which they had found themselves sovereigns in the state of the families, and had united themselves in reigning orders in the state of the cities); and thus they became sovereign civil kingdoms subject to the supreme sovereign God, whose providence is recognized by all sovereign civil powers. This is made plain to human understanding by the explicit avowal of sovereign powers in adding to their titles of majesty such phrases as "by divine providence" or "by the grace of God," through which they must publicly profess to have received their kingdoms. So that if worship of providence were forbidden, the natural consequence would be their fall, for a nation of fatalists or casualists or atheists never existed in the world, and we saw above that all the nations of the world, through four primary religions and no more [paganism, Judaism, Christianity, Islam], believe in a provident divinity. So the plebeians swore by the heroes, and such oaths have survived as *mehercules! mecastor! aedepol!* and *medius-fidius!* "by the god Fidius!" who, as we shall see, was the Roman Hercules; but the heroes swore by Jove. For the plebeians were at first in the power of the heroes (the noble Romans, down to the 419th year of the city, exercised the right of private incarceration over their plebeian debtors), while the heroes, who formed the ruling orders, were in the power of Jove by reason of the auspices. If the auspices seemed to permit, the heroes appointed magistrates, enacted laws and exercised other sovereign rights; if they seemed to forbid, they abstained. All this is that *fides deorum et hominum,* "faith of gods and men," to which pertain the Latin phrases *implorare fidem,* "to implore help and aid"; *recipere in fidem,* "to receive under protection or authority"; and the exclamation *proh deûm atque hominum fidem imploro!* used by the oppressed to implore on their behalf the "force of gods and men," which the Italians rendered in the human sense "the power of the world." For this power in virtue of which civil powers are so called, this force, this faith, for which the oaths just quoted attest the veneration of the subjects, and this protection which the powerful must extend over the weak (in which two things lies the essence of feudalism), are the force which sustains and rules this civil world. The center of this force was sensed if not rationally understood by the Greeks (as we have noted in the

medals of their commonwealths) and by the Latins (as we have observed in their heroic phrases) to be the ground of each civil sphere. Even today the crowns of sovereign powers are surmounted by a sphere, on which is implanted the divine symbol of the cross. The sphere, as we have shown above, is the golden apple, signifying the high dominion which sovereign powers have over the lands of which they are lords; and for this reason it is placed in the left hands of sovereigns in the midst of the solemn rites of coronation. Hence it must be said that civil powers are masters of the substance of their peoples, which sustains, contains and maintains all that is above it and rests upon it. In virtue of its being one part of this substance—a part taken *pro indiviso* or as an undivided whole (to use the scholastic expression for a legal distinction)—in the Roman laws the patrimony of each family father is called *substantia patris* or *paterna substantia*. This is at bottom the reason why sovereign civil powers may dispose of whatever belongs to their subjects: their persons as well as their acquisitions, their works and their labors, and impose thereon tribute or taxes, whenever they have to exercise that dominion over their lands which, from different points of view but with the same meaning in substance, moral theologians and writers on public law now call eminent domain, just as they now speak of the laws concerning this domain as the fundamental laws of the realm. Since this dominion is over the lands themselves, sovereigns naturally may not exercise it save to preserve the substance of their states, on whose stability or collapse hinges the stability or ruin of all the private interests of their peoples.

603   The Romans had an intuitive sense if not a rational understanding of the origin of commonwealths in these eternal principles of fiefs. This is shown by the formula they had for laying claim to a piece of land, which has come down to us as follows: *Aio hunc fundum meum esse ex iure quiritium,* "I declare this piece of land to be mine by the law of the Quirites." By this formula they brought the civil action of vindication to bear on the ownership of the land, an ownership depending on the state and proceeding from the, so to speak, central power by which every Roman citizen is the recognized master of his estate and owns it *pro indiviso* (to use the scholastic phrase for a purely legal distinction), and for that reason called ownership *ex iure quiritium,* "by the law of the Quirites," who, as shown by a thousand proofs already adduced or to be adduced, were originally the Romans armed with spears in public assembly who composed the city. This is the basic reason why the lands and all goods (for all spring from the land), when they have no owner, revert to the public treasury; for every private patrimony *pro indiviso* is public patrimony, and therefore, in default of private owners, it loses its designation as a part and retains only that of the whole. This must be the reason for the technical legal expression by which inheritances, particularly on the part of *heredes legitimi* [those entitled at law in the absence of *sui heredes*], are said to return (*redire*) to the heirs, though in truth they come to them but once. For those who founded Roman law in the process of founding the Roman commonwealth itself gave to all private patri-

monies the status of fiefs, such as writers on feudal law describe as *ex pacto et providentia,* meaning that they all come from the public patrimony and, by pact and providence of the civil laws, devolve from one private owner to another, and in default of private owners must return to the source from which they came. All this that we have been saying is clearly confirmed by the [provisions of the] *Lex Papia Poppaea* concerning lapsed legacies. This law imposed on celibates the just penalty that, because they had neglected to propagate their Roman name through matrimony, if they had made testaments they were to be declared null and void, and further they were to be considered as having no relatives who could inherit *ab intestato.* In both directions, therefore, they were deprived of heirs to preserve their names, and their patrimonies reverted to the public treasury, in the quality not of an inheritance but of a peculium accruing, in the phrase of Tacitus, to the people as the parent of all, *tamquam omnium parentem.* By which phrase this profound writer recalls the reason of all the caducary penalties from the most ancient times when the first fathers of the human race occupied the first vacant lands. Such occupation was the original source of all ownership in the world. Later these fathers, uniting in cities, created the civil power out of their paternal powers, and out of their private patrimonies created the public patrimony called the *aerarium* or public treasury. The patrimonies of the citizens pass from one private owner to another in the quality of inheritances, but, on reverting to the public treasury, they resume their ancient original quality of peculium.

604   Here, at the generation of their heroic commonwealths, the hero poets imagined the eleventh major divinity, Mercury. It is he who carries the law to the mutinous *famuli* in his divine rod (a real word for the auspices), the same rod with which, as Vergil tells, he brings back souls from Orcus. (That is, he restores to social life the clients who, having left the protection of the heroes, were again being scattered and lost in the lawless state which is the Orcus of the poets, waiting to swallow all men, as will be explained later.) The rod is described for us as having one or two serpents wound about it. (These must have been serpent skins signifying the bonitary ownership granted to the *famuli* by the heroes, and the quiritary ownership they reserved for themselves.) There are two wings at the top of the rod (signifying the eminent domain of the heroic orders), and the cap worn by Mercury is also winged (to confirm their high and free sovereign constitution, as the cap remained a hieroglyph of liberty). In addition, Mercury has wings on his heels (signifying that ownership of the fields resided in the reigning senates). He is otherwise naked (because the ownership he carried to the *famuli* was stripped of all civil solemnity and based entirely on the honor of the heroes) just as we have seen Venus and the Graces depicted as naked. Thus from the bird of Idanthyrsus, by which he meant to say to Darius that he was sovereign lord of Scythia in virtue of the auspices he had there, the Greeks took the wings to signify heroic constitutions; and finally, in articulate speech, the Romans used the abstract expression "the auspices are

ours" to show the plebs that all the heroic civil laws and rights belonged to themselves. So that this winged staff of the Greek Mercury, with the serpents removed, is the eagle-headed scepter of the Egyptians, Etruscans, Romans and finally the English, as we have said above. The staff was called *kērykeion* by the Greeks because it carried the agrarian law to the *famuli* of the heroes, called *kērykes* by Homer. It brought also the agrarian law of Servius Tullius ordering the census, so that peasants who came under it are spoken of as *censiti* in the Roman laws. By its serpents it brought the bonitary ownership of the fields, and the land rent paid by the plebeians to the heroes, as we have pointed out above, was called *ōpheleia,* from *ophis,* "serpent." Lastly it brought the famous Herculean knot, by which men paid the tithe of Hercules to the heroes, and plebeian Roman debtors down to the time of the Petelian law were "bound" or liege vassals of the nobles. On all these matters we have much to say farther on.

605   Here it must be added that this Greek Mercury was the Thoth or Mercury who gives laws to the Egyptians, represented by the hieroglyph of Knef. He is described as a serpent, to denote the cultivated land. He has the head of a hawk or eagle, as the hawks of Romulus later became the Roman eagles, representing the heroic auspices. He is girt by a belt as a sign of the Herculean knot, and in his hand he bears a scepter, which signifies the reign of the Egyptian priests. He wears a winged cap, as an indication of their eminent domain over the land. And finally he holds an egg in his mouth, which stood for the sphere of Egypt, if indeed it is not the golden apple which, as we have shown above, signified the eminent domain the priests held over the lands of Egypt. Into this hieroglyph Manetho read the generation of the entire world, and the conceit of the learned reached such an absurd extreme that Athanasius Kircher in his *Obeliscus pamphilius* affirms that this hieroglyph signifies the Holy Trinity.

606   Here began the first commerce in the world, from which this Mercury got his name. He was later regarded as the god of trade, as from his first mission he was held to be the god of ambassadors, and with evident truth it was said that he had been sent by the gods (an appellation, as we have seen, applied to the heroes of the first cities) to men (a name Hotman was amazed to find applied to vassals in the returned barbarism). The wings, which we have noted as signifying heroic constitutions, were later thought to have been used by Mercury to fly from heaven to earth and then to return from earth to heaven. But, to return to commerce, it began with this kind of immovable goods [real estate], and the first payments were, as they could not fail to be, of the most simple and natural sort, that is to say in the produce of the land. Similar payments in labor or goods are still customary in the transactions of peasants.

607   All the above history was preserved by the Greeks in the word *nomos,* signifying both law and pasture; for the first law was the agrarian law in accordance with which the heroic kings were called shepherds of the people, as we have indicated above and as we shall later explain more fully.

608   Thus the plebeians of the first barbarous nations (in the same fashion as among the ancient Germans described by Tacitus, who mistakenly thought they were slaves, for, as we have shown, the heroic *socii* were like slaves) must have been scattered about the countryside by the heroes and have dwelt there in their houses in the fields assigned to them, and by the produce of the farms have contributed whatever was needful to the sustenance of their masters. And to these conditions we must add the oath—also quoted from Tacitus above—requiring them to guard and defend their masters and to serve to their glory. If we look for a legal name to define such relationships, we shall see clearly that there is none that fits them better than our term feudalism.

609   In this fashion the first cities were found to have been based on orders of nobles and multitudes of plebeians, with two contrary eternal properties emerging from this nature of human civil things which we are discussing: namely, [1] that the plebeians always want to change the form of government, as in fact it is always they who do change it, and [2] that the nobles always want to keep it as it is. Hence, in the vicissitudes of civil governments, all those who bend their efforts to maintaining the state are called optimates, and states themselves are so called from this property of standing firm and upright.

610   Here appeared two divisions. The first was that between the wise and the vulgar; for the heroes founded their kingdoms on the wisdom of the auspices, as we stated in the Axioms [250] and as we have fully discussed above. As a result of this division the vulgar received the fixed epithet profane, for the heroes or nobles were the priests of the heroic cities, as certainly they were among the Romans as late as a century after the Law of the Twelve Tables, as we have stated above. Hence the first peoples when they took away citizenship used a kind of excommunication, such as the interdict of water and fire among the Romans, as we shall show later. For the first plebs of the nations were considered foreigners, as we shall presently see, and from this came the eternal property of not granting citizenship to a man of alien religion. And because the plebeians in the first cities, as we have set forth above, had no share in sacred or divine things and for many centuries did not contract solemn matrimony, the term *vulgo quaesiti* came to be used for illegitimate children.

611   The second division was that between citizen and *hostis,* which meant both guest or stranger and enemy, for the first cities were composed of heroes and of those received in their asylums (which we must suppose all heroic hospices to have been). Similarly the returned barbarian times left in Italian *oste* for innkeeper and for soldiers' quarters, and *ostello* for inn. Thus Paris was the guest, that is to say enemy, of the royal house of Argos, for he kidnaped noble Argive maidens, represented by the [poetic] character of Helen. Similarly Theseus was the guest of Ariadne, and Jason of Medea. Both abandoned the women and did not marry them, and their actions were held to be heroic, while to us, with our present feelings, they seem, as indeed they are, the deeds of scoundrels. In like fashion must the piety of Aeneas be defended, for he abandoned Dido whom he had violated (to say nothing of the great kindnesses he had received from her and the magnanimous offer she had made of the kingdom of Carthage as dowry for their marriage) in order to obey the fates who had ordained Lavinia in Italy, though she too was a stranger, as his wife. This heroic custom was preserved by Homer in the person of Achilles, the greatest of the Greek heroes, who refuses to accept any of the three daughters whom Agamemnon offered him in marriage with the royal dowry of seven lands well populated with ploughmen and shepherds, and replies that his wish is to marry whatever woman in his fatherland his father Peleus may give him. In brief, the plebeians were guests in the heroic cities, and against them, to repeat our frequent quotation from Aristotle, the heroes swore eternal enmity. This same division is expressed for us in the terms citizen and peregrine, taking the latter in its original and proper sense of a man wandering through the country, as if *peragrinus* from *ager* in the sense of territory or district (as in such phrases as *ager neapolitanus, ager nolanus*); whereas those strangers who travel through the world do not wander through the country but hold straight to the public highways.

612   The origins herein set forth of heroic guests shed a great light on Greek history where it relates that the Samians, Sybarites, Troezenians, Amphipolitans, Chalcedonians, Cnidians and Chians had their commonwealths changed from aristocratic to popular by strangers. And they give the final touch to what we printed many years ago in our *Principles of Universal Law* concerning the fable that the Law of the Twelve Tables came from Athens to Rome, which is one of the two passages that permit us to believe that that work was not entirely useless. For in the article *De forti sanate nexo soluto* [I, 5], which we proved to have been the subject of that whole contest [between plebeians and nobles], the Latin philologians have said that the *fortes sanates* were the strangers reduced to obedience. Hence they were the Roman plebs which had revolted because they could not obtain from the nobles the certain ownership of the fields. For, as long as the nobles retained the royal power of taking them back again, the ownership could not have lasting certainty unless the law granting it was fixed eternally on a public tablet, determining the rights that had been uncertain and manifesting those that had been secret. This is the true meaning of what Pomponius tells us. It was on this account that the plebs raised such a turmoil that it was necessary to create the decemvirs. These officials gave a new form to the state and brought the rebellious plebs back to obedience by proclaiming them (in the aforesaid article) free from the true bond of bonitary ownership by which they had been bound to the soil (*glebae addicti, adscriptitii* or *censiti*) under the census of Servius Tullius, as we have shown above, and bound only by the fictitious knot of quiritary ownership. But a vestige of the old bond remained until the Petelian law in the right of private imprisonment the nobles had over their plebeian debtors. These were the strangers who under tribunitial incitements, to use Livy's elegant phrase (incitements enumerated in our Note

on the Publilian law [104–114]), finally changed the Roman state from aristocratic to popular.

613   The fact that Rome was not founded on the first agrarian revolts shows us that it must have been a new city, as history tells. It was indeed founded on the asylum where Romulus and his companions, while violence still prevailed everywhere, must first have made themselves strong and then received the refugees and founded the clienteles whose nature we have described above. About two hundred years must have passed before the clients found their condition burdensome, for it was just this length of time that elapsed before king Servius Tullius brought them the first agrarian law. In the ancient cities this period must have extended to five hundred years for the reason that they were composed of simpler men and Rome of a more calculating sort. This is the reason why Rome subjugated Latium, then Italy, and then the world, because their heroism was more youthful than that of the other Latins. It is also the primary reason (as we said in the Axioms [158]) why the Romans wrote their heroic history in the vulgar language, whereas the Greeks had written theirs in fables.

614   All that we have thought out concerning the principles of poetic politics and seen illustrated in Roman history is strikingly confirmed by these four heroic characters: first, the lyre of Orpheus or Apollo; second, the head of Medusa; third, the Roman fasces; fourth and last, the struggle of Hercules with Antaeus.

615   First, the lyre was invented by the Greek Mercury, just as law was invented by the Egyptian Mercury. This lyre was given him by Apollo, god of civil light or of the nobility, for in the heroic commonwealths the nobles dictated the laws, and with this lyre Orpheus, Amphion and other theological poets, who professed knowledge of laws, founded and established the humanity of Greece, as we shall later explain at greater length. So that the lyre was the union of the cords or forces of the fathers, of which the public force was composed which is called civil authority, which finally put an end to all private force and violence. Hence the law was defined with full propriety by the poets as *lyra regnorum,* "the lyre of kingdoms," in which were brought into accord the family kingdoms of the fathers which had hitherto been in disaccord because they were all isolated and divided from one another in the state of the families, as Polyphemus told Ulysses. This glorious history was later raised to the heavens and described in the constellation of the Lyre; and the kingdom of Ireland, on the arms of the king of England, charges its shield with a harp. The philosophers afterwards took it for the harmony of the spheres attuned by the sun; but it was on earth that Apollo played the harp that Pythagoras not only could but must have heard, or rather played himself, if we take him as a theological poet and nation founder instead of the imposture he has hitherto been accused of being.

616   The snakes joined in the head of Medusa, whose temples bear wings, are the high family domains the fathers had in the state of the families, which

later went to make up the civil eminent domain. This head was nailed to the shield of Perseus, which is the same as that borne by Minerva, who, among the arms (that is, in the armed assemblies) of the first nations (among which we found that of Rome), dictates the frightful punishments that turn the spectators to stone. We noted above that one of these snakes was Draco, who is said to have written his laws in blood, because Athens (Athena being [the Greek] Minerva) was armed with them at the time when it was occupied by the optimates, as we have also said above. And among the Chinese, who still write in hieroglyphics, the dragon, as we have also seen above, is the sign of civil authority.

617   The Roman fasces are the *litui* or rods of the fathers in the state of the families. For one such staff in the hand of one of these fathers the pregnant word scepter is used by Homer, and the father is called a king. This is in his description of the shield of Achilles, which contains the history of the world. In this passage the epoch of the families is placed before that of the cities, as will be fully set forth later. Having taken the auspices with these *litui,* the fathers dictated the prescribed punishments to their children, such as that of the impious son which passed into the Law of the Twelve Tables, as we have seen above. Hence the union of these rods or *litui* signifies the generation of the civil authority we are here discussing.

618   Finally Hercules (a character of the Heraclids or nobles of the heroic cities) struggles with Antaeus (a character of the mutinous *famuli*) and, by lifting him into the air (leading the *famuli* back into the first cities on the heights), conquers him and binds him to the earth. From this came a Greek game called the knot, after the Herculean knot by which Hercules founded the heroic nations and by reason of which the plebeians paid to the nobles the tithe of Hercules, which must have been the census [tax] which was the basis of the aristocratic commonwealths. Hence the Roman plebeians under the census of Servius Tullius were *nexi* or bondsmen of the nobles and, by the oath Tacitus tells us was sworn by the ancient Germans to their princes, they were bound to serve them as impressed vassals at their own expense in war; a duty the Roman plebs still complained of under what has been supposed to have been popular liberty. These must have been the first tribute-payers (*assidui*), who fought at their own expense (*suis assibus militabant*); but they were soldiers not of fortune but of harsh necessity.

[CHAPTER III]

THE ORIGINS OF THE CENSUS AND THE TREASURY

619   The plebeians continued to be oppressed by the usurious exactions and the frequent usurpations of their fields by the nobles, to such a point that at the end of the period [Marcius] Philippus, tribune of the plebs, cried out in public that two thousand nobles possessed all the fields that should be divided among a good three hundred thousand citizens, the number counted at Rome in his time. Beginning forty years after the expulsion of Tarquinius Superbus, in the comfortable assurance of his death, the nobility had again begun to be insolent toward the unhappy plebs. The senate of those days had been obliged to put into practice an ordinance requiring the plebeians to pay into the public treasury the census [tax] which previously they had had to pay privately to the nobles, in order that thenceforth the treasury should be able to take care of the costs of war. From this time the census acquires new prominence in Roman history. According to Livy the nobles disdained the administration of it as something unworthy of their dignity. But Livy failed to understand that the nobles did not want it because it was not the census ordained by Servius Tullius, which had been the basis of the liberty of the lords and had been paid privately to them, for Livy, like all the other authorities, was under the false impression that the census of Servius Tullius had been the basis of popular liberty. For certainly there was no magistracy of greater dignity than the censorship, which from the first year had been administered by the consuls. In this fashion the nobles, through their own avaricious machinations, came themselves to set up the census, which later was the basis of popular liberty. So that when the fields had all fallen into their hands in the time of Philippus the tribune, these two thousand nobles had to pay the tribute for three hundred thousand other citizens then counted (just as in Sparta all the land had come into possession of the few), because in the treasury there was a register of the census taxes which the nobles had privately imposed on the fields which, in an uncultivated state, they had of old allotted to the plebeians for cultivation. On account of the inequality referred to there must have been great agitations and revolts among the Roman plebs. These were quelled by Fabius with a most prudent measure which earned him the name Maximus. He ordered that the whole Roman people should be divided into three classes, senators, knights, and plebeians, and that the citizens should be placed in these classes according to their means. This consoled the plebeians, for the senatorial order which previously had consisted solely of nobles and which held all the magistracies, could thenceforward be entered by plebeians of wealth, and thus the regular avenue to all civil honors was open to plebeians.

620   This development gives truth to the tradition that the census of Servius Tullius was the basis of popular liberty, for in it the matter was prepared and from it the occasions were born, as we set forth hypothetically above in the Notes on the Chronological Table, in the passage on the Publilian law. It was this ordinance, originating in Rome itself, that established the democratic commonwealth there, and not the Law of the Twelve Tables [supposed to have been] brought there from Athens. Indeed, what Aristotle calls a democratic commonwealth is rendered in Tuscan by Bernardo Segni as a commonwealth by census, meaning a free popular commonwealth. This is evident even in Livy, for, ignorant as he was of the Roman form of government in those times, he nevertheless states that the nobles complained that by that law they had lost more in the city than they had gained abroad by force of arms in that year, though it was a year of many great victories. And for this reason Publilius, the author of the law, was called the people's dictator.

621   With popular liberty, in which the whole people constitute the city, it came about that civil ownership lost its proper meaning of public ownership (which had been called civil from the word city) and was dispersed among all the private ownerships of the Roman citizens who together now made up the Roman city. The *dominium optimum* or best ownership lost its above stated original meaning of strongest ownership, not weakened by any real encumbrance, even public, and survived in the meaning of owership of property free of any private encumbrance. Quiritary ownership no longer signified such ownership of a piece of land that if the client or plebeian lost possession of it the noble from whom he had title to it was obliged to come to his defense. The first *auctores iuris* or lawmakers in Roman law were those whose duty it was, in connection with these clienteles ordained by Romulus and no others, to expound to the plebeians these and no other laws. For indeed what [other] laws could the nobles have been obliged to set forth to the plebeians, since the latter down to the 309th year of Rome had no privilege of citizenship, and since the laws themselves down to a century after the Law of the Twelve Tables had been kept hidden from the plebs by the nobles in their college of pontiffs? So in those days the nobles were *auctores iuris* in a sense which survived in the *laudatio auctoritatis* by possessors of purchased lands when they are summoned in a suit for recovery by others and "cite the authors" [from whom they have title and] whom they wish to assist and defend them. Quiritary ownership now meant private civil ownership capable of being defended by the action of *rei vindicatio,* whereas bonitary ownership could be maintained by possession only.

622   In the same fashion and not otherwise, by the eternal nature of fiefs, these things recurred in the returned barbarian times. Let us take for example the kingdom of France. Here the various provinces now composing the nation were sovereign seigniories of the princes subject to the king of that realm, and the princes must have held their property without any public encumbrance. Later, through succession, rebellion or failure of heirs, they were incorporated into the kingdom, and all the property *ex iure optimo* of the princes became subject to public exactions. For the lands and houses of the kings, which contained their royal chambers, having passed by marriage or concession to their vassals, are now found subject to taxation and tribute. Thus in hereditary kingdoms ownership *ex iure optimo* was gradually confused with private ownership subject to public charges, just as the fisc, which was the patrimony of the Roman emperor, was gradually confused with the public treasury.

623   Our research into the census and the treasury has been the most difficult of our investigations into Roman things, as we indicated in the Idea of the Work [25].

[CHAPTER IV]

THE ORIGINS OF THE ROMAN ASSEMBLIES

624   Our studies show that the *boulē* and the *agora,* the two above noted heroic assemblies of which Homer speaks, must have corresponded respectively to the Roman *comitia curiata,* the assembly by *curiae* which we read of as the most ancient under the kings, and the *comitia tributa* or assembly by tribes. The former were called *curiata* from *quir,* "spear," whose genitive *quiris* was later used as the nominative, in conformity with what we have set forth in our Origins of the Latin Language [*Scienza nuova,* 1st ed., III, 36]; just as from *cheir,* "hand," which among all nations meant power, must have been derived the Greek *kyria,* with the same meaning as the Latin *curia.* Hence came the Curetes, who were priests armed with spears, for all the heroic peoples were composed of priests and only the heroes had the right to bear arms. The Curetes, as we have seen above, were found by the Greeks in Saturnia or ancient Italy, in Crete, and in Asia. *Kyria* in its ancient sense must have meant seigniory, just as aristocratic commonwealths are now called seigniories. From the *kyria* of these heroic senates came *kyros* for authority, but this authority, as we have observed above and shall observe more closely, was that of ownership. From these origins came the modern *kyrios* for "sir" and *kyria* for "madam." And as the Greek Curetes came from *cheir,* so we saw above that the Roman Quirites came from *quir.* Quirites was the title of Roman majesty given to the people in public assembly, as we have also noted above in a passage in which, comparing [the assemblies of] the Gauls and the ancient Germans with that of the Greek Curetes, we observed that all the first barbarous peoples held their public assemblies under arms.

625   Thus the majestic title of Quirites must have been first used at a time when the people consisted entirely of nobles, who alone had the right to arm. Later, when Rome had become a popular commonwealth, the title passed to the people including the plebeians. For the assemblies of the plebs, who at first did not have the right to arm, were called *comitia tributa* from *tribus*, "tribe." And among the Romans, just as in the state of the families the latter were so called from the *famuli*, so in the later state of the cities the term *tributum*, "tribute," came from *tribus*, "tribe," because the tribes of the plebeians met to receive the orders of the reigning senate, the chief and most frequent of which were demands upon the plebeians for contributions to the treasury.

626   Subsequently, however, Fabius Maximus introduced the [reformed] census which divided the whole Roman people into three classes according to the patrimonies of the citizens. Before this only the senators had been knights, for in heroic times only nobles had the right to arm, and hence in Roman history we read that the ancient Roman commonwealth was divided into fathers and plebs. Thus in those days senator and patrician had been interchangeable terms, and likewise plebeian and ignoble. And as there had thus been only two classes of the Roman people, so there had been only two kinds of assembly: one the *curiata,* consisting of fathers or nobles or senators, the other the *tributa,* consisting of plebeians or the ignoble. But now that Fabius had divided the citizens according to their means into the three classes of senators, knights and plebeians, the nobles ceased to be a separate order in the city and were placed in one or another of the three classes according to their wealth. From that time on patricians were distinguished from senators and knights, and plebeians from the base-born; and plebeians were no longer contrasted with patricians but with knights and senators. A plebeian no longer meant a base-born person but rather a citizen of small patrimony who might well be a noble; and on the other hand a senator no longer meant a patrician but a citizen of ample patrimony who might well be of low birth.

627   Consequently from that time on *comitia centuriata,* the assembly by hundreds, was the term applied to the assemblies in which the entire Roman people of all three classes came together to enact the consular laws among other public business. Those assemblies were still called *comitia tributa* in which the plebs alone enacted tribunitial laws. These were the plebiscites, at first so called in the sense rendered by Cicero as *plebi nota* or laws published to the plebs. (An example cited by Pomponius is Junius Brutus announcing to the plebs that the kings have been forever expelled from Rome.) In monarchies the royal laws might with equal propriety be called *populo nota,* "made known to the people." On this account Baldus, as acute as he was lacking in erudition, expressed surprise that the word *plebiscitum* should have been written with one *s,* since in the sense of a law enacted by the plebs, it should have had two; the *scitum* being in that case from *sciscor,* not *scio* [and taking the genitive *plebis* instead of the dative *plebi*].

628 Lastly, for the certainty of divine ceremonies, there remained the *comitia curiata* or assemblies of the heads of the *curiae* alone, in which sacred matters were dealt with. For in the time of the kings all profane matters were regarded as sacred, and the heroes were everywhere Curetes or armed priests, as we have said above. Hence, down to the last days of Rome, since paternal power was still viewed as sacred (and its regulations are often called *sacra patria* in the laws), adoptions took place in these assemblies by *leges curiatae*.

[CHAPTER V]

COROLLARY

DIVINE PROVIDENCE IS THE ORDAINER OF COMMONWEALTHS AND AT THE SAME TIME OF THE NATURAL LAW OF NATIONS

629 We have seen that the generation of commonwealths began in the age of the gods, in which governments were theocratic, that is, divine. Later they developed into the first human, that is the heroic, governments, here called human to distinguish them from the divine. Within these human governments, even as the mighty current of a kingly river retains far out to sea the momentum of its flow and the sweetness of its waters, the age of the gods continued to run its course, for that religious way of thinking must still have persisted by which whatever men themselves did was attributed to the agency of the gods. (Thus in the state of the families they made a Jove out of the reigning fathers; and out of the same fathers as united in closed orders at the birth of the first cities they made a Minerva; out of their ambassadors sent to the aroused clients they made Mercury; and finally, as we shall shortly see, out of the corsair heroes they made Neptune.) Herein is divine providence to be supremely admired, for, when men's intentions were quite otherwise, it brought them in the first place to the fear of divinity (the cult of which is the first fundamental basis of commonwealths). Their religion in turn led them to remain fixed on the first vacant lands which they occupied before all others (and such occupation is the source of all property rights). When the more robust giants had occupied lands on the mountain tops where the perennial springs arise, providence ordained that thus they should find themselves in healthful and defensible sites and with abundance of water, so that they could safely stop there and put an end to their wanderings; and these are the three qualities that lands must have in order for cities later to arise upon them. Further, again by means of religion, providence led them to unite with chosen women for constant and lifelong companionship; hence the institution of matrimony, the recognized source of all authority.

Later, with these women, they were found to have established the families, which are the seed-plot of the commonwealths. And finally, with the opening of the asylums, they discovered that they had founded the clienteles. Thus the elements were prepared from which, with the first agrarian law, the cities were to be born, based on the two communities of men that composed them, one of nobles to command, the other of plebeians to obey. (The latter are called by Telemachus, in a speech in Homer, the "other people," which is to say a subject people, different from the reigning people which was made up of heroes.) Hence emerges the subject matter of political science, which is nothing other than the science of commanding and obeying in states. And at their very birth providence causes the commonwealths to spring forth aristocratic in form, in conformity with the savage and solitary nature of the first men. This form consists entirely, as writers on political theory point out, in guarding the boundaries and the orders, so that peoples newly come to humanity might, by the very form of their governments, continue for a long time to remain enclosed within these boundaries and orders, and so forget the infamous and nefarious promiscuity of the bestial and feral state. But the minds of men were preoccupied with particulars and incapable of understanding a common good; they were accustomed never to concern themselves with the affairs of others, as Homer makes his Polyphemus tell Ulysses (and in this giant Plato recognizes the fathers of the families in the so-called state of nature preceding the civil state). Providence therefore, by the aforesaid aristocratic form of their governments, led them to unite themselves to their fatherlands in order to preserve such great private interests as their family monarchies were (for this was what they were entirely bent upon), and thus, beyond any design of theirs, they were brought together in a universal civil good called commonwealth.

630   Now here, by those divine proofs we spoke of above in the Method, let us consider and meditate on the simplicity and naturalness with which providence ordered these affairs of men, of which they said truly though in a false sense that they were all the work of the gods. And let us consider in this connection the immense number of civil effects which may all be traced to those four causes which, as will be observed throughout this work, are the four elements as it were of the civil universe; namely, religion, marriage, asylum and the first agrarian law which we have discussed above. Then let us ask ourselves if, among all human possibilities, so many and such various and diverse effects could in any other way have had simpler or more natural beginnings among those very men who are said by Epicurus to have been born of chance and by Zeno to have been creatures of necessity. Yet chance did not divert them nor fate force them out of this natural order. For at the point when the commonwealths were to spring forth, the matter was all prepared and ready to receive the form, and there came forth the formation of the commonwealths, composed of mind and body. The prepared materials were these men's own religions, their own languages, their own lands, their own nuptials, their own names (clans or

houses), their own arms, and hence their own commands, their own magistrates, and finally their own laws. And because these things were their own they were completely free and therefore constitutive of true commonwealths. And all this came about because all the aforesaid institutions had previously belonged to the family fathers as monarchs in the state of nature. The fathers at this juncture, by uniting themselves in an order, came to produce the civil sovereign power, just as in the state of nature they had held the family powers, subject to no one under God. This sovereign civil person was formed of mind and body. The mind was an order of wise men, with such wisdom as could naturally exist in that time of extreme crudeness and simplicity. Hence the eternal property of commonwealths that without an order of wise men states may present the appearance of commonwealths, but are so many dead and soulless bodies. There was also the body, formed of the head and lesser members. Hence this second eternal property of commonwealths: that some men must employ their minds in the tasks of civil wisdom, and others their bodies in the arts and crafts that are needed in peace as well as in war. And there is a third eternal property: that the mind should always command and the body should have perpetually to obey.

631 Yet here is an even greater cause for marveling. By bringing about the birth of the families (all of them born with some awareness of a divinity although, because of their ignorance and disorder, none knew the true one), since each family had its own religion, language, lands, nuptials, name, arms, government and laws, providence had at the same time brought into being the natural law of the *gentes maiores,* with all the aforesaid properties, to be used later by the family fathers over their clients. In like fashion, in creating the commonwealths, by means of the aristocratic form in which they arose, providence caused the natural law of the *gentes maiores* (or families), which had been formerly observed in the state of nature, to be transformed into the natural law of the *gentes minores* (or peoples), to be observed in the time of the cities. For the family fathers, to whom all the aforesaid prerogatives belonged to the exclusion of their clients, at the time when they banded themselves together in a natural order against the latter, came to confine all the aforesaid properties within their civil orders against the plebs. In this consisted the severely aristocratic form of the heroic commonwealths.

632 In this way the natural law of nations, which is now observed among peoples and nations, was born as a property of the sovereign civil powers at the birth of the commonwealths. So a people or nation that has not within itself a sovereign civil power vested with all the aforesaid properties is not properly a nation or people at all, nor can it exercise abroad in its relations with other peoples or nations the natural law of nations, but both the law and its exercise will fall to another people or nation superior to it.

633 What we have here set forth, added to what we have mentioned above of the heroes of the first cities calling themselves gods, will explain the

meaning of the phrase *iura a diis posita,* "laws laid down by the gods," applied to the dictates of the natural law of nations. But when the natural law of human nations ensued, on which we have cited Ulpian several times above, and upon which the philosophers and moral theologians based their understanding of the natural law of fully unfolded eternal reason, the phrase was fitly reinterpreted to mean that the natural law of nations was ordained by the true God.

[CHAPTER VI]

HEROIC POLITICS

634   All the historians date the beginning of the heroic age from the corsair raids of Minos and from Jason's naval expedition to Pontus. It continued through the Trojan war and the wanderings of the heroes and came to an end with the return of Ulysses to Ithaca. Thus in those times the last of the major divinities, Neptune, must have been created. This inference we base on the authority of the historians, reinforced by philosophical reasoning assisted by several golden passages of Homer. The philosophic reason is that the naval and nautical arts were the last inventions of the nations, since it took the flower of genius to invent them; so much so that Daedalus, their inventor, remained a symbol of genius itself, and *daedala tellus* is used by Lucretius in the sense of "the ingenious earth." The Homeric passages to which we refer are in the *Odyssey.* Whenever Ulysses makes a landing or is driven ashore by the tempest, he always mounts a hill to look inland for a trace of smoke which will indicate that the land is inhabited by men. These Homeric passages are reinforced by that golden passage in Plato which we cited from Strabo above in the Axioms [296], in which he tells of the horror the first nations long had of the sea. The reason for this was pointed out by Thucydides where he says that through fear of corsair raids the Greek nations were slow to come down and dwell on the coasts. On this account Neptune is portrayed to us as armed with the trident with which he made the earth shake. The trident must have been a great hook for grappling ships. By a fine metaphor the hook is called a tooth, and the three in the prefix means the superlative, as we have noted above. With this hook he made the lands of men quiver in fear of his raids. Later, already in Homer's day, he was believed to make the physical earth shake, and in this opinion Homer was followed by Plato with his abyss of waters which he placed in the bowels of the earth, with what reason we shall show later.

635   Of such nature must have been the bull in the shape of which Jove abducts Europa, and the Minotaur or bull of Minos by which he steals youths and maidens from the shores of Attica (on which account "horns of ships"

survived in the sense of sails, as used by Vergil). Landsmen thus set forth in all truth that the Minotaur had devoured their children, for to their horror and grief they had seen them swallowed up by the ships. Thus too the Orc seeks to devour Andromeda, lashed to the rock and petrified with terror (so Latin kept the phrase *terrore defixus,* "rigid with fear"); and the winged horse which Perseus rides to her rescue must have been another corsair ship, as the sails were afterwards called the wings of ships. Vergil too, who was acquainted with these heroic antiquities, in speaking of Daedalus, inventor of ships, states that he flies with the machine which he calls *alarum remigium,* "the oarage of wings"; and Daedalus, we are told, was the brother of Theseus. Thus Theseus must be a [poetic] character of the Athenian youths who, under the law of force practiced on them by Minos, are devoured by his bull or pirate ship. He is taught by Ariadne (seafaring art) by means of the thread (of navigation) to escape from the labyrinth of Daedalus (which, before those labyrinths which are the elegant playthings of royal villas, must have been the Aegean Sea because of the great number of islands it bathes and contains). Then, having learned the art from the Cretans, he abandons Ariadne and returns with Phaedra, her sister (that is, with a similar art). Thus he slays the Minotaur and frees Athens from the cruel tribute imposed by Minos (which is to say, the Athenians in their turn took up piratical raiding). And so, as Phaedra was the sister of Ariadne, Theseus was the brother of Daedalus.

636   Apropos of these matters Plutarch in his life of Theseus says that the heroes considered it a great honor and an added prestige to their arms to be called robbers, just as in the returned barbarian times "corsair" was regarded as a title of nobility. It is said that the laws of Solon, who lived about that time, permitted associations for purposes of piracy; so well did Solon understand this complete humanity of ours in which pirates are not protected by the natural law of nations. What is even more astonishing is that Plato and Aristotle made robbery a species of hunting; and with these great philosophers of a most civilized nation the ancient Germans, in their barbarism, are in agreement. For among them, according to Caesar, robbery was not only not regarded as infamous but was reckoned among the exercises of valor by which those who were not brought up to the practice of any art escaped from idleness. This barbarous custom endured for such a long time afterwards among the most enlightened nations that, according to Polybius, one of the terms of peace imposed by the Romans on the Carthaginians was that they were not to pass Cape Pelorum in Sicily either for piracy or for trade. Still the attitude of the Carthaginians and Romans is of minor importance, for they themselves professed to be barbarians in those days, as may be seen from several passages in Plautus in which he says that he has turned the Greek comedies into a "barbarous tongue," meaning Latin. What is more remarkable is that the highly civilized Greeks, in the times of their most cultivated humanity, should have practiced such a barbarous custom, which indeed provided them with almost all the subjects of their comedies. It is perhaps because of this custom, still practiced by the inhabitants against the Christians, that the coast of Africa facing us is called Barbary.

637   The principle of this oldest law of war was the inhospitality of the heroic peoples which we have discussed above, for they looked on strangers as perpetual enemies and rested their own reputation for power on keeping them at the greatest possible distance from their frontiers (as Tacitus tells us of the Suevi, the nation of greatest prestige among the ancient Germans). They thus looked upon strangers as robbers, as we observed not far back. There is a golden passage of Thucydides on this subject in which he remarks that down to his time when travelers met on land or sea they would ask one another if they were robbers, meaning foreigners. But as the Greeks became more civilized they soon cast aside that barbarous custom and called barbarous all the nations that retained it. It was in this sense that the name *Barbaria* remained in use for the land of the Troglodytes, who were supposed to kill foreigners who crossed their borders, as indeed even today there are barbarous nations in which this is the custom. It is certain that civilized nations do not allow strangers to enter without first asking permission.

638   To the nations that the Greeks called barbarous for this reason belongs the Roman. This we know from two golden passages in the Law of the Twelve Tables. One is: *Adversus hostem aeterna auctoritas esto* [III, 7], "against a foreigner the right in property shall be everlasting." The other [II, 2] is reported by Cicero [*De off.* 1.12.37]: *Si status dies sit, cum hoste venito,* "if a day has been appointed, let him appear with the stranger." Here the word *hostis,* on the basis of a conjecture in general terms, is commonly taken as a metaphor for the adversary in the lawsuit. But on this very passage Cicero makes the observation, very much to our point, that the ancients meant by *hostis* what was later meant by *peregrinus.* These two passages taken together give us to understand that the Romans originally regarded strangers as eternal enemies at war. However, the said two passages must be understood as applying to those who were the first *hostes* in the world. These, as noted above, were the foreigners received into the asylums, who later took on the quality of plebeians at the formation of the heroic cities, as shown farther back. Thus the passage in Cicero means that on the appointed day "the noble shall appear with the plebeian to claim his farm for him," as we have also said above. Hence the "everlasting right of property" mentioned in the same law must have been against the plebeians, toward whom, as we learned from Aristotle in the Axioms [271], the heroes swore eternal enmity. This heroic law kept the plebeians, however long in possession, from usucapting any piece of Roman property, for title to such property could pass only from noble to noble. This is a good part of the reason why the Law of the Twelve Tables did not recognize simple possession. Only later, when heroic law was beginning to fall into abeyance and human law was gaining in strength, did the praetors assist the plebeians by [recognizing] simple possession *extra ordinem;* for neither by express provision nor by any interpreta-

tion could they find in the Law [of the Twelve Tables] any basis for ordinary judgments, whether strict or equitable. All this was because that Law held simple possession by a plebeian to be in every case at the pleasure of the nobles. Moreover it took no notice of the underhand or violent acts of the nobles because of that other eternal property of the first commonwealths (on which also we cited Aristotle in the Axioms [269]), namely that they had no laws concerning private wrongs or offenses, which were left to the individuals themselves to settle by force of arms, as we shall show fully in Book IV. Among the formalities of *rei vindicatio* there was a survival of this real force in the feigned force which Aulus Gellius called festucary, "exercised with a straw." All this is confirmed by the interdict *Unde vi* granted by the praetor *extra ordinem* because the Law of the Twelve Tables did not take cognizance of private violence or even mention it; and also by the actions *De vi bonorum raptorum* and *Quod metus caussa,* which came late and were likewise praetorian.

639 Now the heroic custom of holding strangers to be eternal enemies, which was observed by each people privately in peace, when extended abroad, took the form recognized as common to all the heroic nations of carrying on eternal wars with each other, with continual looting and raiding. Thus from the cities, which Plato tells us were born on the basis of arms, as we have seen above, and began to govern themselves in military fashion before the existence of such wars as are waged between cities, we get the term war itself; for the Greek *polemos,* "war," is from *polis,* "city."

640 In proof of what we have said we must make this important observation: that the Romans extended their conquests and gained the victories they won throughout the world on the basis of four laws by which they governed the plebeians at home. In the barbarian provinces they made use of the clienteles of Romulus, sending Roman colonists into them, who took the place of the previous masters of the fields and made laborers of them. In the civilized provinces they applied the agrarian law of Servius Tullius, granting them bonitary ownership of the fields. In Italy they adopted the agrarian law of the Twelve Tables, granting them the quiritary ownership enjoyed by the lands called *sola italica.* And to the municipia or towns which had earned better treatment they accorded the right of *connubium* and the share in the consulship which had been extended to their own plebs.

641 The eternal enmity between the first cities made declarations of war unnecessary, and indiscriminate pillaging was regarded as lawful. Inversely, when the nations had been weaned away from this barbarous custom, undeclared wars came to be regarded as piracy, no longer recognized by the natural law of the nations called human by Ulpian. This same eternal enmity of the first peoples may also explain to us that the long time during which the Romans had waged war on the Albans is to be understood as the entire previous period in which both sides had subjected each other to the pillaging raids of which we are here speaking. Hence it is more reasonable that Horatius should have killed his sister because she was mourning the Curiatius who had abducted her than that she should have been married to him. For Romulus himself could not take a wife from among these same Albans; it in no way availed him that he was of the royal house of Alba nor that he rendered his city a great service by expelling the tyrant Amulius and restoring the legitimate king Numitor. It is well worth noting that victory or defeat in war is decided by the issue of combat between the parties principally interested. In the case of the Alban war this lay between the three Horatii and the three Curiatii; in that of the Trojan war, between Paris and Menelaus. When combat between the latter two was indecisive, the Greeks and Trojans carried on the war to the end. In similar fashion in the last barbarian period the princes would decide the quarrels of their kingdoms by personal combat, on the issue of which the fortunes of their peoples depended. Hence it is clear that Alba was the Latin Troy and Horatia the Roman Helen (of whom the Greeks had a similar story reported by Gerard Jan Vossius in his *Rhetorica*); and the ten years of the siege of Troy among the Greeks must correspond to the ten years of the siege of Veii among the Latins. In both cases we have a finite number standing for the infinity of all preceding time during which the cities had practiced eternal hostilities on each other.

642   For the number system, because of its extreme abstractness, was the last thing to be grasped by the nations (as in this work we set forth in another connection). When their minds had further developed, the Latins used "six hundred" for a number beyond reckoning (just as the Italians at first said "a hundred" and later "a hundred and a thousand"), for the idea of the infinite can be entertained only by the mind of a philosopher. Perhaps it is on this account that the first peoples said "twelve" to signify a large number. For such was the number assigned to the gods of the *gentes maiores*, though Varro and the Greeks counted thirty thousand of them. Twelve also were the labors of Hercules, which must have been countless. The Latins said there were twelve parts of the *as*, though it can be infinitely divided. This must have been the case also of the Law of the Twelve Tables, because of the infinite number of laws which were subsequently from time to time inscribed on tables.

643   At the time of the Trojan war it must have been that, in that part of Greece in which it was waged, the Greeks were called Achaeans. (They had previously been called Pelasgians from Pelasgus, one of the most ancient heroes of Greece, of whom we have spoken above.) The name Achaeans must then have gone on spreading through all Greece (for it lasted down to the time of Lucius Mummius, according to Pliny), even as through all later time they were called Hellenes. Thus the propagation of the name Achaeans must have led by Homer's time to the supposition that all the Greeks had been allied in that war, just as the name of Germany, according to Tacitus, spread ultimately over all that great part of Europe which was thus known by the name of those who had crossed the Rhine, driven out the Gauls, and begun to call themselves Germans.

Thus the glory of this people spread their name over Germany, as the report of the Trojan war spread the name Achaeans over all Greece. For the peoples in their first barbarism were so far from knowing anything of alliances that not even the peoples of offended kings would deign to take up arms to avenge them, as we have observed with regard to the beginning of the Trojan war.

644   Only by understanding this nature of human civil affairs and in no other way can we solve the amazing problem of Spain. For she was the mother of many nations acclaimed by Cicero as most vigorous and warlike, and Caesar found it so by experience, for in all other parts of the world, in which he was everywhere victorious, he fought for the Empire, but in Spain alone he fought for his life. Why then was it that after the fame of Saguntum (which made Hannibal sweat for eight months on end, though he had at his disposal and still fresh the entire forces of Africa, with which later—though much reduced and exhausted—he won the battle of Cannae and came very close to holding a triumph over Rome on the very Capitoline), and after the renown of Numantia (which shook the glory of Rome, though she had already triumphed over Carthage, and perplexed the valiant and wise Scipio, the conqueror of Africa),—why was it that Spain did not then unite all her peoples in an alliance to set up a world empire on the banks of the Tagus? Her failure gave occasion for the unhappy elogium of Lucius Florus, that she realized her strength only after the whole country had been conquered part by part. (Tacitus, in his life of Agricola, making the same observation of the Britons, who at that time were found to be savage fighters, uses the equally apt expression: *dum singuli pugnant, universi vincuntur,* "while they fight singly, all are conquered.") For, so long as they were not attacked, they remained like beasts within the dens of their confines and went on living the savage and solitary life of the Cyclopes, which we have set forth above.

645   The historians have been struck by the fame of heroic naval warfare and so blinded by it as not to take note of heroic land warfare, much less of heroic politics by which in those times the Greeks must have governed themselves. But Thucydides, a most acute and discerning writer, has left us an item of great significance. He tells us that the heroic cities were all without walls, as Sparta continued to be in Greece, and Numantia, the Spanish Sparta, in Spain. And, with their arrogant and violent natures, the heroes were continually ejecting each other from their seats, as Amulius drove out Numitor and Romulus drove out the former and restored the latter to the kingdom of Alba. So much do the genealogies of the heroic royal houses of Greece and a continuous succession of fourteen Latin kings give assurance to the chronologists in their calculations of time! For in the recurrence of barbarism, when it was at its crudest in Europe, we read of nothing more varying and inconstant than the fortune of kingdoms, as we pointed out above in the Notes on the Chronological Table. Indeed Tacitus most knowingly indicates as much in the opening words of his *Annals: Urbem Romam principio reges habuere,* "The city of Rome in the beginning

was held by kings"; for he uses the verb for the weakest of the three degrees of possession distinguished by jurisconsults: *habere, tenere, possidere.*

646   The conduct of civil affairs under such kingdoms is related to us by poetic history in the numerous fables that deal with contests of song (taking song in that sense of the verbs *canere* and *cantare* in which they mean "to predict") and consequently refer to heroic contests over the auspices.

647   Thus the satyr Marsyas (the monster described by Livy as *secum ipse discors*), when overcome by Apollo in a contest of song, is flayed alive by the god (note the savagery of heroic punishments!). Linus, who must be a character of the plebeians (for certainly the other Linus was a poet hero, being numbered with Amphion, Orpheus, Musaeus and others), is slain by Apollo in a similar contest of song. In both these fables the contest is with Apollo, the god of divinity, that is, of the science of divination, or of the auspices; and we found above that he was the god of the nobility also, since the science of the auspices, as we have shown by so many proofs, belonged to the nobles alone.

648   The sirens, who lull sailors to sleep with their song and then cut their throats; the Sphinx, who puts riddles to travelers and slays them on their failure to find the solution; Circe, who by her enchantments turns into swine the comrades of Ulysses (so that *cantare,* singing, was later understood in the sense of practicing witchcraft, as in the phrase *cantando rumpitur anguis,* "the snake is burst by the singing"; whence magic, which in Persia must at first have meant wisdom in divination by auspices, remained with the meaning of the art of magicians, and their spells were known as incantations): all these portray the politics of the heroic cities. The sailors, travelers and wanderers of these fables are the plebeians who, contending with the heroes for a share in the auspices, are vanquished in the attempt and cruelly punished.

649   In the same way Pan the satyr tries to seize the nymph Syrinx, famous in song, as we have said above, and finds himself embracing only reeds; and likewise Ixion, enamored of Juno, goddess of solemn nuptials, attempting to embrace her finds only a cloud in his arms. Here the reeds signify the lightness and the cloud the emptiness of natural marriage; hence from the cloud, the fable tells, were born the centaurs, that is to say the plebeians, who are the monsters of discordant natures that Livy speaks of, who steal their brides from the Lapithae while the latter are still celebrating their weddings. So too Midas (whom we found above to be a plebeian) wears concealed an ass's ears, and the reeds that Pan seizes (that is, natural marriage) reveal them; just as the Roman patricians made out to their plebeians that the latter were all monsters because they practiced marriages like those of wild animals (*agitabant connubia more ferarum*).

650   Vulcan (who here must also be plebeian), attempting to interfere in a contest between Jove and Juno, is precipitated from heaven by a kick of Jove and is left lame as a result of it. This must refer to a struggle by the plebeians to secure from the heroes a share in the auspices of Jove and the solemnized

marriages of Juno, in which, having been worsted, they came out lamed, that is, humiliated.

651   So Phaethon, of the family of Apollo and hence regarded as a child of the Sun, in attempting to drive his father's golden chariot (the cart of poetic gold, that is, grain), strays from the accustomed paths leading to the granary of the father of his family (that is, lays claim to ownership of the fields), and is precipitated from heaven.

652   Most significant of all is the fall from heaven of the apple of discord (the apple which, as we have shown above, signifies the ownership of the fields, for the first discord arose over the fields which the plebeians wanted to cultivate for themselves), and the quarrel of Venus (who must here be plebeian) with Juno (of solemn nuptials) and Minerva (of authority). For, apropos of the judgment of Paris, by good fortune we have a remark of [pseudo-] Plutarch in his *De vita et poesi Homeri* [I, 5] to the effect that the two verses toward the end of the *Iliad* [XXIV, 28-9] which refer to it, are not Homer's but by a later hand.

653   Atalanta, by throwing away the apples of gold, defeats her suitors in the race, just as Hercules, wrestling with Antaeus, overcomes him by lifting him into the air, as we have set forth above. [The meaning here is that] Atalanta first concedes to the plebeians the bonitary and then the quiritary ownership of the fields while withholding *connubium;* just as the Roman patricians [conceded] the first agrarian law of Servius Tullius and the second agrarian law of the Twelve Tables, yet retained *connubium* as a prerogative of their own order in the article *Connubia incommunicata plebi sunto,* "Solemnized marriages shall be withheld from the plebs," which is a direct consequence of the article *Auspicia incommunicata plebi sunto,* "The auspices shall be withheld from the plebs." Wherefore, three years later, the plebs began to lay claim to *connubium* too, and, after a heroic contest of three years, succeeded in winning it.

654   The suitors of Penelope invade the palace of Ulysses (that is the kingdom of the heroes), arrogate to themselves the title of kings, devour the royal substance (having taken over the ownership of the fields), and seek to marry Penelope (claiming the right to *connubium*). In some versions Penelope remains chaste and Ulysses strings up the suitors like thrushes on a net of the sort in which the heroic Vulcan caught the plebeian Mars and Venus. (That is, Ulysses binds them to cultivate the fields like the laborers of Achilles, just as Coriolanus sought to reduce the plebeians who were not satisfied with the agrarian law of Servius Tullius to the condition of the laborers of Romulus, as we have related above.) Again, Ulysses fights Irus, a poor man, and kills him (which must refer to an agrarian contest in which the plebeians were devouring the substance of Ulysses). In other versions Penelope prostitutes herself to the suitors (signifying the extension of *connubium* to the plebs) and gives birth to Pan, a monster of two discordant natures, human and bestial. This is precisely the creature *secum ipse discors* of Livy, for the Roman patricians told the

plebeians that, if they were to share with them the *connubium* of the nobles, the resulting offspring would be like Pan, a monster of two discordant natures brought forth by Penelope who had prostituted herself to the plebeians.

655 From Pasiphaë, who has lain with a bull, is born the minotaur, a monster of two diverse natures. This story must mean that the Cretans extended *connubium* to foreigners, who must have come to Crete in the ship called a bull in which, as we explained above, Minos abducted youths and maidens from Attica, and in which Jove had earlier abducted Europa.

656 The fable of Io is also to be assigned to this kind of civil history. For Jove falls in love with her (is favorable to her with his auspices), and Juno becomes jealous (with that civil jealousy, explained above, with which the heroes guarded their solemn nuptials) and has her watched by Argos of the hundred eyes (that is, by the Argive fathers, each with his eye or clearing, that is, his cultivated land according to the interpretation given above). Then Mercury (who must here be a character of the mercenary plebeians), by the sound of his pipe, or rather by his singing, lulls Argos to sleep (overcomes the Argive fathers in the struggle for the auspices, by which the fortunes were sung or divined in solemn nuptials), whereupon Io is changed into a cow and lies with the bull with which Pasiphaë had lain, and goes wandering into Egypt (that is among those foreign Egyptians with whom Danaus had driven the Inachids from the kingdom of Argos).

657 But Hercules in his old age becomes effeminate and spins at the behest of Iole and Omphale; that is, the heroic right to the fields falls to the plebs. The heroes called themselves *viri,* men, in contrast to the plebeians, and *viri* in Latin has the same meaning as heroes in Greek. Vergil uses the word emphatically in that sense at the beginning of his *Aeneid: Arma virumque cano;* and Horace translates the first verse of the *Odyssey: Dic mihi, Musa, virum. Viri* continued among the Romans to signify husbands by solemn matrimony, magistrates, priests and judges, for, in the poetic aristocracies, solemn matrimony, magistracy, priesthood, and judgeship were all confined to the heroic orders. Thus [the fable relates that] the heroic right to the fields was extended to the plebeians of Greece, just as the Roman patricians conceded to their plebeians the quiritary right by the second agrarian law, which was fought for and won in the Law of the Twelve Tables, as shown above. Precisely in the same way in the returned barbarian times feudal goods were called goods of the lance, and alodial goods were called goods of the distaff, as we find in the laws of the Angles. Hence the royal arms of France (in signification of the Salic law which excludes women from inheriting that kingdom) are supported by two angels clothed in dalmatics and armed with spears, and are adorned with the heroic motto: *Lilia non nent,* "The lilies do not spin." So that just as Baldus, to our good fortune, called the Salic Law *ius gentium Gallorum,* "the law of the Gallic nations," so we may apply the term *ius gentium romanorum* to the Law of the Twelve Tables inasmuch as it rigorously confined intestate succession to *sui* *heredes,* agnates and gentiles. For we shall show later how little truth there is in the belief that in the early times of Rome there had existed a custom whereby daughters could succeed to their fathers *ab intestato,* and that this custom had passed into law in the Twelve Tables.

658   Finally Hercules breaks into a fury on being stained by the blood of the centaur Nessus—the same plebeian monster of two discordant natures mentioned by Livy—that is, in the midst of civil fury he extends *connubium* to the plebs and is contaminated by plebeian blood and so dies, even as the god Fidius, the Roman Hercules, dies with the Petelian law called *De nexu.* By this law *vinculum fidei victum est,* "the bond of faith was broken," although Livy connects it with an event occurring a decade later but similar in substance to the event which had given occasion to the Petelian law, an event in which it was necessary that the matter of the aforesaid phrase should be put into execution and not simply decreed. Livy must have found the phrase in some ancient chronicler whom he follows with as much good faith as ignorance. For when the plebeian debtors were freed from private incarceration by their noble creditors, debtors were still constrained by judicial decisions to pay their debts, but they were released from the feudal law, the law of the Herculean knot, which had had its origin in the first asylums of the world, the bond by which Romulus had founded Rome in his asylum. It seems very likely, therefore, that the chronicler had written *vinculum Fidii,* the bond of the god Fidius, whom Varro asserts to have been the Roman Hercules, and that later historians, not understanding the phrase, erroneously read the word as *fidei.* The same heroic natural law is found among the American Indians, and in our world it still obtains among the Abyssinians of Africa and the Muscovites and Tartars of Europe and Asia. It was practiced with greater mildness by the Hebrews, among whom debtors served only seven years.

659   And, to conclude, in like manner Orpheus, the founder of Greece, with his lyre or cord or force, which signify the same thing as the knot of Hercules (the knot with which the Petelian law was concerned), met his death at the hands of the Bacchantes (the infuriated plebs), who broke his lyre to pieces (the lyre being the law, as we have so often shown above); so that already in Homer's time the heroes were taking foreign women to wife, and bastards were coming into royal successions, showing that Greece had already begun to countenance popular liberty.

660   From all this we must conclude that these heroic contests gave the name to the heroic period; and that in these contests many chieftains, vanquished and humbled, were obliged to take to the sea with their followers and wander in search of other lands. Some of them finally returned to their native countries, like Menelaus and Ulysses. Others settled in foreign parts, like Cecrops, Cadmus, Danaus and Pelops, who settled in Greece (for these heroic contests had arisen many centuries earlier in Phoenicia, Egypt and Phrygia, since civilization had begun earlier in those places). Dido must have been one of the latter sort;

fleeing from Phoenicia to escape the faction of her brother by whom she was pursued, she settled in Carthage, which was called *Punica* as if for *Phoenica*. And of the Trojan refugees after the destruction of their city, Capys stopped at Capua, Aeneas landed in Latium, and Antenor reached Padua.

661   Thus ended the wisdom of the theological poets, the sages or statesmen of the poetic age of the Greeks, such as Orpheus, Amphion, Linus, Musaeus and others. By singing to the Greek plebs of the force of the gods in the auspices (which were the praises that such poets must have sung of the gods, that is the praises of divine providence which it behooved them to sing), they kept the plebs in subjection to their heroic orders. In like fashion Appius [Claudius], the grandson of the decemvir, about the 300th year of Rome, as we have said elsewhere, by singing to the Roman plebeians of the force of the gods in the auspices, of which the nobles claimed to have the science, kept them in obedience to the nobles. And in the same way Amphion, by singing to his lyre, causes the stones to move and the walls of Thebes, which Cadmus had founded three centuries earlier, to arise; that is, he confirms therein the heroic state.

[CHAPTER VII]

COROLLARIES CONCERNING ROMAN ANTIQUITIES, AND IN PARTICULAR THE SUPPOSEDLY MONARCHIC KINGSHIP AT ROME AND THE SUPPOSEDLY POPULAR LIBERTY ORDAINED BY JUNIUS BRUTUS

662   The numerous parallels we have cited in human civil affairs between the Romans and the Greeks, by which we have repeatedly shown that ancient Roman history is a perpetual historic mythology of the many various and diverse fables of the Greeks, must firmly convince anyone of understanding (which is neither memory nor imagination) that from the times of the kings until the extension of *connubium* to the plebs the Roman people (the people of Mars) was composed of nobles alone. To this people of nobles King Tullus, beginning with the case of Horatius, granted the right of persons condemned for crime by the duumvirs or the quaestors to appeal to the entire order. The orders alone were the heroic peoples, and the plebs were accessions to these peoples (as later the provinces were accessions to the conquering nations, as Grotius pointed out) and are in fact the "other people," as Telemachus called his plebeians in the assembly we mentioned above. And hence, by virtue of an invincible metaphysical criticism of these founders of nations, we are able to uproot the error which asserts that such a mass of base-born laborers, held as slaves, had the right, from the time of Romulus, to elect their kings and have their

choice ratified by the fathers. This must be an anachronism of later times when the plebs had a part in the city and shared in the creating of consuls (which was after the extension of *connubium* to the plebs by the fathers), dated back three hundred years to the interregnum of Romulus.

663   Taking the word people in the sense of recent times and applying it to the earliest times of the world of the cities (because of the inability of philosophers and philologians alike to imagine such severe aristocracies) has led to misunderstandings of the words king and liberty as well. As a result, everyone has believed that the Roman kingdom was monarchic and that the liberty ordained by Junius Brutus was popular. Jean Bodin, however, though he too falls into the common vulgar error of all preceding political theorists that monarchies came first, then tyrannies, then popular commonwealths and finally aristocracies (what distortions of human ideas can be and are made when true principles are lacking!), nevertheless, observing the effects of an aristocratic commonwealth in the supposedly popular liberty of ancient Rome, props up his system by distinguishing the form of a government from its administration and asserting that that of ancient Rome was popular in form but aristocratically administered. For all that, since the facts turned out otherwise and even with this prop his political machinery would not stand, he was finally constrained by the force of the truth to confess with gross inconsistency that in ancient times the Roman commonwealth was aristocratic in form as well as in administration.

664   All this is confirmed by Livy, who, in his account of the setting up of two annual consuls by Junius Brutus, openly states and avows that there was no change in the form of government. And indeed how could a wise Brutus have done otherwise than restore the state to its pristine condition from the corruption into which it had fallen! By the institution of two annual consuls, says Livy [II, 1], *nihil quicquam de regia potestate deminutum,* "no diminution was made in the royal power"; for the consuls emerged as two aristocratic annual kings, as indeed Cicero in his *Laws* calls them *reges annuos* (of the same sort as the kings for life at Sparta, which was beyond question an aristocratic commonwealth). And the consuls, as everyone knows, were subject to recall during their period of office (just as the kings of Sparta were subject to correction by the ephors) and at the end of their year's reign could be put on trial (as Spartan kings were condemned to death by the ephors). This one passage of Livy shows both that the Roman kingdom was aristocratic and that the liberty ordained by Brutus was not popular (the freedom of the people from their lords) but aristocratic (the freedom of the lords from the Tarquin tyrants). Brutus would certainly not have been able to accomplish this had it not been for the affair of the Roman Lucretia, which, being offered him, he turned to advantage; for this occasion was clothed with all the sublime circumstances necessary to arouse the plebs against the tyrant Tarquinius, who had so badly handled the nobility that Brutus found it necessary to reconstruct the senate, depleted as it was by the execution of so many senators by [Tarquinius] Superbus. In doing this he

achieved, by prudent consideration, two public advantages: He strengthened the order of the nobles, which was declining; and he won the favor of the plebs, for from their body he had to choose many, and perhaps he chose the boldest, who would otherwise have opposed the reorganization of the nobility. These he caused to enter the order of the nobility, and thus he composed the city, the whole of which was at that time divided *inter patres et plebem,* "between fathers and plebs."

665   If the precurrence of so many varied and diverse causes as we have studied from the age of Saturn onward, if the succession of so many varied and diverse effects as Bodin observes in the ancient Roman commonwealth, and if the perpetual and continuous influence of these causes on these effects as set forth by Livy, are not sufficient to demonstrate that the Roman kingdom was aristocratic and that the liberty ordained by Brutus was the liberty of the aristocracy, then we must say that the Romans, a rough and barbarous people, had a privilege from God withheld from the Greeks, an acute and highly civilized people, who, according to Thucydides, knew nothing of their own antiquities down to the Peloponnesian war, the most illustrious time of Greece as we observed above in the [Notes on the] Chronological Table [101]. There too we showed that the same was true of the Romans down to the second Carthaginian war, from which Livy professes to write the history of Rome with more assurance, while yet confessing ignorance of three circumstances, the most important in the history [of that war], which we also observed there [117]. But, even if we concede such a privilege to the Romans, what survives is still but an obscure memory, a confused imagination, and so reason cannot reject the conclusions we have drawn concerning these Roman antiquities.

[CHAPTER VIII]

COROLLARY CONCERNING THE HEROISM OF THE FIRST PEOPLES

666   The study of the heroic age of the early world which we have here been making leads us perforce to reflect on the heroism of the first peoples. This heroism, by the axioms which we set forth above [196–197] and which have their application here, and by the principles herein established for heroic politics, was a far different thing from what philosophers have hitherto imagined as a consequence of the matchless wisdom of the ancients, misled by the philologians with respect to those three undefined words, people, king and liberty, above referred to. For they have taken the heroic peoples as also including the plebeians; they have taken the kings as monarchs; and they have taken the liberty as popular. On the other hand, they have applied to these matters three

ideas proper to their own refined and learned minds: the first, that of a justice reasoned on maxims of Socratic morals; the second, that of a glory which is the fame of benefits done to the human race; and the third, the desire for immortality. By following these errors and applying these ideas, they have believed that the kings or other great personages of ancient times consecrated themselves and their families (as well as their entire patrimonies and substance) to bring happiness to the poor, who are always the majority in any city or nation.

667   Yet concerning Achilles, the greatest of the Greek heroes, Homer tells us of three of his qualities which were in complete contrast with the three ideas of the philosophers. As regards justice, in speaking with Hector, who proposes that the victor in the fight shall bury the vanquished, he forgets their equality of rank and the common lot [of men] (two considerations which naturally induce men to recognize justice) and makes the following savage reply: "When have men ever made pacts with lions? And when were wolves and lambs ever of one mind?" On the contrary: "If I kill you, I shall drag you naked, bound to my chariot, three days around the walls of Troy," as indeed he did, "and finally I shall give your body to my hunting dogs to eat." This too he would have done if the unhappy father Priam had not himself come to ransom the corpse. And as for glory, this same Achilles because of a personal grievance (Agamemnon having wrongfully taken his Briseis from him) considers himself badly treated by gods and men alike, demands of Jove that he be restored to honor, withdraws his men from the allied army and his ships from the fleet, and allows Hector to make a slaughter of the Greeks. Thus in defiance of the devotion that a man owes his fatherland he insists on avenging a personal offense by the ruin of his entire nation. Indeed he is not ashamed to rejoice with Patroclus over Hector's slaughter of the Greeks, and, what is much graver, this man who carries in his heels the fate of Troy expresses the disgraceful wish to Patroclus that all, Greeks and Trojans alike, may die in the war, leaving only the two of them alive. And as for the third idea, [the desire of immortality,] when Achilles in the lower world is asked by Ulysses if he is content there, he answers that he would rather be the meanest slave in the land of the living. This is the hero that Homer sings of to the Greek peoples as an example of heroic virtue and to whom he gives the fixed epithet, blameless! This epithet, if we are to give Homer credit for making the delight he gives a means of instruction, as poets are supposed to do, can be understood only as meaning a man so arrogant that, as we would say nowadays, he will not let a fly pass the end of his nose. What he preaches is thus the virtue of punctiliousness, on which the duellists of the returned barbarian times based their entire morality, and which gave rise to the proud laws, the lofty duties and the vindictive satisfactions of the knights errant of whom the romancers sing.

668   As against this, let us reflect on the oath of eternal enmity which Aristotle says the heroes swore against the plebs. Let us reflect further on Roman history in the time of Roman virtue, which according to Livy was the time of the war against Pyrrhus, a time he acclaims in the phrase *nulla aetas virtutum feracior,* "there was never an age more productive of virtues." Following Sallust as quoted in St. Augustine's *City of God,* we may extend this period from the expulsion of the kings down to the second Carthaginian war. What of the heroes of this time? Brutus, who consecrates his house in the persons of his two sons to the cause of liberty; Scaevola, who terrifies and routs the Etruscan king Porsena by plunging his own right hand into the flames for its failure to kill him; Manlius called the Imperious, who cuts off the head of his own son for a breach of military discipline though it sprang from love of glory and valor and issued in victory; men like Curtius, who throws himself, mounted and armed, into the fatal abyss; like the Decii who, father and son, sacrifice themselves to save their army; like Fabricius and Curius, who refuse the Samnite gold and the shares of his kingdom offered them by Pyrrhus; like Atilius Regulus, who returns to a certain and most cruel death at Carthage to preserve the sanctity of the Roman oath—what did any of them do for the poor and unhappy Roman plebs? Assuredly they did but increase their burdens by war, plunge them deeper in the sea of usury, in order to bury them to a greater depth in the private prisons of the nobles, where they were beaten with rods on their bare backs like abject slaves. And if anyone in this period of Roman virtue attempted to relieve the lot of the plebs with some sort of agrarian or grain law, he was accused of treason and sent to his death. Such was the fate, to take only one example, of Manlius Capitolinus, though he had saved the capitol from being burned by the ferocious Senonic Gauls. Likewise in Sparta (the city of the heroes of Greece, as Rome was the city of the heroes of the world), the magnanimous king Agis, because of his attempt to relieve the poor Lacedaemonian plebs, oppressed by the usury of the nobles, by a law wiping out debts, and to aid them by another giving them testamentary rights, was strangled by order of the ephors, as before noted. As the valorous Agis was the Manlius Capitolinus of Sparta, so Manlius Capitolinus was the Agis of Rome, and, on the simple suspicion of being somewhat mindful of the poor oppressed Roman plebs, he was thrown from the Tarpeian rock. So that precisely because the nobles of the first peoples considered themselves heroes and of a nature superior to that of their plebeians, as has been fully shown above, they were capable of such misgovernment of the poor masses of the nations. For certainly Roman history will puzzle any intelligent reader who tries to find in it any evidence of Roman virtue where there was so much arrogance, or of moderation in the midst of such avarice, or of justice or mercy where so much inequality and cruelty prevailed.

669   The only principles that can solve the enigma are of necessity the following.

I

670   In consequence of the savage education of the giants which we discussed above, the [heroic] education of the young was severe, harsh and cruel,
as in the case of the unlettered Lacedaemonians, who were the heroes of Greece.
These people, in order to teach their sons to fear neither pain nor death, would
beat them within an inch of their lives in the temple of Diana, so that they often
fell dead in agonies of pain beneath thir fathers' blows. This cyclopean paternal
authority survived among both Greeks and Romans, permitting them to kill
their innocent new-born babes. Whereas the delight we now take in our young
children reveals all the tenderness of our natures.

II

671   Wives were bought with heroic dowries, a usage which survived as
a solemnity in the nuptials of the Roman priests, which were contracted
coëmptione et farre, "by mutual [mock] sale and spelt" [-bread offering].
(This was also the custom among the ancient Germans, according to Tacitus,
and we may therefore assume the same of all the earliest barbarous peoples.)
Wives were maintained as a necessity of nature for the procreation of children.
In other respects they were treated as slaves, as is [still] the custom of nations
in many parts of our [old] world and almost everywhere in the new. When the
wife brings the dowry, it purchases the liberty of her husband and is a public
confession on his part of inability to bear the expense of marriage, which is perhaps the reason for the many privileges with which the emperors favored
dowries.

III

672   Children acquired and wives saved for the benefit of their husbands
and fathers. Not, as nowadays, just the contrary.

IV

673   Games and pleasures were strenuous, such as wrestling and racing
(whence the Homeric fixed epithet of Achilles, swift-footed); and often dangerous too, such as jousting and hunting wild game, to accustom men to steel themselves and to risk and disprize their lives.

V

674   Luxury, refinement and ease were quite unknown.

VI

675   Wars like the ancient heroic ones were all wars of religion, which,
for the reason we have taken as the first principle of this Science, made them
always extremely bitter.

VII

676   Heroic enslavement was also prevalent as a consequence of such wars in which the vanquished were regarded as godless men, so that along with civil liberty they lost natural liberty as well. Here the axiom above proposed [290] finds application: namely, that "natural liberty is fiercer in proportion as property attaches more closely to our persons, and civil servitude is clapped on with goods of fortune not necessary to life."

[VIII]

677   Because of all this the commonwealths were by nature aristocratic, consisting of those who were naturally strongest. They confined all civil honors to the few noble fathers. The public good was the family monarchies preserved by the fatherland; for the true fatherland, as we have often said, meant the interests of the few fathers, and hence the citizens were naturally patricians. And with such natures, customs, commonwealths, orders and laws the heroism of the first peoples is realized. This heroism is now by civil nature impossible, since the causes of it which we have enumerated have given place to their contraries, which have produced the other two kinds of civil states, free popular commonwealths and monarchies; both of these (though the latter more than the former) we have shown above to be human. For throughout the whole period of Roman popular liberty Cato of Utica alone was reputed a hero, and his reputation was that of a spirit of the aristocratic commonwealth whom Pompey's fall left as head of the party of the nobility and who, because he could not bear its humiliation by Caesar, killed himself. In the monarchies the heroes are those who sacrifice themselves for the glory and grandeur of their sovereigns. Wherefore we must conclude that such a hero [as devotes himself to justice and the welfare of mankind (666)] is desired by afflicted peoples, conceived by philosophers and imagined by poets, but is not included among the benefits afforded by civil nature, as covered by our axiom [260].

678   All we have here set forth concerning the heroism of the first peoples receives illumination and illustration from the axioms above proposed concerning Roman heroism [278–281], which will be found to apply also to the heroism of the ancient Athenians at the time when, as Thucydides [i.e. Isocrates] relates, they were governed by the stern Areopagites (an aristocratic senate, as we have seen), and to the heroism of the Spartans, who were a commonwealth of Heraclids or lords, as a thousand proofs above have demonstrated.

[SECTION VI]

[CHAPTER I]

EPITOMES OF POETIC HISTORY

I

679 This whole divine and heroic history of the theological poets was only too unhappily described for us in the fable of Cadmus. For first he slays the great serpent (clears the earth of the great ancient forest). Then he sows the teeth (a fine metaphor, as noted above, for his ploughing the first fields of the world with curved pieces of hard wood, which, before the use of iron was discovered, must have served as the teeth of the first ploughs, and teeth they continued to be called). He throws a heavy stone (the hard earth which the clients or *famuli* wished to plough for themselves, as above explained). From the furrows armed men spring forth (in the heroic contest over the first agrarian law aforementioned, the heroes come forth from their estates to assert their lordship of them, and unite in arms against the plebs, and they fight not among themselves but with the clients that have revolted against them; the furrows signifying the orders in which they unite and thereby give form and stability to the first cities on the basis of arms, as is all set forth above). And Cadmus is changed into a serpent (signifying the origin of the authority of the aristocratic senates, for which the ancient Latins would have used the phrase *Cadmus fundus factus est,* and the Greeks said Cadmus was changed into Draco, the dragon that wrote the laws in blood). All of which is what we above promised to make clear: that the fable of Cadmus contained several centuries of poetic history, and is a grand example of the inarticulateness with which the still infant world labored to express itself, which is one of the seven great sources of the difficulty of the fables which we shall later enumerate [1st ed., Bk. III, Chs. 9–15]. So easy it was for Cadmus to leave a written record of this history in the vulgar characters which he brought to the Greeks from Phoenicia! And Desiderius Erasmus, with a thousand absurdities unworthy of the learned man who was called the Christian Varro, will have it that [the fable] contains the story of the invention of letters by Cadmus. Thus the illustrious history of such a great benefit to the nations as the invention of letters, which must have made itself known far and wide, is concealed by Cadmus from the human race in Greece under the veil of this fable, which remained obscure down to the time of Erasmus, in order to keep hidden from the vulgar such a great invention of vulgar wisdom that from the vulgar these letters received the name of vulgar letters!

II

680   But with admirable brevity and appropriateness Homer tells us the same history compressed in the hieroglyph of the scepter bestowed on Agamemnon. Vulcan made it for Jove (as Jove, with the first thunderbolts after the flood, founded his kingdom over gods and men, which is to say the divine kingdoms in the state of the families). Then Jove gave it to Mercury (in the form of the caduceus with which Mercury brought the first agrarian law to the plebs, whence were born the heroic kingdoms of the first cities). Then Mercury gave it to Pelops, Pelops to Thyestes, Thyestes to Atreus, and Atreus to Agamemnon (that is, it came down through the line of inheritance of the royal house of Argos).

III

681   More full and detailed, however, is the history of the world described by the same Homer as depicted on the shield of Achilles.

682   I. At the beginning there could be seen thereon the sky, the earth, the sea, the sun, the moon and the stars. This is the epoch of the creation of the world.

683   II. Thereafter were depicted two cities. In the one there were songs, hymeneals and nuptials: the epoch of the heroic families composed of children born of solemn nuptials. In the other there were no such things to be seen; this represented the epoch of the heroic families with their *famuli,* who contracted only natural marriages with none of the solemn rites which surrounded heroic nuptials. So that these two cities together represented the state of nature, or of the families. It was to these two cities that Eumaeus, the steward of Ulysses, had reference when he spoke of the two cities in his fatherland, both ruled by his father, in which the citizens had all their goods clearly divided (meaning that no part of citizenship was shared in common between them). Hence the city without hymeneals is exactly the "other people," as Telemachus in assembly calls the plebs of Ithaca. And this is Achilles's meaning in complaining of the outrage done him by Agamemnon, who, he says, has treated him as a common laborer with no part in the governing.

684   III. Then, in this same city of the nuptials, the shield showed parliaments, laws, trials and punishments. This accords with the answer of the Roman patricians to the plebs in the heroic contests, asserting that nuptials, property rights and priesthoods, on which depended the science of laws and hence of

judgments, were all their special prerogatives since the auspices which constituted the chief solemnity of nuptials were theirs. For this reason *viri,* "men"
(which meant among the Latins the same as heroes among the Greeks), was
the term applied to husbands in solemn matrimony, magistrates, priests and
finally judges, as we have said before. This, then, is the epoch of the heroic cities
which, on the basis of families of the *famuli,* arose in strictest aristocratic form.

685   IV. The other city is under armed siege and the two cities prey on
each other by turns; hence the city without nuptials (the plebs of the heroic
cities) becomes a separate and hostile city. This affords striking confirmation of
what we have argued above: that the first foreigners, the first *hostes,* were
the plebs of the heroic peoples, against whom, as we have so often quoted
Aristotle as saying, the heroes swore eternal enmity. Hence the two cities, regarding each other as alien, carried on eternal hostilities against each other with
their heroic raids, as we have explained above.

686   V. And lastly there was portrayed on the shield the history of the
arts of humanity, beginning with the epoch of the families. For, first of all,
there appeared the father king, ordering with his scepter that the roasted ox
be divided among the harvesters. Then there were planted vineyards; then
flocks, shepherds and huts; and last of all, dances were depicted. This picture,
beautifully and truly following the order of human things, indicated that first
of all the necessary arts were invented, agriculture with a view first to bread
and then to wine; then the useful arts, such as herding; then the arts of comfort, like urban architecture; and lastly those of pleasure, represented by the
dance.

[SECTION VII]

[POETIC PHYSICS]

[CHAPTER I]

POETIC PHYSICS

687   Passing now to the other branch of the main trunk of poetic meta-physics, along which poetic wisdom branches off into physics and thence into cosmography and thus into astronomy, whose fruits are chronology and geography, we shall begin this remaining part of our discussion with physics.

688   The theological poets considered the physics of the world of nations, and therefore they first defined Chaos as confusion of human seeds in the period of the abominable sharing of women. It was thence that the physicists were later moved to conceive the confusion of the universal seeds of nature, and to express it they took the word already invented by the poets and hence appropriate. [The poetic Chaos] was confused because there was no order of humanity in it, and obscure because it lacked the civil light in virtue of which the heroes were called *incliti,* "illustrious." Further they imagined it as Orcus, a misshapen monster which devoured all things, because men in this infamous community did not have the proper form of men, and were swallowed up by the void because through the uncertainty of offspring they left nothing of themselves. This [chaos] was later taken by the physicists as the prime matter of natural things, which, formless itself, is greedy for forms and devours all forms. The poets however gave it also the monstrous form of Pan, the wild god who is the divinity of all satyrs inhabiting not the cities but the forests; a character to which they reduced the impious vagabonds wandering through the great forest of the earth and having the appearance of men but the habits of abominable beasts. Afterwards, by forced allegories on which we shall comment later, the philosophers, misled by the name *pan,* "everything," took him as a symbol for the formed universe. Scholars have also held that the poets meant first matter in the fable of Proteus, with whom Ulysses wrestles in Egypt, Proteus in the water and the hero out of it, unable to get a grip on the monster who keeps assuming new forms. But the scholars thus made sublime learning out of what was doltishness and simplicity on the part of the first men, who (just as children, looking in a mirror, will try to seize their own reflections) thought from the various modifications of their own shapes and gestures that there must be a man in the water, forever changing into different shapes.

689   At length the sky broke forth in thunder, and Jove thus gave a beginning to the world of men by arousing in them the impulse which is proper to the liberty of the mind, just as from motion, which is proper to bodies as necessary agents, he began the world of nature. For what seems to be impulse in bodies is but insensible motion, as we said above in the Method. From this impulse came the civil light of which Apollo is the character, by which light was discerned the civil beauty with which the heroes were beautiful. And Venus was the character of this civil beauty, which the physicists later interpreted as the beauty of nature, and even as the whole of formed nature, which is beautifully adorned with all sensible forms.

690   The world of the theological poets was composed of four sacred elements: the air whence Jove's bolts came, the water of the perennial springs whose divinity is Diana, the fire with which Vulcan cleared the forests, and the tilled earth of Cybele or Berecynthia. All four are elements in divine ceremonies: auspices, water, fire and spelt. They are watched over by Vesta, who, as we said before, is the same as Cybele or Berecynthia. She is crowned with the tilled lands protected by hedges and surmounted by the towers of high-placed towns (whence the Latin *extorris,* "exiled," as if *exterris*). This crown encloses all that was signified by the *orbis terrarum,* which is properly the world of men. Thence the physicists were later moved to study the four elements of which the world of nature is composed.

691   The same theological poets gave living and sensible and for the most part human forms to the elements and to the countless special natures arising from them, and thus created many and various divinities, as we have set forth above in the Metaphysics. This gave Plato opportunity to intrude his doctrine of minds or intelligences: that Jove was the mind of ether, Vulcan of fire, and the like. But the theological poets understood so little of these intelligent substances that down to Homer's time they did not understand the human mind itself insofar as, by dint of reflection, it opposes the senses. On this there are two golden passages in the *Odyssey* in which it is called sacred force or occult vigor, which mean the same thing.

[CHAPTER II]

POETIC PHYSICS CONCERNING MAN, OR HEROIC NATURE

692 But the greatest and most important part of physics is the contemplation of the nature of man. We have set forth above in the Poetic Economy how the founders of gentile humanity in a certain sense generated and produced in themselves the proper human form in its two aspects: that is, how by means of frightful religions and terrible paternal powers and sacred ablutions they brought forth from their giant bodies the form of our just corporature, and how by the discipline of their household economy they brought forth from their bestial minds the form of our human mind. Here is a proper place for calling attention again to that development.

693 Now the theological poets in their extremely crude physics saw in man these two metaphysical ideas: being and subsisting. Certainly the Latin heroes understood being quite grossly in the sense of eating. This must have been the first meaning of the verb *sum,* which later was used in both senses, just as nowadays when our peasants want to say that a sick man lives they say he still eats. For *sum* in the sense of being is extremely abstract, transcending all particular beings; most pervasive, penetrating all beings; most pure, as not being circumscribed by any. They apprehended substance, that which stands beneath and sustains, as residing in the heels because a man stands on the base of his feet. Hence Achilles carried his fate in his heel, since there stood his fate or lot of living or dying.

694 The composition of the body they reduced to solids and liquids. Under the head of solids they included in the first place the viscera or flesh (as among the Romans *visceratio* was the term applied to the distribution by the priests to the people of the flesh of sacrificial victims), so that they used the verb *vesci* for taking nourishment when the food was flesh. Next, bones and joints. The latter were called *artus* from *ars,* which to the ancient Latins meant the force of the body, whence *artitus,* "robust of person"; later *ars* was applied to any set of precepts which steadies and directs some faculty of the mind. Then, the sinews. When the poets were still mute and spoke by physical things, they took the sinews for forces (from one of these sinews, called *fides* in the sense of cord, the force of the gods was called their *fides* or "faith," and from this sinew or cord or force they later fashioned the lute of Orpheus); and indeed they justly placed their forces in the sinews, for it is the sinews that stretch the muscles, which is necessary to the exercise of force. And lastly the marrow, in which with an equal sense of fitness they placed the essence of life (whence

medulla was a term applied by the lover to the woman he loved, and *medullitus* was equivalent to our phrase, "with all one's heart," and great love was said to consume the marrow). The liquids, on the other hand, they reduced to blood alone, for the neural or spermatic substance they called also blood (as is shown by the poetic phrase *sanguine cretus* for "begotten"); here too with a just sense, for this substance is the essence of the blood. And again with fine perception they regarded the blood as the juice of the fibers of which the flesh is composed; hence the Latin expression *succiplenus* for fleshy: "steeped in good blood."

695   As for the other part [of our human form], the soul (*anima*), the theological poets placed it in the air (which is also called *anima* by the Latins) and they thought of it as the vehicle of life. (Hence the propriety of the Latin phrase *anima vivimus* and of the poetic locutions *ferri ad vitales auras,* "to be born"; *ducere vitales auras,* "to live"; *vitam referri in auras,* "to die." And in prose Latin: *animam ducere,* to live; *animam trahere,* to be at the point of death; *animam efflare, emittere,* to die.) Whence perhaps the motive of the physicists for placing the world soul in the air. And the theological poets, again with a just sense, put the course of life in the course of the blood, on whose proper flow our life depends.

696   They must with a sense equally just have felt that the spirit (*animus*) is the vehicle of sensation, for in good Latin the phrase survived *animo sentimus.* And again with a just sense they made spirit (*animus*) masculine and soul (*anima*) feminine, for spirit acts on soul (it is the *igneus vigor* of which Vergil speaks); so that spirit must have its subject in the nerves and the neural substance, and soul must have its in the veins and the blood. Thus the vehicle of the spirit is the ether and that of the soul is the air, as accords with the relative swiftness of animal spirits and slowness of vital spirits. And as the soul is the agent of motion, so the spirit is the agent and therefore the principle of voluntary action, as the aforesaid *igneus vigor* of Vergil. The theological poets sensed as much, but without understanding it, and after Homer they used such expressions as sacred force, occult vigor and unknown god; as the Greeks and Latins, when in saying or doing anything they sensed a superior principle within themselves, would say that some god had willed that thing. Such a principle the Latins called *mens animi,* "the mind of the spirit." Thus in a crude fashion they apprehended the lofty truth that ideas come to man from God, which later the natural theology of the metaphysicians proved by invincible reasoning against the Epicureans who would have it that they spring from the body.

697   They understood generation in such a way that it is difficult to say whether later scholars have been able to express it more appropriately. The way in which they understood it is all contained in the word *concipere,* for *concapere,* which expresses the natural activity of physical forms (which must now be supplemented by the weight of the air, demonstrated in our times) in taking from everywhere around them the bodies within their reach, overcoming their resistance, adapting and assimilating them to their own form.

698   Decay they expressed very sagaciously in the verb *corrumpi,* signifying the breaking down of all the parts composing a body, as opposed to *sanum* for the sound and healthy condition of all the parts in which life consists. They must accordingly have thought of disease as bringing on death by corrupting the solids of the body.

699   They reduced all the internal functions of the spirit to three parts of the body: the head, the breast and the heart. To the head they assigned all cognitive functions; as [among them] these were all imaginative, they located memory (*memoria* being the Latin term for *phantasia* or "imagination") in the head. And in the returned barbarian times *fantasia* was used for *ingegno,* and an ingenious or witty man was called a fantastic man. Cola di Rienzo is so described by the author of a contemporary biography in barbarous Italian, a record of natures and customs like those of the ancient heroes we are discussing, which is a great evidence of the recurrence of natures and customs in the course the nations run. Imagination, however, is nothing but the springing up again of reminiscences, and ingenuity or invention is nothing but the working over of what is remembered. Now, since the human mind at the time we are considering had not been refined by any art of writing nor spiritualized by any practice of reckoning or reasoning, and had not developed its powers of abstraction by the many abstract terms in which languages now abound, as we said above in the Method, it exercised all its force in these three excellent faculties which came to it from the body. All three appertain to the primary operation of the mind whose regulating art is topics, just as the regulating art of the second operation of the mind is criticism; and as the latter is the art of judging, so the former is the art of inventing, as has been said above in the last Corollaries of the Poetic Logic. And since naturally the discovery or invention of things comes before criticism of them, it was fitting that the infancy of the world should concern itself with the first operation of the human mind, for the world then had need of all inventions for the necessities and utilities of life, all of which had been provided before the philosophers appeared, as we shall fully show in the Discovery of the True Homer. With reason, then, did the theological poets call Memory the mother of the Muses, which, as we found above, were the arts of humanity.

700   In this connection we must not omit an important observation of great relevance to the statement in the Method that we can now scarcely understand and cannot at all imagine how the first men thought who founded gentile humanity. For their minds were so limited to particulars that they regarded every change of facial expression as a new face, as we observed above in the fable of Proteus, and for every new passion they imagined a new heart, a new breast, a new spirit. Hence the poetic plurals, dictated by this nature of human things rather than by the requirements of counting; *ora, vultus, animi, pectora, corda,* for example, being employed for their singulars.

701   They made the breast the seat of all the passions, and with a due sense

of fitness they placed beneath it the two fomenting principles: (1) the irascible in the stomach, because there we feel the spreading of the bile expressed from the surrounding biliary vessels by the intensification of the peristaltic action of the stomach; and (2) the concupiscible more than anywhere else in the liver, which is defined as the blood factory. The poets called these organs the *praecordia*. The Titan [Prometheus] implanted therein the passions of the other animals, taking from each species its ruling passion. In a rough way they understood that concupiscence is the mother of all the passions, and that the passions have their dwelling in our humors.

702   The heart they made the seat of all counsel, whence the heroes *agitabant, versabant, volutabant corde curas;* for, being stupid and insensate, they gave no thought to things to be done except when shaken by passions. Hence the Latins called wise men *cordati* and simpletons contrariwise *vecordes.* And their resolutions they called *sententiae* because they judged as they felt, whence heroic judgments were always true in form though often false in substance.

[CHAPTER III]

COROLLARY ON HEROIC SENTENCES

703   Now, since the minds of the first men of the gentile world took things one at a time, being in this respect little better than the minds of beasts, for which each new sensation cancels the preceding (which is the cause of their being unable to compare and reason discursively), therefore their sentences must all have been taken as singulars by those who heard them. Hence the sublime sentence admired by Dionysius Longinus in the ode of Sappho which Catullus later turned into Latin, in which the lover in the presence of his mistress expresses himself by the simile: *Ille mi par esse deo videtur,* "Like a god he seems to me," yet falls short of the highest degree of sublimity, because the lover does not make the sentence singular to himself, as Terence does when he says: *Vitam deorum adepti sumus,* "We have attained the life of the gods." This sentiment, though proper to him who speaks, still has the air of a common sentiment because of the Latin usage of plural for singular in the first person. However, in another comedy of the same poet, this sentiment is raised to the highest degree of sublimity by being made singular and appropriated to him who expresses it: *Deus factus sum,* "I am become a god."

704   On this account abstract sentences are the work of philosophers, because they contain universals, and reflections on the passions are the work of false and frigid poets.

[CHAPTER IV]

COROLLARY ON HEROIC DESCRIPTIONS

705   Finally they reduced the external functions of the spirit to the five senses of the body, but senses keen, vivid and strong, for these men were all robust imagination with very little or no reason. Evidence of this may be found in the terms they used for the senses.

706   Their word for hearing was *audire,* as if *haurire,* for the ears drink in the air which has been set in motion by other bodies. Seeing distinctly was called *cernere oculis* (whence perhaps the Italian *scernere*), for the eyes are like a sieve and the pupils like two holes, and as from the sieve streams of dust pour down to touch the earth, so from the eyes, through the pupils, stream forth rays of light to touch the objects which are distinctly seen. (This is the visual ray of which the Stoics later treated, and which in our day has been happily demonstrated by Descartes.) The general expression for seeing was *usurpare oculis,* as if things seen were actually taken possession of by sight. *Tangere,* "to touch," meant also "to steal," for to touch a body is to take something away from it, as our more intelligent physicists are just beginning to understand. Smelling they called *olfacere,* as if by smelling odors they created them; as indeed later the natural philosophers, with their grave observations, found it to be true that the senses make the qualities that are called sensible. And lastly they called tasting *sapere,* a word which properly applies to the things which have savor, because they assayed things for the savor proper to them. Hence later, by a fine metaphor, they used the term *sapientia,* "wisdom," for the faculty of making those uses of things which they have in nature, not those which opinion supposes them to have.

707   Herein is divine providence to be admired, because, having given us the senses for the guarding of our bodies, at a time when men had fallen into the state of brutes (in whom the senses are keener than in men), providence saw to it that by their brutish nature itself they should have the keenest senses for their self-preservation. Later, when they entered the age of reflection, by which they could take counsel for the protection of their bodies, the senses were permitted to become less sharp. Because of all this, the heroic descriptions, as we have them in Homer, are so luminously and splendidly clear that all later poets have been unable to imitate them, to say nothing of equaling them.

[CHAPTER V]

COROLLARY ON HEROIC CUSTOMS

708 By such heroic natures, furnished with such heroic senses, customs of like kind were formed and fixed. Because of their recent gigantic origin, the heroes were in the highest degree awkward and wild, such as we have found the Patagonians described, very limited in understanding but endowed with the vastest imaginations and the most violent passions. Hence they must have been boorish, crude, harsh, wild, proud, difficult and obstinate in their resolves, and at the same time easily diverted when confronted with new and contrary objects; even as we daily observe in our stubborn peasants, who yield to every reasonable argument that is put to them, but, because their powers of reflection are weak, as soon as the argument which has moved them has left their minds, return at once to their original purpose. From this same lack of reflective capacity, the heroes were bluff, touchy, magnanimous and generous, as Homer portrays Achilles, the greatest of all the Greek heroes. It was with such examples of heroic customs in mind that Aristotle made it a precept of the art of poetry that the heroes who are taken as protagonists in tragedies should be neither very good nor very bad but should exhibit a mixture of great vices and great virtues. For that heroism of virtue which realizes its highest idea belongs to philosophy and not to poetry; and gallant heroism is a creation of post-Homeric poets who either made up fables of a new cast or took the old fables, originally grave and severe as becoming the founders of nations, and altered and finally corrupted them to suit the growing effeminacy of later times. We have a great proof of this—and it may well serve as a leading canon of the historical mythology we are discussing—in the example of Achilles. On account of Briseis, taken from him by Agamemnon, he makes such an outcry as to fill heaven and earth and provide matter for the whole *Iliad,* yet nowhere in that entire epic does he give the faintest indication of amorous passion at being deprived of the girl. Similarly Menelaus, though on Helen's account he stirs all Greece to war against Troy, does not show, throughout that whole long and great war, the slightest sign of amorous distress or jealousy of Paris, who has robbed him of her and is enjoying her.

709 All that we have remarked in these three corollaries on heroic sentences, descriptions and customs, belongs properly to the discovery of the true Homer which we shall take up in the following book.

[SECTION VIII]

[CHAPTER I]

POETIC COSMOGRAPHY

710 As the theological poets had set up as principles in physics the substances they imagined to be divine, so they described a cosmography in accord with this physics, regarding the world as composed of gods of the sky, of the underworld (called by the Latins respectively *dii superi* and *dii inferi*), and of gods intermediate between earth and sky (who must have been those whom the Latins at first called *medioxumi*).

711 The first object of their contemplation in the world was the sky, and heavenly things must have been for the Greeks the first *mathēmata* or sublime things and the first *theōrēmata* or divine objects of contemplation. The contemplation of such things was so called by the Latins from the regions of the sky marked off by the augurs for the taking of auspices, which regions they called *templa coeli;* whence in the East the name of the Zoroastrians, which Bochart takes to mean "those who contemplate the stars," for purposes of divination from the paths of falling stars at night.

712 For the poets the first sky was no higher than the summits of the mountains, where the giants were halted in their feral wanderings by Jove's first thunderbolts. This is the Heaven that reigned on earth and, from this beginning, conferred great benefits on mankind, as we have fully explained above. Hence they must have imagined the sky to be the mountain tops (from whose sharpness the Latins applied the term *coelum* also to the burin, a tool used in stone or metal engraving), just as children imagine that mountains are the columns that hold up the roof of the sky (a principle of cosmography found in the Koran of the Arabs). Two of these columns continued to be called the Pillars of Hercules, as we shall see farther on; the original meaning of *columen*, as applied to them, must have been prop or stay; rounded columns were introduced later by architecture. It was from such a roof on Olympus, as Thetis tells Achilles in Homer, that Jove went with the other gods to feast on [Mt.] Atlas. Evidently, as we said above in speaking of the giants, the fable of the Titans warring with the gods and piling up lofty mountains, Ossa on Pelion and Olympus on Ossa, in order to climb up to heaven and cast out the gods, must have been made up after Homer's time, for certainly in the *Iliad* he always speaks of the gods as residing on the summit of Olympus, so that the collapse of Olympus alone would have sufficed to cause their downfall. Nor does this fable really fit in the *Odyssey,* where it is found. For in that poem the lower world in which Ulysses sees and speaks with the departed heroes is no deeper than a ditch; and since the Homer of the *Odyssey* had such a limited notion of the lower world, his idea of heaven must have been equally simple, in conformity with that of the Homer of the *Iliad.* Consequently the fable is not Homer's, as we promised above to demonstrate.

713   It was in this heaven that the gods first reigned on earth and had dealings with the heroes, according to the order of the natural theogony above set forth, beginning with Jove. In this heaven justice was dealt out on earth by Astraea, crowned with ears of grain and holding a balance; for the first human justice was administered by the heroes to men in the first agrarian law above mentioned; and men first became aware of weight, then of measure, and only very slowly of number, in which reason finally came to rest; so that Pythagoras put the essence of the human soul in numbers because he knew of nothing more abstracted from bodies. Through this heaven the heroes go galloping on horseback, like Bellerophon on Pegasus; and *volitare equo* was Latin for going about on horseback. It is in this heaven that Juno whitens the milky way with milk, not her own, for she was sterile, but with the milk of the mothers of the families, who suckled the legitimate offspring of the heroic nuptials of which Juno was the divinity. Over this heaven the gods are carried in carts of the poetic gold or grain after which the golden age was named. In this heaven wings were used, not for flight nor even to signify quickness of wit, but to signify heroic institutions, which were all based on the law of the auspices, as we have fully shown above. Of this sort are the wings of Hymen (heroic Love), Astraea, the Muses, Pegasus, Saturn, Fame, Mercury (who bears them on his heels and at his temples, and whose caduceus is likewise winged, for with it he brought down from this heaven the first agrarian law to the rebellious plebs in the valleys, as above noted), and also the dragon (for the Gorgon also has winged temples, and clearly its wings stand neither for wit nor for flight). It is in this heaven that Prometheus steals fire from the sun, the fire that the heroes must have kindled with flints and set to the thorny underbrush on the mountain tops, dried out by the hot suns of summer; whence, as we are faithfully told, the torch of Hymen was made of thorns. From this heaven Vulcan is precipitated by a kick of Jove; from this heaven Phaethon falls headlong in the chariot of the Sun; and from this heaven the apple of discord drops—all fables that we have explained above. And finally, it is from this heaven that the ancilia or sacred shields of the Romans must have fallen.

714   The first of the deities of the lower world imagined by the theological poets was that of water, and the first water was that of the perennial

springs, which they called Styx and by which the gods swore, as noted above; on which account, perhaps, Plato supposed that the abyss of waters was in the center of the earth. Homer, however, in the contest of the gods, makes Pluto fear that Neptune may open the earth with an earthquake and expose the lower world to the eyes of men and gods. And if we assumed that the abyss was in the deepest entrails of the earth, the earthquakes of Neptune would have quite the contrary effect, for the lower world would be submerged and completely covered with water. So, as we engaged above to do, we have shown that the allegory of Plato is ill-suited to the fable. In view of what we have said, the first lower world must not have been any deeper than the source of the springs. Its first deity was Diana, of whom poetic history says that she was a triformed goddess, for in the heavens she was Diana, on earth the huntress Cynthia and companion to her brother Apollo, and in the underworld Proserpine.

715   With the practice of burial the idea of the underworld was extended, and the poets called the grave the underworld (an expression also found in Holy Scripture). Thus the lower world was no deeper than a ditch, like that in which Ulysses, according to Homer, sees the underworld and the souls of the dead heroes; for in this lower world were placed the Elysian fields, wherein, by virtue of burial, the souls of the dead enjoy eternal peace; and the Elysian fields are the happy dwelling place of the Manes or benevolent spirits of the dead.

716   Later the underworld had the depth of a furrow. It is to this underworld that Ceres (the same as Proserpine, the seed of the grain) is carried off by the god Pluto, to remain there six months and then return to behold the light of heaven. By this will be explained later the golden bough with which Aeneas descends into the lower world; which was Vergil's continuation of the heroic metaphor of the golden apple, which we have already found to be the ears of grain.

717   Finally the underworld was taken to be the plains and the valleys (as opposed to the lofty heaven set on the mountain tops) where the scattered vagrants remained in their infamous promiscuity. The god of this underworld is Erebus, called the son of Chaos, that is of the confusion of human seeds. He is the father of civil night (in which names are obscured), even as the heaven is illuminated by the civil light with which the heroes are resplendent. Through this underworld runs the river Lethe, the stream of oblivion, for these men left no name of themselves to their posterity, whereas the glory of heaven eternalizes the names of the illustrious heroes. From this underworld Mercury with his rod bearing the agrarian law, as we said above in our account of his [poetic] character, recalls the souls from Orcus the all-devouring monster. This is the civil history preserved for us by Vergil in the phrase: *hac ille animas evocat Orco*. That is, he redeems the lives of bestial and lawless men from the feral state which swallows up all mankind in that they leave nothing of themselves to their posterity. The rod was later used by the mages in the vain belief that it had power to bring back the dead. The Roman praetor struck slaves on the

shoulder with his staff in token of their liberation, as if therewith bringing them
back from death to life. Sorcerers also used in their witchcraft the rod which
the wise mages of Persia had used for the divination of the auspices. Wherefore divinity was attributed to the rod, and it was held by the nations to be
divine and capable of performing miracles, as Trogus Pompeius assures us in
Justin's abridgment of his work.

718   This is the underworld guarded by Cerberus, the doglike impudence
of copulating shamelessly in public. Cerberus is three-throated, that is, he has
an enormous gullet (the three is superlative, as noted several times above), because like Orcus he devours everything; and when he comes up on the earth
the sun goes backwards (for when he enters the heroic cities the civil light of
the heroes turns again to civil night).

719   At the bottom of this underworld flows the river Tartarus, and there
the damned are tormented: Ixion forever turns his wheel, Sisyphus rolls his
stone, and Tantalus is forever dying of hunger and thirst—all fables explained
above. And the river that causes the torment of thirst is the same river "without
contentment" which is signified by both Acheron and Phlegethon. Into this
underworld Tityus and Prometheus were later cast by the ignorance of the
mythologers; but actually it was in heaven that they were chained to the crags,
to have their entrails devoured by the mountain eagle (the grievous superstition of the auspices, as above explained).

720   The philosophers later found all these fables convenient for the
meditation and exposition of their moral and metaphysical doctrines. Plato was
stimulated by them to understand the three divine punishments which only the
gods can inflict, and not men: namely, oblivion, infamy and the remorse of a
guilty conscience; and to understand that it is by the *via purgativa* or purga-
torial journey of the passions of the spirit which torment mankind (so he inter-
prets the lower world of the theological poets) that one enters upon the *via
unitiva* by which the human mind attains union with God by means of contemplation of eternal divine things (which he takes the theological poets to
have meant by their Elysian fields).

721   But the theological poets had invented their fables with political matters in mind, as they as founders of nations naturally could not help doing, and
all the gentile founders of peoples descended into the lower world with ideas
quite different from these moral and metaphysical [ideas of Plato]. Orpheus,
who founded the Greek nation, made the descent; and, disobeying the injunc-
tion not to turn his head on leaving, he lost his wife Eurydice (signifying his
return to the infamous sharing of women). Hercules (and every nation tells
of one as its founder) also descended, for the purpose of liberating Theseus, the
founder of Athens, who had descended to bring back Proserpine (that is, since
as we have said she is the same as Ceres, to bring back the sown seed in the form
of ripened grain). But later Vergil, with his profound knowledge of heroic
antiquities (singing of the political hero in the first six books of his *Aeneid* and

of the military hero in the last six), gives us an account of the descent of Aeneas more detailed than any of the others. Aeneas has the advice and safe-conduct of the Cumaean Sybil (that is, since every gentile nation had a sybil and twelve have come down to us by name, his descent was made by divination, which was the vulgar wisdom of the gentiles). With the piety of a bloody religion (the piety professed by the ancient heroes in the fierceness and ruthlessness of their recent bestial origin, as we have shown above) he sacrifices his *socius Misenus* (by the cruel right which the heroes had over their first *socii,* as we have set forth above). He then enters the ancient forest (such as covered the land every-where while it was yet uncultivated), throws the soporific sop to Cerberus and puts him to sleep (just as Orpheus had overcome him with the sound of his lyre, which we have previously seen by abundant evidence to signify law; and just as Hercules had tied him up with the knot with which he had bound Antaeus in Greece, that is with the first agrarian law, in accordance with what we have said above). (Because of his insatiable hunger, Cerberus was imagined as three-throated, that is, as having an enormous gullet, the three standing for the superlative as before noted.) Thus Aeneas descends into the underworld (which we found was at first no deeper than a furrow), comes before Dis (the god of heroic riches, poetic gold or grain, being identical with Pluto the abductor of Proserpine or Ceres, the goddess of grain), and presents the golden bough. (Here the great poet takes the metaphor of the golden apple, signifying the ears of grain, and extends it to the golden bough, signifying the harvest.) When the golden bough is torn from its trunk another grows in its place (because there can be no second harvest until a year after the first has been gathered). And when the gods are well disposed, the bough readily and easily comes off in the hand of him who seizes it, but otherwise no strength in the world is sufficient to pluck it. (For the grain grows up naturally where God wills it, but where he does not will it no human industry can hope to make it grow.) Aeneas then proceeds through the underworld to the Elysian fields (for the heroes, having settled in the cultivated fields, enjoyed eternal peace in death if they had proper burial, as we have set forth above). Here he beholds his ancestors and those who are to come after him (for on the religion of burial, called the underworld by the poets as already noted, were founded the first genealogies, from which, as we have also remarked above, history took its beginning).

722   The earth was associated by the theological poets with the guarding of the boundaries, and hence it was called *terra.* This heroic origin the Latins preserved in the word *territorium,* which signifies the district within which the *imperium* is exercised. The Latin grammarians erroneously derived *ter-ritorium* from the terror of the fasces used by the lictors to disperse the crowds and make way for the Roman magistrates. But at the time when the word *ter-ritorium* arose there were no great crowds in Rome, for, according to Varro as before cited, in two hundred and fifty years of rule she had subdued more than twenty peoples without extending her *imperium* more than twenty miles. In-

stead the word originated in the fact that the boundaries of the cultivated fields, within which the civil powers later arose, were guarded by Vesta with bloody rites, as we have seen above when we noted that the Latin Vesta was the same as the Greek Cybele or Berecynthia, who wears a crown of towers, that is of strongly situated lands. From this crown the so-called *orbis terrarum* began to take form, signifying the world of the nations, later amplified by the cosmographers and called *orbis mundanus* or, in a word, *mundus,* the world of nature.

723   The poetic world was divided into three kingdoms or regions: that of Jove in heaven, that of Saturn on earth, and the underworld kingdom of Pluto, called Dis, god of heroic riches, the first gold or grain, since tilled fields make the true wealth of peoples.

724   Thus the world of the theological poets was formed of four civil elements, later taken by the physicists as natural elements, as we have said not far above: namely, the element of Jove, the air; that of Vulcan, fire; that of Cybele, earth; and that of the underworld Diana, water. For Neptune was late in coming into the acquaintance of the poets, because, as we have said above, the nations were slow in coming down to the seacoasts. Any sea extending beyond the horizon was called Ocean, and any land it surrounded an island, as Homer speaks of the island of Aeolia as surrounded by the Ocean. From such an Ocean must have come the horses of Rhesus, which were made pregnant by Zephyr, the west wind of Greece as we shall shortly show; and on the shores of the same Ocean the horses of Achilles, also begotten by Zephyr, must have been born. Later the geographers, observing that the whole earth, like a great island, was girt by the sea, called Ocean all the waters by which the land is surrounded.

725   Finally, beginning with the idea by which every slight slope was called *mundus* (whence the phrases *in mundo est, in proclivi est,* for "it is easy"; and later everything for the embellishment of a woman came to be called *mundus muliebris*), when they came to understand that the earth and the sky were spherical in form, and that from every point of the circumference there is a slope towards every other, and that the ocean bathes the land on every shore, and that the whole of things is adorned with countless varied and diverse sensible forms, the poets called this universe *mundus* as being that with which, by a fine metaphor, nature adorns herself.

[SECTION IX]

[POETIC ASTRONOMY]

[CHAPTER I]

POETIC ASTRONOMY

726 This world system, somewhat further developed, lasted down to the time of Homer, who always speaks of the gods as settled on Mt. Olympus. We have noted that he has Thetis, the mother of Achilles, tell him that the gods had gone from Olympus to feast on [Mt.] Atlas. So that in Homer's time the highest mountains on the earth were evidently regarded as pillars sustaining the heavens, even as Abyla and Calpe on the straits of Gibraltar continued to be called the Pillars of Hercules because the hero had taken up the burden of Atlas, who had grown tired of supporting the heavens on his shoulders.

[CHAPTER II]

ASTRONOMICAL AND PHYSICO-PHILOLOGICAL DEMONSTRATION OF THE UNIFORMITY OF THE PRINCIPLES [OF ASTRONOMY] AMONG ALL ANCIENT GENTILE NATIONS

727 But as the indefinite force of human minds went on developing, and as the contemplation of the heavens required for taking the auspices obliged the peoples to study the heavens continually, in the minds of the nations the heavens rose ever higher, and with them rose likewise the gods and the heroes. And here for the ascertainment of poetic astronomy it may help us to make use of three items of philological erudition. The first states that astronomy was brought into the world by the Chaldean people; the second, that the Phoenicians carried from the Chaldeans to the Egyptians the use of the quadrant and the

knowledge of the elevation of the pole; and the third, that the Phoenicians, who must have been instructed by the Chaldeans, brought astral theology to the Greeks. To these three bits of philological erudition we may add these two philosophical truths: first, the civil truth that nations, if not emancipated in the extreme of religious liberty (which only comes in the final stages of decadence), are naturally wary of accepting foreign deities; and second, the physical truth that, by an ocular illusion, the planets seem to us larger than the fixed stars.

728 Having premised these principles, we may now say that among all the gentile nations of the East, of Egypt, and of Greece (and we shall see that it holds for Latium too), astronomy sprang from uniform vulgar origins, for by a uniform allocation the gods were raised to the planets and the heroes were assigned to the constellations, because the planets appear much larger than the fixed stars. Hence the Phoenicians found among the Greeks that the gods were already prepared to revolve with the planets and the heroes to compose the constellations, even as later the Greeks found the same to be true among the Latins. And from these examples it is safe to say that the Phoenicians found the same readiness among the Egyptians as among the Greeks. In this way the heroes and the hierogly1phs signifying their institutions or their coats-of-arms, and a goodly number of the major gods, were raised to the heavens and put in readiness for learned astronomy to give to the hitherto nameless heavenly bodies—to their matter, as it were—the form of stars or constellations on the one hand, or of wandering planets on the other.

729 Thus, beginning with vulgar astronomy, the first peoples wrote in the skies the history of their gods and their heroes. Thence there remained this eternal property, that the memories of men full of divinity or of heroism are matter worthy of history, in the one case because of works of genius and of esoteric wisdom, in the other because of works of valor and of vulgar wisdom. And poetic history gave the learned astronomers occasions for depicting the heroes and the heroic hieroglyphs in the sky with one group of stars rather than another, and in one part of the sky rather than another, and for placing in one planet rather than another the major gods by whose names the planets have since been called.

730 To speak somewhat more at length of the planets than of the constellations: Certainly Diana, goddess of the chastity preserved in nuptial relations, who lies all quiet in the night with the sleeping Endymion, was attached to the moon, the giver of nocturnal light. Venus, goddess of civil beauty, was attached to the gayest and brightest of all the planets. Mercury, the divine herald, clothed in civil light, with all the wings (aristocratic hieroglyphs) with which he is adorned (as he bears the agrarian law to the mutinous clients), is lodged in a planet which is so obscured by the rays of the sun as to be rarely visible. Apollo, god of that same civil light (which gave the epithet *incliti* to the heroes), is placed in the sun, the source of natural light. Bloody Mars dwells in a star of the

like hue. Jove, king and father of men and gods, is placed above all the rest, but beneath Saturn, who, since he is the father both of Jove and of Time, has a longer annual course than all the other planets. His wings ill become him if, by a forced allegory, they are taken to mean the swiftness of time, for he runs his year more slowly than any other planet; but he took them to heaven along with his scythe, the latter signifying the reaping not of men's lives but of grain, by the harvests of which the heroes counted the years, and the wings signifying that the cultivated fields were the property of the heroes. Finally the planets or wanderers, with the chariots of gold (that is of grain) with which they went about in heaven when it was on earth, now revolve in their appointed orbits.

731   In view of all that has here been set forth, it must be affirmed that the predominating influences which the stars and planets are supposed to have over sublunar bodies, have been attributed to them from those which the gods and heroes exercised when they were on earth. So little do they depend on natural causes!

[SECTION X]

[POETIC CHRONOLOGY]

[CHAPTER I]

POETIC CHRONOLOGY

732 The theological poets gave beginnings to chronology in conformity with their astronomy. For that same Saturn, who was so called by the Latins from *sati,* "sown" [fields], and who was called Chronos or Time by the Greeks, gives us to understand that the first nations (all composed of farmers) began to count their years by their harvests of grain (the sole or at least the chief thing for which the peasants labored all year). And since they were at first mute, they must have held as many ears or straws and made as many reaping motions as the number of years they meant to signify. Thus in Vergil (as learned as ever man was in heroic antiquities) we find two expressions [407]: the first infelicitous and, by supreme imitative art, infelicitously contorted, to express the infelicity of the first ages in expressing themselves: *Post aliquot mea regna videns mirabor aristas,* meaning simply *post aliquot annos.* The second has somewhat more clarity: *Tertia messis erat.* And indeed even nowadays the peasants of Tuscany, the nation most highly regarded for its speech in all Italy, instead of saying "three years," for example, say "we have harvested three times." The Romans preserved this heroic history of the poetic year signified by the harvest, in using the name *annona* for the management of the stores, particularly of grain.

733 Accordingly Hercules has come down to us as the founder of the Olympiads, the celebrated time-divisions of the Greeks (from whom we get all we know of gentile antiquities), for it was he who set fire to the forests in order to prepare for sowing the lands whereon were gathered the harvests by which the years were reckoned. The games must have been instituted by the Nemeans in celebration of the hero's victory over the Nemean fire-breathing lion, which we have interpreted above as the great forest of the earth, to which, apprehended under the idea of a very powerful animal, they gave the name lion, because so much labor was required to tame it. Later the name was applied to the most

powerful of animals, as set forth above in the Origins of Family Coats-of-Arms [540], and the astronomers assigned to the Lion a house in the zodiac, next to that of Astraea, crowned with ears of grain. This is why in the circuses images of lions were often shown, and images of the sun; it is also the reason for the *metae* with eggs on top, which must originally have been *metae* of grain and the clearings or deforested eyes of the giants, as set forth above. The astronomers later took the egg as signifying the ellipse described by the sun in its annual path through the ecliptic; a meaning that Manetho might more fittingly have given to the egg which Knef holds in his mouth, instead of interpreting it as signifying the generation of the universe.

734   The natural theogony above set forth enables us to determine the successive epochs of the age of the gods, which correspond to certain first necessities or utilities of the human race, which everywhere had its beginnings in religion. The age of the gods must have lasted at least nine hundred years from the appearance of the various Joves among the gentile nations, which is to say from the time when the heavens began to thunder after the universal flood. And the twelve major gods, beginning with Jove, successively imagined within this age, serve to divide it into twelve smaller epochs and thus give some certainty to the chronology of poetic history. By way of example, Deucalion, whom fabulous history places immediately after the flood and the giants, and who with his wife Pyrrha founds the families by means of matrimony, is born of Greek imaginations in the epoch of Juno, goddess of solemn nuptials. Hellen, who founds the Greek language and, through his three sons, divides it into three dialects, is born in the epoch of Apollo, god of song, in whose time poetic speech in verse must have begun. Hercules, who performs the great labor of slaying the Hydra or the Nemean lion (reducing the land to fields for sowing), and who brings back from Hesperia the golden apples (that is, the harvests, an enterprise worthy of history; not pomegranates, an errand for a parasite), distinguished himself in the epoch of Saturn, god of the sown fields. Likewise Perseus must have achieved his fame in the epoch of Minerva when the civil powers were already in existence, since his shield bears the head of Medusa, as does that of Minerva. And finally, Orpheus must have been born after the epoch of Mercury, for by singing to the Greek beasts the force of the gods in the auspices, the science of which belonged to the heroes, he reëstablished the heroic nations of Greece and gave the heroic age its name, for in that age these heroic contests took place. Hence at the same time with Orpheus there flourish such other heroic poets as Linus, Amphion and Musaeus. Amphion uses stones (in the sense in which the Latin word for stone, *lapis,* meant a lout, and signifying therefore the simple-minded plebeians) to erect the walls of Thebes three hundred years after its founding by Cadmus; exactly as, three hundred years after the founding of Rome, Appius, the grandson of the decemvir, as before noted, by singing to the Roman plebs which *agitabat connubia more ferarum* (practiced marriages like those of the beasts of Orpheus) of the force of the gods in

the auspices (the science of which belonged to the nobles) reduces them to obedience and establishes the heroic Roman state.

735   Furthermore we must here take note of four kinds of anachronisms coming under the familiar general head of placing times too early or too late. The first is that of times [for our knowledge] empty of facts which must really have been full of them. Thus the age of the gods, in which we have found almost all the origins of civil human affairs, passes with the learned Varro for the "obscure time." The second is that of times full of facts which must have been empty of them. Thus, under the false belief that the fables were invented by the heroic poets, especially by Homer, the age of the heroes, which runs for two hundred years, is filled with all the facts belonging to the age of the gods, and these facts should be put back into the age to which they belong. The third is that of uniting times which should be divided, lest, for example, Greece should seem to have passed from a state of wild beasts to the splendor of the Trojan war within the single life-span of Orpheus, which is the chronological monstrosity to which we called attention in the Notes on the Chronological Table. The fourth and last is that of dividing times which should be united. By such an anachronism the Greek colonies are brought into Sicily and Italy more than three hundred years after the wanderings of the heroes, whereas they were brought there in the course and as the result of the wanderings of these same heroes.

[CHAPTER II]

CHRONOLOGICAL CANON FOR DETERMINING THE BEGINNINGS OF
UNIVERSAL HISTORY, WHICH MUST PRECEDE THE MONARCHY
OF NINUS, WITH WHICH IT [COMMONLY] STARTS

736   In virtue of the aforesaid natural theogony which has given us our rational poetic chronology, and taking into consideration the kinds of anachronisms noted in poetic history, now, in order to determine the beginnings of universal history, which must precede the monarchy of Ninus from which it [commonly] takes its start, we set up this chronological canon: that from the dispersion of fallen mankind through the great forest of the earth, beginning in Mesopotamia (according to our reasonable postulate in the Axioms [298, 301]), a span of only a hundred years of feral wandering was consumed by the impious [part of the] race of Shem in East Asia, and one of two hundred years by the other two races of Ham and Japheth in the rest of the world. At the end of that time, under the religion of Jove (and the many Joves scattered through the first gentile nations gave us evidence above that the flood was universal), the

princes of the nations began to settle down, each in the land where fortune had placed him. Then ensued the nine hundred years of the age of the gods. Towards the end of that age the nations (which had all been founded inland because they had been dispersed through the world in search of food and [fresh] water, which are not found on the seaboard) must have come down to the coasts. Hence there arose in the minds of the Greeks the idea of Neptune, whom we found to be the last of the twelve major divinities. In like fashion, among the Latins, nine hundred years elapsed between the age of Saturn, the golden age of Latium, and the descent of Ancus Marcius to the coast to take Ostia. After this came the two hundred years which the Greeks assign to the heroic age, beginning with the raids of King Minos, continuing with Jason's naval expedition to Pontus and later with the Trojan war, and ending with the wanderings of the heroes and the return of Ulysses to Ithaca. Thus Tyre, capital of Phoenicia, must have been brought from inland to the shore, and thence to an island near by in the Phoenician sea, more than a thousand years after the flood. And inasmuch as before the Greek heroic age Tyre was already a famous city both for navigation and for its colonies scattered through the Mediterranean and even on the Ocean, it is clearly proved that the beginning of the entire human race was in the East, and that first the feral wanderings through the inland parts of the world, then the heroic law by land and sea, and finally the maritime traffic of the Phoenicians scattered the first nations through the remaining parts of the world. These principles of the commigration of the peoples (as we set forth in an axiom [299]) seem more reasonable than those imagined by Wolfgang Latius.

737   Now, in virtue of the uniform course run by all the nations, which has been proved above by the uniformity of the gods raised to the stars, as brought by the Phoenicians to Egypt and Greece from the East, we must infer that the reign of the Chaldeans in the East covered a like period of time [1100 years], from Zoroaster to Ninus, who founded there the first monarchy in the world, that of Assyria; and correspondingly [in Egypt] from Hermes Trismegistus to Sesostris, the Ramses of Tacitus, who also founded there a great monarchy. And since these were both inland nations, they must have passed through the successive stages of divine and heroic regimes and then of popular liberty in order to reach that of monarchy, which is the last form of human government, if the Egyptian division of the three ages of the world that had elapsed before them is to stand. For, as we shall show later, monarchy cannot arise save as a result of the unchecked liberty of the peoples, to which the optimates subject their power in the course of civil wars. When this authority is thus divided into minimal parts among the peoples, the whole of it is easily taken over by those who, coming forward as partisans of popular liberty, emerge finally as monarchs. Phoenicia, however, as a maritime nation enriched by its commerce, remained in the stage of popular liberty, which is the first form of human government.

738   Thus purely by understanding, without benefit of memory, which

has nothing to go on where facts are not supplied by the senses, we seem to have filled in the beginnings of universal history both in ancient Egypt and in the East, which is more ancient than Egypt; and further, within the East, the beginnings of the Assyrian monarchy. For hitherto this monarchy, for lack of its many and varied antecedent causes, which must have been previously at work in order to produce a monarchy, which is the last of the three forms of civil government, has appeared in history as a sudden birth, as a frog is born of a summer shower.

739   In this way chronology has certainty lent to its successive periods by the progress of customs and deeds through which the human race must have marched. For, by an axiom above stated [314], chronology has here begun her doctrine where her subject matter began: that is, with Chronos or Saturn (after whom time was called *chronos* among the Greeks), the reckoner of the years by the harvests; with Urania, watcher of the skies for the purpose of taking the auspices; and with Zoroaster, contemplator of the stars in order to give his oracles from the paths of falling stars. (For such were the first *mathēmata* and the first *theōrēmata,* the first sublime or divine things contemplated and observed by the nations, as we have said above.) Later, when Saturn ascended to the seventh sphere, Urania became the contemplator of the stars and planets, and the Chaldaeans, with the advantage of their immense open plains, became astronomers and astrologers, measuring the movements and observing the aspects of the heavenly bodies and imagining their influences on so-called sublunar bodies, and even, though vainly, on the free wills of men. This science preserved the first names that had been given to it in full propriety: astronomy, the science of the laws of the stars, and astrology, the science of the speech of the stars. Both names signified divination, even as from the aforesaid theorems came the term theology for the science of the language of the gods in their oracles, auspices and auguries. Thence finally mathematics descended to measure the earth, the measurements of which could not be ascertained save by the already demonstrated measurements of the heavens; and the first and principal part of mathematics bears witness to this origin in the proper name geometry by which it is called.

740   Those two marvelous geniuses, Joseph Justus Scaliger and Denis Petau, with their stupendous erudition, the former in his *De emendatione temporum* and the latter in his *De doctrina temporum,* failed to begin their doctrine at the beginning of their subject matter. For they began with the astronomical year, which, as noted above, was unheard of among the nations for a thousand years, and in any case could have assured them only of conjunctions and oppositions of constellations and planets in the heavens, and not of any of the things that had happened here on earth nor of their sequence (in which the noble efforts of Cardinal Pierre d'Ailly had been expended in vain). And on this account their work has shed little light on the beginnings or on the continuation of universal history.

[SECTION XI]

[POETIC GEOGRAPHY]

[CHAPTER I]

POETIC GEOGRAPHY

741 It remains for us now to cleanse the other eye of poetic history, namely poetic geography. By that property of human nature included among the Axioms [122], that "in describing unknown or distant things, in respect of which they either have not had the true idea themselves or wish to explain it to others who do not have it, men make use of the semblances of things known or near at hand," poetic geography, in all its parts and as a whole, began with restricted ideas within the confines of Greece. Then, as the Greeks went abroad into the world, it was gradually amplified until it reached the form in which it is now described to us. The ancient geographers agree on this truth although they were unable to avail themselves of it, for they affirm that the ancient nations, emigrating to strange and distant lands, gave their own native names to the [new-found] cities, mountains, rivers, hills, straits, isles and promontories.

742 Within Greece itself, accordingly, lay the original East called Asia or India, the West called Europe or Hesperia, the North called Thrace or Scythia, and the South called Libya or Mauretania. And these names for the regions of the little world of Greece were [later] applied to those of the world [at large] in virtue of the correspondence which the Greeks observed between the two. We have clear proof of this in the cardinal winds, which retain in their geography the names which they must certainly have first had within Greece itself. Thus the mares of Rhesus on the shores of the Ocean (a name, as we shall presently find, applied to any sea of unobstructed horizon) must have been impregnated by Zephyr, the west wind of Greece; and likewise on the shores of the Ocean (in the above-noted primary sense) the horses of Achilles must have been generated by Zephyr, even as the mares of Erechtheus—as Aeneas tells Achilles—must have been impregnated by Boreas, the north wind of Greece. This truth concerning the cardinal winds is confirmed by the immense projection to which the Greek mind extended itself in taking from the mountain on which the Homeric gods dwelt and applying to the starry Heaven the name Olympus by which it continued to be known.

743   On these principles, the great peninsula to the east of Greece came to be called Asia Minor when the name Asia was extended to that great eastern part of the world which has continued to be called Asia without qualification. On the other hand, Greece itself, which was to the west of Asia, was called Europe, the Europe which Jove, in the form of a bull, abducted. Later the name was extended to embrace this other great continent as far as the western ocean. They gave the name Hesperia to the western part of Greece, where the evening star Hesperus rises in the fourth quarter of the horizon. Later they saw Italy in the same quarter but much larger than the Hesperia of Greece, and they called it Hesperia Magna. And finally when they reached Spain in the same direction, they called it Hesperia Ultima. Conversely the Greeks of Italy must have called by the name Ionia that part of Greece lying across the sea to the east of them; hence the name Ionian for the sea between the two Greeces [Greece proper and Magna Graecia, the Greek part of southern Italy]. Later, because of the similarity of position of Greece proper and Asiatic Greece, the inhabitants of Greece proper took to calling by the name Ionia the part of Asia Minor to the east of them. It seems reasonable that out of the first Ionia Pythagoras must have come to Italy from Samos [or Cephallenia], one of the islands ruled by Ulysses, and not from the Samos of the second Ionia.

744   From the Thrace within Greece must have come Mars, who was certainly a Greek divinity; and thence too must have come Orpheus, one of the first Greek theological poets.

745   From the Scythia within Greece came Anacharsis, who left the Scythian oracles in Greece. These must have been similar to the oracles of Zoroaster (which must originally have been an oracular history). Anacharsis has been received among the most ancient oracular gods. By imposture, these oracles were later translated into dogmas of philosophy. Similarly the *Orphica* were supposed to be verses of Orpheus, though, like the oracles of Zoroaster, they have no poetic flavor and give forth too distinct an odor of the Platonic and Pythagorean school. So too from this Scythia [within Greece], by way of the original Hyperboreans, the two famous oracles of Delphi and Dodona must have come into Greece, as we suspected in the Notes on the Chronological Table. For in Scythia, that is among these Hyperboreans of Greece proper, Anacharsis, attempting to order humanity by Greek laws, was slain by Caduidas his brother. So little did he profit by the barbarous philosophy of [which] van Heurn [speaks] that he could not devise such laws for them himself! By the same reasoning, Abaris must have been a Scythian too, for he is said to have written the Scythian oracles, which must have been no other than those of Anacharsis just mentioned. And he wrote them in that Scythia in which Idanthyrsus long afterwards wrote with those physical objects. Whence we must conclude that

they were written by an impostor sometime after the introduction of the Greek philosophies. Hence the oracles of Anacharsis were accepted by the conceit of the scholars as oracles of esoteric wisdom, which have not come down to us.

746   Zalmoxis, who, according to Herodotus, brought to the Greeks the dogma of the immortality of the soul, was a Getan in the same sense in which Mars was.

747   It was likewise from a Greek India that Bacchus must have come in triumph from the Indian East (that is, from a Greek land rich in poetic gold). He rides triumphant in a golden chariot (a cart of grain). Hence he is also a tamer of serpents and tigers, as Hercules is of hydras and lions, as set forth above.

748   Certainly the name Morea, preserved by the Peloponnesus down to our days, is ample proof that Perseus, certainly a Greek hero, carried out his enterprises in the Mauretania within Greece; for the Peloponnesus is in the same [geographical] relation to Achaea as Africa is to Europe. Here can be seen how little Herodotus understood of his own antiquities (on which account indeed Thucydides reproves him); for he relates that the Moors were at one time white, as were certainly the Moors of his own Greece, which to this day is called White Morea.

749   It must likewise have been from the pestilence of this Mauretania that Aesculapius saved his island of Cos by his art; for if he had had to save it from the pestilence of the people of Morocco he would have had to save it from all the pestilences in the world.

750   It was in this Mauretania that Hercules must have taken on his shoulders the burden of the sky that old Atlas was tired of bearing; for the name [Atlas] must originally have been used for Mt. Athos, which, on a neck of land later cut through by Xerxes, divides Macedonia from Thrace; and here, as a matter of fact, between Greece and Thrace, there was also a river called Atlas. Later, at the straits of Gibraltar, when it was observed that Mts. Abyla and Calpe on the narrows of the sea similarly separate Africa from Europe, it was said that there Hercules had fixed the columns which, as we have said above, support the heavens, and the name Atlas was applied to the near-by mountain in Africa. And in this way we can find some plausibility in the answer that Thetis gives her son Achilles in Homer: that she cannot carry his complaint to Jove because he and the other gods have gone from Olympus to feast on Atlas (based on the opinion to which we have before alluded that the gods dwelt on the tops of the highest mountains); for if this reply had referred to Mt. Atlas in Africa it would have been beyond belief, in view of the fact that Homer himself tells us that Mercury, even with wings, found the greatest difficulty in reaching the isle of Calypso in the Phoenician sea, much nearer to Greece than the kingdom we now call Morocco.

751   It was likewise from the Greek Hesperia that Hercules must have

brought the golden apples to Attica; and there too dwelt the Hesperides (the daughters of Atlas) who guarded them.

752   In like manner the Eridanus, into which Phaethon fell, must have been the Danube in Greek Thrace, which flows into the Euxine. Later, when the Greeks observed that the Po is the other river in the world which flows from west to east like the Danube, they called it the Eridanus, and the mythologists thus had it that Phaethon fell in Italy. But it was only the tales of their own heroic history, not that of other nations, which the Greeks attached to the stars, among which is Eridanus.

753   Finally, when the Greeks reached the Ocean, they expanded the narrow idea of any sea with an unobstructed prospect (in virtue of which Homer said the isle of Aeolia was girt by the Ocean), and along with the idea the name Ocean was also extended to signify the sea that girds the whole earth, which was conceived as a great island. The power of Neptune was thus immensely enlarged, so that from the abyss of the waters, which Plato placed in the very bowels of the earth, he could shake it with his great trident. The crude principles of this physics have been explained above.

754   By these principles of geography Homer can be completely vindicated against the very grave errors which have been wrongfully imputed to him.

755   I. The Lotus Eaters of Homer, who ate the bark of a plant called lotus, must have been nearer [than in the usual view]. For he says that it was a nine days' journey for Ulysses from Malea to the Lotus Eaters; and if the latter, as has been held, had dwelt beyond the straits of Gibraltar, it would have been not merely difficult but impossible to believe that the journey was made in nine days. This error is charged against Homer by Eratosthenes.

756   II. The Laestrygonians in Homer's time must have been a people of Greece, and when he says that they have the longest days he must mean the longest in Greece and not in the whole world. This passage led Aratus to locate them under the head of Draco. Certainly Thucydides, a serious and precise writer, speaks of the Laestrygonians in Sicily, who must have been the most northerly people of that island.

757   III. By the same reasoning, the Cimmerians had the longest nights of any people [not of the whole world but only] of Greece, because they were situated in its most northerly part. Because of their long nights they were said to dwell near the infernal regions. (Their name was later transferred to the remote inhabitants about the Sea of Azov.) Hence the people of Cumae, since they had their dwelling near the grotto of the Sybil which led to the infernal regions, must have been called Cimmerians because of the supposed similarity of location. For it is not to be believed that Ulysses, sent forth by Circe without any incantation (inasmuch as Mercury had given him a charm against her spells, as we have noted above), in one day could have traveled to the latter-day [and remote] Cimmerians [of the Sea of Azov] to visit the lower regions, and on the

same day have made his return to Circeii, now Mr. Circello, not far from Cumae.

758   On these same principles of poetic Greek geography it is possible to solve many great difficulties in the ancient history of the East, arising from the fact that many peoples who must have been situated in the [Near] East itself have been taken for very distant peoples, particularly toward the north and south.

759   What we have noted of Greek poetic geography is also found to be true of the ancient geography of the Latins. Latium must at first have been a very small country inasmuch as in two hundred and fifty years under the kings Rome subdued a good twenty peoples and yet did not extend her rule more than twenty miles, as we have remarked above. Italy was certainly circumscribed by Cisalpine Gaul and Magna Graecia. Roman conquests later extended the name to its present scope. Similarly the Etruscan [or Tyrrhenian] Sea must have been quite small at the time when Horatius Cocles alone withstood all Etruria on the bridge. Roman victories later extended it to include [the waters bathing] all the lower coast of Italy.

760   In precisely the same way the original Pontus, to which Jason made his naval expedition, must have been the land nearest Europe, from which it is divided by the strait called Propontis. This land must have given its name to the sea of Pontus. Thence the name was extended to its farther shores in Asia, where the kingdom of Mithridates later stood. This same fable [of the Argonauts] tells us that Aeëtes, father of Medea, was born in Chalcis, a city of Euboea, an island within Greece now called Negropont, which must have given its first name to what is certainly still called the Black Sea. The original Crete must have been an island within the [Greek] archipelago, which contains the labyrinth of islands [the Cyclades] above explained, from which Minos must have made his raids on the Athenians. Only later did Crete move out into the Mediterranean, where it still remains.

761   Now, since we have returned from the Latins to the Greeks, we may note that the latter, as they went out over the world, spread everywhere (vainglorious men as they were!) the fame of the Trojan war and the wanderings of the heroes, both those of the Trojans such as Antenor, Capys and Aeneas, and those of the Greeks such as Menelaus, Diomed and Ulysses. They observed scattered through the world a type of nation-founder like their Theban Hercules, and so they spread abroad the name of their Hercules, so that Varro was able to enumerate a good forty Herculeses among the ancient nations, and affirmed that the Latin Hercules had been called the god Fidius. Thus it came about that, with a vainglory equalling that of the Egyptians (who said that their Jove Ammon was the most ancient Jove in the world and that all the Herculeses of the other nations had taken their name from the Egyptian Hercules—in accord with two axioms set forth above [193, 196]—erroneously believing themselves to be the oldest nation in the world), the Greeks caused their Hercules to wander

through all the parts of the earth, freeing it of monsters, but bringing home nothing but the glory.

762   They observed everywhere that there had been a poetic character of shepherds speaking in verse, such as their own Arcadian Evander; and so Evander came from Arcadia to Latium, and there gave shelter to his compatriot Hercules, and took to wife Carmenta, so called from *carmina,* "verses." She was the Latin inventress of letters, that is of the forms of the so-called articulated sounds which are the matter of verses. And finally, in confirmation of all we have been saying, the Greeks observed these poetic characters within Latium at the same time that, as we have seen above, they found their Curetes scattered through Saturnia (ancient Italy), Crete and Asia.

763   But these Greek words and ideas came to the Latins in extremely barbarous times in which the nations were closed to strangers. Livy denies that even the famous name of Pythagoras, to say nothing of the man himself, could have reached Rome from Croton in the days of Servius Tullius through the many nations on the way, with their diverse languages and customs. To meet this very difficulty we have postulated above [306], as a necessary conjecture, that there may have been on the shore of Latium a Greek city, later shrouded in the mists of antiquity, which taught the Latins their letters. These, as Tacitus relates, were at first like the earliest Greek ones, which argues strongly that the Latins received their letters from the Greeks of Latium and not from those of Magna Graecia and much less from those of Greece proper, with whom they had no acquaintance before the war with Tarentum which led into that with Pyrrhus. For otherwise the Latins would have used the latest Greek letters and would not have retained their original letters which were the ancient Greek ones.

764   Thus the names of Hercules, Evander and Aeneas came into Latium from Greece in virtue of the following customs of nations:

765   1. Just as in their barbarism they are enamored of their native customs, so when they begin to become civilized they take pleasure in foreign tongues as well as in foreign wares and fashions. Hence the Latins exchanged their god Fidius for the Greek Hercules, and in place of the native oath *medius fidius* they introduced *mehercule, edepol, mecastor.*

766   2. In virtue of that conceit of nations we have so often noted, which makes them boast illustrious foreign origins, particularly when the traditions of their own barbarous times supply some motive for believing in them, the Latins were pleased to disavow Fidius, their true founder, in favor of Hercules, the true founder of the Greeks, and likewise to exchange the character of their own shepherd poets for Evander of Arcadia. (Similarly, in the returned barbarism, Giovanni Villani relates that Fiesole had been founded by Atlas and that a Trojan king Priam had reigned in Germany.)

767   3. When nations observe foreign things which they cannot explain with certainty in their native vocabulary, they must of necessity make use of foreign terms.

768   4. Lastly, there is the property of the earliest peoples which was discussed above in the Poetic Logic, by which they are incapable of abstracting qualities from subjects and therefore can only designate the qualities by naming the subjects to which they belong. We have clear cases of this in Latin.

769   As the Romans did not know what luxury was until they observed it in the Tarentines, they called a perfumed man a Tarentine. As they did not know what military stratagems were until they observed them in the Carthaginians, they called them *punicas artes,* "Carthaginian arts." As they did not know what pomp was until they observed it in the Capuans, they used the phrase *supercilium campanicum* for pomp and pride. In like fashion, Numa and Ancus were called Sabine because the Romans could not otherwise express a religiousness such as that for which the Sabines were distinguished. Servius Tullius was called Greek because they had no word for astuteness, an idea which must have remained unexpressed until they came to know the Greeks of the conquered city of which we were just speaking [763]; and he was also called a slave because they could not otherwise express his weakness in yielding bonitary ownership of the fields to the plebeians by bringing them the first agrarian law, as shown above, on which account, perhaps, the fathers had him slain. For astuteness is a property which goes with weakness, and both alike were foreign to Roman straightforwardness and valor. For those who affirm that Rome did not have within herself heroes worthy of kingship, so that she had to submit to the rule of a low-born slave, do a great injustice to the origins of Rome and offend overmuch the wisdom of Romulus her founder. Such is the honor done him by the critics who have occupied themselves with the writers. It is of a piece with the later tribute to the effect that the Romans, having founded a powerful empire in Latium and maintained it against all the power of Etruria, had to seek like lawless barbarians through Italy, Magna Graecia and Greece proper for laws to order their liberty: all to sustain the credit of the fable that the Law of the Twelve Tables came to Rome from Athens.

[CHAPTER II]

COROLLARY ON THE COMING OF AENEAS INTO ITALY

770   In the light of all our previous discussion, it can now be shown how Aeneas came into Italy and founded the Roman nation in Alba, from which the Romans draw their origin. Our Greek city on the shore of Latium must have been a Greek city from Asia, where Troy was, and must have been unknown to the Romans until they extended their conquests from the hinterland down to the near-by sea. This they began to do under Ancus Marcius, third of the Roman

kings. He initiated such conquests with Ostia, the maritime city so close to Rome that as the latter afterwards expanded immoderately it made Ostia its port. Thus, just as the Romans had received the Latin Arcadians who were fugitives by land, so later they took under their protection the Phrygians who were fugitives by sea, and by heroic right of war they demolished the city. And thus both Arcadians and Phrygians, by two anachronisms, the former by that of postdating and the latter by that of predating, took refuge in the asylum of Romulus.

771 For if this is not the way things went, then the origin of Rome from Aeneas confounds and baffles any understanding, as we pointed out in the Axioms [307]. In order to avoid such bafflement and confusion, the scholars from Livy on down have treated that origin as fabulous, failing to consider that, as we have said in the Axioms [149], the fables must have had some public motive of truth. For Evander is so powerful in Latium that he receives and shelters Hercules there some five hundred years before the founding of Rome, and Aeneas founds the royal house of Alba, which, under a succession of fourteen kings, so waxes in prestige as to become the capital of Latium; and the Arcadians and Phrygians, after so long a vagabondage, finally repaired to the asylum of Romulus! We may well ask how a shepherd folk knowing nothing of seafaring and coming from Arcadia, an inland part of Greece, could cross such an expanse of water and penetrate into mid-Latium, when Ancus Marcius, third king after Romulus, was the first to take a colony down to the near-by seacoast. And how they got to Latium, along with the dispersed Phrygians, a good two hundred years before the time of which Livy writes when he tells us that not even the name of Pythagoras, so celebrated in Magna Graecia, could reach Rome from Croton through the many intervening nations of diverse languages and customs. And, for that matter, four hundred years before the Tarentines had heard of the Romans, who were already a powerful people in Italy.

772 Nevertheless, as we have often stated in conformity with one of the axioms set forth above [149], these vulgar traditions must from the beginning have had great public grounds of truth, since an entire nation has so long preserved them. What then must we say? We must assume that some Greek city had stood on the shore of Latium, just as so many others stood and remained afterward on the shores of the Tyrrhenian Sea. This city must have been conquered by the Romans before the time of the Law of the Twelve Tables, and, by the heroic right of such barbarous victories, the Romans must have demolished it and received the vanquished inhabitants in the quality of heroic *socii*. And in the language of poetic characters these Greeks must have called Arcadians the vagabonds who wandered by land through the forests, and Phrygians those who wandered by sea, just as the Romans described as received into the asylum of Romulus the vanquished who surrendered to them and whom they took in as laborers under the clienteles established by Romulus when he opened the asylum in the clearing for those who came thither as refugees. Out of such conquered and surrendered men (whom we may assign to the period between

the expulsion of the kings and the Law of the Twelve Tables) the Roman plebeians must have emerged under the agrarian law of Servius Tullius, who had granted them bonitary ownership of the fields. Because this was not to the liking of Coriolanus, he sought, as we said above, to reduce [the plebeians to their previous condition as] Romulus's laborers. Subsequently, as the Greeks broadcast everywhere the tale of the Trojan war and the wanderings of the heroes, and particularly in Italy the voyage of Aeneas because in that country they had already discovered their Hercules, their Evander and their Curetes (as noted above), it thus came about in the course of time that these traditions were altered and finally corrupted on the lips of a barbarous people. So, as we say, Aeneas became the founder of the Roman people in Latium, though according to Bochart he never set foot in Italy, though Strabo says he never left Troy, and though Homer, of more weight here, relates that he died in Troy and left his kingdom to his descendants. Thus, by two different manifestations of the conceit of the nations—that of the Greeks in making such a stir about the Trojan war, and that of the Romans in boasting an illustrious foreign origin—the Greeks foisted their Aeneas upon the Romans and the latter finally accepted him as their founder.

773   This fable could not have arisen before the time of the war with Pyrrhus, for it was only then that the Romans began to find pleasure in Greek things. It is a habit we find nations acquiring only after long and extensive dealings with foreigners.

. [CHAPTER III]

THE DENOMINATION AND DESCRIPTION OF THE HEROIC CITIES

774   Now, since the parts of geography are nomenclature and chorography, that is to say the denomination and description of places, principally of cities, it remains for us to examine these matters in order to complete our discussion of poetic wisdom.

775   We have seen above that the heroic cities were founded by providence in natural strongholds, to which the ancient Latins in their divine age must have given the sacred name *arae*, "altars." They must also have called these strong positions *arces*, "fortresses"; for in the returned barbarian times the seigniories were called [in Italian] *rocche*, from *rocce*, "steep and precipitous rocks," and later *castella*. In like manner the name *arae* must have been extended to the whole district held by a heroic city, which, as above noted, was called *ager* when considered with reference to the frontiers dividing it from foreigners, and *territorium* when considered with reference to the jurisdiction of the city over

its citizens. On all this there is a golden passage in Tacitus describing the *ara maxima* of Hercules in Rome, and because this passage gives strong support to these principles we shall quote it in full: *Igitur a foro boario, ubi aeneum bovis simulacrum adspicimus, quia id genus animalium aratro subditur, sulcus designandi oppidi captus, ut magnam Herculis aram complecteretur, ara Herculis erat* [1]—"From the ox market, then, where we see the brazen statue of a bull because that is the animal commonly yoked to the plough, a furrow was drawn to mark out the town, so as to embrace the great altar of Hercules [and the land itself within that furrowed circuit] was the [original] altar of Hercules." There is another golden passage in Sallust telling of the famous altar of the brothers Philaeni [Philaenorum Arae] left as a boundary marker between the Carthaginian and Cyrenaic empires.

776   All ancient geography is strewn with such altars. To begin with Asia, Keller in his *Notitia orbis antiqui* states that all the cities of Syria had the word Aram placed before or after their specific designations, whence Syria itself was called Aramea or Aramia. But in Greece Theseus founded the city of Athens on the famous altar of the unhappy, properly considering unhappy those lawless and impious men who, from the brawling of their infamous communism, took recourse to the fortified lands of the strong, as we have said above, all solitary, weak and needful of all the benefits that the pious had derived from their humanity. And thus in Greek the word *ara* also meant "vow," because on these first altars of the gentile world, as we have also set forth above, the first victims (called *Saturni hostiae,* as noted above)—the first *anathēmata* (translated into Latin as *diris devoti*)—who were the violent and impious men who dared to enter the cultivated fields of the strong in pursuit of the weak who had fled thither to escape them (whence perhaps the use of *campare* in the sense of saving oneself), were consecrated to Vesta and slain. Hence in Latin *supplicium* meant both punishment and sacrifice, as used by Sallust among others. To this double meaning in Latin there is a close correspondence in Greek, for the word *ara,* which as we have said means "vow," has also the sense of *noxa,* "the body that has done the harm," and also that of *dirae,* "the Furies"; and precisely such were these first *devoti,* the vowed or devoted men of whom we just spoke (and of whom we shall have more to say in Book IV), for they were consecrated to the Furies and then sacrificed on these first altars of the gentile world. So the word *hara,* which survived in the sense of "coop" or "pen," must have meant to the ancient Latins the victim. From this word, certainly, is derived *aruspex,* he who divines from the entrails of victims slain before the altars.

777   From what we were saying of the *ara maxima* of Hercules, it was on an altar similar to that of Theseus that Romulus must have founded Rome within the asylum opened in the grove; for it remained true among the Latins that never was there mention of a *lucus* or "sacred wood" without allusion to an

---

[1] *Annals* XII 24; *ara Herculis erat* added by Vico.

altar erected therein to some divinity. So by telling us that in general the asylums were an ancient counsel of founders of cities, *vetus urbes condentium consilium,* Livy discloses to us the reason why in ancient geography we read of so many cities with the name *Arae.* Whence too we must admit that it was with knowledge of this antiquity that Cicero called the Senate *ara sociorum,* for it was to the Senate that the provinces carried their complaints regarding accounting against governors that had governed them avariciously, thereby recalling the origin of the provinces from these first *socii* in the world.

778   We have already shown that the heroic cities in Asia and, as regards Europe, in Greece and Italy were called *Arae* or altars. In Africa, according to Sallust, the aforesaid altar of the brothers Philaeni, *Arae Philaenorum,* remained famous. In the north, coming back to Europe, Altars of the Sicilians [Szekelyek Retze] is still the term applied to the cities in Transylvania inhabited by an ancient Hunnish nation made up of noble farmers and shepherds, which, with the Hungarians and the Saxons, compose that province. For Germany, we read of an *Ara Ubiorum* in Tacitus. In Spain *ara* is still a part of the names of many cities. But in the Syrian language the word *ari* means lion; and above, in the natural theogony of the twelve major divinities, we showed that from the defense of their altars the Greeks conceived the idea of Mars, whom they called Ares; so that, with the same idea of strength, in the returned barbarian times many cities and noble houses charged their arms with lions. This word *ara,* uniform in sound and meaning in so many nations widely separated from each other by space, time and customs, must have been the root of the Latin word *aratrum,* plough, the moldboard of which was called *urbs.* And the Latins must also have derived from *ara* the words *arx,* "fortress," and *arceo,* "to repel," whence the phrase *ager arcifinius* used by writers on the boundaries of fields. Hence also the words *arma* and *arcus,* "arms" and "bow." For they justly conceived strength to consist in thrusting back harm and holding it at a distance.

[CONCLUSION]

779 We have shown that poetic wisdom justly deserves two great and sovereign tributes. The one, clearly and constantly accorded to it, is that of having founded gentile mankind, though the conceit of the nations on the one hand and that of the scholars on the other, the former with ideas of an empty magnificence and the latter with ideas of an impertinent philosophical wisdom, have in effect denied it this honor by their very efforts to affirm it. The other, concerning which a vulgar tradition has come down to us, is that the wisdom of the ancients made its wise men, by a single inspiration, equally great as philosophers, lawmakers, captains, historians, orators and poets, on which account it has been so greatly sought after. But in fact it made or rather sketched them such as we have found them in the fables. For in these, as in embryos or matrices, we have discovered the outlines of all esoteric wisdom. And it may be said that in the fables the nations have in a rough way and in the language of the human senses described the beginnings of this world of sciences, which the specialized studies of scholars have since clarified for us by reasoning and generalization. From all this we may conclude what we set out to show in this [second] book: that the theological poets were the sense and the philosophers the intellect of human wisdom.

BOOK THREE

DISCOVERY OF THE TRUE HOMER

[SECTION I]

[SEARCH FOR THE TRUE HOMER]

[INTRODUCTION]

780 Although our demonstration in the preceding book that poetic wisdom was the vulgar wisdom of the peoples of Greece, who were first theological and later heroic poets, should carry as a necessary consequence that the wisdom of Homer was not at all different in kind, yet, as Plato left firmly fixed the opinion that Homer was endowed with sublime esoteric wisdom (and all the other philosophers have followed in his train, with [pseudo-] Plutarch foremost, writing an entire book on the matter), we shall here examine particularly if Homer was ever a philosopher. On this question another complete book was written by Dionysius Longinus, which is mentioned by Diogenes Laertius in his life of Pyrrho.

[CHAPTER I]

THE ESOTERIC WISDOM ATTRIBUTED TO HOMER

781 Let us concede to Homer what certainly must be granted, that he had to conform to the quite vulgar sensibilities and hence the vulgar customs of the barbarous Greece of his day, for such vulgar perceptions and vulgar customs provide the poets with their proper materials. Let us therefore concede to him what he narrates: that the gods are esteemed according to their strength, as by his supreme strength Jove attempts to show, in the fable of the great chain, that he is the king of men and gods, as we have observed above. On the basis of this vulgar opinion he makes it credible that Diomed can wound Venus and Mars with the help of Minerva, who, in the contest of the gods, despoils Venus and strikes Mars with a rock (and Minerva forsooth was the goddess of philosophy in vulgar belief, and uses weapons so worthy of the wisdom of Jove!). Let us allow him to tell of the inhuman custom (so contrary to what the writers on the natural law of nations claim to have been eternally practiced among the nations) which then prevailed among the barbarous peoples of Greece (who are held to have spread humanity through the world): to wit, that of poisoning arrows (for Ulysses goes to Ephyra to seek poisonous herbs for this purpose), and further, that of denying burial to enemies slain in battle, leaving their unburied bodies instead as a prey to dogs and vultures (on which account the unhappy Priam found so costly the ransom of his son's body, though the naked corpse of Hector had already been dragged by Achilles's chariot three times around the walls of Troy).

782   Nevertheless, if the purpose of poetry is to tame the ferocity of the vulgar whose teachers the poets are, it was not the part of a wise man, versed in such fierce sensibilities and customs, to arouse admiration of them in the vulgar in order that they should take pleasure in them and be confirmed in them by that pleasure. Nor was it the part of a wise man to arouse pleasure in the villainous vulgar at the villainies of the gods, to say nothing of the heroes. As for example we read of Mars in the midst of the contest calling Minerva a dog-fly, and of Minerva punching Diana, and of Agamemnon and Achilles, the latter the greatest of the Greek heroes and the former the head of the Greek league, and both of them kings, calling each other dogs, as servants in popular comedies would scarcely do nowadays.

783   But what name under Heaven more appropriate than sheer stupidity can be given to the wisdom of his captain Agamemnon? For he has to be compelled by Achilles to do his duty in restoring Chryseis to Chryses, her father, priest of Apollo, the god who, on account of this rape, was decimating the Greek army with a cruel pestilence. And then, holding himself offended, Agamemnon thought to regain his honor by an act of justice of a piece with his wisdom, by wrongfully stealing Briseis from Achilles, who bore in his person the fate of Troy, so that, on his withdrawing in anger with his men and ships, Hector might make short work of the Greeks still surviving the pestilence. Here is the Homer hitherto considered the architect of Greek policy or civilization, beginning with such an episode the thread with which he weaves the whole *Iliad,* the principal actors of which are such a captain and a hero such as we have shown Achilles to be when we spoke of the Heroism of the First Peoples. Here is the Homer unrivaled in creating poetic characters, as we shall show him to be farther on, of whom the very greatest are so discordant with this civil human nature of ours. Yet they are perfectly decorous in relation to the punctilious heroic nature, as we have said above.

784   What are we then to say of his representing his heroes as delighting so much in wine, and, whenever they are troubled in spirit, finding all their comfort, yes, and above all others the prudent Ulysses, in getting drunk? Fine precepts for consolation, most worthy of a philosopher!

785   Scaliger is indignant at finding almost all his comparisons to be taken from beasts and other savage things. But even if we admit that they were necessary to Homer in order to make himself better understood by the wild and savage vulgar, nevertheless to attain such success in them—for his comparisons are incomparable—is certainly not characteristic of a mind chastened and civilized by any sort of philosophy. Nor could the truculent and savage style in which he describes so many, such varied and such bloody battles, so many and such extravagantly cruel kinds of butchery as make up all the sublimity of the *Iliad* in particular, have originated in a mind humanized and softened by any philosophy.

786   The constancy, moreover, which is developed and fixed by the study of the wisdom of the philosophers, could not have depicted gods and heroes of such instability. For some, at the slightest suggestion of contrary sentiment, however deeply moved or distressed they may be, become quiet and tranquil; others, while burning with violent wrath, if they chance to recall some sad event, break into bitter tears. (Just so, in the returned barbarism of Italy, at the end of which came Dante, the Tuscan Homer, who also sang only of history, we read of Cola di Rienzo, whose biography we said above exhibited vividly the customs of the Greek heroes as described by Homer, that when he spoke of the unhappy Roman state oppressed by the great of that time, both he and his hearers broke down in uncontrollable tears.) Others, conversely, when deep in grief, if some pleasant diversion offers itself, like the banquet of Alcinous in the case of the wise Ulysses, completely forget their troubles and give themselves over to hilarity. Others, quiet and calm, at some innocent remark which is not to their humor, react with such violence and fly into such a blind rage as to threaten the speaker with a frightful death. So it is with Achilles when he receives Priam in his tent on the aforementioned occasion when the latter, protected by Mercury, has come through the Greek camp by night and all alone in order to ransom the body of Hector. Achilles receives him at dinner and, because of a little phrase that does not please him and which has fallen inadvertently from the mouth of the unhappy father grieving for such a valorous son, flies into a rage. Forgetting the sacred laws of hospitality, unmindful of the simple faith in which Priam has come all alone to him because he trusts completely in him alone, unmoved by the many great misfortunes of such a king or by pity for such a father or by the veneration due to so old a man, heedless of the common lot which avails more than anything else to arouse compassion, he allows his bestial wrath to reach such a point as to thunder at him that he "will cut off his head." The same Achilles, even while impiously determined not to forgive a private injury at the hands of Agamemnon (which grave though it was could not justly be avenged by the ruin of their fatherland and of their entire nation), is pleased—he who carries with him the fate of Troy—to see all the Greeks fall to ruin and suffer miserable defeat at Hector's hands, nor is he moved by love of country or by his nation's glory to bring them any aid. He does

it finally only to satisfy a purely private grief, the slaying of his friend Patroclus by Hector. And not even in death is he placated for the loss of his Briseis until the unhappy beautiful royal maiden Polyxena, of the ruined house of the once rich and puissant Priam, but now become a miserable slave, has been sacrificed before his tomb, and his ashes, thirsting for vengeance, have drunk up the last drop of her blood. To say nothing of what is really past understanding: that a philosopher's gravity and propriety of thought could have been possessed by a man who amused himself by inventing so many fables worthy of old women entertaining children, as those with which Homer stuffed his other poem, the *Odyssey*.

787   Such crude, coarse, wild, savage, volatile, unreasonable or unreasonably obstinate, frivolous and foolish customs as we set forth in the second book in the Corollaries on the Heroic Nature, can pertain only to men who are like children in the weakness of their minds, like women in the vigor of their imaginations and like violent youths in the turbulence of their passions; whence we must deny to Homer any kind of esoteric wisdom. These are the considerations which first gave rise to the doubts that put us under the necessity of seeking out the true Homer.

[CHAPTER II]

HOMER'S FATHERLAND

788   Such was the esoteric wisdom hitherto attributed to Homer; let us now examine his origin. Almost all the cities of Greece claimed to be his birthplace and there were not lacking those who asserted that he was an Italian Greek. To determine his native land Leo Allacci in his *De patria Homeri* spends much effort in vain. But since there has come down to us no writer more ancient than Homer, as Josephus stoutly maintains against the grammarian Apion, and since the writers came long after him, we are obliged to apply our metaphysical criticism, treating him as the founder of a nation as he is held to be of Greece, and to discover the truth, both as to his age and as to his fatherland, from Homer himself.

789   Certainly, as regards the Homer who was author of the *Odyssey*, we are assured that he must have come from the west of Greece and a little toward the south, as evidenced by that golden passage in which Alcinous, king of the Phaeacians in what is now Corfu, offers to Ulysses, who is anxious to be on his way, a well-fitted ship manned by his vassals. These, he says, are expert mariners who could take the hero, if need were, as far as Euboea (now Negropont), which, by the report of those whom chance had taken thither, was a land far

away, a sort of Ultima Thule of the Greeks. This passage shows clearly that the Homer of the *Odyssey* was not the same as the Homer of the *Iliad,* for Euboea was not far from Troy, which was situated in Asia near the shore of the Helles-pont, on the narrow strait of which there are now two fortresses called the Dardanelles, a name recalling to this day its origin from that of Dardania, the ancient territory of Troy. And certainly we find in Seneca that there was a celebrated debate among the grammarians as to whether the *Iliad* and the *Odyssey* were by the same author.

790   As for the contest among the Greek cities for the honor of claiming Homer as citizen, it came about because almost all of them observed in his poems words and phrases and dialectical locutions that belonged to their own vernaculars.

791   What has been said here will serve for the discovery of the true Homer.

[CHAPTER III]

THE AGE OF HOMER

792   We find evidence regarding the age of Homer in the following passages of his poems.

I

793   For the funeral of Patroclus, Achilles causes to be played almost all the kinds of games that were later played in the Olympics when Greek civiliza-tion was at its height.

II

794   The arts of casting in bas-relief and of engraving on metals had already been invented, as is shown, among other examples, by the shield of Achilles, to which we have referred above. Painting had not yet been invented. For casting abstracts the surfaces of things along with some relief, and en-graving does the same with some depth; but painting abstracts the surfaces absolutely, and this is a labor calling for the greatest ingenuity. Hence neither Homer nor Moses ever mentions anything painted, and this is an argument of their antiquity.

III

795   The delights of the gardens of Alcinous, the magnificence of his palace and the sumptuousness of his banquets indicate to us that the Greeks had reached the stage of admiring luxury and pomp.

IV

796   The Phoenicians were already bringing to Greek shores ivory, purple, Arabian incense used to perfume the grotto of Venus; further, a linen finer than the outer skin of an onion, embroidered garments, and, among the gifts of the suitors, one [such garment] for the adornment of Penelope, draped on a frame contrived with such delicate springs that they stretched it out in the fuller places and drew it in in the slender places. An invention worthy of the effeminacy of our day!

V

797   The coach of Priam, in which he drives to Achilles, is made of cedar wood, and the cave of Calypso is fragrant with its perfumes, which betrays a sensuous refinement that was still foreign to the pleasure of the Romans when they were most bent on wasting their substance in luxury in the days of Nero and Heliogabalus.

VI

798   We read of voluptuous baths in the dwelling of Circe.

VII

799   The youthful servants of the suitors are handsome, graceful and blonde-haired, even as the amenity of our present customs would demand.

VIII

800   The men care for their hair like women; this is a reproach brought against the effeminate Paris by Hector and Diomed.

IX

801   It is true that Homer describes his heroes as always eating roast meats. This is the simplest and easiest way of cooking them, since it requires nothing but live coals. This practice was retained in the case of sacrifices, and the Romans used the term *prosiicia* for the meat of the victims roasted on the altars, which was then cut up and divided among the guests. In later times, however, it was roasted on spits just like unconsecrated meat. So Achilles on the occasion of the dinner with Priam cuts up the lamb and Patroclus then roasts it [on a spit], prepares the table and puts bread upon it in the serving baskets; for the heroes celebrated no banquets which were not sacrificial in nature, with themselves in the character of priests. Among the Latins these survived in the *epulae,* sumptuous banquets given usually by the great, in the *epulum,* a public feast for the people, and in the sacred banquet of which the priests called *epulones* partook. Agamemnon himself, accordingly, kills the two lambs whose sacrifice consecrates the terms of the war with Priam. Such was the magnificence at that time of an idea we would now associate with a butcher! Only after this stage must have come boiled meats, for in addition to fire they require water, a kettle and along with it a tripod. Vergil has his heroes eat this kind of meat also, and he has them roast meat on spits. Last of all came seasoned foods, which, besides the things already mentioned, called also for condiments. Now, to get back to the heroic banquets of Homer, though he describes the most delicate food of the Greeks as made of flour, cheese and honey, yet two of his similes are drawn from fishing. And Ulysses, when pretending to be poor and asking alms of one of the suitors, tells him that the gods give to hospitable kings, that is those who are charitable to poor wanderers, seas abounding in fish, which are the greatest delight of the table.

X

802 Lastly (and what is more to our purpose), Homer seems to have appeared at a time when heroic law had already decayed in Greece and the period of popular liberty had begun, for his heroes contract marriages with foreigners and bastards succeed to kingdoms. And so indeed it must have been, for, long since, Hercules, stained by the blood of the ugly centaur Nessus, had gone forth in madness and died; signifying, as we explained in the second book, the end of heroic law.

803 As therefore with regard to the age of Homer we are unwilling to scorn authority altogether, in all these matters gathered and noted from his poems themselves (not as much from the *Iliad* as from the *Odyssey,* which Dionysius Longinus holds was composed in Homer's old age), we find support for the opinion of those who place him long after the Trojan war. The time runs to the extent of 460 years, or until about the period of Numa. Indeed, we believe we are humoring them in not assigning him to a time even nearer our own. For they say it was after Numa's time that Psammeticus opened Egypt to the Greeks. Yet the Greeks, as appears from numerous passages particularly in the *Odyssey,* had long since opened their own country to commerce with the Phoenicians, whose tales no less than their merchandise the Greek peoples had come to delight in, just as Europeans do now in those of the Indies. There is thus no contradiction between these two facts: on the one hand that Homer never saw Egypt, and on the other that he recounts so many things of Egypt and Libya, of Phoenicia and Asia, and above all of Italy and Sicily; for these things had been related to the Greeks by the Phoenicians.

804 Yet we do not see how to reconcile so many refined customs with the many wild and savage ones which he attributes to his heroes at the same time, and particularly in the *Iliad*. So that, lest barbarous acts be confounded with gentle ones—*ne placidis coëant immitia*—we must suppose that the two poems were composed and compiled by various hands through successive ages.

805 Thus, from what we have here said of the fatherland and of the age of Homer as he has hitherto been held to be, our doubts take courage for the search for the true Homer.

[CHAPTER IV] .

HOMER'S MATCHLESS FACULTY FOR HEROIC POETRY

806   The complete absence of philosophy which we have shown in Homer, and our discoveries concerning his fatherland and his age, arouse in us a strong suspicion that he may perhaps have been quite simply a man of the people. This suspicion is confirmed by Horace's observation in his *Art of Poetry* concerning the desperate difficulty of creating fresh characters or persons of tragedy after Homer, on account of which he advises poets to take their characters from Homer's poems. Now this grave difficulty must be taken in conjunction with the fact that the personages of the New Comedy are all of artificial creation; indeed there was an Athenian law requiring the New Comedy to appear on the stage with characters entirely fictitious, and the Greeks managed this so successfully that the Latins, for all their pride, despaired of competing, as Quintilian acknowledged in saying: *Cum graecis de comoedia non contendimus,* "We do not contend with the Greeks in comedy."

807   To Horace's difficulty we must add two others of wider scope. For one thing, how is it that Homer, who came first, was such an inimitable heroic poet, while tragedy, which was born later, began with the crudeness familiar to everybody and which we shall later describe more in detail? And for another, how is it that Homer, who preceded philosophy and the poetic and critical arts, was yet the most sublime of all the sublime poets, and that after the invention of philosophies and of the arts of poetry and criticism there was no poet who could come within a long distance of competing with him? However, putting aside our two difficulties, that of Horace combined with what we have said of the New Comedy should have spurred scholars like Patrizzi, Scaliger and Castelvetro and other valiant masters of the poetic art to investigate the reason for the difference.

808   The reason cannot be found elsewhere than in the origin of poetry, as discovered above in the Poetic Wisdom, and consequently in the discovery of the poetic characters in which alone consists the essence of poetry itself. For the New Comedy portrays our present human customs, on which the Socratic philosophy had meditated, and hence, from the latter's general maxims concerning human morals, the Greek poets, profoundly steeped in that doctrine (as was Menander for example, in comparison with whom Terence was called even by the Latins "half a Menander"), could create certain luminous examples of ideal men, by the light and splendor of which they might awaken the vulgar, who are as quick to learn from convincing examples as they are incapable of

understanding from reasoned maxims. The Old Comedy took arguments or subjects from real life and made plays of them just as they were, as the wicked Aristophanes once did with the good Socrates, thus bringing on his ruin. But tragedy puts on the scene heroic hatred, scorn, wrath and revenge, which spring from sublime natures which naturally are the source of sentiments, modes of speech and actions in general that are wild, crude and terrible. Such arguments are clothed with an air of marvel, and all these matters are in closest conformity among themselves and uniform in their subjects. Such works the Greeks could produce only in the time of their heroism, at the end of which Homer must have come. This is shown by the following metaphysical criticism. The fables, which at their birth had come forth direct and proper, reached Homer distorted and perverted. As may be seen throughout the Poetic Wisdom above set forth, they were all at first true histories, which were gradually altered and corrupted, and in their corrupt form finally came down to Homer. Hence he must be assigned to the third age of the heroic poets. The first age invented the fables to serve as true narratives, the primary and proper meaning of the word *mythos,* as defined by the Greeks themselves, being "true narration." The second altered and corrupted them. The third and last, that of Homer, received them thus corrupted.

809   But, to return to our purpose, for the reason assigned by us to this effect, Aristotle in his *Poetics* says that only Homer knew how to invent poetic falsehoods. For his poetic characters, which are incomparable for the sublime appropriateness which Horace admires in them, were imaginative universals, as defined above in the Poetic Metaphysics, to which the peoples of Greece attached all the various particulars belonging to each genus. To Achilles, for example, who is the subject of the *Iliad,* they attached all the properties of heroic valor, and all the sentiments and customs arising from these natural properties, such as those of quick temper, punctiliousness, wrathfulness, implacability, violence, the arrogation of all right to might, as they are summed up by Horace in his description of this character. To Ulysses, the subject of the *Odyssey,* they attached all the sentiments and customs of heroic wisdom, that is, those of wariness, patience, dissimulation, duplicity, deceit, always preserving propriety of speech and indifference of action, so that others may of themselves fall into error and may be the causes of their own deception. And to these two characters, according to kind, they attached those actions of particular men which were conspicuous enough to arouse and move the still dull and stupid Greeks to note them and refer them to their kinds. These two characters, since they had been created by an entire nation, could only be conceived as naturally uniform (in which uniformity, agreeable to the common sense of an entire nation, alone consists the decorum or beauty and charm of a fable); and, since they were created by powerful imaginations, they could not be created as anything but sublime. Hence derive two eternal properties of poetry: one that poetic sublimity is inseparable from popularity, and the other that peoples who have first

created heroic characters for themselves will afterwards apprehend human [or civilized] customs only in terms of characters made famous by luminous examples.

[CHAPTER V]

PHILOSOPHICAL PROOFS FOR THE DISCOVERY OF THE TRUE HOMER

810   In view of what we have stated, the following philosophical proofs may be assembled.

I

811   First of all, the one enumerated above among the Axioms [201], which states that men are naturally led to preserve the memories of the orders and laws that keep them within their societies.

II

812   The truth understood by Castelvetro, that history must have come first and then poetry, for history is a simple statement of the truth but poetry is an imitation at a second remove. Yet this scholar, though otherwise most acute, failed to make use of this truth to discover the true principles of poetry by combining it with the other philosophical proof which follows here.

III

813   Inasmuch as the poets came certainly before the vulgar historians, the first history must have been poetic.

IV

814   The fables in their origin were true and severe narrations (whence *mythos*, "fable," was defined as *vera narratio,* as we have frequently noted). But because for the most part they were originally monstrous, they were later misappropriated, then altered, subsequently became improbable, after that obscure, then scandalous and finally incredible. These are the seven sources of the difficulties of the fables, which can all easily be found throughout the second book.

V

815   And, as we have shown in the same book, they were received by Homer in this corrupt and distorted form.

VI

816   The poetic characters, in which the essence of the fables consists, were born of the need of a nature incapable of abstracting forms and properties from subjects. Consequently they must have been the manner of thinking of entire peoples, who had been placed under this natural necessity in the times of their greatest barbarism. It is an eternal property of the fables always to magnify the ideas of particulars. On this there is a fine passage in Aristotle's *Ethics* in which he remarks that men of limited ideas erect every particular into a maxim. The reason must be that the human mind, which is indefinite, being constricted by the vigor of the senses, cannot otherwise express its almost divine nature than by thus magnifying particulars in imagination. It is perhaps on this account that in both the Greek and the Latin poets the images of gods and heroes always appear larger than those of men, and that in the returned barbarian times the paintings particularly of the Eternal Father, of Jesus Christ and of the Virgin Mary are exceedingly large.

VII

817   Since barbarians lack reflection, which, when ill used, is the mother of falsehood, the first heroic Latin poets sang true histories, that is, the Roman wars. And in the returned barbarian times, in virtue of this nature of barbarism, the Latin poets like Gunther, William of Apulia and others again sang nothing but history, and the romancers of the same period thought they were writing true histories. Even Boiardo and Ariosto, who came in an age illuminated by philosophy, took the subjects of their poems from the history of Bishop Turpin of Paris. And in virtue of this same nature of barbarism, which for lack of reflection does not know how to feign (whence it is naturally truthful, open, faithful, generous and magnanimous), even Dante, though learned in the loftiest esoteric knowledge, filled the scenes of his *Comedy* with real persons and portrayed real events in the lives of the dead. For that reason he gave the name *Comedy* to his poem, for the Old Comedy of the Greeks, as we have said above, portrayed real persons in its plays. In this respect Dante was like the Homer of the *Iliad,* which Dionysius Longinus says is all dramatic or representative, as the *Odyssey* is all narrative. Francesco Petrarca too, though a most learned man, yet sang in Latin of the second Carthaginian war, and his *Trionfi,* in Tuscan, which have a heroic note, are nothing but a collection of histories. And here we have a luminous proof of the fact that the first fables were histories. For satire spoke ill of persons not only real but well known; tragedy took for its arguments characters of poetic history; the Old Comedy put into its plots illustrious living persons; the New Comedy, born in times of the most lively reflection, finally invented characters entirely fictitious (just as in the Italian language the New Comedy came in again only with the marvelously learned Cinquecento):

and neither among the Greeks nor among the Latins was an entirely fictitious character ever the protagonist of a tragedy. Strong confirmation of this is found in the popular taste which will not accept musical dramas, the arguments of which are always tragic, unless they are taken from history, whereas it will tolerate fictitious plots in comedies because, since they deal with private life which is not public knowledge, it believes them true.

VIII

818   Since poetic characters are of this nature, their poetic allegories, as we have shown above throughout the Poetic Wisdom, must necessarily contain historical significations referring only to the earliest times of Greece.

IX

819   Such histories must naturally have been preserved in the memories of the communities of the peoples, in virtue of the first philosophical proof just mentioned; for, as the children of the nations, they must have had marvelously strong memories. And this was not without divine providence, for up to the time of Homer and indeed somewhat afterwards, common script had not yet been invented (on the authority of Josephus against Apion, which we have already cited several times). In that human indigence, the peoples, who were almost all body and almost no reflection, must have been all vivid sensation in perceiving particulars, strong imagination in apprehending and magnifying them, sharp wit in referring them to their imaginative genera and robust memory in retaining them. It is true that these faculties appertain to the mind, but they have their roots in the body and draw their strength from it. Hence memory is the same as imagination, which for that reason is called *memoria* in Latin. (In Terence, for example, we find *memorabile* in the sense of "imaginable," and commonly we find *comminisci* for "feigning," which is proper to the imagination, and thence *commentum* for a fiction.) Imagination is likewise taken for wit or ingenuity. (In the returned barbarian times an ingenious man was called imaginative [*fantastico*]; so, for example, Cola di Rienzo is described by his contemporary biographer.) Memory thus has three different aspects: memory when it remembers things, imagination when it alters or imitates them and invention when it gives them a new turn or puts them into proper arrangement and relationship. For these reasons the theological poets called Memory the mother of the Muses.

X

820   The poets must therefore have been the first historians of the nations. This is why Castelvetro failed to make use of his dictum for finding the true origins of poetry; for he and all others who have discussed the matter (from Plato and Aristotle on down) could easily have observed that all gentile histories

have their beginnings in fables, as we set forth in the Axioms [202] and demonstrated in the Poetic Wisdom.

XI

821   By the very nature of poetry it is impossible for anyone to be at the same time a sublime poet and a sublime metaphysician, for metaphysics abstracts the mind from the senses, and the poetic faculty must submerge the whole mind in the senses; metaphysics soars up to universals, and the poetic faculty must plunge deep into particulars.

XII

822   In virtue of the axiom set forth above [213]—that he who has not the natural gift may by industry succeed in every [other] capacity, but that in poetry success by industry is completely denied to him who lacks the natural gift—the poetic and critical "arts" serve to make minds cultivated but not great. For delicacy is a small virtue and greatness naturally disdains all small things. Indeed, as a great rushing torrent cannot fail to carry turbid waters and roll stones and trunks along in the violence of its course, so his very greatness accounts for the low expressions we so often find in Homer.

XIII

823   But this does not make Homer any the less the father and prince of all sublime poets.

XIV

824   For we have seen that Aristotle regarded the Homeric lies as without equal, which is equivalent to Horace's opinion that his characters are inimitable.

XV

825   He is celestially sublime in his poetic sentences, which, as we have shown in our Corollaries on the Heroic Nature in the second book, must be conceived of true passions, or in virtue of a burning imagination must make themselves truly felt by us, and they must therefore be individualized in those who feel them. Hence maxims of life, as being general, were defined by us as sentences of philosophers; and reflections on the passions themselves are the work of false and frigid poets.

XVI

826   The poetic comparisons taken from wild and savage things, as we observed above, are certainly incomparable in Homer.

XVII

827　　The frightfulness of the Homeric battles and deaths, as we also noted above, gives to the *Iliad* all its marvelousness.

XVIII

828　　But these sentences, comparisons and descriptions, as we also proved above, could not have been the natural product of a calm, cultivated and gentle philosopher.

XIX

829　　For in their customs the Homeric heroes are like boys in the frivolity of their minds, like women in the vigor of their imaginations and like turbulent youths in the boiling fervor of their wrath, as was also shown above, and therefore it is impossible that a philosopher should have conceived them so naturally and felicitously.

XX

830　　The ineptitudes and indecencies, as we have already proved, are effects of the awkwardness with which the Greek peoples had labored to express themselves in the extreme poverty of their language in its formative period.

XXI

831　　And even if the Homeric poems contained the most sublime mysteries of esoteric wisdom, as we have shown in the Poetic Wisdom that they certainly do not, the form in which they are expressed could not have been conceived by a straightforward, orderly and serious mind such as befits a philosopher.

XXII

832　　The heroic language, as we have seen above in the Origins of Languages in the second book, was a language of similes, images and comparisons, born of the lack of genera and species, which are necessary for the proper definition of things, and hence born of a necessity of nature common to all peoples.

XXIII

833　　It was by a necessity of nature, as we also said in the second book, that the first nations spoke in heroic verse. Here too we must admire the providence which, in the time when the characters of common script were not yet invented, ordained that the nations should speak in verses so that their memories might be aided by meter and rhythm to preserve more easily the histories of their families and cities.

XXIV

834   These fables, sentences and customs, this language and verse, were all called heroic, and were current in the times to which history has assigned the heroes, as has been fully shown above in the Poetic Wisdom.

XXV

835   Hence all the aforesaid were properties of entire peoples and consequently common to all the individual men of these peoples.

XXVI

836   In virtue, however, of the very nature from which sprang all the aforesaid properties, which made Homer the greatest of poets, we denied that he was ever a philosopher.

XXVII

837   Further we showed above in the Poetic Wisdom that the meanings of esoteric wisdom were intruded into the Homeric fables by the philosophers who came later.

XXVIII

838   But, as esoteric wisdom appertains to but few individual men, so we have just seen that the very decorum of the heroic poetic characters, in which consists all the essence of the heroic fables, cannot be achieved today by men most learned in philosophy, in the art of poetry and in the art of criticism. It is for this decorum that Aristotle and Horace give the palm to Homer, the former saying that his lies are beyond equal and the latter that his characters are inimitable, which comes to the same thing.

[CHAPTER VI]

PHILOLOGICAL PROOFS FOR THE DISCOVERY OF THE TRUE HOMER

839   With this great number of philosophical proofs, resulting in large part from the metaphysical criticism of the founders of the gentile nations, among whom we must number Homer since certainly we have no more ancient profane writer than he (as Josephus the Jew stoutly maintains), we may conjoin the following philological proofs.

I

840   All ancient profane histories have fabulous beginnings.

II

841   Barbarous peoples, cut off from all the other nations of the world, as were the Germans and the American Indians, have been found to preserve in verses the beginnings of their history, as we have seen above.

III

842   It was the poets who began to write Roman history.

IV

843   In the returned barbarian times, the histories were written by the poets who wrote in Latin.

V

844   Manetho, high priest of the Egyptians, interpreted the ancient history of Egypt, written in hieroglyphics, as a sublime natural theology.

VI

845   In the Poetic Wisdom we showed that the Greek philosophers did the same with the early history of Greece recounted in fables.

VII

846   Wherefore above in the Poetic Wisdom we were obliged to reverse the path of Manetho and, taking our point of departure from the mystical interpretations, to restore to the fables their original historical meanings; and the naturalness and ease, free of violence, subterfuge or distortion, with which we were able to do so, show that the historical allegories which they contained were proper to them.

VIII

847   All of which strongly confirms the assertion of Strabo, in a golden passage, that before Herodotus, or rather before Hecataeus of Miletus, the history of the peoples of Greece was all written by their poets.

IX

848   And in the second book we showed that the first writers of both ancient and modern nations were poets.

X

849   There are two golden passages in the *Odyssey* in which it is said, in praise of a speaker who has told a story well, that he has told it like a musician or singer. Just such indeed were the Homeric rhapsodes, who were vulgar men, each preserving by memory some part of the Homeric poems.

XI

850   Homer left none of his poems in writing, according to the firm assertion of Flavius Josephus the Jew against Apion the Greek grammarian, which we have several times cited.

XII

851   The rhapsodes went about the cities of Greece singing the books of Homer at the fairs and festivals, one singing one of them, another another.

XIII

852   By the etymology of their name from the two words which compose it, rhapsodes were stitchers together of songs, and these songs they must certainly have collected from none other than their own peoples. Similarly [the common noun] *homēros* is said to come from *homou,* "together," and *eirein,* "to link"; thus signifying a guarantor, as being one who binds creditor and debtor together. This derivation is as far-fetched and forced [when applied to a guarantor] as it is natural and proper when applied to our Homer as a tier or putter together of fables.

XIV

853   The Pisistratids, tyrants of Athens, divided and arranged the poems of Homer, or had them divided and arranged, into [two groups,] the *Iliad* and *Odyssey.* Hence we may understand what a confused mass of material they must have been before, when the difference we can observe between the styles of the two poems is infinite.

XV

854   The Pisistratids also ordered that from that time on the poems should be sung by the rhapsodes at the Panathenaic festivals, as Cicero writes in his *On the Nature of the Gods,* and Aelian also, who is followed on this point by [his editor] Scheffer.

XVI

855   But the Pisistratids were expelled from Athens only a few years before the expulsion of the Tarquins from Rome. So, if we assume that Homer lived at the time of Numa, as we have proved above, a long time must still have ensued after the Pisistratids during which the rhapsodes continued to preserve his poems by memory. This tradition takes away all credit from the other according to which it was at the time of the Pisistratids that Aristarchus purged, divided and arranged the poems of Homer, for that could not have been done without vulgar writing, and so from then on there would have been no need of rhapsodes to sing the several parts of them from memory.

XVII

856   By this reasoning, Hesiod, who left his works in writing, would have
to be placed after the Pisistratids, since we have no authority for supposing that
he was preserved by the memory of the rhapsodes as Homer was, though the
vain diligence of the chronologists has placed him thirty years before Homer.
Like the Homeric rhapsodes, however, were the cyclic poets, who preserved all
the fabulous history of Greece from the origins of their gods down to the return
of Ulysses to Ithaca. These cyclic poets, so called from *kyklos*, "circle," could
have been no other than simple men who would sing the fables to the common
people gathered in a circle around them on festive days. The circle is precisely
the one alluded to by Horace in his *Art of Poetry* in the phrase *vilem patulumque
orbem*, "the base and large circle," concerning which Dacier is not at all satisfied
with the commentators who assert that Horace here means long episodes or di-
gressions. And perhaps the reason for his dissatisfaction is this: that it is not necessary that an episode in a plot be base simply because it is long. To cite examples,
the episode of the joys of Rinaldo and Armida in the enchanted garden, and
that of the conversation of the old shepherd with Erminia, are indeed long but
are not therefore base; for the former is ornate and the latter tenuous and delicate,
and both are noble. But in this passage Horace, having advised the tragic poets
to take their arguments from the poems of Homer, runs into the difficulty that
in that case they would not be [creative] poets, since their plots would be those
invented by Homer. So Horace answers them that the epic stories of Homer
will become tragic plots of their own if they will bear three things in mind.
The first is to refrain from making idle paraphrases, in the way we still see men
read the *Orlando furioso* or the [*Orlando*] *innamorato* or some other rhymed
romance to the "base and large circles" of idle people on feast days, and, after
reciting each stanza, explain it to them in prose with more words. The second is
not to be faithful translators. The third and last is not to be servile imitators, but,
adhering to the characters that Homer attributes to his heroes, to bring forth
from them new sentiments, speeches and actions in conformity with them; thus
on the same subjects they will be new poets in the style of Homer. So, in the same
work, Horace speaks of a "cyclical poet" as a trivial market-place poet. Authors
of this sort are ordinarily called *kyklioi* and *enkyklioi,* and their collective work
was called *kyklos epikos, kyklia epē, poiēma enkyklikon,* and sometimes *kyklos*
without qualification, as Gerard Langbaine observes in his preface to Dionysius
Longinus. So in this way it may be that Hesiod, who contains all the fables of
the gods, is earlier than Homer.

XVIII

857   For this reason the same may be said of Hippocrates, who left many
great works, written not indeed in verse but in prose, so that they naturally

could not have been preserved by memory; whence he is to be assigned to about the time of Herodotus.

XIX

858   From all this [it is evident that] Vossius placed an excess of good faith in the three heroic inscriptions with which he thought he could confute Josephus. For these inscriptions, the first of Amphitryon, the second of Hippocoon, and the third of Laomedon [i.e. Laodamas], are impostures similar to those still committed by falsifiers of medals. Martin Schoock supports Josephus against Vossius.

XX

859   We may add that Homer never mentions vulgar Greek letters, and the epistle written by Proetus to Eureia as a trap for Bellerophon is said by Homer to have been written in *sēmata,* as we noted above.

XXI

860   Though Aristarchus emended Homer's poems, they still retain a great variety of dialects and many improprieties of speech, which must have been idiomatic expressions of various peoples of Greece, and many licenses in meter besides.

XXII

861   The fatherland of Homer is not known, as we observed above.

XXIII

862   Almost all the cities of Greece laid claim to him, as has also been noted above.

XXIV

863   Above we have brought forward strong conjectures that the Homer of the *Odyssey* was from the west of Greece and toward the south, and that the Homer of the *Iliad* was from the east and toward the north.

XXV

864   Not even Homer's age is known.

XXVI

865   The opinions on this point are so numerous and so varied that the divergence extends to 460 years, the extreme estimates putting it as early as the Trojan war and as late as the time of Numa.

XXVII

866   Dionysius Longinus, being unable to ignore the great diversity in the styles of the two poems, says that Homer composed the *Iliad* in his youth and the *Odyssey* in his old age: a strange detail to be known about a man of whom we do not know the two most important historical facts, namely when and where he lived, regarding which Longinus has left us in the dark in his discussion of the greatest luminary of Greece.

XXVIII

867   This consideration should destroy all faith in Herodotus or whoever was the author of the *Life of Homer,* in which so many delightful minor details are narrated as to fill an entire volume, and all trust as well in the *Life* of him written by Plutarch, who, being a philosopher, spoke of him with greater sobriety.

XXIX

868   But perhaps Longinus based his conjecture on the fact that in the *Iliad* Homer depicts the wrath and pride of Achilles, which are properties of youth, while in the *Odyssey* he relates the wiles and stratagems of Ulysses, which are characteristic of the aged.

XXX

869   Tradition says that Homer was blind and that from his blindness he took his name, which in the Ionic dialect means blind.

XXXI

870   Homer himself describes as blind the poets who sing at the banquets of the great, such as the one who sings at the banquet of Alcinous for Ulysses, and the one who sings at the feast of the suitors.

XXXII

871   It is a property of human nature that the blind have marvelously retentive memories.

XXXIII

872   And finally [tradition says] that he was poor and wandered through the market places of Greece singing his own poems.

[SECTION II]

DISCOVERY OF THE TRUE HOMER

[INTRODUCTION]

873   Now all these things reasoned out by us or related by others concerning Homer and his poems, without our having intentionally aimed at any
such result—indeed it had not even entered into our reflections when readers of
the first edition of this *New Science* (which was not worked out on the same
method as the present), men of acute minds and excelling in scholarship and
learning, suspected that the Homer believed in up to now was not real—all
these things, I say, now compel us to affirm that the same thing has happened
in the case of Homer as in that of the Trojan war, of which the most judicious
critics hold that though it marks a famous epoch in history it never in the world
took place. And certainly if, as in the case of the Trojan war, there did not remain
of Homer certain great vestiges in the form of his poems, the great difficulties
would lead us to conclude that he was a purely ideal poet who never existed as
a particular man in the world of nature. But the many great difficulties on
the one hand, taken together with the surviving poems on the other, seem to
force us to take the middle ground that Homer was an idea or a heroic character of Grecian men insofar as they told their history in song.

[CHAPTER I]

THE IMPROPRIETIES AND IMPROBABILITIES OF THE HOMER
HITHERTO BELIEVED IN BECOME PROPER AND NECESSARY
IN THE HOMER HEREIN DISCOVERED

874   In the light of this discovery, all the things in the speeches and in the
narrative which are improprieties and improbabilities in the Homer hitherto

believed in become proper and necessary in the Homer herein discovered. And
first of all, those most important matters concerning Homer on which we are
left in uncertainty compel us to say:

I

875   That the reason why the Greek peoples so vied with each other for
the honor of being his fatherland, and why almost all claimed him as citizen,
is that the Greek peoples were themselves Homer.

II

876   That the reason why opinions as to his age vary so much is that
our Homer truly lived on the lips and in the memories of the peoples of Greece
throughout the whole period from the Trojan war down to the time of Numa,
a span of 460 years.

III

877   And the blindness

IV

878   and the poverty of Homer were characteristics of the rhapsodes, who,
being blind, whence each of them was called *homēros,* had exceptionally retentive memories, and, being poor, sustained life by singing the poems of Homer
throughout the cities of Greece; and they were the authors of these poems inasmuch as they were a part of these peoples who had composed their histories in
the poems.

V

879   Thus Homer composed the *Iliad* in his youth, that is when Greece
was young and consequently seething with sublime passions, such as pride,
wrath and lust for vengeance, passions which do not tolerate dissimulation but
which love magnanimity; and hence this Greece admired Achilles, the hero of
violence. But he wrote the *Odyssey* in his old age, that is when the spirits of
Greece had been somewhat cooled by reflection, which is the mother of prudence,
so that it admired Ulysses, the hero of wisdom. Thus in the time of Homer's
youth the peoples of Greece found pleasure in coarseness, villainy, ferocity,
savagery and cruelty, while in the time of his old age they found delight in the
luxury of Alcinous, the joys of Calypso, the pleasures of Circe, the songs of the
Sirens, the pastimes of the suitors, and the attempts, nay the siege and the as-
saults on the chastity of Penelope: two sets of customs which, conceived above as
existing at the same time, seemed to us incompatible. This difficulty was enough
to cause the divine Plato to declare, in order to solve it, that Homer had fore-
seen by inspiration these nauseating, morbid and dissolute customs. Yet in this
way he merely made of Homer a stupid organizer of Greek civilization, for,

however much he may condemn, he nevertheless teaches these corrupt and decadent customs which were to come long after the nations of Greece had been organized, to the end that, by an acceleration of the natural course of human affairs, the Greeks might hasten on toward corruption.

VI

880   In this fashion we show that the Homer who was the author of the *Iliad* preceded by many centuries the Homer who was the author of the *Odyssey*.

VII

881   And we show that it was from the northeastern part of Greece that the Homer came who sang of the Trojan war, which took place in his country, and that it was from the southwestern part of Greece that the Homer came who sang of Ulysses, whose kingdom was in that region.

VIII

882   Thus Homer, lost in the crowd of the Greek peoples, is justified against all the accusations leveled at him by the critics, and particularly [against those made] on account of his

IX

883   base sentences,

X

884   vulgar customs,

XI

885   crude comparisons,

XII

886   local idioms,

XIII

887   licenses in meter,

XIV

888   variations in dialect,

XV

889   and his having made men of gods and gods of men.

890   These last-mentioned fables Dionysius Longinus does not trust himself to sustain save by the props of philosophical allegories, which amounts to admitting that, as they sounded when sung to the Greeks, they cannot have brought Homer the glory of having been the organizer of Greek civilization.

The same difficulty recurs in Homer's case which, above in the Notes on the Chronological Table, we raised against Orpheus as the founder of Greek humanity. But the aforesaid properties and particularly the last all appertained to the Greek peoples themselves. For inasmuch as at their founding they were themselves pious, religious, chaste, strong, just and magnanimous, they made their gods so also, as our natural theogony has demonstrated above; then later, in the long passage of the years, as the fables became obscure and customs decayed, from their own character they judged the gods too to be dissolute, as we have set forth at length in the Poetic Wisdom. This in virtue of the axiom laid down above [220], that men naturally bend obscure or dubious laws to their own passions and utilities. For they feared that the gods would not be agreeable to their desires if they were not like them in customs, as we have already said.

XVI

891   But more than ever to Homer belong by right the two great preeminences which are really one: that poetic falsehoods, as Aristotle says, and heroic characters, as Horace says, could be created only by him. On this account Horace avows himself to be no poet because he lacks the knack or the wit to maintain what he calls the colors of works, *colores operum,* which means the same thing as the poetic untruths of Aristotle's phrase, for in Plautus we find *obtinere colorem* in the sense of telling a lie that under every aspect has the appearance of truth, which is what a good fable must be.

892   In addition to these, all those other preëminences fall to him which have been ascribed to him by all the masters of the art of poetry, declaring him incomparable

XVII

893   in his wild and savage comparisons,

XVIII

894   in his cruel and fearful descriptions of battles and deaths,

XIX

895   in his sentences filled with sublime passions,

XX

896   in the clarity and splendor of his style. All these were properties of the heroic age of the Greeks, in which and throughout which Homer was an incomparable poet, just because, in the age of vigorous memory, robust imagination and sublime invention, he was in no sense a philosopher.

XXI

897   Wherefore neither philosophies, arts of poetry, nor arts of criticism, which came later, could create a poet who could come anywhere near to rivaling Homer.

898   And, what is more, his title is assured to the three immortal eulogies that are given him:

XXII

899   first, of having been the organizer of Greek polity or civilization;

XXIII

900   second, of having been the father of all other poets;

XXIV

901   and third, of having been the source of all Greek philosophies. None of these eulogies could have been given to the Homer hitherto believed in. Not the first, for, counting from the time of Deucalion and Pyrrha, Homer comes eighteen hundred years after the institution of marriage had laid the first foundations of Greek civil life, as we have shown throughout the Poetic Wisdom. Not the second, for it was certainly before Homer's time that the theological poets flourished, such as Orpheus, Amphion, Linus, Musaeus and others, among whom the chronologists have placed Hesiod, putting him three hundred years before Homer. And Cicero affirms in his *Brutus* that there were other heroic poets before Homer, whom Eusebius mentions by name in his *Praeparatio evangelica,* such as Philammon, Thamyris, Demodocus, Epimenides, Aristaeus and others. And, finally, not the third, for, as we have shown fully and at length in the Poetic Wisdom, the philosophers did not discover their philosophies in the Homeric fables but rather inserted them therein. But it was poetic wisdom itself whose fables provided occasions for the philosophers to meditate their lofty truths, and supplied them also with means for expounding them, as we showed throughout the second book in fulfilment of the promise made at its beginning.

[CHAPTER II]

THE POEMS OF HOMER REVEALED AS TWO GREAT TREASURE STORES OF THE NATURAL LAW OF THE NATIONS OF GREECE

902   But above all, in virtue of our discovery we may ascribe to him an additional and most dazzling glory:

XXV

903   that of having been the first historian of the entire gentile world who has come down to us.

XXVI

904   Wherefore his poems should henceforth be highly prized as being two great treasure stores of the customs of early Greece. But the same fate has befallen the poems of Homer as the Law of the Twelve Tables; for, just as the latter, having been held to be the laws given by Solon to the Athenians and subsequently taken over by the Romans, has up to now concealed from us the history of the natural law of the heroic nations of Latium, so the Homeric poems, having been regarded as works produced by a single supreme poet, have hitherto concealed from us the history of the natural law of the nations of Greece.

[APPENDIX]

RATIONAL HISTORY OF THE DRAMATIC AND LYRIC POETS

905 We have already shown above that there were three ages of poets before Homer. The first was the age of the theological poets, who were themselves heroes and sang true and austere fables; the second, that of the heroic poets who altered and corrupted the fables; and the third that of Homer, who received them in their altered and corrupted form. Now the same metaphysical criticism of the history of the obscurest antiquity, that is, the explanation of the ideas the earliest nations naturally formed, can illuminate and distinguish for us the history of the dramatic and lyric poets, on which the philosophers have written only in an obscure and confused fashion.

906 The philosophers class among the lyric poets Amphion [i.e. Arion] of Methymna, a most ancient poet of heroic times, and affirm that he discovered the dithyramb and therewith the chorus, and that he introduced the singing of verses by satyrs, and that the dithyramb was a chorus led about singing verses in praise of Bacchus. They say that noteworthy tragic poets flourished within the period of the lyric; and Diogenes Laertius affirms that the first tragedy was represented by the chorus alone. They say that Aeschylus was the first tragic poet, and Pausanias relates that he was commanded by Bacchus to write tragedies (although Horace says that Thespis was their originator, in that passage of his *Art of Poetry* where he begins his treatment of tragedy with satire, and that Thespis introduced satire [i.e. the satyr play] on carts at vintage time). Later, they say, came Sophocles, called by Palaemon the Homer of the tragic poets; and the cycle was completed by Euripides, whom Aristotle calls *tragikōtaton,* the most tragic of them all. They say that in the same period came Aristophanes, who invented the Old Comedy and opened the way for the New (which was later traveled by Menander), with his play entitled *The Clouds,* which was the ruin of Socrates. Then some of them put Hippocrates in the time of the tragic poets, others in the lyric period. But Sophocles and Euripides lived somewhat before the time of the Law of the Twelve Tables, and the lyric poets came even later; which would seem to upset the chronology which puts Hippocrates in the age of the Seven Sages of Greece.

907   To solve this difficulty we must declare that there were two kinds of tragic poets and two kinds of lyric poets.

908   The ancient lyric poets must in the first place have been the authors of hymns in honor of the gods, like those attributed to Homer, composed in heroic verse. They must later have been the poets of that lyric vein in which Achilles sings to his lyre the praises of the heroes who have gone before. Similarly among the Latins the first poets were the authors of the Salian verses, which were hymns sung by the priests called Salii on the festival days of the gods. (The priests were perhaps so called from *salio,* "to leap," even as the first Greek choruses danced in a circle.) The fragments of these verses are the most ancient memorials of the Latin language that have come down to us, and they have something of the feeling of heroic verse, as we have already observed. All of which is in accord with the beginnings of the humanity of the nations, which in the first or religious period must have offered praise only to the gods (even as in the returned barbarian times this religious custom returned, and the priests, the only literate men of the time, composed only sacred hymns); whereas later, in the heroic period, they must have admired and celebrated only the great deeds of heroes, such as those sung by Achilles. It is to this kind of sacred lyric poets that Amphion [i.e. Arion] of Methymna must have belonged. He was also the originator of the dithyramb, which was the first rough beginning of tragedy, composed in heroic verse (the first kind of verse in which the Greeks sang, as shown above). Thus the dithyramb of Amphion was the first satire, and it is with satire that Horace begins his discussion of tragedy.

909   The new lyric poets were the melic poets, whose prince is Pindar, and who wrote in verse what we in Italian call *arie per musica.* This sort of verse must have come later than the iambic, which in turn, as we have shown above, was the kind of verse in which the Greeks commonly spoke after the heroic verse. Thus Pindar came in the times of the pompous bravery of Greece admired at the Olympic games, at which these lyric poets sang. In the same way Horace came in the most sumptuous times of Rome, under the reign of Augustus; and among the Italians the melic period came in the times of the greatest softness and tenderness.

910   The tragic and comic poets ran their course between the following limits. Thespis in one part of Greece and Amphion [i.e Arion] in another originated at vintage time the satire or satyr play, the primitive form of tragedy, with satyrs for its characters. In the rough and simple fashion of those days they must have invented the first mask by covering their feet, legs and thighs with goat skins which they must have had at hand, and painting their breasts and faces with the lees of wine and fitting their foreheads with horns (on which account perhaps in our own day the vintagers are still vulgarly called "horned," *cornuti*). In this sense it may well be true that Bacchus, god of the vintage, commanded Aeschylus to compose tragedies. All of which accords well with the times when the heroes were asserting that the plebeians were monsters of two

natures, half man, half goat, as we have fully set forth above. Thus there is strong ground for conjecture that tragedy had its beginnings in this chorus of satyrs and that it took its name from the primitive mask we have described, rather than from the award of a *tragos* or goat to the winner in a competition in this sort of verse. (Horace glances at this latter possibility without making anything of it, and calls the goat paltry.) And the satire preserved this eternal property with which it was born: that of expressing invective and insult; for the peasants, thus roughly masked and riding in the carts in which they carried the grapes, had the license—as the vintagers still have in our happy Campania (once called the dwelling of Bacchus)—of hurling abuse at their betters. Hence we may understand with how little truth the learned later inserted into the fable of Pan (for *pan* signifies "all") the philosophical mythology to the effect that he signifies the universe, and that the hairy nether parts mean the earth, the red breast and face the element of fire and the horns the sun and the moon. The Romans, however, preserved for us the historical mythology concerning him in the word *satyra,* which, according to Festus, was a dish made of various kinds of foods. Hence the later expression *lex per satyram* for an omnibus law. So, in dramatic satire, which we are discussing here, according to Horace (for no examples of this form have come down to us either from the Greeks or from the Latins) various types of characters made their appearance, such as gods, heroes, kings, artisans and slaves. But the satire that survived among the Romans does not treat of varied matters, since each poem is devoted to a separate argument.

911   Then Aeschylus brought about the transition from the Old Tragedy, that is the satyr play, to Middle Tragedy by using human masks and by converting the dithyramb of Amphion, which was a chorus of satyrs, into a chorus of men. And Middle Tragedy must have been the origin of Old Comedy, in which great personages were portrayed and the chorus was therefore fitting. Afterwards came first Sophocles and then Euripides, who left us the final form of tragedy. The Old Comedy ended with Aristophanes, because of the scandal about Socrates; and Menander bequeathed us the New Comedy, built around private and fictitious personages, who could be fictitious because they were private, and could therefore be believed to be real, as we have explained above. Hence there was no longer any room for the chorus, which is a public that comments and comments only on public matters.

912   In this way the satire was composed in heroic verse, as the Latins afterwards preserved it, because the first peoples spoke in heroic verse. Later they spoke in iambic verse, so that tragedy was composed in iambic verse quite naturally, and comedy only by an empty adherence to precedent when the Greek peoples were already speaking in prose. The iambic meter was certainly appropriate to tragedy, for it is a verse born to give vent to anger, and its movement is that of what Horace calls a swift foot (as noted in an axiom [233]). Vulgar tradition says that it was invented by Archilochus to vent his wrath against Lycambes, who had refused to give him his daughter in marriage, and that the

bitterness of his verses drove father and daughter to hang themselves in despera-
tion. This must have been a history of the heroic contest over *connubium,* in
which the rebellious plebeians must have hanged the nobles along with their
daughters.

913   So was born that monstrosity of poetic art by which the same violent,
rapid and excited verse is made to fit such grand poetry as that of tragedy, considered by Plato even more lofty than the epic, and at the same time such delicate
poetry as that of comedy; and the same metric foot, well adapted, as we have
said, to express wrath and rage, in which tragedy must break forth so fearfully,
is considered equally good as a vehicle for jests, games and sentimental love
affairs, which must make up all the grace and charm of comedy.

914   As a result of the indiscriminate use of the terms lyric and tragic,
Hippocrates was placed in the time of the Seven Sages; but he should rather be
put about the time of Herodotus, since he came at a time when men still spoke
largely in fables (for his own life has a tinge of the fabulous, and Herodotus's
History is largely narrated in the form of fables), yet not only had speech in
prose been introduced but also writing in vulgar characters, in which Herodotus
wrote his history and Hippocrates wrote the many works on medicine that have
come down to us, as we have already said above.

BOOK FOUR

THE COURSE OF NATIONS

[INTRODUCTION]

915   In virtue of the principles of this Science established in the first book, and of the origins of all the divine and human things of the gentile world which we investigated and discovered in the second book, and of the discovery in the third book that the poems of Homer are two great treasure stores of the natural law of the nations of Greece (just as we had already found the Law of the Twelve Tables to be a great monument of the natural law of the nations of Latium), we shall now, by the aid of this philosophical and philological illumination, and relying on the Axioms above stated concerning the ideal eternal history [241–245], in this fourth book discuss the course the nations take, proceeding in all their various and diverse customs with constant uniformity upon the division of the three ages which the Egyptians said had elapsed before them in their world, namely, the successive ages of gods, heroes and men. For the nations will be seen to develop in conformity with this division by a constant and uninterrupted order of causes and effects present in every nation, through three kinds of natures. From these natures arise three kinds of customs; and in virtue of these customs three kinds of natural laws of nations are observed; and in consequence of these laws three kinds of civil states or commonwealths are established. And in order that men, having reached the stage of human society, may on the one hand communicate to each other the aforesaid three most important matters [customs, laws, commonwealths], three kinds of languages and as many of characters are formed; and in order that they may on the other hand justify them, three kinds of jurisprudence assisted by three kinds of authority and three kinds of reason in as many of judgments. The three kinds of jurisprudence prevail in three sects of times, which the nations profess in the course of their history. These [groups of] three special unities, with many others that derive from them and will also be enumerated in this book, all lead to one general unity. This is the unity of the religion of a provident divinity, which is the unity of the spirit informing and giving life to this world of nations. Having discussed these matters above in fragmentary fashion, we shall here exhibit the order of their development.

[SECTION I]

THREE KINDS OF NATURES

916   The first nature, by an illusion of imagination, which is most robust in those weakest in reasoning power, was a poetic or creative nature which we may be allowed to call divine, as it ascribed to physical things the being of substances animated by gods, assigning the gods to them according to its idea of each. This nature was that of the theological poets, who were the earliest wise men in all the gentile nations, when all the gentile nations were founded on the belief which each of them had in certain gods of its own. Furthermore it was a nature all fierce and cruel; but, through that same error of their imagination, men had a terrible fear of the gods whom they themselves had created. From this period there remained two eternal properties: one, that religion is the only means powerful enough to restrain the fierceness of peoples; and the other, that religions prosper when those who preside over them are themselves inwardly reverent.

917   The second was the heroic nature, believed by the heroes themselves to be of divine origin; for, since they believed that the gods made everything, they held themselves to be children of Jove, as having been generated under his auspices. Being thus of the human [not a bestial] species, they regarded their heroism as including the natural nobility in virtue of which they were the princes of the human race. And this natural nobility they made their boast over those who had fled from the infamous and bestial communism to save themselves from the strife it entailed, and had taken refuge in their asylums; for, since they had come thither without gods, the heroes regarded them as beasts. We have discussed these two natures above.

918   The third was human nature, intelligent and hence modest, benign and reasonable, recognizing for laws conscience, reason and duty.

[SECTION II]

THREE KINDS OF CUSTOMS

919   The first customs were all tinged with religion and piety, like those of Deucalion and Pyrrha, fresh from the flood.

920   The second were choleric and punctilious, like those related of Achilles.

921   The third are dutiful, taught by one's own sense of civil duty.

[SECTION III]

THREE KINDS OF NATURAL LAW

922 The first law was divine, for men believed themselves and all their property to depend on the gods, since they thought everything was a god or was made or done by a god.

923 The second was heroic law, the law of force, but controlled by religion, which alone can keep force within bounds where there are no human laws or none strong enough to curb it. Hence providence ordained that the first peoples, ferocious by nature, should be persuaded by this their religion to acquiesce naturally in force, and that, being as yet incapable of reason, they should measure right by fortune, with a view to which they took counsel by auspicial divination. This law of force is the law of Achilles, who referred every right to the tip of his spear.

924 The third is the human law dictated by fully developed human reason.

[SECTION IV]

THREE KINDS OF GOVERNMENTS

925   The first were divine, or, as the Greeks would say, theocratic, in which men believed that everything was commanded by the gods. This was the age of oracles, which are the earliest thing we read of in history.

926   The second were heroic or aristocratic governments, which is as much as to say governments of the optimates in the sense of the most powerful. In Greek they were called governments of Heraclids (men sprung from the race of Hercules), in the sense of nobles; these were scattered throughout early Greece, and survived at Sparta. They were also called governments of Curetes, which the Greeks found scattered in Saturnia (ancient Italy), Crete and Asia; and hence governments of Quirites among the Romans, that is of armed priests in public assembly. In governments of this kind, in virtue of the distinction of a nobler nature ascribed to divine origin, as we have noted above, all civil rights were confined to the ruling orders of the heroes themselves, and the plebeians, being considered of bestial origin, were only permitted to enjoy life and natural liberty.

927   The third are human governments, in which, in virtue of the equality of the intelligent nature which is the proper nature of man, all are accounted equal under the laws, inasmuch as all are born free in their cities. This is the case in the free popular cities in which all or the majority make up the just forces of the city, in virtue of which they are the lords of popular liberty. It is also the case in monarchies, in which the monarchs make all their subjects equal under their laws, and, having all the force of arms in their own hands, are themselves the only bearers of any distinction in civil nature.

[SECTION V]

THREE KINDS OF LANGUAGES

928   Three kinds of languages.

929   The first of these was a divine mental language by mute religious acts or divine ceremonies, from which there survived in Roman civil law the *actus legitimi* which accompanied all their civil transactions. This language belongs to religions by the eternal property that it concerns them more to be reverenced than to be reasoned, and it was necessary in the earliest times when men did not yet possess articulate speech.

930   Th second was by heroic blazonings, with which arms are made to speak; this kind of speech, as we have said above, survived in military discipline.

931   The third is by articulate speech, which is used by all nations today.

[SECTION VI]

THREE KINDS OF CHARACTERS

932   Three kinds of characters.

933   The first were divine, properly called hieroglyphics, used, as we have shown above, by all nations in their beginnings. And they were certain imaginative universals, dictated naturally by the human mind's innate property of delighting in the uniform (on which we set forth an axiom [204]). When they could not achieve this by logical abstraction, they did it by imaginative representation. To these poetic universals they reduced all the particular species belonging to each genus, as to Jove everything concerning the auspices, to Juno everything touching marriage, and so on.

934   The second were heroic characters, which were also imaginative universals to which they reduced the various species of heroic things, as to Achilles all the deeds of valiant fighters and to Ulysses all the devices of clever men. These imaginative genera, as the human mind later learned to abstract forms and properties from subjects, passed over into intelligible genera, which prepared the way for the philosophers, from whom the authors of the New Comedy, which came in the most civilized times of Greece, took the intelligible genera of human customs and portrayed them in their comedies.

935   Finally, there were invented the vulgar characters which went along with the vulgar languages. The latter are composed of words, which are genera as it were of the particulars previously employed by the heroic languages; as, to repeat an example cited above, from the heroic phrase "the blood boils in my heart" they made the word "I am angry." In like fashion, of a hundred and twenty thousand hieroglyphic characters (the number still used, for example, by the Chinese) they made a few letters, to which, as to genera, they reduced the hundred and twenty thousand words (of which the Chinese vulgar spoken language is composed). This invention certainly is the work of a mind more than human; whence, as we learned above, Bernard von Mallinckrodt and Ingewald Eling held it to be a divine invention. It is easy to understand how the common sense of marvel led the nations to believe that men eminent in divinity had invented these letters, as St. Jerome among the Illyrians, St. Cyril

among the Slavs, and so on, as Angelo Roccha observes in his *Bibliotheca Vaticana,* where the authors of what we call vulgar letters are depicted along with their alphabets. But such an opinion can be convicted of manifest falsity if we pose the simple question: Why did they not teach letters of their own creation? We have raised this difficulty in the case of Cadmus above, who brought letters from Phoenicia to the Greeks, and the latter afterwards used letters of very different forms from the Phoenician.

936   Above we affirmed that such languages and letters were under the sovereignty of the vulgar of the various peoples, whence both are called vulgar. In virtue of this sovereignty over languages and letters, the free peoples must also be masters of their laws, for they impose on the laws the senses in which they constrain the powerful to observe them, even against their will, as we noted in the Axioms [283]. It is naturally not in the power of monarchs to deprive the people of this sovereignty, but, in virtue of this very inalienable nature of human civil affairs, such sovereignty, inseparable from the people, contributes largely to the power of the monarchs, for they may issue their royal laws, which the nobles must accept, according to the senses that their peoples give to them. This sovereignty over vulgar letters and languages implies that, in the order of civil nature, the free popular commonwealths preceded the monarchies.

[SECTION VII]

THREE KINDS OF JURISPRUDENCE

937   Three kinds of jurisprudence or [legal] wisdom.

938   The first was a divine wisdom, called, as we have seen, mystic theology, which means the science of divine speech or the understanding of the divine mysteries of divination. This science of auspicial divinity was the vulgar wisdom whose sages were the theological poets, who were the first sages of the gentile world. From this mystic theology they were called *mystai* or mystics, which the well-informed Horace translates as interpreters of the gods. To this first jurisprudence therefore belonged the first and proper interpreting, called *interpretari* for *interpatrari*, that is, "to enter into the fathers," as the gods were at first called as we observed above. Dante would call it *indiarsi*, "to enter into the mind of God." This sort of jurisprudence measured justice only by the solemnity of the divine ceremonies, whence the Romans preserved such a superstitious regard for the *actus legitimi* and they retained in their language the phrases *iustae nuptiae, iustum testamentum* for solemnized nuptials and testaments.

939   The second was the heroic jurisprudence, taking precautions by the use of certain proper words. Such is the wisdom of Ulysses who speaks so adroitly in Homer that he obtains the advantages he seeks while always observing the propriety of his words. Hence all the reputation of the ancient Roman jurisconsults rested in their *cavere*, their taking care or making sure; and their *de iure respondere* was nothing but cautioning clients who had to present their cases in court to set forth the facts to the praetor with such circumstances that the formulae for action would be satisfied and the praetor would be unable to withhold them. Similarly in the returned barbarian times all the reputation of the doctors rested on finding safeguards for contracts and wills and on knowing how to draw up pleas at law and articles; which correspond exactly to the *cavere* and the *de iure respondere* of the Roman jurisconsults.

940   The third is human jurisprudence, which looks to the truth of the facts themselves and benignly bends the rule of law to all the requirements of the equity of the causes. This kind of jurisprudence is observed in the free popular

commonwealths and even more under the monarchies, which are both human governments.

941   Thus divine and heroic jurisprudence laid hold of the certain when the nations were rude, and human jurisprudence looked to the true when they had become enlightened. All this in consequence of the definitions of the certain and the true, and of the axioms set forth on the matter in our Elements [137, 138, 321, 324].

[SECTION VIII]

THREE KINDS OF AUTHORITY

942   There were three kinds of authority. The first is divine, and of this we ask no accounting by providence. The second is heroic, resting entirely on the solemn formulae of the laws. The third is human, based on the trust placed in persons of experience, of singular prudence in practical matters, and of sublime wisdom in intellectual matters.

943   These three kinds of authority employed by jurisprudence in the course which the nations take, correspond to three sorts of authority appertaining to senates, which succeed one another in the aforesaid course.

944   The first was the authority of property ownership, in virtue of which those from whom we derive title to property were called *auctores,* and such ownership is itself always called *auctoritas* in the Law of the Twelve Tables. This authority had its roots in divine governments from the time of the family state, in which divine authority must have been vested in the gods, for it was believed, fairly enough, that everything belonged to the gods. Afterwards in the heroic aristocracies in which the senates were the seat of sovereignty (as they are in the aristocracies of our own time), authority quite properly was vested in these reigning senates. Hence the heroic senates gave their approval to that which the peoples had previously devised; as Livy puts it, *eius, quod populus iussisset, deinde patres fierent auctores.* This does not, however, date from the interregnum of Romulus, as history relates, but from the declining period of the aristocracy when citizenship had been extended to the plebs, as explained above. This arrangement, as Livy himself says, *saepe spectabat ad vim,* frequently threatened to issue in revolt; so that, if the people wanted their proposals confirmed, they had, for example, to nominate for consuls those who were favored by the senate, just as is the case when magistrates are nominated by the people under monarchies.

945   From the time of the law of Publilius Philo, which declared the Roman people free and absolute sovereign of the empire, as stated above, the authority of the senate was that of guardianship, just as the approval given by guardians to the transactions of their wards, who are masters of their own

patrimonies, is called *auctoritas tutorum.* This [tutorial] authority was conferred by the senate on the people in the formula of the law drafted beforehand in the senate, by which, just as the authority of the guardian has to be conferred on the ward, so the senate was to be present in the people, present in the great assemblies, present in the act of decreeing the law if they decided to decree it; otherwise they might reject ("antiquate") it, *probaret antiqua,* that is, declare that they wished no change. All this in order that the people, in decreeing the laws, might not, by reason of their weak counsel, do any harm to the commonwealth, and in order that, in decreeing them, they might be regulated by the senate. Thus the formulae of the laws brought by the senate to the people to be decreed by them are advisedly defined by Cicero as *perscriptae auctoritates:* not personal authorizations, like that of guardians who by their presence approve the acts of their wards, but authority set out at length in writing (for such is the sense of *perscribere*), as distinguished from the formulae of actions, written *per notas* or employing abbreviations which are not understood by the people. This is what was ordained by the Publilian law: that henceforth the authority of the senate, in Livy's words, *valeret in incertum comitiorum eventum,* should be committed while the outcome in the assembly is as yet uncertain.

946   Finally the commonwealth passed from popular liberty to monarchy, and there ensued the third kind of authority, which is that of credit or reputation for wisdom; and hence the authority of counsel, in respect of which the jurisconsults under the emperors were said to be *auctores.* Such also must be the authority of senates under monarchs, who have full and absolute liberty to follow or not to follow the counsel their senates give them.

[SECTION IX]

THREE KINDS OF REASON

[CHAPTER I]

[DIVINE REASON AND REASON OF STATE]

947   There were three kinds of reason.

948   The first is divine and understood only by God; men know of it only what has been revealed to them. To the Hebrews first and then to the Christians, this has been by internal speech to their minds as the proper expression of a God all mind; but [also] by external speech through the prophets and through Jesus Christ to the apostles, by whom it was declared to the Church. To the gentiles it has been through the auspices, the oracles and other corporeal signs regarded as divine messages because they were supposed to come from the gods, whom the gentiles believed to be corporeal. So that in God who is all reason, reason and authority are the same thing; whence in good theology divine authority holds the same place as reason. Here providence is to be admired because, in the earliest times when the men of the gentile world did not understand reason (which must have been the case above all in the family state), it permitted them to fall into the error of following in place of reason the authority of the auspices, and to govern themselves by what they believed to be the divine counsels thereby communicated. This by the eternal property that when men fail to see reason in human affairs, and much more if they see it opposed, they take refuge in the inscrutable counsels hidden in the abyss of divine providence.

949   The second was reason of state, called by the Romans *civilis aequitas*, which Ulpian, as cited above in the Axioms [320], defined for us as not naturally known to all men but only to the few experts in government who are able to discern what is necessary for the preservation of mankind. In this the heroic senates were naturally wise, and above them all the Roman senate was most wise both in the times of aristocratic liberty, when the plebs was not permitted to take part in public affairs, and in the times of popular liberty, so long as the people were guided by the senate in public matters, which is to say down to the times of the Gracchi.

[CHAPTER II]

COROLLARY ON THE POLITICAL WISDOM OF THE ANCIENT ROMANS

950   Here arises a problem which seems very difficult to solve. How is it that the Romans could have been so wise in statecraft in the rude times of Rome, when in their enlightened times Ulpian says that "today only a few experts in government understand statecraft"? The answer is that, by virtue of the same natural causes which produced the heroism of the first peoples, the ancient Romans, who were the heroes of the world, naturally looked to civil equity, which was most scrupulous about the words in which the laws were expressed. By this superstitious observance of their words, they made the laws march straight through all the facts, even where the laws turned out to be severe, harsh and cruel (in accordance with what we have said above), just as reason of state operates today. Thus civil equity naturally subordinated everything to that law, queen of all others, conceived by Cicero with a gravity adequate to the matter: *Suprema lex populi salus esto,* "Let the safety of the people be the supreme law." For in heroic times, in which the states were aristocratic, as we have fully shown above, the heroes each possessed privately a large share of the public utility in the form of the family monarchies preserved for them by the fatherland; and in view of this great particular interest preserved for them by the commonwealth, they naturally subordinated their minor private interests. Hence naturally as magnanimous men they defended the public good, which is that of the state, and as wise men they gave counsel on affairs of state. This was a high counsel of divine providence, for the cyclopic fathers (such as we have found them in Homer and Plato), if they had not had such a great private interest identified with that of the state, could not have been induced to abandon their savage life in favor of civilization, as we have already observed above.

951   It is quite otherwise in the human times in which free popular states or monarchies develop. In the former the citizens have command of the public wealth, which is divided among them in as many minute parts as there are citizens making up the people who have command of it. In the second the subjects are commanded to look after their own private interests and leave the care of the public interest to the sovereign prince. To this we must add the natural causes which produced these forms of state (which are quite opposite to those which had produced heroism); namely, as we have shown above, love of ease, tenderness toward children, love of women and desire for life. By reason of all this, men are today naturally led to attend to the smallest details which may bring their private utilities into equality with those of others. This is the *aequum bonum* considered by the third kind of reason to be discussed here, namely, natural reason, which is called *aequitas naturalis* by the jurisconsults. This is the only reason of which the multitude are capable, for, when they are themselves involved, they attend to the smallest considerations of the justice which is called for by cases when the facts are reduced to their individual species. And in monarchies there are needed a few men skilled in statecraft to give counsel according to civil equity on public emergencies in the cabinets, and a great many jurists of private jurisprudence to administer justice to the peoples by professing natural equity.

[CHAPTER III]

COROLLARY: FUNDAMENTAL HISTORY OF ROMAN LAW

952   What has here been set forth concerning the three kinds of reason may serve as a foundation on which to establish the history of Roman law. For governments must conform to the nature of the governed, as we have laid down above in an axiom [246]; inasmuch as the governments are born of the nature of the governed, as has been shown above by our Principles. So too the laws must be administered in conformity with the governments, and on that account must be interpreted according to the form of the governments. (This seems not to have been done by any of the jurisconsults or interpreters, who have fallen into the same error into which the historians of Roman affairs had previously fallen. The latter tell of laws decreed at various times in the Roman commonwealth but fail to point out the relations which these laws must have had to the forms of government through which that commonwealth passed. Hence the facts emerge so denuded of the proper causes which must naturally have produced them, that Jean Bodin, equally learned as jurist and as statesman, argues that the things done by the ancient Romans in the period of the liberty which the historians falsely describe as popular were instead the effects of an aristocratic commonwealth, as in the present work we have shown to be the fact.) In view of all this, if all the embellishers of the history of Roman law are asked: Why did the old jurisprudence practice such rigors in applying the Law of the Twelve Tables? Why did the middle jurisprudence, by the edicts of the praetors, begin to exercise a benignity of reason while still respecting that Law? Why did the new jurisprudence, without even a pretense of regard for that Law, adopt the generous profession of natural equity?—then, in order to give an explanation of some kind, they put forward one which is very offensive to Roman generosity, for they say that the rigors, the solemnities, the scruples, the verbal subtleties and

finally the secrecy of the laws themselves were impostures on the part of the nobles in order to keep the laws in their own hands, for the reason that the laws make up a great part of civil power.

953 Yet these practices were so far from being impostures that they were customs born of their very natures, which through such customs produced such states as naturally dictated such practices and no others. For in the time of the extreme savagery of earliest mankind, when religion was the only means sufficiently powerful to tame it, providence, as we have seen above, ordained that men should live under divine governments and that the laws everywhere reigning should be sacred, which is as much as to say mysterious and hidden from the masses of the peoples. The laws in the state of the families were so naturally of this sort that they were preserved in mute languages expressed in consecrated solemnities (which survived in the *actus legitimi*), which those simple minds held necessary to assure one man of the effective will of another in the exchange of utilities, whereas now, in the natural intelligence of our minds, it is sufficient to assure oneself by the spoken word or even by mere gestures. Then came the human governments of aristocratic civil states, and, naturally continuing to practice the religious customs, they religiously continued to keep the laws mysterious and secret (this secrecy being the soul and life of aristocratic commonwealths), and religion insured the strict observance of the laws which is the rigor of civil equity by which aristocracies are principally preserved. Afterwards, when the time came for popular commonwealths, which are naturally open, generous and magnanimous (being commanded by the multitude, whom we have shown to be naturally intent on natural equity), the so-called vulgar languages and letters (of which, as we said above, the multitude are masters) developed at the same pace, and in these they ordered that the laws be written down, and thus what had been secret came naturally to be published. This is [the history of] the *ius latens* of which Pomponius relates that the Roman plebs would have no more of it and hence insisted that the laws be inscribed on tablets, since vulgar letters had come from the Greeks to Rome, as noted above. This order of civil human things was finally found ready for the monarchic states, in which the monarchs wish the laws administered according to natural equity and consequently in harmony with the understanding of the multitude, and thus make the powerful and the weak equal before the law, which monarchy alone can do. And civil equity or reason of state was understood by a few men wise in public reason, and, by virtue of its eternal property, is preserved secret within cabinets.

[SECTION X]

THREE KINDS OF JUDGMENTS

[CHAPTER I]

[FIRST KIND: DIVINE JUDGMENTS]

954   There were three kinds of judgments.

955   The first were divine judgments. In the so-called state of nature (which was that of the families), as there were no civil authorities ruling by law, the family fathers complained to the gods of the wrongs done them (which was the first and proper meaning of the phrase *implorare deorum fidem*) and called the gods to bear witness to the justice of their causes (the first and proper meaning of *deos obtestari*). Such accusations and defenses were the world's first orations, in the primary and proper sense of that word, and *oratio* continued to be used in Latin for accusation or defense. There are fine examples of this usage in Plautus and Terence, and the Law of the Twelve Tables preserved two golden passages in which *furto orare* and *pacto orare* (not *adorare,* which is Lipsius's reading) are used respectively for *agere* and *excipere,* "to bring suit" and "to enter an exception." From these orations the term *oratores* survived in Latin for those who plead cases in court. The original appeals to the gods were made by simple and rude people in the belief that they were heard by the gods whom they imagined to dwell on the tops of the mountains, as Homer places them on Olympus; and Tacitus tells of a war waged between the Hermunduri and the Chatti under the superstition that, except from the mountain tops, mortal prayers are nowhere more closely listened to by the gods—*preces mortalium nusquam propius audiri*—[than at the river between these two peoples].

956   The rights secured by these divine judgments were themselves gods, for in those times the gentiles imagined that all things were gods. For example, *Lar* was the ownership of the household; *dii Hospitales,* the right of shelter; *dii Penates,* the paternal power; *deus Genius,* the right of marriage; *deus Terminus,* the ownership of the farm; *dii Manes,* the right of burial. Of the last, a golden vestige survived in the Law of the Twelve Tables: *ius deorum manium.*

957   After such orations (or obsecrations or implorations) and after such obtestations, they proceeded to the act of execrating the criminals. Hence among the Greeks, as was certainly the case at Argos, there were temples of execration, and the execrated men were called *anathēmata,* or, as we say, excommunicates. And against them they made vows (this was the first *nuncupare vota,* which means to make solemn vows with consecrated formulae) and they consecrated them to the Furies (who were truly *diris devoti*) and then killed them. (The custom of the Scythians, as we noted above, was to fix a knife in the ground, adore it as a god and then kill the man with it.) This kind of execution the Latins called *mactare,* which remained a sacred term used in sacrifices; this is the source of the Spanish *matar* and the Italian *ammazzare,* to kill. We saw above that among the Greeks *ara* remained in the senses of "harmful body," "vow," and "fury," and among the Latins it meant both "altar" and "victim." Some kind of excommunication survived among all nations. Caesar left us a detailed account of the Gallic ceremony, and the interdict of fire and water was preserved among the Romans, as set forth above. Many of these consecrations passed into the Law of the Twelve Tables; for example, he who violated a tribune of the plebs was "consecrated to Jove"; an impious son was "consecrated to the gods of the fathers"; he who set fire to another's grain was "consecrated to Ceres" and burned alive. Such must have been those whom Plautus called Saturn's victims, *Saturni hostiae.* It may be seen that the cruelty of these divine punishments was like that mentioned in the Axioms [190] as characteristic of the cruelest witches.

958   From the practice of these judgments in private affairs, the peoples went forth to wage wars which were called pure and pious, *pura et pia bella,* and they waged them *pro aris et focis,* "for altar and hearth"; that is, for civil concerns both public and private, for they regarded all human things as divine. Hence the heroic wars were all wars of religion, and the heralds, in delivering a declaration of war, called forth the gods from the enemy city, and consecrated the enemy to the gods. Wherefore defeated kings were presented by the triumphant Romans to Jove Feretrius on the Capitoline and thereafter slain, after the pattern of the impious violent who had been the first hosts, the first victims, which Vesta had consecrated on the first altars of the world. And the surrendered peoples were considered men without gods, after the pattern of the first *famuli;* whence slaves, like inanimate things, were called *mancipia* in the Roman language, and in Roman jurisprudence they were held *in loco rerum.*

[CHAPTER II]

COROLLARY ON DUELS AND REPRISALS

959 One sort of divine judgments, in the barbarous period of the nations, were duels, which must have begun under the earliest government of the gods and continued for a long time under the heroic commonwealths. Concerning the latter we cited in the Axioms [269] the golden passage in Aristotle's *Politics* where he says that these commonwealths had no judiciary laws for punishing private wrongs and making restitution for private injuries. Until now this has not been believed, because of the false opinion hitherto held by the conceit of scholars concerning the philosophic heroism of the first peoples which was supposed to follow from the matchless wisdom of the ancients.

960 Certainly among the Romans the interdict *Unde vi* and the actions *De vi bonorum raptorum* and *Quod metus caussa* were introduced late and only by the praetor, as we have already noted. And in the return of barbarism private reprisals lasted down to the time of Bartolus. Such must have been the condictions or personal actions of the ancient Romans, for *condicere,* according to Festus, means to denounce or serve notice. (Thus a family father had to make formal demand for restitution on one who had unjustly taken from him something that belonged to him, in order to proceed to reprisals.) Such a denunciation remained a formality of personal actions, as Ulrich Zasius acutely discerned.

961 But duels contained real judgments, which, because they took place *re praesenti,* had no need of the formal denunciation. From these developed the *vindiciae,* in which a clod taken from the wrongful possessor with a feigned show of force, which Aulus Gellius calls *festucaria,* of straw (but the name *vindiciae* must have come from the real force originally used), was taken to the judge, before whom the claimant spoke over the *gleba* or clod the words: *Aio hunc fundum meum esse ex iure quiritium,* "I declare this farm to be mine by the law of the Quirites." Hence those who write that duels were introduced for lack of proofs are wrong; they should say rather for lack of judiciary laws. For certainly Frotho, king of Denmark, ordered that all disputes should be settled by duels, thereby forbidding their settlement by legitimate judgments. And, to avoid litigation, the laws of the Lombards, Salians, Englishmen, Burgundians, Normans, Danes and Germans are all alike full of duels. On this account Cujas in his *De feudis* says: *Et hoc genere purgationis diu usi sunt christiani tam in civilibus quam in criminalibus caussis, re omni duello commissa:* "Christians made use of this sort of purgation for a long time in both civil and criminal cases, everything being settled by duel." From this it came about that those who

are called *Ritter* or knights in Germany profess the science of dueling and oblige the prospective adversaries to tell the truth; for duels, if witnesses were admitted and consequently judges had to intervene, would come under either civil or criminal judgments.

962   It has not been believed that the first barbarism practiced dueling, because no record of it has come down to us. But it passes our understanding how the Homeric Cyclopes, in whom Plato recognizes the earliest family fathers in the state of nature, can have endured being wronged, to say nothing of showing humanity in the matter. Certainly Aristotle, as cited in the Axioms [269], tells us that in the earliest commonwealths, not to speak of the still earlier state of the families, there were no laws to right wrongs and punish offenses suffered by private citizens (as we have just proved was the case in the ancient Roman commonwealth); and therefore Aristotle also tells us, as cited in the same place, that this was the custom of barbarous peoples, for, as we noted in that connection, peoples are barbarous in their beginnings because they are not yet chastened by laws.

963   However, there are two great vestiges of such duels, one from Greek and one from Roman history, showing that the peoples must have begun their wars (called *duella* by the ancient Latins) with combats between the offended individuals, even if they were kings, waged in the presence of their respective peoples whom they wished publicly to defend or avenge their offenses. In this fashion certainly the Trojan war began with the combat of Menelaus and Paris (the former the wronged husband and the latter the seducer of his wife Helen); and when the duel was indecisive the Greeks and Trojans proceeded to wage war with each other. And we have already noted the same custom among the Latin nations in the war between the Romans and the Albans, which was effectively settled by the combat between the three Horatii and the three Curiatii, one of whom must have abducted Horatia. In such armed judgments right was measured by the fortune of victory. This was a counsel of divine providence, to the end that, among barbarous peoples with little capacity for reason and no understanding of justice, wars might not breed further wars, and that they might thus have some notion of the justice or injustice of men from the favor or disfavor of the gods: even as the gentiles scorned the saintly Job when he had fallen from his royal estate because God was against him. And on the same principle in the returned barbarian times the barbarous custom was to cut off the hand of the loser, however just his cause.

964   From this sort of custom observed by the peoples in private affairs, there emerged what the moral theologians call the external justice of wars, whereby the nations might rest in the certainty of their dominions. In this fashion the auspices which had founded the monarchical paternal authority of the fathers in the state of the families, and had prepared and preserved for them their aristocratic reigns in the heroic cities, and which, when shared with the

plebs, produced the free popular commonwealths (as Roman history openly relates), finally legitimized by the fortune of arms the conquests of the lucky victors. All this can have no other source than the innate concept of providence which all nations possess and to which they must bow when they see the just afflicted and the wicked prospering, as we have said before in the Idea of the Work.

[CHAPTER III]

[SECOND KIND: ORDINARY JUDGMENTS]

965   The second kind of judgments, because of their recent origin from divine judgments, were all ordinary, observed with an extreme verbal scrupulousness which must have carried over from the previous divine judgments the name *religio verborum,* even as divine things are universally conceived in sacred formulae which cannot be altered by as much as one little letter; whence it was said of the ancient formulae for actions:; *qui cadit virgula, caussa cadit,* "he who drops a comma loses his case." This is the natural law of heroic nations, observed naturally by ancient Roman jurisprudence; and it was the praetor's *fari,* which was an unalterable utterance, from which the days on which he dispensed justice were called *dies fasti.* This justice, because only the heroes shared in it under the heroic aristocracies, must have been the *fas deorum* of the times in which, as we have explained above, the heroes had taken to themselves the name of gods; whence later the name *Fatum* was given to the ineluctable order of causes producing the things of nature, as being the utterance of God. Hence perhaps the Italian verb *ordinare,* as applied especially to laws, in the sense of giving commands which must necessarily be carried out.

966   In virtue of this order (which in connection with judgments signifies the solemn formula for an action), that had dictated the cruel and shameful punishment against the illustrious defendant Horatius, the duumvirs themselves could not have absolved him even had he been found innocent, and the people, to whom he appealed, absolved him, as Livy tells us, *magis admiratione virtutis quam iure caussae,* "rather because of admiration of his valor than because of the justice of his cause." This order of judgments was necessary in the times of Achilles, who measured all right by force, in virtue of that property of the powerful described by Plautus with his usual elegance: *pactum non pactum, non pactum pactum*—"an agreement is no agreement, and no agreement is an agreement"—where promises are not fulfilled according to their proud desires or where they themselves are not willing to keep their promises. So, in

order that they should not break out into disputes, quarrels and killings, it was a counsel of providence that they should naturally adopt as their notion of justice that precisely such and so much was their right as had been set forth in solemn verbal formulae; whence the reputation of Roman jurisprudence and of our own ancient [i.e. medieval] doctors lay in safeguarding their clients. This natural law of heroic nations provided Plautus with plots for several comedies, in which panders, through deceptions devised against them by young men enamored of their slave girls, are unjustly defrauded of the girls by being innocently found guilty under some legal formula, and not only are they unable to bring an action for fraud, but one of them reimburses the deceitful youth for the price of the slave, another begs another youth to be content with half the penalty he has incurred for theft not proved by direct evidence, another flies the city for fear of being convicted for having corrupted another's slave. Such was the reign of natural equity in the judgments of Plautus's times!

967   Not only was this strict law naturally observed among men, but, judging the gods from their own natures, men thought that they too observed it in their oaths. So Homer relates that Juno swears to Jove, who is not only witness but also judge in the matter of oaths, that she had not urged Neptune to rouse up a tempest against the Trojans, since the god Somnus had acted as her intermediary, and Jove remains satisfied with her oath. So Mercury, disguised as Sosia, swears to the real Sosia, "If I deceive you, let Mercury be against Sosia"; and we can hardly believe that it was Plautus's intention in the *Amphitryon* to bring in the gods to teach perjury to the people in the theater. It is even less credible in the case of Scipio Africanus and Laelius (who was called the Roman Socrates), two most wise princes of the Roman republic with whose collaboration Terence is said to have composed his comedies; yet in the *Andria* Davus is represented as having the baby placed before Simo's door by the hands of Mysis so that if perchance his master should ask him about it, he may with a clear conscience deny having put it there.

968   But a very grave proof is the fact that in Athens, a city of discerning and intelligent men, on hearing the verse of Euripides which Cicero rendered in Latin: *Iuravi lingua, mentem iniuratam habui*—"I swore with my tongue, but my mind I kept unsworn"—the spectators in the theater murmured in disgust, for naturally they held the opinion that *uti lingua nuncupassit, ita ius esto*—"as the tongue has declared, so let it be binding"—as the Law of the Twelve Tables commanded. And what release could the unhappy Agamemnon find from the rash vow in fulfilment of which he consecrated and slew his innocent and pious daughter Iphigenia? Hence we can understand how ingratitude to providence led Lucretius impiously to exclaim upon this deed of Agamemnon: *Tantum religio potuit suadere malorum!*—"So great were the evils religion could prompt!"—as we set forth above in the Axioms [191].

969   In final confirmation of our argument here, we adduce two certain

facts from Roman history and jurisprudence: one, that it was in very late [re-
publican] times that Gallus Aquilius introduced the action *de dolo;* and the
other, that Augustus gave judges discretion to absolve those who had been
tricked or seduced.

970   Being used to this custom in peace, nations defeated in war, according to the terms of surrender, either suffered miserable oppression or by good
fortune mocked the wrath of their conquerors.

971   Miserable oppression was the lot of the Carthaginians, who had
accepted the Roman peace under the provision that they would have left to
them life, their city and their substance. For they understood by the city its buildings, for which sense the Latin word is *urbs,* but the Romans had used the word
civitas, which means the community of citizens. So when in fulfilment of the
peace terms the Carthaginians were commanded to abandon their city on the
coast and retire inland, they refused to obey and took up their arms again in defense. The Romans then declared them rebels, took Carthage and, by the heroic
law of war, barbarously set fire to it. The Carthaginians repudiated the terms of
peace granted them by the Romans, which they had not understood in negotiat-
ing them; for they had become intelligent before their time, partly through
African sharpness and partly through maritime trading which quickens the
wit of nations. But the Romans did not therefore consider that war unjust; for,
excepting a few who regard the Romans as having begun to wage unjust wars
with that against Numantia which was brought to an end by Scipio Africanus,
all agree that they began with the later one against Corinth.

972   A still better proof of what we are arguing is afforded by the returned
barbarian times. When the Emperor Conrad III dictated the terms of surrender to
Weinsberg, whose resistance had been fomented by his rival for the empire, he
specified that only the women should be allowed to come out of the city with
whatever they could carry away on their backs; whereupon the pious women
of Weinsberg came out carrying their children, husbands and fathers. The victorious emperor stood before the city gate, in the very moment of triumph which
is naturally tempting to insolence, and yet restrained his anger (which is terrify-
ing in the great and must be most ominous when caused by impediments to
acquiring or retaining their sovereignty). While the army under his command
stood by with swords drawn and lances in rest, prepared to slaughter the men
of Weinsberg, he looked on and permitted all to pass safely by him whom he
had intended to put to the sword. So far was the natural law of the developed
human reason of Grotius, Selden and Pufendorf from being current by nature
through all times in all nations!

973   All that we have so far set forth, and all that we shall have to say
later, springs from the definitions we have laid down above in the Axioms [321,
324] concerning the truth and the certitude of laws and pacts; and [from the
fact] that the strict law observed in words, which is properly the *fas gentium,* is

as natural in barbarous times as that benign law is in human times which is measured by the equal utility of causes, which should properly be called *fas naturae,* the immutable law of rational humanity which is the true and proper nature of man.

[CHAPTER IV]

[THIRD KIND: HUMAN JUDGMENTS]

974   The third kind of judgments are all extraordinary. In these the governing consideration is the truth of the facts, to which, according to the dictates of conscience, the laws benignly give aid when needed in everything demanded by the equal utility of causes. These are all imbued with natural modesty (which is the child of intelligence) and therefore guaranteed by good faith (the daughter of humanity), which is appropriate to the openness of popular commonwealths and much more to the generosity of monarchies, wherein the monarchs, in these judgments, make it their pride to be above the laws and subject only to God and their conscience. And from these judgments, practiced in modern times during peace, have arisen the three systems of the law of war which we owe to Grotius, Selden and Pufendorf. And Father Nicola Concina, having observed many errors and defects in them, has constructed another system more in conformity with good philosophy and more useful to human society. This system of his, to the glory of Italy, he still teaches in the illustrious university of Padua, in addition to metaphysics, in which he holds the principal chair.

[SECTION XI]

THREE SECTS OF TIMES

[CHAPTER I]

[SECTS OF RELIGIOUS, PUNCTILIOUS AND CIVIL TIMES]

975   All the aforesaid things have been practiced through three sects of times.

976   The first was that of religious times which was observed under the divine governments.

977   The second was that of the punctilious, like Achilles. In the returned barbarian times it was that of the duellists.

978   The third was that of civil or modest times, the times of the natural law of nations, which Ulpian, adding the specific epithet human, calls *ius naturale gentium humanarum*. Hence the Latin writers under the emperors call the duty of subjects *officium civile,* and every offense against natural equity in the interpretation of the laws is called *incivile*. It is the last sect of times in Roman jurisprudence, beginning with the time of popular liberty. Hence the praetors, to accommodate the laws to the Roman nature, customs and government, which had now suffered change, had first of all to soften the severity and temper the rigidity of the Law of the Twelve Tables, which had been decreed when it was natural in the heroic times of Rome. And later the emperors had to remove all the veils in which the praetors had cloaked it and reveal natural equity in all the openness and generosity which was appropriate to the gentleness to which the nations had become accustomed.

979   The jurisconsults accordingly justify their views as to what is just by appealing to the sect of their times, as we may observe. For these [three sects of times] are the proper sects of Roman jurisprudence, in which the Romans concurred with all other nations of the world; sects taught them by divine providence, which the Roman jurisconsults set up as the principle of the natural law of nations; and not the sects of the philosophers, which some learned interpreters of Roman law have forcibly intruded therein, as we have said above in the

Axioms [326-329?]. And the emperors, when they wish to give a reason for their laws or for other orders issued by them, say that they have been guided by the sect of their times, as in the passages collected by Barnabé Brisson in his *De formulis et solemnibus populi Romani verbis*. For the customs of the age are the school of princes, to use the term [*saeculum,* age] applied by Tacitus to the decayed sect of his own times, where he says *corrumpere et corrumpi seculum vocatur*—"they call it the spirit of the age to corrupt and to be corrupted"—or, as we would now say, the fashion.

[SECTION XII]

OTHER PROOFS DRAWN FROM THE PROPERTIES OF THE HEROIC ARISTOCRACIES

[INTRODUCTION]

980   Such a constant and perpetual orderly succession of civil human things, within the strong chain of so many and such various causes and effects as we have observed in the course taken by the nations, should constrain our minds to receive the truth of these principles. But, in order to leave no room for doubt, we shall add the explanation of other civil phenomena which can be explained only by the discovery, made above, of the heroic commonwealths.

[CHAPTER I]

THE SAFEGUARDING OF THE FRONTIERS

981   The two greatest eternal properties of the aristocratic commonwealths, as we have said above, are the guarding of the frontiers and the guarding of the orders.

982   The guarding of the frontiers began to be observed, as we have seen above, by bloody religions under the divine governments, for it was necessary to set up boundaries to the fields in order to put a stop to the infamous sharing of things in the bestial state. On these boundaries were to be fixed the frontiers first of families, then of clans or houses, later of peoples, and finally of nations. Hence the giants, as Polyphemus tells Ulysses, lived separately, each in his own cave with his wife and children, and did not meddle in one another's affairs, thus following the habits of their recent savage origin; and they savagely slew any who entered within their boundaries, as Polyphemus attempted to slay Ulysses and his companions. (In this giant, as we have remarked several times,

Plato discerns the fathers in the state of the families.) From this, as we showed above, the custom was derived whereby the cities for a long period of time looked upon each other as enemies. So much for the harmonious division of the fields described by Hermogenianus the jurisconsult and received in good faith by all interpreters of Roman law. From this first and most ancient principle of human things, with which its subject matter began, it would be reasonable to begin also the doctrine which teaches *De rerum divisione et acquirendo earum dominio*—"Of the classification of things and of acquiring ownership of them." This guarding of the frontiers is naturally practiced in the aristocratic commonwealths, which, as political writers point out, are not established by conquest. But later, when the infamous communism of things had ceased and the boundaries of the peoples were well fixed, came the popular commonwealths which are made for the expansion of empires, and finally the monarchies which are even more efficient in that respect.

983   This and no other must be the reason why the Law of the Twelve Tables did not recognize simple possession, and usucapion in heroic times served to solemnize natural transfers, the best interpreters defining it as *dominii adiectio,* the addition of civil ownership to the natural ownership previously acquired. But afterwards in the time of popular liberty the praetors came to the assistance of bare possession with the interdicts, and usucapion began to be *dominii adeptio,* a way of acquiring civil ownership from the beginning; and while at first cases of possession did not come up for judgment because the praetor took extrajudicial cognizance of them, in accordance with what we have said on the subject above, today the most certain judgments are those called possessory.

984   Thus there came about in the period of popular liberty at Rome a fading, and under the monarchy a complete disappearance, of the distinction between bonitary, quiritary, optimum and civil ownership. Originally these terms carried meanings very different from their present ones. The first meant natural ownership, maintained by perpetual physical possession. The second meant ownership that could be vindicated; it was current among the plebeians, having been extended to them by the nobles in the Law of the Twelve Tables, but a plebeian could vindicate it only by calling in as *auctor* the noble from whom he had acquired title, as we have fully shown above. The third meant ownership free of any encumbrance public or private; it was enjoyed by the patricians among themselves before the establishment of the census which was the basis of popular liberty, as we have said above. The fourth and last meant the ownership belonging to the cities themselves, which today is called eminent domain. The difference between optimum and quiritary ownership had already been obscured in the times of liberty, so that the jurisconsults of the latest period took no account of it. But under the monarchy what is called bonitary ownership (born of bare natural transfer) and the so-called quiritary ownership (born of mancipation or civil conveyance) were quite confused by Justinian in the con-

stitutions *De nudo iure quiritium tollendo* and *De usucapione transformanda,* and the famous distinction between *res mancipi* and *res nec mancipi* was completely obliterated. There remained civil ownership in the sense of ownership yielding an action of *rei vindicatio,* and optimum ownership in the sense of ownership not subject to any private encumbrance.

[CHAPTER II]

THE SAFEGUARDING OF THE ORDERS

985   The guarding of the orders began in divine times from jealousy (the jealousy of Juno, the goddess of solemn matrimony, as noted above) with a view to the certainty of the families as against the nefarious communism of women. Such vigilance is a natural property of the aristocratic commonwealths, desirous of keeping family relationships, successions, and consequently wealth and through it power, within the order of the nobles. On this account testamentary laws were late in appearing among the nations. (Tacitus says that there was no testament among the ancient Germans.) This is the reason why, when King Agis tried to introduce such laws at Sparta, he was strangled by command of the ephors, the custodians of the liberty of the Lacedaemonian nobles, as we have already stated. We may understand from this with how much discernment the embellishers of the Law of the Twelve Tables fixed in the eleventh table the article *Auspicia incommunicata plebi sunto*—"Let the auspices be withheld from the plebs"—for on these originally depended all civil rights both public and private, which were thus all kept within the order of the nobles. The private rights were solemn matrimony, paternal power, *heredes sui,* agnates, gentiles, legitimate succession, testaments and guardianships, as we have set forth above. Thus, after having extended all these rights to the plebs in the first table and thereby established the laws proper to a popular commonwealth, and particularly the testamentary law, they proceed by a single article in the eleventh table to give it a completely aristocratic form. However, in such confusion of things they say this too, which, though a guess on their part, is true: that in the last two tables some ancient customs of the Romans passed into law. This statement verifies the aristocratic nature of the ancient Roman state.

986   Now, to come back to the subject, when the human race was everywhere settled by the solemnizing of matrimony, there appeared the popular commonwealths, and much later the monarchies. In these, as a result of intermarriage with the plebs of the peoples and as a result of testamentary successions, the orders of the nobility were disorganized, and so, little by little, wealth began to pass from the noble houses. For it has been fully shown above that the Roman

plebeians contracted only natural marriages down to the 309th year of Rome, when they finally obtained from the patricians the grant of *connubium* or the right of contracting solemn nuptials; nor in their miserable state, like that of abject slaves as Roman history represents it to us, could they have made any pretension to intermarriage with the nobles. This is one of the most important considerations which led us to say in the first edition of this work that unless we assign these principles to Roman jurisprudence, Roman history is more incredible than the fabulous history of the Greeks, as it has hitherto been related to us. For we could not understand what the latter meant, but we feel instinctively that the former is in direct opposition to the order of human desires. For it shows us men of the basest condition aspiring first to nobility in the struggle over *connubium,* then to honors in the struggle for the consulate, and finally to wealth by laying claim to the high priesthood; whereas, by the eternal common civil nature, men first seek wealth, then honors, and lastly nobility.

987   Thus we are compelled to say that, when the plebeians had won from the nobles the certain ownership of the fields by the Law of the Twelve Tables (which we showed above to be the second agrarian law of the world), as they were still strangers (for such ownership can be granted to strangers), they learned by experience that they could not leave their fields intestate to their kin, for, as they could not contract solemn matrimony, they had no *heredes sui,* agnates or gentiles; much less could they dispose of them by testament, as they were not citizens. And there is no reason to wonder at this, since they were men of little or no intelligence, as is evident from the Furian, Voconian and Falcidian laws, which were all plebiscites; for it took all three of them in order that by the Falcidian law the desired end should finally be achieved, namely that estates should not be absorbed by legacies. Because the plebeians perceived, in the case of those of their number who died during the three years [following the Law of the Twelve Tables], that the fields which had been assigned to them reverted to the nobles by reason of the aforesaid disabilities, they laid claim to *connubium* and thereby to citizenship, as we have explained above. But the grammarians, confused by all the political writers who imagined Rome to have been founded by Romulus with the form of government which cities now have, did not know that the plebs of the heroic cities had been for several centuries considered as foreigners and had therefore contracted only natural marriages among themselves. Hence they did not observe either the factual impropriety or the poor Latinity of taking the historical phrase *plebei tentarunt connubia patrum* as if it read *cum patribus* (after the manner of the marriage laws, such as: *patruus non habet cum fratris filia connubium*), as we have noted above. For, if they had noticed this, they would certainly have understood that the plebeians did not claim the right of intermarrying with the nobles, but the right, which belonged to the nobles, of contracting solemn nuptials.

988   Hence, if we consider legitimate successions as determined by the Law of the Twelve Tables—that the deceased father of a family should be suc-

ceeded in the first place by *heredes sui,* in their default by his agnates, and in defect of these by his gentiles—the Law of the Twelve Tables will seem to have been precisely a Salic Law of the Romans. This law was also observed by Germany in its earliest times (whence we may assume the like for the other first nations of the returned barbarism), and it finally survived in France and Savoy. Baldus, quite agreeably to our thesis, calls this law of succession *ius gentium Gallorum.* By the same token, the Roman law of agnate and gentile successions may rightfully be called *ius gentium romanarum,* with the addition of the epithet *heroicarum,* and, to put it more properly, *romanum.* This would be precisely the *ius quiritium romanorum* which we showed above to have been the natural law common to all the heroic nations.

989   What we have said here about the Salic Law, so far as it excludes women from the royal succession, is not, as may appear, contradicted by the statement that Tanaquil, a woman, governed the Roman kingdom. For that was a heroic phrase to describe a weak-spirited king who allowed himself to be dominated by the crafty Servius Tullius, who invaded the Roman kingdom with the favor of the plebs, on whom he had bestowed the first agrarian law, as shown above. A parallel to the Tanaquil story, with the same heroic manner of speaking, occurred in the returned barbarian times when Pope John was called a woman (against which fable Leo Allacci wrote an entire book) because of the great weakness he showed in yielding to Photius, patriarch of Constantinople, as pointed out by Baronio and after him by de Sponde.

990   Having resolved this difficulty, we may now state that in the same way as the phrase *ius quiritium romanorum* had first been used in the sense of *ius naturale gentium heroicarum romanarum,* just so, when Ulpian under the emperors defines the law current in the free commonwealths and much more under the monarchies, he calls it, weighing his words, *ius naturale gentium humanarum.* And in view of all this the title in the *Institutes* [I.2: *De iure naturali, gentium, et civili*] ought to read, it would seem, *De iure naturali gentium civili,* not only removing with Hermann Vulteius the comma between *naturali* and *gentium* (and with Ulpian supplying *humanarum* in place of the second comma), but suppressing as well the particle *et* before *civili.* For the Romans must have had reference to their own law as they had preserved it from the time of its introduction in the age of Saturn, first by their customs and later by their legislation, just as Varro in his great work *Antiquitates rerum divinarum et humanarum* treated of Roman things with reference to their purely native origins, with no admixture of anything foreign.

991   Now, returning to the Roman heroic successions, we have many strong reasons for doubting that, in ancient Roman times, daughters were exceptions to the exclusion of women. For we have no reason to believe that the hero fathers had any spark of tenderness, but rather many weighty ones to the contrary. The Law of the Twelve Tables called an agnate as remote as the seventh degree in order to exclude an emancipated son from succeeding to his father.

The family fathers had a sovereign right of life and death over their children and hence a despotic dominion over the acquisitions of their sons. They contracted alliances on behalf of their sons in order to bring into their houses women worthy of the family. (This is evidenced by the verb *spondere,* which properly means to promise for another, whence betrothals were called *sponsalia.*) They regarded adoptions in the same light as marriages, as a means of reinforcing decaying families by choosing scions from noble stocks. They regarded emancipation as chastisement or punishment. They had no notion of legitimation, since concubinage was practiced only with freed slaves and foreigners, with whom in heroic times solemn matrimony could not be contracted lest the children degenerate from the nobility of their sires. For the most frivolous reasons, testaments were either null or nullified or broken or of no effect, in order to clear the way for legitimate successions. To such an extent were they naturally dazzled by the brightness of their own private names, whence they were naturally inflamed for the glory of the common name of Roman! All these are customs proper to aristocratic commonwealths such as the heroic commonwealths were, and they are all properties in accord with the heroism of the first peoples.

992   A matter worthy of reflection is this glaring error committed by the erudite embellishers of the Law of the Twelve Tables who assert that it was brought from Athens to Rome: namely that inheritances left intestate by Roman family fathers, during all the time before that Law brought in testamentary and legitimate successions, must have gone under the category of the things called *res nullius.* Providence, on the contrary, in order that the world should not relapse into the infamous communism of things, ordained that the certainty of ownership should be preserved by and through the very form of the aristocratic commonwealths. Hence legitimate successions must naturally have been observed by all the first nations before they had any notion of testaments, which are proper to the popular commonwealths and much more to the monarchies, as indeed Tacitus clearly tells us was the case among the ancient Germans (whose practice gives us reason to assume the same of all the first barbarous peoples). This was the basis for the conjecture we have just made that the Salic Law, which was certainly observed in Germany, was observed universally by the nations in the time of the second barbarism.

993   However, the jurisconsults of the last [period of Roman] jurisprudence, by estimating the things of the unknown earliest times by those of their own quite late times, which is the source of innumerable errors noted in this work, believed that the Law of the Twelve Tables had called the daughters of families to the inheritances of their fathers who had died intestate, in virtue of the word *suus* [in the phrase *sui heredes*], following the rule that the masculine gender includes women also. But heroic jurisprudence, of which we have had so much to say in this work, took the words of the laws in their strictest meaning, so that the word *suus* meant only the son of a family. Invincible proof

of this is afforded by the formula for the institution of posthumous children, introduced many centuries later by Gallus Aquilius, which is phrased *Si quis natus natave erit,* lest from the word *natus* alone it should not be understood that a posthumous daughter is included. Because of his ignorance of these matters, Justinian in the *Institutes* affirms that the Law of the Twelve Tables by the use of the word *adgnatus* had called male and female agnates alike, but that later the middle jurisprudence had made the law more rigid by restricting it to sisters of the same blood. Thus by chance and yet happily this jurisprudence came to be called middle for the reason that, beginning with these cases, it mitigated the rigors of the Law of the Twelve Tables, whereas the ancient jurisprudence which preceded it had guarded its words with the greatest scrupulousness. Both have been fully described above.

994   But when sovereignty had passed from the nobles to the people, since for the plebs all its strength, wealth and power depends on the multitude of its children, the tenderness of blood ties began to make itself felt. Before that the plebeians of the heroic cities cannot have had this feeling, for they generated children to make them slaves of the nobles, by whom indeed they were bidden to propagate at such a time as would result in springtime births so that the young would be born not only healthy but robust. (Hence they were called *vernae,* as the Latin etymologists tell us, and from this name, as we said above, the vulgar tongues were called *vernaculae.*) The mothers must have hated rather than loved their children, for they had only the pain of bearing and the trouble of nursing them, without having from them any joy or profit. But the multitude of the plebeians, while it had been dangerous to the aristocratic commonwealths, which are and profess to be the property of the few, added to the greatness of the popular commonwealths and much more to that of the monarchies (which is why the imperial laws are so favorably disposed to women because of the dangers and pains of childbirth). Hence from the times of popular liberty the praetors began to consider the rights of blood and to satisfy them by means of the *bonorum possessiones.* They began with their remedies to repair the faults and shortcomings of testaments in order to facilitate the diffusion of wealth, which alone is admired by the vulgar.

995   Finally came the emperors, who, taking umbrage at the splendor of the nobles, devoted themselves to promoting the rights of human nature, common to plebeian and noble alike. This began with Augustus, who bent his efforts to the protection of trusteeships (by which formerly property had passed to persons incapable of inheritance thanks only to the conscientiousness of the injured heirs) and gave them such great assistance that within his lifetime he endowed them with legal compulsion, obliging the heirs to give effect to them. A great many *senatusconsulta* followed which placed cognates on a level with agnates. Finally Justinian abolished the distinction between legacies and trusteeships, merged the Falcidian [i.e. Pegasian] fourth [part of an estate reserved to the heir] with the Trebellian, minimized the distinction between testaments and

codicils, and put agnates and cognates on precisely the same footing as regards inheritance *ab intestato*. And the latest Roman laws went to such lengths in favor of last wills that, whereas in ancient times they were declared invalid on the slightest pretext, nowadays they must always be interpreted in such a way as to favor their validity.

996   Because of the humanity of the times (as displayed in the affection of popular commonwealths for their sons and the desire of monarchies to see fathers devoted to their sons), since the cyclopean authority of the family fathers over the persons of their children had already vanished, the emperors sought to do away also with the authority they still had over their acquisitions. To this end, they introduced first the *peculium castrense* to attract young men to war, then extended it to the *peculium quasi castrense* to attract them to the imperial service, and finally, to satisfy the sons who were neither soldiers nor clerks, introduced the *peculium adventitium*. They deprived the paternal power of its influence over adoptions, now no longer restricted to a few close relations. They universally encouraged formal adoptions (*adrogationes*), which were somewhat difficult in that citizens who were family fathers in their own right thereby became subordinate members of others' families. They counted emancipations as benefits. They gave to legitimation by a subsequent marriage all the efficacy of solemn nuptials. But above all, since the *imperium paternum* seemed to detract from their own majesty, they directed that it should be called the *patria potestas*. This was in accordance with their own example, introduced with great sagacity by Augustus; for in order not to arouse the jealousy of the people, who might want to take from him some part of his *imperium,* he assumed the *tribunicia potestas,* thus declaring himself the protector of Roman liberty. In the tribunes of the plebs this had been a *de facto* power, for they had never held *imperium* in the republic. Indeed in the time of Augustus himself, when Labeo was summoned by a tribune of the plebs to appear before him, this prince of one of the two sects of Roman jurisconsults was within his rights in refusing to obey, since the tribunes of the plebs did not have *imperium*. Yet neither grammarians nor jurists nor writers on politics have observed the reason why the patricians, in the contest over extending the consulship to the plebs, in order to satisfy the latter without yielding any part of the *imperium,* hit upon the device of creating the military tribunes, some of them nobles and some of them plebeians, *cum consulari potestate,* as history always puts it, and not *cum imperio consulari,* of which we never read.

997   Hence the free Roman commonwealth was entirely conceived in the triple formula: *senatus auctoritas, populi imperium, tribunorum plebis potestas.* And the two terms *imperium* and *potestas* retained in the laws this original exactness of meaning, the former being ascribed to the major magistrates, such as consuls and praetors, and extended to all who had the right to impose the death penalty, and the latter being ascribed to the minor magistrates such as

the aediles, as it was supported by but modest powers of coercion—*modica coërcitione continetur*.

998   Finally, displaying all their clemency toward humanity, the Roman emperors began to show favor to slaves and to restrain the cruelty of their masters. They extended the efficacy of manumission and diminished its formalities. Citizenship, which had originally been conferred only on distinguished foreigners who had deserved well of the Roman people, was now granted to everyone born in Rome, even if born of a slave father provided the mother was free by birth or by enfranchisement. It was from the fact that men were thus born free in the cities that the natural law which had previously been called that of the clans [*gentium*] or noble houses (because in heroic times all commonwealths had been aristocratic and such a law was proper to them, as we have set forth above), was now called the natural law of nations, after the rise of the popular commonwealths (in which the entire nations are masters of the *imperium*), and later of the monarchies (in which the monarchs represent the entire nations subject to them).

[CHAPTER III]

THE SAFEGUARDING OF THE LAWS

999   The safeguarding of the orders carries with it that of the magistracies and priesthoods, and hence also that of the laws and of the science of their interpretation. Hence we read in Roman history that in the times of the aristocratic commonwealth *connubia,* consulships and priesthoods were all confined to the senatorial order (which was then made up entirely of nobles), and the science of their laws was kept sacred or secret (which are the same thing) within the college of pontiffs (to which only patricians were admitted), as in all the other heroic nations. This lasted among the Romans down to a hundred years after the Law of the Twelve Tables, according to the account of the jurisconsult Pomponius. And the name *viri,* men, which among the Romans of those times had the same meaning as *hērōes* among the Greeks, was applied to husbands in solemn wedlock, to magistrates, priests and judges, as we have said before. Here, however, we shall discuss the safeguarding of the laws, since that was a principal property of the heroic aristocracies and hence was the last to be extended by the patricians to the plebs.

1000   In divine times this custody was scrupulously practiced, so that the observance of the divine laws is called religion. This was perpetuated through all subsequent governments, in which the divine laws have to be observed with certain unalterable formulae of consecrated words and solemn ceremonies. There is nothing so characteristic of the aristocratic commonwealths as this guarding of the laws. The reason why Athens (and, on her example, almost all the cities of Greece) passed quickly to popular liberty was that, as the Spartans (whose commonwealth was aristocratic) used to say to the Athenians, the many laws at Athens were written and the few laws at Sparta were observed.

1001   In the aristocratic commonwealth the Romans were very strict guardians of the Law of the Twelve Tables, as we have seen above. It was called by Tacitus *finis omnis aequi iuris,* because after these laws which were considered sufficient to equalize liberty (and which must have been enacted after the decemvirs, for whom, in the manner the ancient peoples had of thinking in poetic characters, they were named), there were no consular enactments of private law, or very few. For the same reason it was called by Livy *fons omnis aequi iuris,* for it must have been the source of all interpretation. The Roman plebs, like the Athenian, passed new laws every day for particular occasions, because it was incapable of universals. Sulla, leader of the nobles, when he had defeated Marius, leader of the plebs, repaired the disorder somewhat with the *quaestiones perpetuae* or permanent courts, but, once he had resigned the dictatorship, particular laws began to multiply again no less than before, as Tacitus relates. And, as political writers point out, there is no readier way to arrive at monarchy than through such a multitude of laws. Hence Augustus, for the purpose of establishing it, enacted a great number of them, and succeeding emperors used the senate above all to issue *senatusconsulta* in the field of private law. Nevertheless, even in these times of popular liberty, the formulae for actions were so strictly guarded that it took all the eloquence of Crassus (whom Cicero called the Roman Demosthenes) to get an expressed pupillary substitution interpreted as containing an unexpressed vulgar or common substitution; and it took all Cicero's eloquence to prevent Sextus Aebutius from keeping a farm of Aulus Caecina's because of the omission of a "d" from the formula. Finally things reached such a point, when Constantine had done away entirely with the formulae, that every particular motive of equity prevailed over the laws; so willing are human minds under human governments to recognize natural equity. Thus, passing from that article of the Law of the Twelve Tables: *Privilegia ne irroganto,* observed in the Roman aristocracy, through the great many particular laws enacted, as we have said, under popular liberty, a point was reached under the monarchy where the emperors did nothing but grant privileges, than which, if proportioned to merit, there is nothing more in harmony with natural equity. Indeed all the exceptions to the laws which are made nowadays can truly be called privileges dictated by the particular merit of the facts, which removes them from the general disposition of the laws.

1002   Hence, as we believe, it came about that in the rude days of the returned barbarism the nations forgot the Roman laws, so much so that whoever invoked one on his behalf was severely punished in France, and in Spain even suffered death. Certainly in Italy the nobles counted it a disgrace to regulate their affairs by Roman laws and professed to be subject to those of the Lombards. The plebeians, who were slow in shaking off their old customs, continued to observe some Roman laws by force of habit. This is the reason why the corpus of the laws of Justinian and other monuments of western Roman law were lost to us in Italy, and the Basilica and other monuments of eastern Roman law fell into oblivion among the Greeks. But later, when the monarchies were reëstablished and popular liberty reintroduced, the Roman law comprised in the books of Justinian was universally received, so that Grotius declares that it is now a natural law of the nations of Europe.

1003   The Roman gravity and wisdom is much to be admired in this: that, in these constitutional changes, the praetors and the jurisconsults put forth every effort to insure that the words of the Law of the Twelve Tables should be shifted from their original and proper meanings as little and as slowly as possible. Perhaps it was principally for this reason that the Roman Empire grew so great and endured so long; for in its changes of constitution it made every effort to stand firm by its principles, which were the same as those of this world of nations, and all political theorists agree that there is no better policy for making a state endure and grow great. Thus the cause which produced among the Romans the wisest jurisprudence in the world (of which we have spoken above) is the same that made the Roman Empire the greatest in the world. And it is the cause of the Roman greatness which Polybius, in too general a sense, attributes to the religion of the nobles; Machiavelli, on the contrary, to the magnanimity of the plebs; and Plutarch, envious of Roman virtue and wisdom, to their good fortune; this last in his book *De fortuna romanorum,* to which, in other and more indirect ways [than ours], Tasso gave answer in his noble *Risposta.*

[SECTION XIII]

[CHAPTER I]

OTHER PROOFS TAKEN FROM [MIXED COMMONWEALTHS, THAT IS FROM] THE TEMPERING OF THE STATE OF A SUCCEEDING COMMONWEALTH BY THE GOVERNMENT OF THE PRECEDING ONE

1004   All that we have had to say in this [fourth] book is so much evidence to prove that in the course of the entire lifetime of nations they follow this order through these three kinds of commonwealths or civil states, and no more. They all have their roots in the first, which were the divine governments, and from this beginning all nations (by the axioms above posited [241–245] as principles of the ideal eternal history) must proced through this sequence of human things: first becoming commonwealths of optimates, later free popular commonwealths, and finally monarchies. Hence Tacitus, though he does not see them in this order, affirms (as we pointed out in the Idea of the Work) that, outside of these three forms of public states, ordained by the nature of peoples, the others compounded of these three by human design are more to be desired of heaven than ever to be attained by effort, and if by chance any such exist they are not enduring. But, to leave no point of doubt concerning this natural succession of political or civil states, we shall find that the succession naturally admits of mixtures, not of form with form (for such mixtures would be monsters), but of a succeeding form with a preceding government. Such mixtures are founded on the axiom above [249], that when men change they retain for some time the impression of their previous customs.

1005   Hence we say that the first gentile fathers, passing from the bestial life to the human, retained, in the religious times in the state of nature under the divine governments, much of the savagery and cruelty of their recent origins (so that Plato recognizes in the Cyclopes of Homer the first family fathers of the world); and that likewise in the formation of the first aristocratic commonwealths the private sovereign powers remained intact in the hands of the family fathers, just as they had held them in the previous state of nature. And because they were intensely proud and there was no reason for one to yield to another when all were equal, they made themselves subject in aristocratic form to the public sovereignty of their own reigning orders. Thus the high private dominion of each family father went to make up the superior high public dominion of the senates, just as out of the private sovereignties which they had over their families they composed the civil sovereignties of their orders themselves. In no other way is it possible to conceive how the cities were composed of the families. The cities must therefore have originated as aristocratic commonwealths with a natural admixture of family sovereignties.

1006   The commonwealths remained aristocratic as long as the fathers preserved this authority of ownership within their reigning orders, and until the plebs of the heroic peoples had obtained from the fathers themselves laws extending to them the certain ownership of the fields, the right to solemn nuptials, the sovereign powers, the priesthoods and thereby the science of the laws. But as soon as the plebs of the heroic cities became numerous and inured to war (to the alarm of the fathers, who in the oligarchic commonwealths must have been few), and, with force on their side (the force of their numbers), began to enact laws without the authority of the senates, then the commonwealths changed from aristocratic to popular. For no one of them could have lived for a moment with two supreme legislative powers without distinction of subjects, times and territories, concerning which, during which and within which their laws were to be enacted. Hence the dictator Philo declared by the Publilian law that the Roman commonwealth had already become popular by nature. In this revolution, in order that the authority of ownership might retain what it could of the form that had suffered change, it naturally became the authority of guardianship (just as the power that fathers have over their minor children is transferred, on the death of the fathers, to others in the form of the authority of guardians). In virtue of this authority, the free peoples, masters of their sovereignties, as it were reigning wards, being weak in public counsel, naturally allow themselves to be governed by their guardians, the senates. Thus they were by nature free commonwealths, governed aristocratically. But when the powerful in the popular commonwealths directed this public counsel to the private interests of their power, and the free peoples, for the sake of private utilities, let themselves be seduced by the powerful to subject their public liberty to the ambition of the latter, then factions, seditions and civil wars, ruinous to their very nations, brought on the monarchical form.

[CHAPTER II]

AN ETERNAL NATURAL ROYAL LAW BY WHICH THE NATIONS
COME TO REST UNDER MONARCHIES

1007   The monarchical form was introduced in accordance with this eternal natural royal law, felt by all the nations which recognize in Augustus the founder of the Roman monarchy. This law has escaped the notice of the interpreters of Roman law, preoccupied as they have all been with the fable of the "royal law" of Tribonian, of which he openly professes himself the author in the *Institutes,* but which he attributes to Ulpian at one point in the *Pandects.* Yet it was well understood by the Roman jurisconsults, who were well acquainted with the natural law of nations. For Pomponius, in his brief history of Roman law, discussing the royal law of which we speak, described it for us in the well-considered phrase: *rebus ipsis dictantibus, regna condita*—"kingdoms were founded at the dictation of things themselves."

1008   This natural royal law is conceived under this natural formula of eternal utility: Since in the free commonwealths all look out for their own private interests, into the service of which they press their public arms at the risk of ruin to their nations, to preserve the latter from destruction a single man must arise, as Augustus did at Rome, and take all public concerns by force of arms into his own hands, leaving his subjects free to look after their private affairs and after just so much public business, and of just such kinds, as the monarch may entrust to them. Thus are the peoples saved when they would otherwise rush to their own destruction. In this truth the professors of modern law concur when they say that *universitates sub rege habentur loco privatorum*—"corporations are treated as private persons under the king"—because the majority of the citizens no longer concern themselves with the public welfare. Tacitus, most learned in the natural law of nations, points out as much in his *Annals* within the family of the Caesars itself, by this order of human civil ideas: As the death of Augustus became imminent, *pauci bona libertatis incassum disserere*—"a few spoke in vain of the blessings of liberty"; as soon as Tiberius came, *omnes principis iussa adspectare*—"all looked to the commands of the emperor"; under the three subsequent Caesars first came *incuria* or indifference and finally *ignorantia reipublicae tanquam alienae,* ignorance of public affairs as something foreign. Thus, as the citizens have become aliens in their own nations, it becomes necessary for the monarchs to sustain and represent the latter in their own persons. Now in free commonwealths if a powerful man is to become monarch the people must take his side, and for that reason monarchies are by nature popularly governed:

first through the laws by which the monarchs seek to make their subjects all equal; then by that property of monarchies whereby sovereigns humble the powerful and thus keep the masses safe and free from their oppressions; further by that other property of keeping the multitude satisfied and content as regards the necessaries of life and the enjoyment of natural liberty; and finally by the privileges conceded by monarchs to entire classes (called privileges of liberty) or to particular persons by awarding extraordinary civil honors to men of exceptional merit (these being singular laws dictated by natural equity). Hence monarchy is the form of government best adapted to human nature when reason is fully developed, as we have said before.

[CHAPTER III]

REFUTATION OF THE PRINCIPLES OF POLITICAL THEORY AS REPRESENTED BY THE SYSTEM OF JEAN BODIN

1009   In the light of what has been set forth up to this point, we can see how much scientific foundation there is for the political theory of Jean Bodin which places the successive forms of civil states in this order: they were first monarchic, then, having passed through a stage of tyranny, became free and popular, and finally became aristocratic. We might here content ourselves with having refuted him completely by the natural succession of political forms which we have established by such numberless proofs, particularly in this [fourth] book. But it pleases us to add, *ad exuberantiam,* a refutation based on the impossibilities and absurdities of his own position.

1010   He certainly admits the truth that the families were the elements of which the cities were composed. However, by a common error which we have corrected above, he has assumed that the families included only the children. How, we ask him, could monarchies have developed from such families?

1011   There are two possible ways: by force or by fraud.

1012   But how could one family father subdue the rest by force? For if in the free commonwealths (which, according to Bodin, came after the tyrannies) the family fathers consecrated themselves and their families to the fatherlands by which their families were preserved to them (and, according to him, these fathers had already been tamed under the monarchies), must we not suppose that the family fathers, when they were still Cyclopes but recently emerged from their savage bestial liberty, would have allowed themselves to be slain along with their entire families rather than endure inequality?

1013   By fraud, then? This is used by those who, aiming at rule in the free commonwealths, offer to those whom they would seduce either liberty or power or wealth. But as for liberty, in the family state the fathers were all sovereigns. Power? But the nature of the Cyclopes was to live apart in their caves and take care of their own families, with no concern for those of others, in accordance with the habits of their savage origin. And wealth, in those simple and frugal first times, had no meaning at all.

1014   The difficulty grows out of all proportion when we add that in the first barbarian times there were no fortresses, and the heroic cities, made up of families, were for a long time unwalled, as we learned above from Thucydides. And in the midst of the jealousies of state, which were all consuming in the heroic aristocracies as above described, Valerius Publicola, suspected of plotting tyranny because he had built a house on high ground, in order to justify himself had it dismantled in one night, and the next day, calling a public assembly, had his lictors lay the consular fasces at the feet of the people. The custom of leaving cities unwalled lasted longest among the most savage nations; thus we read that Henry the Fowler was the first in Germany to bring in the people from the villages in which they had previously been dispersed, to dwell in cities and to gird them with walls. So much for the notion that the first founders of the cities were those who marked out with the plough the walls and the gates, the name *porta* for gate being derived, according to the Latin etymologists, from their lifting and carrying the plough, *a portando aratro,* over the places where they wanted the gates to be! Thus between the savagery of the barbarous times and the insecurity of the palaces, at the court of Spain more than eighty persons of royal blood were slain within sixty years, so that the fathers of the Illiberitan council, one of the earliest of the Latin Church, condemned this frequently recurring wickedness under penalty of solemn excommunication.

1015   But the difficulty mounts to infinity if we assume the families to include only the children. For in that case, whether by force or by fraud, the children must have been the instruments of the ambitions of others and have betrayed and slain their own fathers. Thus the first states would not have been monarchies but impious and wicked tyrannies. But when the young nobles of Rome conspired against their fathers on behalf of the tyrant Tarquin, it was because of their hatred for the severity of the laws which is characteristic of aristocratic commonwealths (as benign laws are of popular commonwealths, clement ones of legitimate kingdoms, and dissolute ones of tyrannies); a severity of which these young conspirators made trial at the cost of their lives. The two sons of Brutus, numbered among the conspirators, were beheaded, their own father dictating the severe penalty. Thus we may see how monarchic the Roman commonwealth was and how popular the liberty established therein by Brutus!

1016   In face of such and so many difficulties, Bodin (and with him all other political writers) ought to recognize the family monarchies in the state of the families as here shown, and to admit that the families included not only children but famuli (after whom they were called families in the first place). We have seen that these famuli foreshadowed the slaves who appeared after the

founding of cities as a result of their wars. In this way free men and slaves are
the matter of commonwealths, as Bodin will have it, though they cannot be so
on his premises.

1017   Because of this difficulty on Bodin's premises of making free men
and slaves the matter of commonwealths, he himself is surprised that his own
people should have been called Franks or freemen, when, as he observes, in their
earliest times they were treated as baseborn slaves. This is because, from his
position, he could not see that the nations were brought to completion by those
who were freed from bondage by the Petelian law. Thus the Franks, the source
of Bodin's surprise, are the same as the rustic vassals whom Hotman is surprised
to find called *homines* or men, and of whom, as we have shown in this work,
the plebs of the first heroic peoples were composed. It was these masses, as we
have also shown, that moved the aristocracies to popular liberty and finally to
monarchy, and did so in virtue of the vulgar tongue in which, under these last
two forms of government, the laws are conceived, as explained above. On this
account the vulgar language was called vernacular by the Latins, as being the
tongue of houseborn slaves, for such a houseborn slave, and not one taken in
war, is what is meant by *verna*. And we have shown above that these houseborn
slaves existed among all the ancient nations from the time of the family state.
For this same reason the Greeks ceased to be called Achaeans (whence the
Homeric phrase for the heroes: sons of the Achaeans) and took the name
Hellenes from Hellen who started the Greek vulgar tongue, just as the sons of
Israel dropped that name of their earliest times and took on that of the Hebrew
people from Heber, whom the fathers declare to have been the propagator of the
sacred tongue. So well did Bodin and all the other writers on political theory
see this most luminous truth which has been clearly demonstrated throughout
this entire work, with particular reference to Roman history: namely, that the
plebs of the peoples, always and in all nations, have changed states from aristocratic to popular and from popular to monarchic, and that by founding the vulgar languages (as fully proved above in the Origins of Languages) they gave
their names to the nations, as we have just seen! It was in this way that the
ancient Franks, to the surprise of Bodin, gave their name to France.

1018   Finally, to apply the test of present experience, the aristocratic states
are very few and are survivals from barbarian times—Venice, Genoa and Lucca
in Italy, Ragusa in Dalmatia and Nuremberg in Germany. The others are
popular states governed aristocratically. Wherefore Bodin—whose theory obliges
him to hold that the Roman kingdom was monarchic and that the expulsion
of the tyrants was followed by the introduction of popular liberty at Rome—
fails to find in the first period of Roman freedom the effects called for by his
principles (because the actual effects were those proper to an aristocratic commonwealth), and in order to come creditably out of it, as we observed above, says
at first that the Roman state was popular but its government was aristocratic,
and then, constrained by the force of the truth, confesses in another passage,

with crass inconsistency, that the state as well as the government was aristocratic.

1019 Such errors in political theory spring from a failure to define the three terms people, kingdom and liberty, as we have noted several times already. Thus it has been believed that the first peoples were composed of plebeian as well as noble citizens, whereas we have shown by a thousand proofs that only the nobles were included. The liberty of ancient Rome has been thought to be popular liberty, meaning the freedom of the people from the nobles, whereas we have found it to be aristocratic liberty, that is, freedom of the nobles from the tyrant Tarquins; and statues were erected to the slayers of such tyrants because they had acted by order of the reigning senates. The kings, in the savagery of the first peoples and the insecurity of the palaces, were aristocratic, such as the two life-term kings at Sparta (an aristocratic commonwealth beyond doubt, as we have shown), and later the two annual consuls at Rome whom Cicero calls annual kings in his *Laws*. This institution due to Junius Brutus, as Livy plainly declares, entailed no change in the Roman kingdom so far as the royal power was concerned; and we have already observed that there was appeal to the people from these annual kings during their reign, and that when their reign expired, they had to render an accounting of their administration to the people. And we remarked too that in heroic times it was a daily occurrence for one king to drive another from the throne, as Thucydides said; and we noted in this the resemblance to the returned barbarian times, in which we read of nothing more uncertain and variable than the fortune of kingdoms. We pondered the opening words of the *Annals* of Tacitus, who often conveys his views by the propriety and force of the words he chooses. *Urbem Romam principio reges habuere*—"The city of Rome in the beginning was held by kings." This is the weakest of the three degrees of possession distinguished by the jurisconsults, for which the verbs are *habere, tenere* and *possidere*. And he uses the word *urbem*, which means, strictly speaking, the buildings, in order to signify a physical possession; and not *civitatem*, which is the community of the citizens, all or the majority of whom make up spiritually the public constitution.

[SECTION XIV]

FINAL PROOFS TO CONFIRM THE COURSE OF NATIONS

[CHAPTER I]

[PUNISHMENTS, WARS, ORDER OF NUMBERS]

1020   There are other instances of the congruity of effects with the causes assigned to them in the principles of this Science, which confirm the natural course of the lives of nations. We have already mentioned most of them in scattered passages without any order. Here we shall bring them together and arrange them according to the natural succession of human things.

1021   Punishments, for example, in the time of the families were of a cyclopean cruelty: it is in this state that Marsyas is flayed by Apollo. They continued so in the aristocratic commonwealths; thus the shield of Perseus turned its beholders to stone, as explained above. Punishments were called *paradeigmata* by the Greeks in the same sense in which the Latins called them *exempla,* that is, exemplary chastisements. And, as we have also observed before, in the returned barbarian times punishments by death were called ordinary punishments. So the laws of Sparta (a commonwealth we have shown by a thousand proofs to be aristocratic), which were judged savage and cruel by Plato and Aristotle alike, required that the illustrious king Agis should be strangled to death. And the laws of Rome, while it was an aristocratic state, condemned the noble and victorious Horatius to be stripped, beaten with rods and hanged to the unhappy tree. We have spoken of both these incidents above in another connection. Under the Law of the Twelve Tables, those who had set fire to another's grain were condemned to be burned alive, false witnesses were cast from the Tarpeian Rock and defaulting debtors were torn to pieces while still alive. This last-named punishment Tullus Hostilius did not spare his peer Metius Fufetius, king of Alba, because he had failed to keep his pledge of alliance; and Romulus himself, before that time, had been torn to pieces by the fathers on a mere suspicion of treason to the state. Let this suffice for those who contend that such punishments were never dealt out in Rome.

1022   Later came the mild punishments practiced in the popular commonwealths commanded by the multitude, which, being made up of the weak, is naturally inclined to compassion. Thus the Roman people, more from admiration of his valor than from the justice of his cause—*magis admiratione virtutis quam iure caussae* in the elegant phrase of Livy already cited above—absolved Horatius when he was condemned for killing his sister in heroic rage at seeing her weeping over the public good fortune. And just as Plato and Aristotle in the times of Athenian freedom censured the Spartan laws (as we noted a little while ago), so in the mildness of Roman popular liberty Cicero protests against the inhuman cruelty of the death penalty in the case of a private Roman knight, Rabirius, who had been found guilty of treason. Finally came the monarchies, in which princes rejoice to receive the grateful title, clement.

1023   Again, the barbaric wars of the heroic times meant the ruin of conquered cities, and the surrendered foes became herds of laborers scattered over the countryside to cultivate the fields of the victors. (Such, as we explained above, were the heroic inland colonies.) Then the magnanimity of the popular commonwealths, as long as they were ruled by their senates, took from the vanquished the law of heroic nations but left them in free enjoyment of the natural law of human nations of which Ulpian speaks. (As conquests were extended, all the rights later called *propriae civium romanorum* were restricted to Roman citizens. These rights, such as solemn nuptials, paternal power, *sui heredes,* agnates, gentiles, quiritary or civil ownership, mancipation, usucapion, stipulation, testaments, guardianship and inheritance, must all have been possessed as civil law rights of their own by the subject nations when they were still free.) Finally came the monarchies, which seek, as under Antoninus Pius [i.e. Caracalla], to make one Rome of all the Roman world. For it is a vow characteristic of great monarchs to make one city of the whole world, as Alexander the Great used to say that for him all the world was a single city of which his phalanx was the citadel. Thus the natural law of nations, developed in the provinces by the Roman praetors, came home at long last to dictate laws in the Romans' own house. The heroic law which the Romans had exercised over the provinces was relinquished, because monarchs desire all their subjects to be made equal by their laws. And Roman jurisprudence, which in heroic times had been based entirely on the Law of the Twelve Tables, and which in the times of Cicero (as he notes in his *Laws*) had begun to follow the edict of the Roman praetor, finally, from the days of the emperor Hadrian on down, concerned itself entirely with the *Edictum perpetuum* or "Perpetual Edict," composed and arranged by Salvius Julianus almost wholly from the provincial edicts.

1024   Again, from the little districts which could be well governed by the aristocratic commonwealths, through expansion by the conquests to which the free commonwealths are disposed, we finally arrive at monarchies, which are beautiful and magnificent in proportion as they are big.

1025   From the brooding suspicions of aristocracies, through the turbulence of popular commonwealths, nations come at last to rest under monarchies.

1026   But lastly we wish to show how, on this concrete and composite order of human civil things, we may superimpose the order of numbers, which are the purest abstracts. Governments began with the one, in the family monarchies; passed to the few in the heroic aristocracies; went on to the many and the all in the popular commonwealths, in which all or the majority make up the body politic; and finally in civil monarchies return again to the one. By the nature of numbers we cannot conceive a more adequate division or another order than one, few, many and all, with the few, many and all retaining, each in its kind, the principle of the one; just as numbers consist of indivisibles according to Aristotle, and, when we have passed the all, we must begin again with the one. And thus the history of humanity is all contained between the family monarchies and the civil monarchies.

[CHAPTER II]

COROLLARY: THAT THE ANCIENT ROMAN LAW WAS A SERIOUS POEM, AND THE ANCIENT JURISPRUDENCE A SEVERE KIND OF POETRY, WITHIN WHICH ARE FOUND THE FIRST OUTLINES OF LEGAL METAPHYSICS IN THE ROUGH; AND HOW, AMONG THE GREEKS, PHILOSOPHY WAS BORN OF THE LAWS

1027   There are many other great effects, particularly in Roman jurisprudence, which find their causes only in these same principles. Above all, by the axiom [137] that as men are naturally drawn to the pursuit of the true, their desire of it, when they cannot attain it, causes them to cling to the certain, mancipations began *vera manu,* with the actual hand, that is with real force, since force is abstract and hand is concrete. Among all nations the hand signified power; hence the *cheirothesiai* ("hand-placings") and *cheirotoniai* ("hand-raisings") of the Greeks. In the former, those elected to power had it bestowed upon them by the laying of hands on their heads; in the latter, powers already bestowed were acclaimed by the raising of hands. Such ceremonial gestures are proper to mute times; the election of kings in the returned barbarian times was similarly acclaimed. Such actual mancipation occurs in the case of occupation, the first great natural source of all property rights, of which *occupatio bellica* was a survival among the Romans; hence slaves were called *mancipia,* and the booty and the conquests *res mancipi,* of the Romans, having become by the victory *res nec mancipi* in relation to the vanquished. So true is it that mancipation began within the walls of the single city of Rome as a way of acquiring civil ownership in private transactions between Romans!

1028   This actual mancipation was accompanied by a correspondingly actual usucapion, that is, acquisition of ownership (for such is the meaning of *capio*) by actual use (in the sense in which *usus* signifies *possessio*). Possession was originally exercised by continuous physical tenure of the thing possessed. *Possessio* must have come from *porro sessio* (as domiciles were called *sedes* in Latin from this continual act of sitting or standing firm) and not from *pedum positio* as the Latin etymologists say, for the praetor assists the former and not the latter kind of possession and upholds it by interdicts. From this position, called *thesis* by the Greeks, Theseus must have taken his name, and not from his handsome posture as the Greek etymologists say, for the men of Attica founded Athens by remaining fixed there a long time. This is the usucapion which legitimizes states among all nations.

1029   Further, in Aristotle's heroic commonwealths which had no laws for redress of private wrongs, *rei vindicationes* were carried out with real force (such were the first duels or private wars of the world), and *condictiones* were private reprisals, which in the returned barbarism lasted down to the times of Bartolus.

1030   As the savagery of the times began to abate, as private violence began to be forbidden by judiciary laws, and all private forces were becoming united in the public force called civil sovereignty, the first peoples, by nature poets, must naturally have imitated the real forces that they had previously employed to preserve their rights and institutions. And so they made a fable of natural mancipation and created from it the solemn civil conveyance represented by the handing over of a symbolic knot in imitation of the chain whereby Jove had bound the giants to the first unoccupied lands, and by which they themselves had later bound thereto their clients or *famuli*. With this symbolic mancipation they consecrated all their civil transactions by *actus legitimi*, which must have been solemn ceremonies of peoples still mute. Later (articulate speech having meanwhile been formed), in order to make certain of one another's wills in contracts, they determined that agreements, at the moment of handing over this knot, should be clothed with solemn words in which certain and precise stipulations were conceived. Thus later in war they conceived the terms under which they accepted the surrender of vanquished cities. These were called "peaces" from *pacio* which means the same as *pactum*. A notable survival of this remains in the formula for the surrender of Collatia. In Livy's account it is a contract of receiving under one's power, in the form of solemn questions and answers. Hence it was with full propriety that those who had surrendered were called *recepti*, as the Roman herald said to the representatives of Collatia: *Et ego recipio*. So much for the notion that in heroic times stipulation was restricted to Roman citizens! And so much for the discernment of those who have hitherto believed that Tarquinius Priscus, in the formula for the surrender of Collatia, meant to teach the nations how surrenders were to be conducted!

1031   In this way the law of the heroic nations of Latium remained fixed in the famous article of the Law of the Twelve Tables which reads: *Si quis nexum faciet mancipiumque, uti lingua nuncupassit, ita ius esto*—"If one executes a bond or conveyance, as his tongue has declared, so let it be binding." This is the great fount of all ancient Roman law, which those who compare it with Attic law confess did not come from Athens to Rome.

1032   Usucapion [at first] extended [only] as far as physical possession. Later this was feigned and the intent to possess sufficed. In the same way they symbolized vindications by a feigned force, and heroic reprisals were transformed into personal actions preserving the solemnity of denunciation of debtors. The childhood of the world could have followed no other path; for children, as we have set forth in an axiom [215], have a powerful faculty for imitating the truth in matters within their capacity, and it is in this that poetry consists, which is nothing but imitation.

1033   Thus there appeared in the market place as many masks as there were persons (for *persona* properly means simply a mask) or as there were names. The names, which in the times of mute speech took the form of real words, must have been the family coats-of-arms, by which families were found to be distinguished among the American Indians, as above said. And under the person or mask of the father of a family were concealed all his children and servants, and under the real name or emblem of a house were concealed all its agnates and gentiles. Thus we saw Ajax the tower of the Greeks, and Horatius alone on the bridge withstanding the whole of Tuscany, and in the returned barbarian times we encountered forty Norman heroes driving an entire army of Saracens from Salerno. Hence the reputation for amazing strength of the paladins of France (who were sovereign princes and whose name survived in [the counts palatine of] Germany), and above all of Count Roland, later called Orlando. The reason for this springs from the principles of poetry discovered above. The founders of Roman law, at a time when they could not understand intelligible universals, fashioned imaginative universals. And just as the poets later by art brought personages and masks onto the stage, so these men by nature had previously brought the aforesaid names and persons into the forum.

1034   The word *persona* must not have been derived from *personare,* "to resound everywhere," for it was not necessary in the quite small theaters of the first cities (when, as Horace says, the spectators were so few as to be easily counted) to use masks for resonance to enable the voice to fill a large theater. And besides, the quantity of the [second] syllable does not admit of this derivation, for if it came from *sono* it would have to be short. It must rather have come from *personari,* a verb which we conjecture meant to wear the skins of wild beasts, which was permitted only to heroes. The companion verb *opsonari* has come down to us. It must at first have meant to feed on the meat of hunted game, which must have been the first rich fare on which Vergil describes his heroes as feasting. Hence the first rich spoils must have been these skins of slain beasts brought back by the heroes from their first wars, which were waged against the beasts in defense of themselves and their families, as set forth above. The poets clothe their heroes in these pelts, and above all Hercules, who wears that of the lion. To such an origin of the verb *personari,* in the primary meaning which we have restored to it, is to be traced, we conjecture, the Italian application of the term *personaggi,* "personages," to men of high station and great representations.

1035 On these same principles, because they did not understand abstract forms, they imagined corporeal forms, and they imagined them, after their own nature, as animate. *Hereditas* or "inheritance" they imagined as mistress of hereditary property, and they recognized her as entire in every particular item of inherited goods, just as when they presented to the judge a lump or clod from a farm, they called it *hunc fundum* in the formula of *rei vindicatio.* Thus, if they did not understand, they at least sensed in a rough way that rights were indivisible.

1036 In conformity with such natures, ancient jurisprudence was throughout poetic. By its fictions what had happened was taken as not having happened, and what had not happened as having happened; those not yet born as already born; the living as dead; and the dead as still living in their estates pending acceptance. It introduced so many empty masks without subjects, *iura imaginaria,* rights invented by imagination. It rested its entire reputation on inventing such fables as might preserve the gravity of the laws and do justice to the facts. Thus all the fictions of ancient jurisprudence were truths under masks, and the formulae in which the laws were expressed, because of their strict measures of such and so many words—admitting neither addition, subtraction, nor alteration—were called *carmina* or "songs," as above we found Livy terming the formula dictating the punishment of Horatius. This is confirmed by a golden passage in the *Asinaria* of Plautus, where Diabolus says that the parasite is a great poet, for he knows better than anybody how to invent verbal safeguards or formulae, which we have just seen were called *carmina.*

1037 Thus all ancient Roman law was a serious poem, represented by the Romans in the forum, and ancient jurisprudence was a severe poetry. Very conveniently to our argument, Justinian in the proemium of the *Institutes* speaks of the fables of the ancient law—*antiqui iuris fabulas.* He uses the phrase in derision but he must have taken it from some ancient jurisconsult who had understood the matters we have been discussing. From these ancient fables, as we here prove, Roman jurisprudence drew its principles. And from the masks called *personae* which were used in these dramatic fables, so true and severe, derive the first origins of the doctrine of the law of persons—*De iure personarum.*

1038 With the coming of the human times of the popular commonwealths, the intellect was brought into play in the great assemblies, and universal legal concepts abstracted by the intellect were thenceforward said to have their being in the understanding of the law—*consistere in intellectu iuris.* This understanding is concerned with the intention which the lawmaker has expressed in his law (this intention being called *ius*), an intention which was that of the citizens brought into agreement upon an idea of a common rational utility. This they must have understood as spiritual in nature, because all those rights which did not attach to corporeal things over which they could be exercised (and which were called *nuda iura,* rights not corporeally vested) were said *in intellectu iuris consistere.* Since rights are thus modes of spiritual substance, they are therefore indivisible, and hence also eternal, for corruption is nothing else than division of parts.

1039   The interpreters of Roman law have rested the entire reputation of legal metaphysics on the consideration of the indivisibility of rights in their treatment of the famous subject of divisibles and indivisibles—*De dividuis et individuis.* But they have not considered the other and no less important attribute of eternity. Yet they should have noted it in the following two rules of law. The first establishes that, *cessante fine legis, cessat lex.* It does not read *cessante ratione,* for the *finis* or end of the law is the equal utility of causes, which may fail of realization; but the *ratio* or reason of the law is a conformity of the law to the fact, clothed in such and such circumstances, and whenever the fact is so clothed the reason of the law lives and governs it. The other rule establishes that *tempus non est modus constituendi vel dissolvendi iuris.* For time cannot give a beginning or put an end to the eternal, and in usucapion and prescription time neither produces nor terminates the rights, but is proof that he who held them intended to relinquish them. From the fact that the usufruct, for example, is said to terminate, it does not follow that the right terminates, but only that it is detached from the servitude and becomes free as before. Herefrom spring two very important corollaries. First, that as rights are eternal in the intelligence of them or in their idea, whereas men have their being in time, the rights can come to men only from God. And second, that all the countless various rights that have been, now are or ever will be in the world, are divers modifications of the power of the first man, who was the prince of the human race, and of the ownership which he held over the whole earth.

1040   Now, because laws certainly came first and philosophies later, it must have been from observing that the enactment of laws by the Athenian citizens involved their coming to agreement in an idea of an equal utility common to all of them severally, that Socrates began to adumbrate intelligible genera or abstract universals by induction, that is by collecting uniform particulars which go to make up a genus of that in respect of which the particulars are uniform among themselves.

1041   Plato, reflecting that in such public assemblies the minds of particular men, each passionately bent on his private utility, are brought together in a dispassionate idea of common utility (according to the saying that men individually are swayed by their private interests but collectively they seek justice), raised himself to the meditation of the highest intelligible ideas of created minds, ideas which are distinct from these created minds and can reside only in God, and thus he reached the height of conceiving the philosophical hero who commands his passions at will.

1042   The way was thus prepared for the divine definition which Aristotle later gave us of a good law as a will free of passion, which is to say the will of a hero. He understood justice as queen of the virtues, seated in the spirit of the hero and commanding all the others. For he had observed legal justice seated in the spirit of the sovereign civil power and dictating prudence in the senate, fortitude in the armies and temperance at festivals, as well as the two forms of particular justice: distributive justice in the public treasuries and commutative justice for the most part in the forum; the latter employing arithmetic proportion and the former geometric. He must have observed distributive justice in the census which is the basis of the popular commonwealths and which distributes honors and burdens in geometric proportion according to the patrimonies of the citizens. For previously only arithmetic proportion had been understood; wherefore Astraea, heroic justice, was depicted for us with the scales, and in the Law of the Twelve Tables all the punishments—which philosophers, moral theologians and professors writing on public law now say must be dispensed by distributive justice in geometric proportion—all the punishments, we read, reduce either to the double (*duplio*) if pecuniary and to the like (*talio*) if corporal. And since the law of retaliation was invented by Rhadamanthus, he was made judge in the lower world, in which punishments are certainly distributed. In Aristotle's *Ethics* retaliation was called Pythagorean justice, invented by the Pythagoras whom we have revealed as founder of a nation in Magna Graecia, whose nobles were called Pythagoreans, as above noted. This invention would be a disgrace to the Pythagoras who later became a sublime philosopher and mathematician.

1043   From all the above we conclude that these principles of metaphysics, logic and morals issued from the market place of Athens. From Solon's advice to the Athenians, "Know thyself" (as set forth above in one of the corollaries of our Poetic Logic), came forth the popular commonwealths, from the popular commonwealths the laws, and from the laws emerged philosophy; and Solon, who had been wise in vulgar wisdom, came to be held wise in esoteric wisdom. This may serve as a fragment of the history of philosophy told philosophically, and a last reproof, of the many brought forth in this work, against Polybius who said that if there were philosophers in the world there would be no need of religions. For [the fact is that] if there had not been religions and hence commonwealths, there would have been no philosophers in the world, and if human affairs had not been thus guided by divine providence there would have been no idea of either science or virtue.

1044   Now, to return to our subject and conclude the argument under discussion, in these human times in which the popular commonwealths and afterwards the monarchies appeared, it was understood that the causes [of legal obligation], which had at first been formulae safeguarded by precise and proper words (for *cavere* is the origin of *cavissae,* of which *caussae* is the shortened form), were the affairs or transactions themselves in the case of [consensual] contracts (which affairs or transactions are now solemnized by pacts, which in the act of contract are agreed upon so that they will produce the actions). In the case of those contracts which are valid titles for the conveyance of property, they solemnized the natural delivery in order to effect the transfer. And only in the contracts which are said to be completed by word of mouth (that is to say in stipulations) did the verbal safeguards remain causes in the strict ancient sense. What we have said here illustrates further the principles above set forth for the obligations arising from contracts and pacts.

1045   To sum up, a man is properly only mind, body and speech, and speech stands as it were midway between mind and body. Hence the certitude of law began in mute times with the body. Then when the so-called articulate languages were invented, it passed to certain ideas or verbal formulae. And finally, when our human reason was fully developed, it reached its end in the truth of ideas concerning justice, determined by reason from the detailed circumstances of the facts. This is a formula devoid of any particular form, called by the learned Varro *formula naturae,* which, like light, of itself informs in all the minutest details of their surface the opaque bodies of the facts over which it is diffused, as we have fully indicated in the Elements [321-325].

BOOK FIVE

THE RECURRENCE OF HUMAN THINGS

IN THE RESURGENCE OF THE NATIONS

1046 In countless passages scattered throughout this work and dealing with countless subjects, we have observed the marvelous correspondence between the first and the returned barbarian times. From these passages we can easily understand the recurrence of human things in the resurgence of the nations. For greater confirmation, however, we wish in this last book to give a special place to this argument. Thus we shall bring more light to bear on the period of the second barbarism, which has remained more obscure than that of the first, though Varro, most learned student of the earliest antiquities, in his chronological division called this the "obscure" time. And we shall also show how the Best and Greatest God has made the counsels of his providence, by which he has guided the human things of all nations, serve the ineffable decrees of his grace.

[CHAPTER I]

[THE LATEST BARBARIC HISTORY ILLUMINATED BY THE
RECURRENCE OF THE FIRST BARBARIC HISTORY]

1047 When, working in superhuman ways, God had revealed and confirmed the truth of the Christian religion by opposing the virtue of the martyrs to the power of Rome, and the teaching of the Fathers, together with the miracles, to the empty wisdom of Greece, and when armed nations were about to arise on every hand destined to combat the true divinity of its Founder, He permitted a new order of humanity to emerge among the nations in order that [the true religion] might be firmly established according to the natural course of human affairs.

1048 Following this eternal counsel, He brought back the truly divine times, in which Catholic kings everywhere, in order to defend the Christian religion of which they are protectors, donned the dalmatics of deacons and consecrated their royal persons (whence they preserve the title Sacred Royal Majesty). They assumed ecclesiastical dignities, as Hugh Capet, according to Symphorien

Champier in his *Genealogy of the Kings of France* (*Regum Francorum genealogia*), took the title of Count and Abbot of Paris, and Paradin in his *Annales de Bourgogne* refers to ancient documents in which the princes of France were commonly entitled Duke and Abbot or Count and Abbot. Thus the first Christian kings founded armed religions by which they reëstablished in their realms the Catholic Christian religion against the Arians (by whom St. Jerome says almost the whole Christian world was befouled), and against the Saracens and numerous other infidels.

1049   Thus there was a return in truth of what were called the pure and pious wars—*pura et pia bella*—of the heroic peoples, and hence all Christian powers still bear on the globe surmounting their crowns the cross which they had earlier displayed on their banners when they waged the wars called crusades.

1050   Amazing indeed is the recurrence of these civil human things in the returned barbarian times. The ancient heralds, for example, called out the gods—*evocabant deos*—from the cities on which they were declaring war, using the elegant and splendid formula preserved for us by Macrobius; for they believed that thereby the conquered peoples would be left without gods and hence without auspices, which are the first principle of everything that we have discussed in this work. For, by the heroic law of victory, the conquered were left without any civil rights, public or private, all of which, as we have already fully proved principally from Roman history, were dependent in heroic times on the divine auspices. All this was comprised in the heroic formula of surrender, applied by Tarquinius Priscus to Collatia, whereby the vanquished owed all things divine and human—*debebant divina et humana omnia*—to the conquering peoples. In the same way, the latest barbarians in taking a city made it their principal concern to seek out and carry off famous remains or relics of saints. So the peoples of those times were very careful to bury or hide them, and such repositories are everywhere found in the innermost and deepest parts of churches. That is the reason why almost all the removals of the bodies of the saints took place in those times. A trace of this custom survives in the rule by which conquered peoples must ransom from the victorious commanders all the bells of the cities they have taken.

1051   Moreover, from the fifth century onward, when so many barbarous nations began to inundate Europe and Asia and Africa as well, and the conquering peoples could not make themselves understood by the conquered, it came about from the barbarism of the enemies of the Catholic religion that in those iron times we can find no contemporary documents in the vulgar tongues, whether Italian, French, Spanish, or even German. (As for the Germans, they did not begin to write documents in their language until the times of Frederick of Swabia, according to Johann Aventinus in his *Annals of Bavaria* [*Annales Boiorum*], or even until those of the Emperor Rudolph of Hapsburg according to others, as we have already mentioned.) Among all the aforesaid nations we find documents only in barbarous Latin, understood only by a very few nobles who were also ecclesiastics. Hence we may assume that in all those unhappy centuries the nations had reverted to communicating with each other in a mute language. Because of this paucity of vulgar letters, there must everywhere have been a return to the hieroglyphic writing of family coats-of-arms, which, in order to give certainty to ownership (as above explained), signified seigniorial rights usually over houses, tombs, fields and flocks.

1052   There was a return of certain kinds of divine judgments called "canonical purgations." One kind of these judgments, as we have shown above, was the duels of the first barbarian times, though these were not recognized by the sacred canons.

1053   There was a return of heroic raids. We saw above that, as the heroes had counted it an honor to be called robbers, so now it was a title of nobility to be a corsair.

1054   There was a return of heroic reprisals, which, as we have observed, lasted down to the times of Bartolus.

1055   And since the wars of the latest barbarian times, like those of the first, were all wars of religion, as we have just seen, there was a return of heroic slavery, which lasted a long time among Christian nations themselves. For because of the practice of duels in those times, the conquerors believed that the conquered had no God (as we remarked above in discussing duels), and hence held them no better than beasts. This national feeling is still preserved between Christians and Turks. To a Christian the name Turk means a dog (whence Christians when they desire or are obliged to treat civilly with Turks call them Moslems, which means true believers); the Turks, on the other hand, call the Christians swine. Hence in their wars both sides practice heroic slavery, though the Christians do so with more mildness.

1056   But the most striking recurrence of human things in this connection was the resumption in these divine times of the first asylums of the ancient world, within which, as we learned from Livy, all the first cities were founded. For everywhere violence, rapine and murder were rampant, because of the extreme ferocity and savagery of these most barbarous centuries. Nor, as we said in the Axioms [177], was there any efficacious way of restraining men who had shaken off all human laws save by the divine laws dictated by religion. Naturally, therefore, men in fear of being oppressed or destroyed betook themselves to the bishops and abbots of those violent centuries, as being comparatively humane in the midst of such barbarism, and put themselves, their families and their patrimonies under their protection, and were received by them. Such submission and such protection are the principal constitutive elements of fiefs. Hence in Germany, which must have been the wildest and most savage of all the nations of Europe, there remained almost more ecclesiastical sovereigns (bishops or abbots) than secular; and, as we have said, in France all sovereign princes assumed the title of counts or dukes and abbots. Thus it came about that such an immense number of cities, towns and castles in Europe were named after saints; for in high or hidden places, in order to hear mass and perform the other offices of piety commanded by our religion, little churches were opened, which may be defined as the natural asylums of Christians in those times. Close by they built their dwellings. Hence everywhere the most ancient things we see of this second barbarism are little churches in such places as we have described, for the most part in ruins. A famous example of all this is our own Abbey of San Lorenzo of Aversa, with which was incorporated the Abbey of San Lorenzo of Capua. This Abbey governed either directly or through abbots or monks dependent upon it a hundred and ten churches in Campania, Samnium, Apulia and old Calabria, from the river Volturno to the gulf of Taranto; and the abbots of San Lorenzo were barons of almost all the aforesaid places.

[CHAPTER II]

RECURRENCE OF THE NATIONS IN CONFORMITY WITH THE ETERNAL NATURE OF FIEFS, AND RECURRENCE OF ANCIENT ROMAN LAW IN FEUDAL LAW

1057   These divine times were followed by certain heroic times, in consequence of the return of a certain distinction between almost opposite natures, the heroic and the human. Hence arises the cause of the effect so surprising to Hotman, that in feudal terminology the rustic vassals are called *homines*, "men." This word must be the origin of the two feudal terms, *hominium* and *homagium*, which have the same meaning. *Hominium* stands for *hominis dominium*, the baron's ownership of his man or vassal. Helmodius, according to Cujas, considers this term more elegant than the second, *homagium*, which stands for *hominis agium*, the baron's right to lead his vassal where he pleases. Learned writers on feudal law translate this barbarous term into classical Latin as *obsequium*, which is an exact equivalent, since it originally meant the readiness of the man to follow the hero wherever he led in order to till the latter's fields. The word *obsequium* emphasizes the fealty owed by the vassal to the baron, so that the *obsequium* of the Latins signifies at once the homage and the fealty which must be sworn at the investiture of fiefs; and among the ancient Romans the *obsequium* was inseparable from what they called *opera militaris* and our writers on feudal law call *militare servitium*, the service which the Roman plebeians over a long period rendered to the nobles in war at their own expense, as we found above to be certain from Roman history. *Liberti* or "freedmen" continued to owe to their patrons this *obsequium* and the services it entailed. As we observed above with reference to Roman history, this duty goes back to the time when Romulus founded Rome on the clienteles, which we found to be the form of protection extended to laboring peasants received by him into his asylum. These clienteles of ancient history, as we pointed out in the Axioms [263], cannot more properly be explained than as fiefs, and indeed the learned feudists translate the barbarous *feudum* by the elegant Latin *clientela*.

1058   These principles of things are clearly confirmed by the origins of the words *opera* and *servitium*. *Opera* in its original sense is the day's labor of a peasant, whom the Latins therefore called *operarius,* for which the Italian equivalent is *giornaliere*. It is as such a day laborer, without any privilege of citizenship, that Achilles complains of having been treated by Agamemnon when the latter wrongfully took from him his Briseis. The Latins applied to these laborers the term herd—*greges operarum,* or even *greges servorum*—because both they and the later slaves were regarded as beasts, which are said to feed in herds—*pasci gregatim*. [Herds of men must have come first, and herds of beasts later;] and, correspondingly, there must first have been the shepherds of such men (whence the Homeric fixed epithet for the heroes, shepherds of the people), and only later the shepherds of flocks and herds. This is confirmed by the Greek word *nomos,* which means both law and pasturage, as noted above; for by the first agrarian law the rebellious *famuli* were accorded sustenance on lands assigned to them by the heroes, and this sustenance was called *nomos* or pasturage, as being appropriate to such beasts, even as food is proper to men.

1059   The property of pasturing these first herds of the world must have appertained to Apollo, whom we found to be the god of civil light, that is of the nobility; for fabulous history tells of him as a shepherd at the river Amphrysus, just as Paris, who was certainly of the royal house of Troy, was also a shepherd. So also is the family father (whom Homer calls a king) who with his scepter orders the roasted ox to be divided among the harvesters, as portrayed on the shield of Achilles, on which, as we showed above, the history of the world was represented, with the epoch of the families fixed in this scene. Now it is not the business of our shepherds to feed the flocks but to guide and watch over them, but pasturing [in this later sense] could have been introduced only after the confines of the first cities had been made somewhat secure because of the prevalence of raiding in heroic times. This must be why bucolic or pastoral poetry appeared only in the most civilized times, among the Greeks with Theocritus, the Latins with Vergil, and the Italians with Sannazaro.

1060   The word *servitium* or service shows that these same things returned in the latest barbarian times; and in the converse of this relationship the baron was called *senior* in the sense of lord. Thus the ancient Franks who so surprised Bodin must be these servants born in the household, whom we found above to be everywhere the same as those whom the ancient Romans called *vernae,* who gave the name *vernaculae* to the vulgar tongues introduced by the vulgar of the peoples, that is, as we found above, by the plebs of the heroic cities, just as the poetic language had been introduced by the heroes or nobles of the first commonwealths.

1061   Once the power of the barons had been dispersed and dissipated among the peoples in the civil wars in which the powerful must depend on the people, and had hence been easily concentrated again in the persons of the monarchical kings, the *obsequium* of the freedmen passed over into what is called *obsequium principis,* in which, according to Tacitus, consists the entire duty of subjects to their monarchies. On the other hand, because of the supposed difference of the two natures, heroic and human, the lords of the fiefs were called barons in the same sense in which, as we found above, they were called heroes by the Greek poets and men (*viri*) by the ancient Latins. A trace of this survives in the Spanish *varon* for a man; the vassals, because of their weakness, being regarded as women in the heroic sense above explained.

1062   In addition to what we have just set forth, the term *signori* for the barons can only come from the Latin *seniores,* for of such elders the first public parliaments of the new realms of Europe must have been composed, just as Romulus had applied the term *senatum* to the public council, which he must naturally have composed of the older members of the nobility. And as, from these who thus were and were called *patres,* those who give slaves their liberty came to be called *patroni,* so, in Italian, the term *padroni* must have come to mean protectors from [its original reference to] these [slaves]. This term *padroni* retains the full elegance and propriety of its Latin original. Conversely, with equal Latin elegance and propriety the word *clientes* is used in the sense of the rustic vassals to whom Servius Tullius, in decreeing the census as explained above, conceded such fiefs by taking the shortest possible step from the clienteles of Romulus, as was fully shown above. These *clientes* are precisely the freedmen who later gave the nation of the Franks its name, as we said in the preceding book in reply to Bodin.

1063   In this fashion the fiefs came back, springing from the eternal source assigned to them in the Axioms [260-262], where we indicated the benefits which may be hoped for in the nature of civil things, whence with full Latin elegance and propriety the fiefs are called *beneficia* by the learned feudists. Hotman indeed observes, but without making use of the point, that the victors kept for themselves the cultivated fields in conquered lands and left to the unhappy vanquished the untilled fields for their sustenance. Thus the fiefs of the first world, as described in our second book, returned, taking their new beginning, however (as by their nature we showed above that they must), from the personal rustic fiefs which we found the clienteles of Romulus at first to have been, and of which we remarked in the Axioms [263] that they were scattered all over the ancient world of peoples. These heroic clienteles, in the splendor of Roman popular liberty, passed over into the custom by which the plebeians in their togas betook themselves in the morning to pay court to the great lords, saluted them with the title of the ancient heroes, *Ave rex*—"Hail, king!"—accompanied them into the forum, returned home with them in the evening, and were there given their evening meal by the lords, in conformity with the practice which gave the ancient heroes the title of shepherds of the people.

1064 Such personal vassals must have been the first *vades* or "sureties" among the ancient Romans. This term was preserved for the defendants who were obliged to appear with the plaintiffs in court, the obligation being called *vadimonium*. The name of these *vades,* according to our Origins of the Latin Language [*Scienza nuova,* 1st ed., III, 36], must have been derived from the nominative *vas,* the *bas* of the Greeks and the *was* of the barbarians, whence *wassus* and eventually *vassalus*. Vassals of this kind are even now to be found everywhere in the kingdoms of the colder north, which still retain a great deal of barbarism, particularly in Poland where they are called *ķmet* and are a kind of slaves, whole families of whom are gambled away by their lords and obliged to pass into the service of other masters. In these vassals we must recognize those who were chained by their ears and whom the Gallic Hercules leads whither he will by the chains of poetic gold (that is, grain) which issue from his mouth.

1065 Then came real rustic fiefs, reached by way of the first agrarian law of the nations, which we found to have been among the Romans the law by which Servius Tullius decreed the first census, by which, as we found, he conceded to the plebeians the bonitary ownership of the fields assigned to them by the nobles under certain burdens not only personal as before but also real. These plebeians must have been the first *mancipes,* a term which later designated those under real estate bond to the public treasury. Of the same nature must have been the vanquished to whom the victors gave the uncultivated fields to till for sustenance, as we found Hotman saying a short way back. Thus returned the Antaeuses bound to the soil by the Greek Hercules, and the *nexi* or bondmen of the god Fidius, the Roman Hercules as we found above, who were finally freed by the Petelian law.

1066 These *nexi* freed by the Petelian law, in virtue of what we have set forth above concerning them, correspond exactly to the vassals who must at first have been called liege men as being bound (*legati*) by this knot. Liege men are now defined by the writers on feudal law as those who must recognize as friends or enemies all the friends or enemies of their lord. This is precisely the oath sworn by the ancient German vassals (according to Tacitus as before cited) when they pledged themselves to serve the glory of their princes. Later when these fiefs developed into the full splendor of sovereign civil fiefs, the liege vassals were the conquered kings, to whom the Roman people, in the words of the solemn formula recounted in Roman history, gave their kingdoms in gift—*regna dono dabat*—which is as much as to say in fief—*beneficio dabat*. They became allies of the Roman people under the kind of alliance which the Latins called unequal league—*foedus inaequale*—and they were called royal friends of the Roman people in the sense in which the emperors spoke of their noble courtiers as friends. Such an unequal alliance was nothing but the investiture of a sovereign fief, which was conceived under the formula set forth by Livy, that the allied king was to uphold the majesty of the Roman people—*servaret maiestatem populi romani*—just as the jurisconsult Paulus says that the praetor renders justice *servata maiestate populi romani;* that is, he renders justice to those to whom the law grants it and withholds it from those to whom the law denies it. These allied kings were thus lords of sovereign fiefs subject to a greater sovereignty. This reappeared in Europe in the common usage by which, generally speaking, the title of Majesty is applied only to great kings who are lords of great kingdoms and numerous provinces.

1067   Along with these rustic fiefs, from which these things took their beginnings, returned the emphyteusis under which the great ancient forest of the earth had been cultivated; whence the *laudimia* came to signify both the payment made by the vassal to his lord and that made by the emphyteuticary to his immediate landlord.

1068   There was a return of the ancient Roman clienteles called commendations, as we showed not far back, so that the vassals, with Latin elegance and propriety, are called *clientes* by the learned feudists and the fiefs themselves are called *clientelae.*

1069   There was a return of the kind of census decreed by Servius Tullius, by which the Roman plebeians were for a long time obliged to serve the nobles in war at their own expense. The vassals now called *angarii* and *perangarii* were the equivalent of the ancient Roman *assidui,* who, as we found above, *suis assibus militabant;* the nobles having moreover the right of private imprisonment over their plebeian debtors down to the time of the Petelian law, which freed the Roman plebs from the feudal law of *nexum.*

1070   There was a return of the *precaria,* which must originally have been lands granted by the lords in response to the entreaties of the poor, so that they might find their sustenance by cultivating them; for precisely such are the possessions which the Law of the Twelve Tables never recognized, as has been shown above.

1071   And since barbarism with its violence destroys the confidence necessary to commerce and leaves the people with no other concern than the bare necessities of natural life, and since all rents had to be in the form of so-called natural fruits, there appeared at the same time also the *libelli* as transferences of immovable goods. Their utility must have been apparent, as we have already noted, from the fact that one man had an abundance of fields yielding a kind of fruit which another man lacked, and vice versa, and hence they made exchanges one with another.

1072   There was a return of mancipations, the vassal placing his hands between the hands of his lord to signify fealty and subjection. The rustic vassals under the census of Servius Tullius, as we noted not far back, were thus the first *mancipes* of the Romans. Along with mancipation there returned the division of things into *res mancipi* and *res nec mancipi;* for feudal estates are *res nec mancipi* for the vassal, who cannot alienate them, but *res mancipi* for the lord, just as the lands of the Roman provinces were *res nec mancipi* for the provincials but *res mancipi* for the Romans. In the act of mancipation there was a return of stipulations in the form of infestucations or investitures, which we showed above to be identical. Along with stipulations there was a return of what in ancient Roman jurisprudence (as noted above) were at first properly called *cavissae,* later shortened to *caussae,* which in the second barbarian times were called *cautelae* from the same Latin origin. The solemnizing of pacts and contracts by means of such *cautelae* was called *homologare* after the *homines* or men [i.e. vassals] to whom, at the beginning of this chapter, we traced *hominium* and *homagium;* for all the contracts of those times must have been feudal. Thus, with the *cautelae,* there was a return of pacts safeguarded [by precautionary phrases] in the act of mancipation, *pacta stipulata* as they were called by the Roman jurisconsults, from the *stipula* or blade which sheathes the grain, as we saw above; and thus in the same sense in which the barbarous doctors derived the expression *pacta vestita* from the investitures which were also called infestucations. Pacts not thus safeguarded were called by both [ancient and medieval lawyers], using the same phrase in the same sense, *pacta nuda.*

1073 There was a return of the two kinds of ownership, direct and useful —*dominium directum* and *dominium utile*—which correspond exactly to the quiritary and bonitary ownership of the ancient Romans. Direct ownership arose just as quiritary ownership first arose among the Romans. We saw above that the latter was originally ownership of the lands granted to the plebeians by the nobles. If they lost possession of them, they had to resort to *rei vindicatio,* employing the formula, *Aio hunc fundum meum esse ex iure quiritium,* "I declare this field to be mine by the law of the Quirites." Such a revindication, as we have shown above, was nothing less than a citation of the whole order of nobles (who made up the city in the Roman aristocracy) as the *auctores* from whom the plebeians derived the title of civil ownership in virtue of which they could vindicate the fields in question. Such ownership was always called *auctoritas* in the Law of the Twelve Tables, from the authority of ownership enjoyed by the reigning Senate over the Roman territory at large, over which later the people, with the coming of popular liberty, held the sovereign *imperium,* as set forth above.

1074 This "authority" of the second barbarism, which we illuminate in this work as we do innumerable other things by reference to the antiquities of the first barbarism (so much more obscure have we found the times of the second barbarism than those of the first!), has left three very clear traces in three feudal terms. First, the adjective *directus,* which confirms that the action [of *rei vindicatio*] was originally authorized by the direct or immediate overlord. Next, the noun *laudimia* for the payment [made by the vassal] on taking possession of the fief to which he had laid claim by the aforesaid citation [*lauda-*

tio] [of his lord] as *auctor*. Lastly, the noun *lodo,* which must originally have signified the judicial decision in this sort of case, and which later came to mean an arbitrated decision; for these cases [concerning fiefs] seem to have been concluded on friendly terms, in contrast with cases litigated concerning *alodia* (which Budé believes to have been so called from *alaudia,* just as *laus* becomes *lode* in Italian), over which the lords had originally had to meet in duels, as shown above. This custom has lasted down to my time in our Kingdom of Naples, where the barons used to avenge not by civil suits but by duels the invasions of their feudal territories by other barons. And like the quiritary ownership of the ancient Romans, the direct ownership of the early barbarians came finally to mean ownership which gives rise to a real civil action.

1075   And here is a very clear occasion for observing in the recurrence of nations a recurrence also of the lot of the later Roman jurisconsults in that of the later barbarian doctors. For just as the former in their times had already lost sight of early Roman law (as we have shown above by a thousand proofs), so the latter in their most recent times lost sight of early feudal law. For the erudite [humanist] interpreters of Roman law resolutely deny that these two barbarian types of ownership [direct and useful] were recognized by Roman law, being misled by the difference in names and failing to understand the identity of the things themselves.

1076   There was a return of goods *ex iure optimo* in the alodial goods which the learned feudists define as goods free of every encumbrance public or private, comparing them with the few houses held *ex iure optimo* which Cicero says still remained at Rome in his time. However, just as all notion of this sort of goods was lost in the latest Roman legislation, so in our times not a single example of these *alodia* can be found. And like the estates *ex iure optimo* of the Romans, the *alodia* finally became immovable goods free of every real private encumbrance but subject to real public encumbrances. For there was a recurrence of the transition from the census decreed by Servius Tullius to the census which was the basis of the Roman public treasury, a transition which we have traced above. Alods and fiefs, then, which are the two great divisions of things in feudal law, were originally distinguished by the fact that feudal goods were protected by citation of the lord and alodial goods were not. Here, for lack of these principles, all the learned feudists cannot help being at a loss as to how the *alodia,* which they latinize with Cicero as *bona ex iure optimo,* came to be called "goods of the spindle." In their proper meaning, as we said above, these were goods held under a very strong title, not weakened even by any public encumbrance. Such, as we also said above, were the goods of the fathers in the family state and continuing for a long time into the state of the first cities, which goods they had acquired by the labors of Hercules. The difficulty is easily solved if, following our principles, we observe that this same Hercules, when he became a slave of Iole and Omphale, took to the spinning wheel. That is, the heroes became effeminate and yielded their heroic rights to the plebeians whom they had regarded as women (holding and calling themselves in contrast *viri* or "men," as explained above), and allowed their goods to become subject to the public treasury through the census which was first the basis of the popular commonwealths and later lent itself to the establishment of the monarchies.

1077   Thus through this early feudal law which was lost sight of in later times, there was a return of estates *ex iure quiritium,* which we explained as "the law of the Romans in public assembly, armed with lances," which they called *quires.* From these Quirites was conceived the formula of *rei vindicatio: Aio hunc fundum meum esse ex iure quiritium,* which was, as we have said, a citation of the entire heroic city of Rome as *auctor.* Now in the second barbarism fiefs were certainly called "goods of the lance," which required the citation of the lords as *auctores,* in contrast with the later alods called "goods of the spindle" (with which Hercules, dispirited and enslaved to women, does his spinning); whence above we discovered the heroic origin of the motto of the royal arms of France, *Lilia non nent,* for in that kingdom women may not inherit. For there was a return of the gentilitial successions of the Law of the Twelve Tables, which we found to be *ius gentium Romanorum,* as we noted that Baldus called the Salic Law *ius gentium Gallorum.* The latter was certainly observed throughout Germany, and thus must have been observed throughout all the other first barbarous nations of Europe, but was later confined to France and Savoy.

1078   Lastly, there was a return of armed courts such as we found above that the heroic assemblies were which were held under arms, and which were called by the Greeks assemblies of Curetes and by the Romans assemblies of Quirites. The first parliaments of the realms of Europe must have consisted of barons, as that of France certainly was of peers. French history tells us clearly that kings were heads of its parliament in the beginning and created the peers of the courts to adjudicate cases in the capacity of commissioners; whence they continued to be called the dukes and peers of France. Just as the first trial in which, according to Cicero, the life of a Roman citizen was at stake, was that in which the king Tullus Hostilius created the duumvirs to act as commissioners and, in the formula preserved for us by Livy, to charge Horatius with treason— *in Horatium perduellionem dicerent*—for having slain his sister.

1079   This was because in the severity of those heroic times every killing of a citizen (when the cities were composed of heroes only, as fully shown above) was considered an act of hostility against the fatherland, which is precisely the meaning of *perduellio;* and every such killing was called a *parricidium,* for the victim was a father, that is, a noble, as we saw above that in those days Rome was divided into fathers and plebs. For that reason from the time of Romulus down to that of Tullus Hostilius there was no trial for the slaying of a noble, for the nobles must have been careful not to commit such offenses, having among themselves the practice of dueling discussed above. But since in the case of Horatius there was no one who could privately avenge by a duel the slaying of Horatia, a trial was then for the first time ordered by Tullus Hostilius. Killings of plebeians, on the other hand, were either committed by their own lords against whom no accusation could be brought, or by others who could indemnify the man's own lord for the loss as if he had been a slave, as is still the custom in Poland, Lithuania, Sweden, Denmark and Norway. But the learned interpreters of Roman law did not see this difficulty because they relied on the vain opinion of the innocence of the golden age, just as the political theorists for the same reason relied on Aristotle's statement that in the ancient commonwealths there were no laws concerning private wrongs and offenses; whence Tacitus, Sallust and other writers who are otherwise most discerning, when they speak of the origin of commonwealths and laws, relate that in the primitive state preceding the cities men led lives like so many Adams in the state of innocence. But once the cities had admitted those *homines* or men who so surprised Hotman and from whom comes the natural law of the nations called *humanae* by Ulpian, from then on the killing of any man was called *homicidium*.

1080   In these parliaments were discussed feudal causes concerning rights or successions or devolutions of fiefs by reason of felony or default of heirs. Such causes, when they had been confirmed many times by such adjudications, formed the customs of feudalism which are the most ancient of all the customs of Europe and which prove to us that the natural law of nations was born of these human customs of the fiefs, as has been fully shown above.

1081   Finally, just as King Tullus granted Horatius an appeal to the people (which then consisted of nobles only, as shown above) from the verdict by which he had been condemned, since against a reigning senate there was no remedy for the condemned save appeal to the senate itself; even so and in no other way the nobles of the returned barbarian times must have made appeals to the kings in their parliaments, for instance to the kings of France who at first were heads of parliament.

1082   There is a notable vestige of these heroic parliaments in the Sacred Council of Naples, for its president is given the title of Sacred Royal Majesty, the councilors are called *milites* and serve in the capacity of commissioners (for in the second barbarian times the nobles alone were soldiers and the plebeians served them in war, as we found from Homer and from ancient Roman history to have been the case in the first barbarian times), and its decisions admit of no appeal to any other tribunal, but only a request for revision by the Council itself.

1083   From all the matters here enumerated, we must conclude that the realms were everywhere aristocratic, we do not say in constitution but in government, as in the cold north that of Poland still is (and as those of Sweden and Denmark were until a century and a half ago). In time, if extraordinary causes do not impede its natural course, Poland will arrive at perfect monarchy.

1084   So true is this that Bodin himself goes so far as to say of his kingdom of France that it was aristocratic, not in government as we assert but in constitution, during the Merovingian and Carlovingian dynasties. But here we may ask Bodin how the kingdom of France became perfectly monarchical as it now is? Perhaps by some royal law by which the paladins of France divested themselves of their power and conferred it upon the kings of the Capetian dynasty?—If he has recourse to the fable of the royal law invented by Tribonian, by which the Roman people supposedly divested itself of its free sovereignty and conferred it on Augustus, to prove it a fable it suffices to read the first pages of the *Annals* of Tacitus in which he narrates the last acts of Augustus, legitimizing the beginning of the Roman monarchy in his own person, as indeed all nations perceived that it began with Augustus.—Perhaps because France was conquered through force of arms by one of the Capetian kings?—But all the histories keep it at a safe distance from such an unhappy fate. Bodin therefore, and with him all the other political and legal authorities who have written on public law, must recognize this eternal natural royal law by which the free power of a state, just because it is free, must be actualized. Namely, that in proportion as the optimates lose their grip the strength of the people increases until they become free; and in proportion as the free peoples relax their hold the kings gain in strength until they become monarchs. Wherefore, just as the natural law of the philosophers (or moral theologians) is that of reason, so this natural law of nations is that of utility and of force, which, as the jurisconsults say, is observed by the nations *usu exigente humanisque necessitatibus expostulantibus,* "as use requires and human necessities demand."

1085   From all these beautiful and elegant expressions of ancient Roman jurisprudence, with which the learned feudists do in fact mitigate and might even further mitigate the barbarousness of feudal doctrine (since the ideas of the latter fit the expressions of the former in their full propriety, as we have shown), let Oldendorp (and all the others with him) consider whether feudal law was born from the sparks of the fire set by the barbarians to Roman law. On the contrary, Roman law was born from the sparks of the fiefs observed in the first barbarism of Latium, such fiefs as were the origin of all the commonwealths in the world. As we have demonstrated this in a particular discussion above of the Poetic Politics of the first commonwealths, so in this [fifth] book (in a demonstration promised in the Idea of the Work) we have seen that the new realms of Europe have their origins within the eternal nature of fiefs.

1086   But finally, with the studies undertaken in the universities of Italy and the teaching of the Roman laws contained in the books of Justinian, laws therein based on the natural law of human nations, minds already developed and grown more intelligent were dedicated to the cultivation of the jurisprudence of natural equity, which makes the common people and the nobles equal in civil rights, just as they are equal in human nature. And just as from the time when Tiberius Coruncanius began to teach the laws publicly in Rome their secrecy began to slip from the hands of the nobles, and the power of the nobles gradually declined, so it happened in the case of the nobles of the realms of Europe, which had been ruled by aristocratic governments before passing into free commonwealths and thence into perfect monarchies.

1087   These last two forms of state, since both involve human governments, readily admit of change from either to the other, but a return from either
to an aristocratic state is almost impossible in the nature of civil things. So much
so that Dion of Syracuse, although he was a member of the royal family and
had driven into exile a monster of princes, Dionysius the tyrant, and although
he was so well favored with civil virtues as to be worthy of the friendship of the
divine Plato, was nevertheless barbarously slain when he attempted to restore the
aristocratic state. And the Pythagoreans (that is, as above explained, the nobles
of Magna Graecia), for the same attempt, were all cut in pieces save for the
few who had taken refuge in strongholds and were burned alive by the multitude. For the plebeians, once they know themselves to be of equal nature with
the nobles, naturally will not submit to remaining their inferiors in civil rights;
and the equality they seek may be found either in free commonwealths or under
monarchies. Wherefore, in the present humanity of the nations, the few remaining aristocratic commonwealths must take infinite pains and shrewd and
prudent measures to keep the multitude at the same time dutiful and content.

[CHAPTER III]

THE ANCIENT AND MODERN WORLD OF NATIONS DESCRIBED IN
CONFORMITY WITH THE PLAN OF THE PRINCIPLES OF THIS
[NEW] SCIENCE

1088   Carthage, Capua and Numantia, the three cities which caused
Rome to fear for her empire of the world, failed to accomplish this course of
human civil things. The Carthaginians were prevented by their native African
shrewdness which was further sharpened by their maritime trade; the Capuans
by the mild climate and the fertility of this happy Campania; and the Numan-
tians, finally, in the first flower of their heroism were suppressed by the power
of Rome under a Scipio Africanus, the conqueror of Carthage, assisted by the
forces of the world. But the Romans, having none of these obstacles, proceeded
with even steps, being ruled by providence through the medium of vulgar
wisdom. Through all three forms of civil states, in the natural order which
has been demonstrated by so many proofs in this work, they persisted in each
until it was naturally succeeded by the next. They retained the aristocracy down
to the Publilian and Petelian laws; they preserved popular liberty down to the
times of Augustus; and they clung to the monarchy as long as they could
humanly withstand the internal and external causes which destroy that form
of state.

1089   Today a complete humanity seems to be spread abroad through all nations, for a few great monarchs rule over this world of peoples. If there are still some barbarous peoples surviving, it is because their monarchies have persisted in the vulgar wisdom of imaginative and cruel religions, in some cases with the less balanced nature of their subject nations as an added factor.

1090   Beginning with the cold north, the Czar of Muscovy, although Christian, rules over men of sluggish minds. The Knyaz or Khan of Tartary dominates an effeminate people, like to the ancient Seres who formed the larger part of his great empire, a part which is now united with that of China. The Negus of Ethiopia and the powerful kings of Fez and Morocco reign over peoples too weak and sparse.

1091   In the mid-temperate zone, however, where the nature of men is better balanced, to begin with the Far East, the Emperor of Japan practices a humanity similar to that of the Romans at the time of the Carthaginian wars. He imitates their ferocity in arms, and, as learned travelers observe, his language has a Latin ring about it. Yet, through a religion of fierce and terrible imagination with dreadful gods all armed with frightful weapons, he retains much of the heroic nature. For the missionary fathers who have been there report that the greatest difficulty they have encountered in converting the people to Christianity is that the nobles cannot be persuaded that the plebeians have the same human nature as themselves. The Emperor of the Chinese, who reigns under a mild religion and cultivates letters, is most humane. The Emperor of the Indies is rather humane than otherwise, and practices in the main the arts of peace. The Persian and the Turk have mingled the rude doctrine of their religion with the softness of Asia, which they rule; and thus both, and particularly the Turks, temper their arrogance with magnificence, pomp, liberality and gratitude.

1092   But in Europe, where the Christian religion is everywhere professed, inculcating an infinitely pure and perfect idea of God and commanding charity to all mankind, there are great monarchies most humane in their customs. It is true that those situated in the cold north, such as Sweden and Denmark until a hundred and fifty years ago, and Poland and even England still today, although they are monarchic in constitution yet seem to be governed aristocratically; but if the natural course of human civil things is not impeded in their case by extraordinary causes they will arrive at perfect monarchies. In this part of the world alone, because it cultivates the sciences, there are furthermore a great number of popular commonwealths, which are not found at all in the other three parts. Indeed, because of the recurrence of the same public utilities and necessities, there has been a revival of the form of the Aetolian and Achaean leagues. Just as the latter were conceived by the Greeks because of the necessity of protecting themselves against the overwhelming power of the Romans, so the Swiss cantons and the united provinces or states of Holland have organized a number of free popular cities into two aristocracies, in which they stand united in a perpetual league of peace and war. And the body of the German empire is a system of many free cities and sovereign princes. Its head is the emperor, and in matters concerning the state of the empire it is governed aristocratically.

1093   We must observe here that sovereign powers uniting in leagues, whether perpetual or temporary, come of themselves to form aristocratic states into which enter the anxious suspicions characteristic of aristocracies, as above shown. Hence, as this is the last form of civil states (for we cannot conceive in civil nature a state superior to such aristocracies), this same form must have been the first, which, as we have shown by so many proofs in this work, was that of the aristocracies of the fathers, sovereign family kings united in reigning orders in the first cities. For this is the nature of principles, that things begin and end in them.

1094   Now to come back to our subject, in Europe today there are only five aristocracies: namely, Venice, Genoa and Lucca in Italy, Ragusa in Dalmatia and Nuremberg in Germany. Almost all of them have small territories. But Christian Europe is everywhere radiant with such humanity that it abounds in all the good things that make for the happiness of human life, ministering to the comforts of the body as well as to the pleasures of mind and spirit. And all this in virtue of the Christian religion, which teaches truths so sublime that it receives into its service the most learned philosophies of the gentiles and cultivates three languages as its own: Hebrew, the most ancient in the world; Greek, the most delicate; and Latin, the grandest. Thus, even for human ends, the Christian religion is the best in the world, because it unites a wisdom of [revealed] authority with that of reason, basing the latter on the choicest doctrine of the philosophers and the most cultivated erudition of the philologists.

1095   Lastly, crossing the ocean, in the new world the American Indians would now be following this course of human things if they had not been discovered by the Europeans.

1096   Now, in the light of the recurrence of human civil things to which we have given particular attention in this [fifth] book, let us reflect on the comparisons we have made throughout this work in a great many respects between the first and last times of the ancient and modern nations. There will then be fully unfolded, not the particular history in time of the laws and deeds of the Romans or the Greeks, but (in virtue of the substantial identity of meaning in the diversity of modes of expression) the ideal of the eternal laws in accordance with which the affairs of all nations proceed in their rise, progress, mature state, decline and fall, and would do so even if (as is certainly not the case) there were infinite worlds being born from time to time throughout eternity. Hence we could not refrain from giving this work the invidious title of a *New Science,* for it was too much to defraud it unjustly of the rightful claim it had over an argument so universal as that concerning the common nature of nations, in virtue of that property which belongs to every science that is perfect in its idea, and which Seneca has set forth for us in his vast expression: *Pusilla res hic mundus est, nisi id, quod quaerit, omnis mundus habeat* —"This world is a paltry thing unless all the world may find therein what it seeks." [1]

---

[1] *Naturales Quaestiones* VII, 31: *Pusilla res mundus est, nisi in illo quod quaerat omnis mundus habeat.*—"The world is a paltry thing unless it offers matter for the researches of all the world."

CONCLUSION OF THE WORK

ON AN ETERNAL NATURAL COMMONWEALTH, IN EACH

KIND BEST, ORDAINED BY DIVINE PROVIDENCE

1097   Let us now conclude this work with Plato, who conceives a fourth kind of commonwealth in which good honest men would be supreme lords. This would be the true natural aristocracy. This commonwealth conceived by Plato was brought into being by providence from the first beginnings of the nations. For it ordained that men of gigantic stature, stronger than the rest, who were to wander on the mountain heights as do the beasts of stronger natures, should, at the first thunderclaps after the universal flood, take refuge in the caves of the mountains, subject themselves to a higher power which they imagined as Jove, and, all amazement as they were all pride and cruelty, humble themselves before a divinity. For in this order of human things we cannot conceive how divine providence could have employed any other counsel to halt them in their bestial wandering through the great forest of the earth, in order to introduce among them the order of human civil things.

1098   Here was formed a state so to speak of monastic commonwealths or of solitary sovereigns under the government of a Greatest and Best whom they themselves created for their faith out of the flash of the thunderbolts, in which this true light of God shone forth for them: that He governs mankind. Hence they came to imagine that all the human benefits supplied to them and all the aids provided for their human needs were so many gods, and feared and revered them as such. Then, between the powerful restraints of frightful superstition and all the goading stimuli of bestial lust (which must both have been extremely violent in such men), as they felt the aspect of the heavens to be terrible to them and hence to inhibit their use of venery, they must have learned to hold in check the impulse of the bodily motion of lust. Thus they began to use human liberty, which consists in controlling the motions of concupiscence and giving them another direction; for since this liberty does not come from the body, whence comes concupiscence, it must come from the mind and is therefore properly human. The new direction took the form of forcibly seizing their women, who were naturally shy and unruly, dragging them into their caves, and, in order to have intercourse with them, keeping them there as perpetual lifelong companions. Thus, with the first human, which is to say chaste and religious, couplings, they gave a beginning to matrimony. Thereby they became certain fathers of certain children by certain women. Thus they founded the families and governed them with a cyclopean family sovereignty over their children and their wives, such as was proper to such proud and savage natures, so that later as cities arose men might be found disposed to stand in awe of the civil sovereignty. Thus providence ordained certain household commonwealths of monarchic form under fathers (in that state princes) best in sex, age and virtue. These fathers, in the state we must call that of nature (which was identical with the state of the families), must have formed the first natural orders, as being those who were pious, chaste and strong. Since they were settled on their lands and could no longer escape by flight (as they had previously done in their feral wanderings), in order to defend themselves and their families they had to kill the wild beasts that attacked them. And in order to provide sustenance for themselves and their families, as they had ceased foraging, they had to tame the earth and sow grain. All this for the salvation of the nascent human race.

1099   Meanwhile, scattered through the plains and valleys and preserving the infamous communism of things and of women, there remained a great number of the impious, the unchaste and the nefarious—impious in having no fear of gods, unchaste in their use of shameless bestial venery, and nefarious in their frequent intercourse with their own mothers and daughters. After a long time, driven by the ills occasioned by their bestial society, weak, astray and solitary, relentlessly pursued by the robust and violent because of quarrels engendered by their infamous communism, they came at last to seek refuge in the asylums of the fathers. The latter, taking them under their protection, proceeded to extend their family kingdoms to include these *famuli* through the clienteles. Thus they developed commonwealths on the basis of orders naturally superior by reason of virtues certainly heroic. First, piety, for they adored divinity, though because of their little light they multiplied and divided it into many gods formed according to their various apprehensions. (This is worked out and confirmed by Diodorus Siculus and more clearly by Eusebius in his *De praeparatione Evangelica* and by St. Cyril of Alexandria in his *Adversus Iulianum imperatorem*.) And in the virtue of their piety they were also endowed with prudence, taking counsel from the auspices of the gods; with temperance, coupling each with the one woman whom he had taken under the divine auspices as a perpetual companion for life; with strength for slaying beasts and taming the earth; and with magnanimity in giving succor to the weak and aid to those in danger. Such was the nature of the Herculean commonwealths, in which the pious, wise, chaste, strong and magnanimous cast down the proud and defended the weak, which is the mark of excellence in civil governments.

1100   But finally the family fathers, having become great by the religion and virtue of their ancestors and through the labors of their clients, began to abuse the laws of protection and to govern the clients harshly. When they had thus departed from the natural order, which is that of justice, their clients rose in mutiny against them. But since without order (which is to say without God) human society cannot stand for a moment, providence led the family fathers naturally to unite themselves with their kindred in orders against their clients. To pacify the latter, they conceded to them, in the world's first agrarian law, the bonitary ownership of the fields, retaining for themselves the optimum or sovereign family ownership. Thus the first cities arose upon reigning orders of nobles. And as the natural order declined which had been based, in accordance with the then state of nature, on [superiority of] kind, sex, age and virtue, providence called the civil order into being along with the cities. And first of all [civil orders], that which approximated most closely to nature: that in virtue of nobility of humankind (for in that state of affairs nobility could be based only on generating in human fashion with wives taken under divine auspices) and thus in virtue of a heroism, the nobles should rule over the plebeians (who did not contract marriage with such solemnities), and now that divine rules had ceased (under which the families had been governed by divine auspices) and the heroes had to rule in virtue of the form of the heroic governments themselves, that the principal basis of these commonwealths should be religion safeguarded within the heroic orders, and that through this religion all civil laws and rights should belong to the heroes alone. But since nobility had now become a gift of fortune, providence caused to arise among the nobles the order of the family fathers themselves, as being naturally more worthy because of age. And among the fathers it caused the most spirited and robust to arise as kings whose duty it should be to lead the others and gird them in orders to resist and overawe the rebellious clients.

1101   But with the passage of the years and the far greater development of human minds, the plebs of the peoples finally became suspicious of the pretensions of such heroism and understood themselves to be of equal human nature with the nobles, and therefore insisted that they too should be taken into the civil orders of the cities. Since in due time the peoples were to become sovereign, providence permitted a long antecedent struggle of plebs with nobility over piety and religion in the heroic contests for the extension of the auspices by the nobles to the plebeians, with a view to securing thereby the extension of all public and private rights regarded as dependent on the auspices. Thus the very care for piety and attachment to religion brought the people to civil sovereignty. In this respect the Roman people went beyond all others in the world, and for that reason it became the master people of the world. In this way, as the natural order merged more and more with the civil orders, the popular commonwealths were born. In these everything had to be reduced to lot or balance, and providence therefore, in order that neither chance nor fate should rule, ordained that the census should be the measure of fitness for office. Thereby the industrious and not the lazy, the frugal and not the prodigal, the provident and not the idle, the magnanimous and not the faint-hearted—in a word, the rich with some virtue or semblance thereof, and not the poor with their many shameless vices—were considered the best for governing. In such commonwealths the entire peoples,

who have in common the desire for justice, command laws that are just because
they are good for all. Such a law Aristotle divinely defines as will without passions, which would be the will of a hero who has command of his passions.
These commonwealths gave birth to philosophy. By their very form they inspired it to fashion the hero, and for that purpose to interest itself in truth. All
this was ordained by providence to the end that, since virtuous actions were no
longer prompted by religious sentiments as formerly, philosophy should make
the virtues understood in their idea, and by dint of reflection thereon, if men
were without virtue they should at least be ashamed of their vices. Only so can
peoples prone to ill-doing be held to their duty. And from the philosophies
providence permitted eloquence to arise and, from the very form of these popular
commonwealths in which good laws are commanded, to become impassioned for
justice, and from these ideas of virtue to inflame the peoples to command good
laws. Such eloquence, we resolutely affirm, flourished in Rome in the time of
Scipio Africanus, when civil wisdom and military valor, which happily united
in establishing at Rome on the ruins of Carthage the empire of the world, must
necessarily have brought in their train a robust and most prudent eloquence.

1102   But as the popular states became corrupt, so also did the philosophies. They descended to skepticism. Learned fools fell to calumniating the truth.
Thence arose a false eloquence, ready to uphold either of the opposed sides of
a case indifferently. Thus it came about that, by abuse of eloquence like that of
the tribunes of the plebs at Rome, when the citizens were no longer content with
making wealth the basis of rank, they strove to make it an instrument of power.
And as furious south winds whip up the sea, so these citizens provoked civil
wars in their commonwealths and drove them to total disorder. Thus they caused
the commonwealths to fall from a perfect liberty into the perfect tyranny of an-
archy or the unchecked liberty of the free peoples, which is the worst of all
tyrannies.

1103   To this great disease of cities providence applies one of these three
great remedies in the following order of human civil things.

1104   It first ordains that there be found among these peoples a man like
Augustus to arise and establish himself as a monarch and, by force of arms, take
in hand all the orders and all the laws, which, though sprung from liberty, no
longer avail to regulate and hold it within bounds. On the other hand providence
ordains that the very form of the monarchic state shall confine the will of the
monarchs, in spite of their unlimited sovereignty, within the natural order of
keeping the peoples content and satisfied with both their religion and their
natural liberty. For without this universal satisfaction and content of the peoples,
monarchic states are neither lasting nor secure.

1105   Then, if providence does not find such a remedy within, it seeks it
outside. And since peoples so far corrupted had already become naturally slaves
of their unrestrained passions—of luxury, effeminacy, avarice, envy, pride and
vanity—and in pursuit of the pleasures of their dissolute life were falling back

into all the vices characteristic of the most abject slaves (having become liars, tricksters, calumniators, thieves, cowards and pretenders), providence decrees that they become slaves by the natural law of nations which springs from the nature of such nations, and that they become subject to better nations which, having conquered them by arms, preserve them as subject provinces. Herein two great lights of natural order shine forth. First, that he who cannot govern himself must let himself be governed by another who can. Second, that the world is always governed by those who are naturally fittest.

1106 But if the peoples are rotting in this last civil illness and cannot agree upon a monarch from within, and are not conquered and preserved by better nations from without, then providence for their extreme ill has its extreme remedy at hand. For such peoples, like so many beasts, have fallen into the custom of each man thinking only of his own private interests and have reached the extreme of delicacy, or better of pride, in which like wild animals they bristle and lash out at the slightest displeasure. Thus in the midst of their greatest festivities, though physically thronging together, they live like wild beasts in a deep solitude of spirit and will, scarcely any two being able to agree since each follows his own pleasure or caprice. By reason of all this, providence decrees that, through obstinate factions and desperate civil wars, they shall turn their cities into forests and the forests into dens and lairs of men. In this way, through long centuries of barbarism, rust will consume the misbegotten subtleties of malicious wits, that have turned them into beasts made more inhuman by the barbarism of reflection than the first men had been made by the barbarism of sense. For the latter displayed a generous savagery, against which one could defend oneself or take flight or be on one's guard; but the former, with a base savagery, under soft words and embraces, plots against the life and fortune of friends and intimates. Hence peoples who have reached this point of premeditated malice, when they receive this last remedy of providence and are thereby stunned and brutalized, are sensible no longer of comforts, delicacies, pleasures and pomp, but only of the sheer necessities of life. And the few survivors in the midst of an abundance of the things necessary for life naturally become well behaved and, returning to the primitive simplicity of the first world of peoples, are again religious, truthful and faithful. Thus providence brings back among them the piety, faith and truth which are the natural foundations of justice as well as the graces and beauties of the eternal order of God.

1107 The clear and simple observation we have made on the affairs of the entire human race, if we had been told nothing more by the philosophers, historians, grammarians and jurisconsults, would lead us to say certainly that this is the great city of the nations founded and governed by God. Lycurgus, Solon, the decemvirs and the like have been eternally praised to the skies as wise legislators, because it has hitherto been believed that by their good measures and laws they had founded Sparta, Athens and Rome, the three cities that outshone all others in the fairest and greatest civil virtues. Yet they were all of short duration and even of small extent as compared with the universe of peoples, which was constituted by such orders and secured by such laws that even in its decay it assumes those forms of states by which alone it may everywhere be preserved and perpetually endure. And must we not then say that this is a counsel of a super-human wisdom? For without the force of laws (whose force, according to Dio as cited in the Axioms [308], is like that of a tyrant), but making use of the very customs of men (in the practice of which they are as free of all force as in the expression of their own nature, whence the same Dio said that customs were like kings in commanding by pleasure), it divinely rules and conducts [the aforesaid city].

1108   It is true that men have themselves made this world of nations (and we took this as the first incontestable principle of our Science, since we despaired of finding it from the philosophers and philologists), but this world without doubt has issued from a mind often diverse, at times quite contrary, and always superior to the particular ends that men had proposed to themselves; which narrow ends, made means to serve wider ends, it has always employed to preserve the human race upon this earth. Men mean to gratify their bestial lust and abandon their offspring, and they inaugurate the chastity of marriage from which the families arise. The fathers mean to exercise without restraint their paternal power over their clients, and they subject them to the civil powers from which the cities arise. The reigning orders of nobles mean to abuse their lordly freedom over the plebeians, and they are obliged to submit to the laws which establish popular liberty. The free peoples mean to shake off the yoke of their laws, and they become subject to monarchs. The monarchs mean to strengthen their own positions by debasing their subjects with all the vices of dissoluteness, and they dispose them to endure slavery at the hands of stronger nations. The nations mean to dissolve themselves, and their remnants flee for safety to the wilderness, whence, like the phoenix, they rise again. That which did all this was mind, for men did it with intelligence; it was not fate, for they did it by choice; not chance, for the results of their always so acting are perpetually the same.

1109   Hence Epicurus, who believes in chance, is refuted by the facts, along with his followers Hobbes and Machiavelli; and so are Zeno and Spinoza, who believe in fate. The evidence is clearly in favor of the contrary position of the political philosophers, whose prince is the divine Plato, who affirms that providence rules the affairs of men. It was therefore with good reason that Cicero refused to discuss laws with Atticus unless the latter would give up his Epicureanism and first concede that providence governed human affairs. Pufendorf ignored it in his hypothesis, Selden assumed it, and Grotius excluded it; but the Roman jurisconsults established it as the first principle of the natural law of nations. For in this work it has been fully demonstrated that through providence the first governments of the world had as their entire form religion, on which alone the state of the families was based; and passing thence to the heroic or aristocratic civil governments, religion must have been their principal firm basis. Advancing then to the popular governments, it was again religion that served the peoples as means for attaining them. And coming to rest at last in monarchic governments, this same religion must be the shield of princes. Hence, if religion is lost among the peoples, they have nothing left to enable them to live in society: no shield of defense, nor means of counsel, nor basis of support, nor even a form by which they may exist in the world at all.

1110   Let Bayle consider then whether in fact there can be nations in the world without any knowledge of God! And let Polybius weigh the truth of his statement that if the world had philosophers it would have no need of religions! For religions alone have the power to cause the peoples to do virtuous works by stimulation of the senses, which alone move men to perform them; and the reasoned maxims of the philosophers concerning virtue are of use only when employed by a good eloquence for kindling the senses to do the duties of virtue. There is, however, an essential difference between our Christian religion, which is true, and all the others, which are false. In our religion, divine grace causes virtuous action for the sake of an eternal and infinite good. This good cannot fall under the senses, and it is consequently the mind that, for its sake, moves the senses to virtuous actions. The false religions, on the contrary, have proposed to themselves finite and transitory goods, in this life as in the other (where they expect a beatitude of sensual pleasures), and hence the senses must drive the mind to do virtuous works.

1111   But providence, through the order of civil things discussed in this work, makes itself clearly felt by us in these three feelings: the first, marvel; the second, veneration, hitherto felt by all the learned for the matchless wisdom of the ancients; and the third, the ardent desire with which they burned to seek and attain it. These are in fact three lights of divine providence, which aroused in them the aforesaid three beautiful and just sentiments, which were later perverted by the conceit of scholars along with that of nations (which we set forth among our first axioms [125, 127] and have sought throughout this work to discredit). Their true meaning is that all the learned should admire, venerate and desire to unite themselves to the infinite wisdom of God.

1112   To sum up, from all that we have set forth in this work, it is to be finally concluded that this Science carries inseparably with it the study of piety, and that if one be not pious he cannot really be wise.

INDEX OF NAMES

(Numbers refer to paragraphs, not to pages. "Greece," "Greek," "Rome," "Latin" are omitted.)

Joseph A. Morse